Berlitz® HANDBOOK

THAILAND

Contents

Top 25 Attractions	4
Thailand Fact File	10
Trip Planner	12
UNIQUE EXPERIENCES	20
Backpacking	22
Beaches and Islands	28
Adventures in Thailand	36
Shopping	44
Spa Treatments	50
Culinary Experiences	56
PLACES	60
Getting Your Bearings	62
Bangkok and Surroundings	64
Bangkok	66
🚶 Tour of Rattanakosin	70
🚶 Tour of Chinatown	80
Around Bangkok	82
Listings	*84*
Central Thailand	92
West of Bangkok	93
North of Bangkok	95
🚶 Tour of Ayutthaya	96
⭐ Thai Boxing	98

South of Bangkok	100
Listings	*102*
Eastern Seaboard	106
Bang Saen to Pattaya	106
Ko Samet	110
Ko Chang	112
⭐ Lady-Boy Culture	114
Ko Chang Archipelago	116
Listings	*117*
The Gulf Coast	122
Northern Gulf Coast	123
Ko Samui	126
🚶 Tour of Phetchaburi	128
Ko Phangan	131
Ko Tao	134
Listings	*136*
Northern Andaman Coast	142
Ranong to Khao Lak	143
Phuket	147
Krabi	153
Ko Phi Phi	155
Ko Lanta Yai	157
Listings	*160*

The Deep South	170	
Nakhon Si Thammarat	171	
Songkhla	172	
Satun	173	
★ Performance Art	174	
Trang	176	
Listings	178	
Chiang Mai and Around	182	
Chiang Mai City	183	
★ Elephants	186	
Around Chiang Mai	189	
Lamphun	191	
Lampang	192	
Listings	193	
Northern Thailand	198	
Chiang Rai and East	199	
★ Buddhism	204	
The Northwest	206	
Lower North	211	
Listings	216	
Northeast Thailand	222	
Nakhon Ratchasima to		
Ubon Ratchathani	223	
★ Khmer Connection	230	

North to Loei	232
The Mekong River	237
Listings	241
PRACTICAL ADVICE	248
Accommodation	250
Transport	253
Health and Safety	258
Money and Budgeting	260
Responsible Travel	262
Family Holidays	264
SETTING THE SCENE	266
History	268
Culture	276
Food and Drink	283
PHRASEBOOK	288
INDEX	298

FAMILY FRIENDLY SYMBOL 👪

This symbol is used throughout the Handbook to indicate a sight, hotel, restaurant or activity that is suitable for families with children.

Top **25** Attractions

1 **Ayutthaya Historical Park** The remains of Thailand's capital until 1767, then one of the finest cities in Asia *(see p.95)*

2 **Sukhothai Historical Park** The ruins of Thailand's first capital are some of the best in the country *(see p.212)*

3 **Chiang Mai** Capital of the ancient kingdom of Lanna with an old city of historic temples *(see p.182)*

4 **Beach Parties** Anything goes at the beach raves of Ko Phangan (see p.26)

5 **Thai Cooking Schools** The authentic way to cook Thailand's wonderful food (see p.58)

6 **Wat Pho** Bangkok's oldest and largest temple is home to the serene Reclining Buddha (see p.72)

7 **Silk Weaving in Isaan** Northeastern villages produce some of Thailand's finest textiles (see p.226)

8 **Grand Palace and Wat Phra Kaew** Gold facades that appear to be straight from a fairy tale (see p.67)

9 Tiger Temple A forest retreat that adopted tigers and invites visitors inside to pet them *(see p.15)*

10 Phuket Vegetarian Festival Penitents pierce their flesh during this religious festival *(see p.169)*

11 Diving in Surin The pick of the Andaman sites, with sharks, sea turtles and dolphins *(see p.144)*

12 The Karsts at Ao Phang Nga Majestic limestone rock towers that rise from the sea *(see p.153)*

13 Chatuchak Weekend Market The world's biggest flea market, with nearly 10,000 stalls *(see p.82)*

15 **Bangkok's Chinatown** The city's earliest trade centre, with a 200-year-old market *(see p.74)*

14 **Phee Ta Khon Festival** Masked men wave red tipped phalluses around the village of Dan Saï *(see p.237)*

16 **Songkran** Thai New Year is one giant water-splashing street party *(see p.14)*

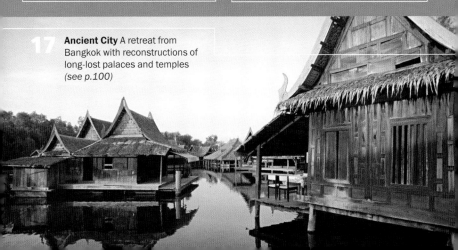

17 **Ancient City** A retreat from Bangkok with reconstructions of long-lost palaces and temples *(see p.100)*

18 **Thai Massage** A healing experience that combines elements of yoga and acupressure *(see p.50)*

19 **Lopburi** An old centre of Mon and Khmer civilisations and famed for its annual Monkey Buffet *(see p.105)*

20 **National Museum** Includes a beautiful Sukhothai Walking Buddha amid its huge collection *(see p.72)*

21 **Hill Tribe Treks** Stay overnight with villagers who live outside the fringes of Thai society *(see p.37)*

22 **Lampang** Take a horse and carriage to visit old Burmese-style temples *(see p.192)*

23 **Canal Trips** Float past old country temples and fast-disappearing traditional lifestyles *(see p.90)*

24 **Tattoo Festival** Chanting monks induce trances and ink their followers with tattoos *(see p.26)*

25 **Thai Boxing** A brutal but beautiful martial art accompanied by ritual dance and music *(see p.98)*

Thailand Fact File

Thailand is a country of four distinct regions – North, Central Plains, Northeast and South – in a landscape that covers 1,800km (1,125 miles) from the foothills of the Tibetan Plateau in the north to tropical islands and rainforests a few degrees from the equator. Almost 20 percent of the population lives in rapidly expanding Bangkok, while the regions still have many small agricultural villages.

 BASICS
Population: 66.5 million (20th in world)
Area: 513,120 sq km (200,437 sq miles/50th in world)
Official language: Thai
State religion: Buddhism
Capital city: Bangkok
Prime minister: Abhisit Vejjajiva
National anthem: Phleng Chat Thai
National symbol: Elephant
National sports: Muay Thai
National airline: THAI

 CURRENCY
Baht (B)
B1 = 100 satang

The following figures are approximate:
£1 = B49
€1 = B41
$1 = B32.50

 TIME ZONE
GMT +7 throughout the year

In January:
New York: midnight
London: 7am
Bangkok: noon
Sydney: 4pm
Auckland: 6pm

In July:
New York: 1am
London: 6am
Bangkok: noon
Sydney: 3pm
Auckland: 5pm

KEY TELEPHONE NUMBERS
Country code: +66
International calls: 001 + country code + number
Police: 191
Ambulance: 191
Fire: 191
Tourist police: 1155

AGE RESTRICTIONS
Driving: 18
Drinking: 18
Age of consent: 18 (15 in law; 18 in practice)

Smoking is banned inside public buildings, including bars cafés and restaurants.

ELECTRICITY
220 volts, 50 Hertz
2-pin plug

OPENING HOURS
Banks: Mon–Fri 8.30am–3pm
Shops: Daily 10am–9 or 10pm
Businesses in Bangkok's Chinatown close on Sundays

POSTAL SERVICE
Thailand Post Office
Post Offices:
Mon–Fri 8.30am–4.30pm,
Sat 9am–noon
Postboxes: red
Standard post: B3
Airmail: B17

Trip Planner

WHEN TO GO

Climate

There are three main seasons in Thailand: hot, with temperatures of 27–35°C (80–95°F), rainy (24–32°C/75–90°F) and cool (22–30°C/72–86°F). But to the tourist winging in from more temperate regions, it is just plain hot. To make things worse, humidity levels are above 70 percent. But the countryside is generally cooler, and nights everywhere during the cool season are very comfortable.

Chiang Mai enjoys lower temperatures and is less humid, with cool-season temperatures ranging between 13°C and 28°C (55°F and 82°F). In the northern hills, however, the mercury can plummet much lower, occasionally close to zero. The height of the rainy season is

Public Holidays	
1 Jan	New Year's Day
6 Apr	Chakri Day
13–15 Apr	Songkran
1 May	Labour Day
5 May	Coronation Day
12 Aug	Queen's Birthday
23 Oct	Chulalongkorn Day
5 Dec	King's Birthday
10 Dec	Constitution Day
Jan/Feb (full moon)	Magha Puja
May (full moon)	Visakha Puja
July (full moon)	Asanha Puja

Government offices and banks close for holiday periods, but many shops and attractions remain open.

Caught in a monsoon downpour along an alleyway in Bangkok's Chinatown

September, when you can expect over 300mm (11.8ins) of rainfall.

There are regional variations along Thailand's coastline, but generally the Eastern Seaboard and northern Gulf coast have a weather pattern similar to Bangkok, with temperatures close to 40°C (104°F) in April, dropping to 32°C (89.6°F) in December. The southern Gulf, around Ko Samui, is a little different: it receives light intermittent rain from June to October; from November to January, however, the northeast monsoon brings the heaviest rains, with November being the wettest month. Phuket and the Andaman coast experience their wettest months from May to October.

Sunbathing on the white sands of magnificent Maya Bay, Ko Phi Phi Ley

High/Low Season

The hot season runs from March to May, followed by the rainy season (June–Oct), and the cool season (Nov–Feb). Most tourists arrive for the cool season, when centres like Phuket, Pattaya and Chiang Mai will be crowded and prices will double. By April, the Andaman coast is virtually deserted and many hotels close. During the rainy season, part of most days will still be sunny, so visiting then is not a disaster. It is also cooler for city sightseeing and waterfalls gush their strongest at that time of year. Weather-wise, April to May is the worst time to visit Thailand, as the heat can be unbearable.

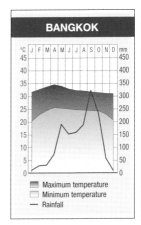

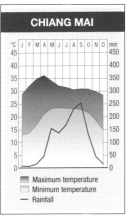

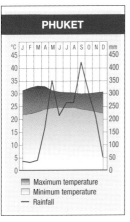

ESSENTIAL EVENTS

The riotous three-day Phee Ta Khon festival in Dan Sai features devilish masks

January–February

Chinese New Year (lunar), countrywide, but particularly Bangkok. Many Thais have Chinese ancestry, and this week-long celebration sees colourful parades with dragon dances through the streets. Many shops and businesses will close for several days.

Songkran 13–15 April, countrywide. Thais mark Songkran, the lunar new year, with the traditional, good-natured practice of gently sprinkling water to make merit at temples. The custom has become a giant water street fight in many places, such as Bangkok's Khao San Road.

May

Royal Ploughing Ceremony Bangkok. Held at Sanam Luang in early May. The King presides at this Brahman ritual which marks the start of the rice-planting season. Crimson-cad attendants lead buffaloes drawing a plough over specially consecrated ground.

June

La Fete various dates, Bangkok. A month-long French multicultural festival at various venues around the city. It takes in film, fashion, art, music, street theatre and all points between.

July

Phee Ta Khon Festival lunar, Dan Sai, Loei Province. This part Buddhist celebration, part animist fertility rite, sees the men of the village dressed as ghosts waving large phalluses around the streets.

Bangkok International Festival of Dance and Music various dates, Bangkok. Usually running for around a month, this cultural festival has mainly classical music and ballet performances by companies from around the world, plus some jazz and folk.

Bangkok International Film Festival various dates, Bangkok. Up to 100 films from across the globe, and guest appearances by directors and actors. Also has seminars and workshops on film-making.

October

Phuket Vegetarian Festival lunar, Phuket Town. A Tao Chinese cleansing festival in which people give up meat and sex. It also involves male penitents piercing their bodies with knives, needles and other sharp objects.

November

Loi Krathong November full moon, nationwide. People across the country launch small banana-leaf floats with lighted candles on rivers and lakes to thank the water spirits. It is perhaps Thailand's most beautiful festival.

River Kwai Festival various dates, Kanchanaburi. The Bridge on the River Kwai is the focal point for folk entertainment and a sound and light show that re-enacts the Allied bombing in World War II.

Elephant Round-up Surin. Thailand's iconic elephants are the subject of this popular festival, attracting visitors from far and wide.

December

The King's Birthday 5 December, Bangkok. People honour the revered monarch with an elaborate parade on Ratchadamnoen Klang Avenue and a culture festival on the royal grounds of Sanam Luang, opposite the Grand Palace.

Ayutthaya World Heritage Fair various dates, Ayutthaya. Parades, sound-and-light shows, folk performances and handicrafts commemorate the city's status as a Unesco World Heritage Site.

15

Trip Planner

The Loi Krathong festival gives thanks for the country's life-bringing rivers and lakes

ITINERARIES

Thailand is full of interesting cultural pockets, not to mention activities like diving, trekking and shopping, so for somebody with broad interests, to 'do' the whole country could realistically take several months (or years). But if you plan your time, a two-week stay could take in three days in Bangkok and four days seeing Chiang Mai, with some jungle trekking, and still leave a week to relax on the beach. Alternatively, you could theme your stay and achieve a lot in a relatively short time.

One Week for Shoppers

Days 1–2: Check out northern Thai crafts at Chiang Mai Night Bazaar; ceramics, antiques and wooden furniture at Hang Dong village; plus silverware and painted umbrellas at Bo Sang.

Days 3–4: head south of Nakhon Ratchasima, to Pak Thong Chai, where some 70 factories weave and silk clothing and accessories. Nearby, at the village of Dan Khwian, are traditional red ceramics.

Days 5–7: Trawl the stalls of Chinatown and Chatuchak, the world's biggest flea market, then move to the upmarket Pathumwan malls.

Two Weeks for Culture Buffs

Days 1–4: Bangkok's Rattanakosin, with its Grand Palace, National Museum and Wat Po's Reclining Buddha, then stroll the Old City temples and Chinatown markets. Later, maybe a boat trip past traditional canal-side homes.

The lively Chiang Mai Night Bazaar is an ideal venue for souvenir shopping

Days 5–6: Walk around the ruined temples of Thailand's old capital, Ayutthaya.

Days 7–8: Even older are the restored ruins of Thailand's first capital, Sukhothai.

Days 9–11: Visit Chiang Mai's old city temples, such as Wat Phra Singh, the one million artefacts at Chiang Mai National Museum, and the cultural gems at the Tribal Museum.

Days 12–14: Do a tour of the northeast's ancient Khmer sites, such as Phimai and Prasat Hin Khao Phanom Rung Historical Park, the largest and best-restored Khmer monument in Thailand.

Three Weeks for Adventurers

Days 1–7: Explore island dive sites, such as Similan and Surin, in the Andaman Sea off the coast of Phuket.

Days 8–14: Head north for hill tribe trekking and off-road biking out of Chiang Mai. Go whitewater rafting from Pai, and, when you reach Mae Hong Son, take a trip to the coffin caves near Sopporot.

Days 15–21: Take an AFF (Accelerated Freefall) Programme with Thai Sky Adventures, in Pattaya.

One Month for the Grand Tour

Days 1–3: Get over the jet lag with pampering treatments at one of Hua Hin's luxury spas.

Days 4–7: Head north to Chiang Rai, where the Hill Tribe Museum and Education Centre is a primer for hill tribe treks.

Days 8–10: North of Chiang Rai is

Andaman Sea dive sites are hard to beat for reef and marine diversity, and water clarity

Trip Planner

the Golden Triangle, the point where Thailand, Laos and Myanmar meet, and once the centre of the opium trade. The small towns here are just a hop across the Mekong River to market communities in Myanmar and Laos.

Days 11–14: Move south for a few days' shopping, dining and old city sights in Chiang Mai.

Days 15–22: Get some sun on the island beaches of Ko Samui in the Gulf of Thailand, where dive trips, yoga retreats and nightlong parties are all nearby.

Days 23–25: The southern province of Satun has boat trips to the deserted islands of Tarutao.

Days 26–30: See the historical sights of Bangkok, catch some clubbing and fine dining, and grab those last-minute souvenirs.

BEFORE YOU LEAVE

Visas and Entry Requirements

The various visa regulations for different nationalities are listed at the Thai Ministry of Foreign Affairs website (www.mfa.go.th).

Foreign nationals must have passports with at least six months' validity. You can get 60-day tourist visas at the Thai embassy in your home country, or at the airport. Nationals from most countries can get visas-on-arrival, valid for 15–90 days, depending on the country. Visas can be extended for 30 days or you can leave the country (even for half an hour) and return to receive another visa on entry.

Tourists can stay in Thailand for a cumulative time not exceeding 90 days within any six-month period. Overstaying carries a daily fine of B500, up to B20,000, or possible imprisonment.

Embassies and Consulates

UK 29 Queen's Gate, London; tel: 0-20-7589-2944, ext. 5500; www.thaiembassyuk.org.uk

Nationality	Visa Required
UK	✗
US	✗
Canada	✗
Australia	✗
New Zealand	✗
Ireland	✗
South Africa	✗

US 351 East 52nd Street, New York; tel: 212-754-1770; www.thaiconsulnewyork.com
Australia Level 8, 131 Macquarie Street, Sydney; tel: 6-12-9241-2542; www.thaiconsulatesydney.org
Canada 17 Isabella St, Unit 100, Toronto; tel: 416-850-0110; www.thaiconsulatetoronto.com
Ireland PO Box 9863, Dublin 14; tel: 00353-1-478-6412; www.thaiconsulateireland.com
New Zealand 2 Cook Street, Karori, Wellington; tel: 64-4-476-8616; www.thaiembassynz.org.nz
South Africa 248 Hill Street, Arcadia, Pretoria; tel: 27-12-342-4600; www.thaiembassy.co.za

Pack your swimsuit, sandals and sunblock and head for one of Thailand's idyllic beaches

Vaccinations and Insurance
No vaccinations are required to enter Thailand. However, immunisation against cholera, and hepatitis A and B are recommended. Malaria prophylaxis is a wise precaution if you are travelling to remote areas. Buy travel insurance with adequate medical cover in advance of your journey.

Tourist Information
Tourism Authority of Thailand (TAT)
www.tourismthailand.org
Tourism Authority of Thailand offices abroad
UK 1st Floor, 17–19 Cockspur Street, Trafalgar Square, London; tel: 0-870-900-2007; www.tourismthailand.co.uk
US 61 Broadway, Suite 2810, New York; tel: 1-212-432-0433; www.tatny.com
Australia 2002, Level 20, 56 Pitt Street, Sydney; tel: 61-2-9247-7549; www.thailand.net.au

Maps and Books
Periplus and Borch are good standard maps; Nancy Chandler's does hand-drawn maps of Bangkok and Chiang Mai with tourist tips.

Books
Very Thai: Everyday Popular Culture, Philip Cornwel-Smith. Everyday Thailand, from spirit houses to insect foods.
A History of Thailand second edition, Dr Pasuk Phongpaichit and Chris Baker. Informed history, mainly from the Rattanakosin period.
The King Never Smiles: A Biography of Thailand's Bhumibol Adulyadej, Paul M. Handley. An unauthorised portrait. The book is banned throughout Southeast Asia.
Travellers' Tales Thailand, edited by James O'Reilly and Larry Habegger. A collection of observations and true stories from 50 writers.
Bangkok 8, John Burdett. The best of several foreign-penned hard-boiled Bangkok crime fiction.

Websites
www.tourismthailand.org The Tourism Authority of Thailand.
www.nationmultimedia.com *The Nation* daily newspaper.
www.langhub.com/en-th Audio and video files to learn Thai.
www.bkmagazine.com Bangkok free listings mag with events and reviews.
www.khaosanroad.com Backpacker resource with accommodation, forums, etc.
www.customs.go.th The Thai Customs Department.
www.utopia-asia.com Gay resource for Thailand and Asia.

Packing List
- Swimsuit
- Shorts
- Mosquito repellent
- Sunblock
- Sunglasses
- Sturdy shoes
- Sandals
- Phrase book
- Sun hat
- Jumper
- Light cotton clothes

UNIQUE EXPERIENCES

Backpacking – *p.22* **Beaches and Islands** – *p.28*
Adventures in Thailand – *p.36* **Shopping** – *p.44*
Spa Treatments – *p.50* **Culinary Experiences** – *p.56*

Backpacking

For the freewheeling traveller, Bangkok's Khao San Road is the gateway to the world, to a bustling experience of beach parties, hill tribes, tattoo festivals, meditation and buckets of cheap beer. And when it's time to move on, there are cut-rate connections to Laos, Cambodia and the rest of Asia.

For lucky people with spare months, or even years, to build flexibility into their travel experience, Thailand has long been irresistible. For one, it's cheap; two, it's safe; and three, it's very close to other countries in the region, so you can skip to Vietnam, Laos, Malaysia, Myanmar and Cambodia without breaking sweat. For all these reasons, and many more, Thailand has one of the world's main jump-off points for the global traveller: Bangkok's Khao San Road.

It is many years since the term backpacker conjured images of unwashed hippies on the road to enlightenment, and Khao San Road has moved with the times. The ease of travel and communications means the area is now a temporary home for gap-year students and workers, migrants taking their time getting to pastures new in the UK, US or Australia, and flashpackers, who have the money to afford a little extra comfort, but prefer to maintain the informality and personal touch rarely shown by traditional hotels.

People leaving home with merely conservative plans often find a freedom of spirit comes with 'the road' experience, and Thailand has plenty of alternative pleasures to broaden the horizon. For a start, it's a Buddhist country, and countless travellers

Bangkok's Khao San Road is a legendary stopover for backpackers

seek fresh inspiration by enrolling in a meditation course. Others head for the Tattoo Festival, visit the Tiger Temple or hang out at a Muay Thai training camp.

And of course, there are some that are so smitten, they stay in Khao San for years.

Practical Information

Thailand is a very safe destination to travel in, but the freedom to change plans on the fly brings a few risks that you should take care of. It is vital to get health insurance as hospitals won't treat you without it. Don't attract attention by flashing money around: get a money belt for valuables, including passport and backups of important details like insurance, credit cards, and a photocopy of your passport. Also, get into the habit of letting someone know your plans. If anything bad happens it's good that someone suspects there might be a problem.

There a few common scams to look out for. It is best not to accept food or drink from strangers, as these are sometimes spiked, on rare occasions lethally so. And if anyone asks you to a card game, saying someone has been set up to lose a lot of money, remember, that someone is you. Motorbike bag

Taking a break from the road on one of Thailand's many fine beaches

23

Backpacking

snatches also happen occasionally, so carry your bag away from the road side.

Khao San Road

Khao San until the late 1990s was mainly foreigners only, but once Thai film crews started using it as an 'exotic' location, young Thais headed there attracted by the bohemian lifestyle. Many of them opened bars, lending a healthy local flavour that adds to one of the liveliest scenes in Bangkok.

The area's success means that when people now talk of 'Khao San,' they likely mean a half square kilometre of bars and shops, cafés and restaurants bounded by Thanons Ratchadamnoen, Tanao, Phra Sumen and Phra Arthit. However, most of the action is on Khao San Road itself, a walking street of around 400m/yds.

Cheap Bangkok Bars

- **Ad Here the 13th** (13 Thanon Samsen; tel: 08-9769-4613) Tiny place with big live blues
- **Cheap Charlie's** (1 Sukhumvit Soi 11; tel: 0-2253-4648) No walls, no ceiling, just a bar
- **Phranakorn Bar** (58/2 Soi Damnoen Klang Tai; tel: 0-2222-0282) Laid-back, alfresco rooftop vibe
- **Poh Bar & Restaurant** (Tha Tien Pier; no phone) Pierside watering hole with sunset river views
- **Wong's Place** (27/3 Soi Si Bamphen, off Soi Ngam Duphli; tel: 0-2286-1558) Monster selection of music DVDs from the 1950s onwards

It's a great place to find your feet and shake off the jet lag at venues like **Bangkok Bar** (100 Soi Rambuttri; tel: 0-2281-2899; www.bkkbar.com), **Café Democ** (78 Thanon Ratchadamnoen; tel: 0-2622-2572; www.café-democ. com) and the newly relocated **Club Culture** (Thanon Ratchadamnoen; tel: 08-9497-8422; www.club-culture-bkk.com), which has some very hot nights with imported DJs.

Cheap digs still exist, but there's an upward trend that includes spa treatments at the area's original 'boutique' hotel, **Buddy Lodge** (265 Thanon Khao San; tel: 0-2629-4477; www.buddylodge.com) and in-room computers at the **Old Bangkok Inn** (609 Thanon Phra Sumen; tel: 0-2629-1785; www.oldbangkokinn.com).

Most people stay here three or four days before heading on, perhaps practising Muay Thai training at **Sor Vorapin** (3 Trok Kasab, near Thanon Khao San; tel: 0-2243-3651; daily 8am–5.30pm); getting some inkwork from **Max Body Art** (70/3 D&D Hotel, Thanon Khao San; tel: 0-2629-1642; www.maxtattoobangkok.com); or buying juggling sticks from **Chuchep Poi Shop** (Bayon Building, 249 Thanon Khao San; tel: 08-1510-1611).

When the time comes to leave, there are good coach, train or plane services to all parts of the country, and there are lots of travel agents in Khao San, so prices are very competitive.

There's no tradition of hitching in Thailand, but upcountry buses run regularly between towns. For shorter journeys, take motorbike taxis or songthaews. These are small vans with benches in the back, which are shared, like buses. Just hail one at the road side and tell the driver where you want to go.

If you plan to explore and then return to fly on somewhere from Bangkok, consider packing light and leaving some stuff in your guesthouse – most have storeroom facilities for a small fee. You won't need much in the way of clothes on the islands, but if you're going north, take a jumper or jacket, since the mountains can be chilly, especially in the cool season. If you haven't already got a small pack, they're cheap to buy.

Moving On

There are several popular routes around the country, with hopping-off points to other destinations of the region, and some with an established

In training for the punishing and brutal ancient martial art of Muay Thai

Vendors sell everything from artwork to hill-tribe clothing at the Chiang Mai Night Bazaar

traveller scene that are good places to meet like-minded people. Chiang Mai – a great centre for exploring the north – is known for its laid-back atmosphere and has long thrived on backpacker trade. Many people who thought they were just travelling through have stayed on or returned to settle.

In the last decade Chiang Mai has built towards high-end tourism, with sumptuous accommodation like the **Mandarin Oriental Dhara Dhevi** (51/4 Thanon Chiang Mai-San Kamphaeng; tel: 0-5388-8888; www. mandarinoriental.com). But the city retains an otherness, and relaxed places like **Gap's House** (3 Ratchad-amnoen Soi 4; tel: 0-5327-8140; www. gaps-house.com) offer good accommodation at reasonable prices. The nightlife leans more toward live music than clubbing. One of the country's best guitar players runs **Chai Blues House** (Thanon Suthep Soi 4; tel: 0-5332-8296; www.chaiblueshouse. com). After Chiang Mai, many head for the very chilled small town of Pai, a few hours away in a plateau in the mountains, and hang out at **Bebop** (188 M 8, Vieng Tai; tel: 0-5369-8046).

A popular stopoff west of Bangkok is Kanchanaburi. There's a good scene at Thanon Mae Nam Kwai, where

The Tiger Temple

The **Tiger Temple** (Wat Pa Luanta Bua Yannasampanno; Km 21, Route 323; tel: 0-3453-1557) is a popular draw an hour from Kanchanaburi. The forest monastery adopted two cubs abandoned in the wild, and after breeding they are now in double figures. They come out of their cages daily, around 3pm, when people can pet them.

Full Moon Parties

The Full Moon Party on Ko Phangan is an essential stop for many. Dubbed the 'world's biggest beach party', it draws hundreds of people for its all-night raves on Hat Rin Nok, known as Sunrise Beach. The big action happens in front of Paradise Resort, although all the main beach bars have DJs spinning, so the crowd gravitates towards the hottest grooves. At sunrise, when it all seems over, head up the hill to Backyard Bar for the traditional after-party. December and January have the wildest nights; guesthouses charge highest prices, and some take only four-night minimum bookings. Don't stay on Hat Rin Nok if you intend to sleep – that is most nights, never mind Full Moon.

guesthouses such as **The Jolly Frog** (28 Soi China; tel: 0-3451-4579) overlook the river. As well as several World War II museums honouring the prisoners who died building the 'Death Railway' over the Bridge on the River Kwai, an hour out of town you can cuddle the big cats at the **Tiger Temple** *(see p.25)*, and if you travel in March, on the road to Kanchanaburi check out the **Tattoo Festival** (Wat Bang Phra, Nakhon Chaisi; tel: 034-389-3333), where hundreds go to be tattooed by monks in the traditional manner, with magic incantations that induce trances.

The other major backpack destination is the Gulf of Thailand and, in particular, the island of Ko Phangan, famous for its Full Moon Parties.

Full moon entertainment, Hat Rin

See www.fullmoon.phangan.info for a list of party dates. The action happens on Hat Rin beach *(see box, opposite)*, but **Cocohut Village** (Ban Tai, Leela Beach; tel: 0-7737-5368; www.cocohut.com), which is walkable to Hat Rin, is a good place to stay because it is on another beach, so you'll get some sleep if you need it. The main party has DJs all up the beach, with the traditional after-party at **Backyard Bar** (Hat Rin Nok; tel: 0-7737-5244). When you are partied out, there are lots of quieter places on the island, such as **Sheesha Bar** (Ao Chalok Lam; tel: 0-7737-4161; www.sheesha-bar.com), where you relax on the beach.

A volunteer veterinarian tending a tiger cub in Kanchanaburi Province

Eco Travel

Travellers, now more aware of environmental issues, increasingly opt for eco-friendly travel or volunteer programmes. This type of journey emphasises local communities by spending money with them rather than with large multinationals, and not disturbing the environment by feeding wildlife, for instance, or removing objects such as coral. *(See Responsible Travel p.262–3.)*

People also share their skills in a wide variety of projects. **The Educational Travel Centre** (www.etc.co.th) has options such as volunteering at the **Children's Village Project**, which provides a home for kids with family or social problems. Volunteers live in the village and teach the children whatever their abilities allow, or help in vocational workshops. Some donate teaching materials like books or posters. Volunteers work,

too, in wildlife sanctuaries, on animal healthcare, cage cleaning or office work; some go to hill-tribe villages and help with museum facilities, develop websites or write reports. Other sources of ecotourism and volunteering information are **North by North East Tours** (www.north-by-north-east.com) and **East West Siam** (www.ewsiam.com).

Projects exist to protect endangered species

Beaches and Islands

Thailand's scorching sun is best enjoyed beside the sea, where the splash of surf, the shade of coconut palms, and a refreshing cocktail are always close at hand to cool you down. And if you want some action, there are scary wakeboards, world-class dive sites and dancing on the beach.

With almost 3,000km (2,000 miles) of coastline, nearly 1,500 islands, and warm, clear, aquamarine waters, Thailand truly is the beach-lover's proverbial paradise. There is an impressive array of natural features and man-made attractions to suit all types of visitor, whether you are in search of raucous parties, family entertainment or just longing to get away from it all.

Although heavy monsoon weather around Phuket and the rest of the Andaman coast makes most activities a washout from May to October, the Gulf of Thailand, which has two official high seasons, from December to January and June to July, frequently has good weather even in the low season. This means that, apart from very windy Novembers, islands such as Ko Samui, Ko Tao and Ko Phangan give practically year-round opportunities to enjoy the fun.

The northern Gulf Coast has some charming towns and secluded bays that are within a few hours of Bangkok, likewise the Eastern Seaboard, where islands such as Ko Samet and Ko Chang are a complete contrast to the full-on nightlife and sexual shenanigans of notorious Pattaya. That

Ao Maya on the island of Koh Phi Phi Ley was the main filming location for *The Beach*

said, Pattaya is very much on the family holiday radar, with numerous sports facilities and cultural shows.

Other distractions from sunbathing include A-grade dive sites, such as the Similan Islands and Surin, with spectacular coral and wildlife such as sharks, sea turtles and dolphins that leap through the water beside your boat. First-class dive operators know all the best spots; they teach PADI standard courses for beginners upwards, and often have job opportunities if you want to stay on.

There's a rapidly expanding boating community, too, with a wide choice of motor launches and sailing yachts for hire, some of which are available for deep-sea fishing, as laid-back or as rod-pumping as you like. Most major resorts can arrange charters, where the evening meal depends on how well you do battle with a powerful barracuda. Those who want to stay closer to shore might try sea canoes, water-skis or kite-boarding.

And there's a good range of accommodation for most pockets, from lavish teak villas to simple huts and camping on the beach.

Thailand's second-largest island, Ko Chang, is part of a national marine park

Accommodation

Given the soft white sand of Thailand's beaches, many people choose to sleep under the stars, lulled by the calming rhythm of the waves. However, if you want the security of a roof over your head and a few modern conveniences, there is waterside accommodation galore to suit all kinds of traveller and budget.

Top Five: Film and TV Locations

The Man with the Golden Gun (1974) Roger Moore, as James Bond, confronts the villainous Scaramanga (Christopher Lee) at his hideout on Ko Ping-Kan (since known as James Bond Island), in Phan Nga Bay.

The Killing Fields (1984) The film, based in Khmer Rouge-era Cambodia, was shot in Hua Hin and Phuket.

The Beach (2000), with Leonardo di Caprio, was filmed on Ko Phi Phi Lay, much to the chagrin of environmentalists, who protested that the crew had damaged the beach there.

Survivor (2002) The remote terrain of Ko Tarutao was a shoe-in for the fifth series of this 'deserted island' reality TV show.

Bridget Jones: The Edge of Reason (2004) Starring Renée Zellweger and Colin Firth, made in Phuket and Bangkok.

High Style

Contemporary beachside villas forego the traditional hotel layout in favour of an opulent home-from-home, as found at **Pimalai Resort & Spa** (99 Moo 5, Ba Kan Tiang Beach, Ko Lanta, Krabi; tel: 075-607-999; www.pimalai.com), on Ko Lanta, and **Amanpuri** (Pansea Beach, Phuket; tel: 076-324-333; www.amanresorts.com), in Phuket. Both provide exquisite luxury, with multi-bedroom Thai-style teak houses with designer silk interiors, art on the walls and infinity pools. Amanpuri even provides live-in maids. Facilities include spa treatments, restaurants and water sports, without ever having to leave the complex.

Boutique Stays

Despite a lower design budget than their high-society sisters, Thailand's increasing number of 'boutique' resorts are often tastefully executed, and of course are much cheaper. Some are located off the beaten track, where

Soaking in the Hot Springs Waterfall at Thanboke Koranee National Park on Krabi

---

Beachside Events

Many boating locations in Thailand have annual regattas during which there are chances to crew in race conditions, or at the very least enjoy the beachside parties. These include Pattaya's Top of the Gulf Regatta (May); Ko Samui Regatta (May–June); Hua Hin Regatta (July–August); and the Phuket King's Cup (December). Other major beachside events include the Pattaya Music Festival (March), the Hua Hin Jazz Festival (June) and the Phuket Vegetarian Festival (September–October).

---

larger chains might find profits too low, such as **Fisherman's Village** (170 Moo 1, Had Chao Samran, Petchaburi; tel: 032-441-370; www.fishermans village.net), near the historic town of Petchaburi. And often they make up for reduced luxury with a personalised, quirky touch. **Birds and Bees Resort** (366/11 Moo 12, Thanon Phra Tam Nak Soi 4, Pattaya; tel: 038-250-556; www.cabbagesandcondoms.co.th) is part of the local Cabbages & Condoms chain that gives part of its proceeds to family planning associations. Where hotels might leave chocolates on your pillow, they give you condoms.

Sea Huts

Traditionally Thais build houses on stilts, particularly in waterside communities, with the living quarters sitting above the waves. Buildings of this type, such as those at **Le Paradis Resort** (101/1 Moo 3, Chaweng Beach, Bophut, Ko Samui; tel: 077-239-041; www.leparadisresort.com), are becoming popular as holiday stays. **Bang Bao Sea Hut** (53 Moo 1, Bang Bao Village, Ko Chang; tel: 039-558-098) is located in the fishing village of Bang Bao, on Ko Chang, where the whole community lives above the sea.

Splendid Isolation

The Robinson Crusoe dream of finding your own deserted beach is still possible in Thailand, where marine national parks offer white sands far from the tourist crowds. The islands can be relatively difficult to get to and many are completely uninhabited. **Ko Tarutao Marine National Park**, 60km (36 miles) off the coast of Satun, still retains the remoteness that made it an ideal choice for former roles as a penal colony and a hideout for pirates. Only five of its 51 islands have regular boat services; for the rest you hire a long-tail boat. The rewards are glorious deserted beaches and wildlife that includes dolphins, sea turtles and rare dugong, said to be the origin of mermaid legends. Most people stay on the main island, Ko Tarutao, camping or in very basic rangers' huts, or at one of the modest resorts on **Ko Lipe**. South of Ko Lanta, **Ko Rok** is so undeveloped you need to take your own food (there is a single shop, but not much in it).

There's a full list of national parks at www.dnp.go.th, where you can also book accommodation.

For merely quiet, rather than completely deserted, there are many options close to civilisation, so you can find some action if things get lonely. For instance, **Pranburi**, south of Hua Hin, has quiet beaches, and

A beach bar on one of the idyllic island resorts in the Andaman Sea

on Phuket you need to hire a longtail boat to get to **Freedom Beach**, which is only accessible by sea.

Good for Families

Successful holidays with the kids in tow are more likely where there are plenty of attractions on offer, and despite a somewhat sleazy reputation, Pattaya is popular with families for facilities such as the Pattaya Kart Speedway (248/2 Moo 12 Thepprasit Road; tel: 0-3842-2044) and Nong Nooch Tropical Garden (34/1 Moo 7, Km 18 Thanon Sukhumvit Rd; tel. 0-3870-9358; www.nongnoochgarden.com), which has mini zoos and elephant shows.

Phuket has the circus and cultural shows of Phuket Fantasea (99 Moo 3, Kamala Kathu, Phuket; tel: 0-7638-5111; www.phuket-fantasea.com), and a mix of dinosaurs and mini golf at Dino Park Mini Golf (47 Thanon Karon, Karon Beach, Phuket; tel: 0-7633-0625; www.dinopark.com).

Good For Nightlife

The beach nightlife is legendary on the Gulf islands of **Ko Samui**, **Ko Tao** and **Ko Phangan**. The last hosts the world-famous Full Moon Parties every month at Hat Rin, when the beach heaves with revellers in all states of intoxication dancing to house, hip-hop and all points between. They also do Half Moon Parties and Black Moon Parties.

The best bars on Ko Tao are located in the villages of Mae Haad and Sairee, which also have Moon parties. The main action in Samui is at Chaweng Beach.

Diving

Don your wetsuit, dive deep into Thailand's clear, warm waters and you experience another world of colourful coral, clown fish, sharks and rays. Most dive operators have PADI Open Water certification courses for beginners to dive master level, and day trips or longer with live-aboard facilities to the best sites. Before embarking, ask a few key questions, such as whether they offer insurance and hotel pick-ups, how many people will be in your class, and if there an instructor who speaks your language.

The Andaman Sea on the west coast is known for some of the best

Many overseas visitors learn how to dive while holidaying in Thailand

Unique Experiences

diving on the planet, particularly around the Similan and Surin island chains. Reach them with Phuket live-aboard operators such as **Dive Asia** (24 Thanon Karon, Kata; tel: 076-330-598; www.diveasia.com), which has multilingual training programmes, and **Scuba Cat Diving** (94 Thanon Thawiwong, Patong; tel: 076-293-120; www.scubacat.com), a Canadian-owned, English-managed National Geographic dive centre with an out-door training pool. On Ko Phi Phi, another premier site, **Island Divers** (157 Moo 7, Ao Nang, Ko Phi Phi; tel: 089-873-2205; www.islanddiverspp.com) has beginner to dive master courses. In the Gulf of Thailand many good firms, like **Big Blue Diving** (Hat Sai Ree and Mae Hat, tel: 077-456-050; www.bigbluediving.com), operate from Ko Tao. If you're staying on the nearby islands of Ko Samui or Ko Phangan, most operators head to Ko Tao anyway, so there's no need to switch accommodation. The 50-island archipelago of Ko Chang has many schools, including the professional and well-equipped **Water World Diving** (Ko Chang Plaza, 17/3 Moo 4, Hat Chai Chet; tel: 08-6139-1117; www.waterworldkohchang.com), which has competitive prices and multilingual courses.

Wind- and Kite-surfing

For a full-throttle adrenalin rush there's nothing like racing at 30 km/h (20mph) behind a speedboat with nothing but a sliver of wood between you and the chopping waves. **Wake Up! Wakeboarding** (71/3 Moo 7, Cha-loklum, Ko Phangan; tel: 08-7283-6755;

Windsurfing is a very popular activity on Ko Chang and other islands

Sea Gypsies

The Andaman Sea is home to three groups of nearly 5,000 'Sea Gypsies', known in Thai as *Chao Lay*. They principally live in coastal shacks, from Ranong to Ko Tarutao, and subsist by fishing and beachcombing, although the most famous, the Moken, lead a mainly nomadic life on boats moving between islands. The other two communities, the Urak Lawoi and the Moklen, are fairly well integrated into Thai society.

Little is known of the *Chao Lay*'s past, as they have no written language or records. Their spoken languages are mainly related to Malay, though the Moken, living furthest north, have borrowed a much larger vocabulary from Thai and Burmese.

The *Chao Lay*'s intimacy with their environment is said to have saved many from the 2004 tsunami, when they understood early-warning signs in the sea's behaviour and fled to higher ground.

Beaches and Islands

Hat Than Phra Nang and karsts viewed from Railay Bay

www.wakeupwakeboarding.com) has good boards, water-skis, mono-skis, kneeboards and even wake-skates to simulate a half-pipe experience. Their boat carries an elevated rope for easier jumps.

For an even bigger high, attach yourself to a parachute behind a boat and be lifted heavenwards with some kite-surfing. **Kite Boarding Asia** (www.kiteboardingasia.com) runs 1- to 3-day training from offices in seven locations, including Hua Hin, Samui, Pattaya and Phuket.

Sailing

What better way to experience Thailand's dramatic scenery than sailing beside jaw-dropping limestone karsts that rise from the water like prehistoric sculptures? It's a fun activity to do with friends or family, safe for kids of most ages, and you can usually learn how to hoist the sails and take the tiller. Then drop anchor in the silvery bay of an uninhabited isle for a swim and picnic lunch.

Sailing from Phuket, **SY Stressbreaker** (tel: 08-1894-3966; www.thailand-sail.com) has adventure sailing in the Mergui Archipelago with experienced skippers and four boats sleeping up to ten. Sideshows include sea fishing, diving, kayaking and wind-surfing. **Samui Boat Charters** (tel: 08-7276-7598; www.samuiboatcharter.com) has a small fleet sailing from half-day cruises to multiday island tours, including luxury motorised cruisers, speedboats and sporting yachts. Fishing and diving are options, and they even have charters to the monthly Full Moon Parties on Ko Phangan. On the Eastern Seaboard, **Blue Wave/Yacht Pro** (Ocean Marina Yacht Club, Jomtien; tel:

08-1622-9372; www.sailing-pattaya.com) has half-day to multi-day sailing in several boats, plus a sailing school, and **Sea Adventures** (Hat Sai Khao, Ko Chang; tel: 08-4728-6387) takes day trips around Ko Chang and the neighbouring islands Ko Klum and Ko Wai on their 13m (40ft) catamaran.

Deep-sea Fishing

Hard-core deep-sea thrills that satisfy your hidden Ernest Hemingway

Sea-kayaking around Krabi's impressive limestone karsts, Railay Bay

involve strapping yourself to a chair and grappling big fish such as tuna, which you catch and then eat for dinner. **Phuket Deep Sea Fishing** (Chalong Bay, Phuket; tel: 08-7269-7383; www.phuketdeepseafishing.com) rolls around the Andaman and Similan Islands. If you don't eat what you catch you can use it as shark bait on a night fishing trip. **Seaduction** (551/2 Moo 10 Tambon Nongprue, Banglamung; tel: 038-710-029; www.seaductiondiving.com) has a wooden boat for single day trips or three days' night fishing 80km (50 miles) offshore, where you'll hunt barracuda, marlin and sailfish.

Sea-Kayaking

Kayaking is a rewarding, eco-friendly and scenic way to explore the many limestone crags, secluded lagoons and tidal caves (known as *hong*) that are scattered around the Andaman Sea and the Gulf of Thailand. The original, run by the charismatic John Gray out of Phuket, is **John Gray Sea Canoe** (124 Soi 1 Thanon Yaowarat, Phuket Town; tel: 0-7625-4505; www.johngray-seacanoe.com). On Samui, **Blue Stars** (83/23 Moo 2, Thanon Chaweng Lake, Chaweng, Samui; tel: 0-7741-3231; www.bluestars.info) has one- and two-day trips around Ang Thong Marine National Park, the latter with barbecue dinner and overnight camping on a desolate beach. And from Krabi, **Sea Kayak Krabi** (40 Thanon Maharat, Krabi Town; tel: 0-7563-0270; www.seakayak-krabi.com) has trips to Ao Thalane and Ao Luk, where monkeys, otters and tropical birds are common companions.

Adventures in Thailand

Hunger for the jungle experience has driven travellers for centuries, and for the modern-day adventurer Thailand has a range of tasty exploits to excite the senses. Along with wildlife watching on forest treks, there's freefall parachuting, deep-water climbing, bungy jumping, and much else besides to make the adrenalin rush.

Thailand's diverse terrain has some breathtaking experiences for sports and adventure enthusiasts. The jungle offers elephant treks, whitewater rafting, off-road biking and – particularly in the north of the country – visits to the hill-tribe settlements.

Elephants are the symbol of Thailand, and in the past played a very important role in the country, transporting heavy goods such as logs, and carrying mounted troops into battle. Riding an elephant on treks gives a small hint at age-old modes of travel, when much movement through the jungle involved climbing on an elephant's back. A few minutes will give you an appreciation of an experience that often entailed journeys lasting days or weeks.

In centuries past, elephant travellers will have encountered the several tribes that live in the mountains of northern Thailand, Myanmar and Laos, some of which began settling in Thailand over 500 years ago. In the modern era, most hill tribes have been accepting tourists for decades, so there is little chance of a truly 'authentic' experience. However, in many cases they retain a very traditional way of life and hill-tribe trekking can be an interesting and rewarding encounter.

Thailand has been very proactive in preserving areas on both land and water as national parks, although policing the resources within them has, to a wide degree, failed. Fish, coral, wildlife and forest areas are all under threat from illegal poaching, logging, development and poor environmental practices.

Elephant-back trekking is a fun way to experience the jungle around Chiang Mai

Nonetheless, recent developments in ecotourism leave some scope for optimism in the tourism industry, and there are many chances to experience the country's natural environments through activities such as wildlife safaris and birdwatching. The rocky limestone karsts of southern Thailand offer challenging cliffs for climbers, some of them out at sea, and Thailand's long coastline has spawned a famous (sometimes notorious) beach life that extends to snorkelling and diving, sailing and paragliding.

Many energetic sports enthusiasts take the time to learn Muay Thai, which was developed as the martial art of the elite forces of ancient Siam, particularly during the many wars with neighbouring Burma.

Hill Tribes & Trekking

In the jungle, the floor is cluttered with tree roots that trip you at every step; it's steep, and the trees and bushes clamp you to the stifling heat like a baker's oven. Then, just when you think you can't take another step, there's a clearing, a few iron pots smoking over open fires and a cluster of bamboo huts on stilts. Your accommodation in a local hill-tribe village.

Chiang Mai and Chiang Rai are major centres where dozens of agencies arrange hikes to hill-tribe villages. Prices should range from B2,000 to B3,000 per person per day, and include all transport, lodging, food and guide services.

Most guides are freelance, so it's best to speak to them before you sign up with any tour agency. Find out exactly what the itinerary will be, and

Organised north Thailand hill-tribe treks include visits to Karen communities

Adventures in Thailand

ask lots of questions: What can they tell you about the culture and lifestyle of the tribes? How many hours' walking will there be and over what type of ground? What activities will you see or be allowed to experience?

Typically you'll take a minivan or four-wheeled drive to start the trek, two or three hours away, before setting off up the mountainside. Each section of walk will be at least four hours, and it's hot during the day. So pack light but do include long trousers as well as shorts as some areas have leeches. A jumper is handy (it gets cold up there at night), and insect repellent, too. Ask the agency for their advice on what to take.

When you reach the village, you should expect some souvenir selling, but in many you will witness normal daily life, staying in a traditional home, eating and (possibly) cooking with the family. You may experience other chores, like planting crops.

The best place to learn about hilltribe cultures before a trek is the **Hilltribe Museum & Education Centre** (620/1 Thanon Thanalai, Chiang Rai; tel: 0-5374-0088; www.pda.or.th/chiangrai/hilltribe_museum.htm; Mon–Fri 9am–7pm, Sat–Sun 10am–7pm; charge). Run by the non-profit Population & Community Development Association, it also conducts environmentally friendly and culturally sensitive tours. In Chiang Mai, **Trekking Collective** (3/5 Thanon Loy Kroh, Chiang Mai; tel: 0-5320-8340; www.trekkingcollective.com) appeals to many because it pumps part of its profits into funding community projects, although its tours are more expensive than the norm. Treks last one to six days and cater to all levels of fitness.

Many say the best place for trekking is Mae Hong Son, where **Nam Rim Tours** (Thanon Khunlum Praphat, Mae Hong Son; tel: 0-5361-4454) include stopovers with the longneck Karen tribe, so called because of the stack of rings worn by women to elongate their necks. In Mae Sot, guided trips to Um Phang District by **Eco-Trekking** (No 4 Guest House, 736 Thanon Intharakhiri, Mae Sot; tel: 0-5554-4976; http://th.88db.com/Travel/Travel-Agencies/ad-506214/) include hot springs and bat caves.

The vast expanse of Kaeng Krachan and Khao Sam Roi Yot national parks are accessible with **Hua Hin Adventure Tour** (69/8 Thanon Petchkasem, tel: 0-3235-0314; www.huahinadventuretour.com), who have one-day to three-day excursions that may feature kayaking and rock climbing.

Khao Sam Roi Yot National Park

National Parks

When your guide points to scratches on a tree and says: "Claw marks. Probably made by a Malaysian Sun Bear", a nervous glance into the jungle is acceptable. If you are lucky you might also see tigers in Kaeng Krachan National Park, and Kitti's Hog-nosed Bat (the world's smallest mammal) in Sai Yok. And elephants, deer, gibbons and monkeys are common.

Visits are available to most of Thailand's 110 marine and land-based **National Parks** (http://web2.dnp.go.th). The official website has good information about everything from geography and climate to flora and fauna. Most parks have accommodation, which you can book online.

Off-Road Tours

The exhilaration is hard to describe as you leave the tarmac and cars behind and your bike hits the dirt road for the first time. The rush of splashing through the mud and bouncing

Tigers inhabit Kaeng Krachan National Park

And in Kanchanaburi **AS Mixed Travel** (153/4 Moo 4 Sutjai Bridge; tel: 0-3451-2017; www.guesthousekanchanaburi.com), owned by Apple's Retreat & Guesthouse, has tours of the surrounding attractions as well as the chance to trek through Erawan National Park, ride on an elephant and raft on the river.

Best National Parks

Doi Inthanon National Park Thailand's highest mountain.

Erawan National Park: Kanchanaburi Province The seven-level Erawan Waterfall is the star attraction at this national park to the west of Bangkok.

Kaeng Krachan National Park: Phetchaburi Province Thailand's largest national park is surprisingly one of the least explored.

Khao Sam Roi Yot National Park: Gulf of Thailand Expect varied topography at this vast reserve, with beaches, marshes, lush forests and mountains.

Khao Sok National Park: Northern Andaman Coast South Thailand's most popular national park is unique in many ways, and has an amazing variety of flora and fauna.

Khao Yai National Park: Nakhon Ratchasima Although located in northeastern Thailand, this popular national park is easily accessed from Bangkok.

Phu Kradung National Park: Loei A high-altitude forest and mountain reserve that is one of the most memorable escapes in northeastern Thailand.

Thai Sky Adventures offers tandem and solo parachute jumps

over the crest of a hill is balanced by the fourth time you hit the ground, as you drop your bike, yet again. This is a tough game. **Green Earth Adventure** (88/8 Thanon Sridonchai, Chiang Mai; tel: 0-5381-8876; www. greenearthadventure.in.th) organises custom adventure tours by Jeep or motorbike that can take in white-water rafting and elephant riding as well as trips into Laos. The company also offers pre-planned tours lasting from 1 to 15 days.

Whitewater Rafting

You need to hang on tight as the boat tips 45 degrees over the edge of the rapids or you end up in the drink. Which is actually a small price to

Top Five: Adrenalin Rush

- Sky Diving
- Bungy Jumping
- Whitewater Rafting
- Jungle Zip Line
- Ballooning

pay for a superb journey with **Thai Adventure Rafting** (Moo 4 Thanon Rongsianoon, Pai; tel: 0-5369-9111; www.thairafting.com) through 60 rapids along a 110km (69-mile) stretch of the Pai River. You spend a night in the jungle and finish in Mae Hong Son. They also have trekking, four-wheel drive and mountain-bike options.

Sky High

The wind rattles around your ears; the clouds are wisps beneath your feet; and all you have is a little backpack between you and the tiny specks 4km (2½ miles) below. You drop at 190k/ph (120mph) for the first minute on the freefall course with **Thai Sky Adventures** (Pattaya Sports Apartments, 142/162 Soi Banluekanka, Thanon Sukhumvit 21, Pattaya; tel: 08-5900-3412; www. thaiskyadventures.com), before opening your parachute for a more leisurely 20-minute drift on the wind. Alternatively, they will give you a tandem leap strapped to the back of an instructor.

Maybe start with something less scary, but equally breathtaking. **Earth Wind & Fire** (158/60 Moo 6 Cheungdoi, Doi Saket, Chiang Mai; tel: 0-5329-2224; http://balloon.wind-and-fire.com) arrange hot-air balloon flights over the villages, temples and rice paddies nestled between mountains along the Pai River valley. The company can also provide pilot training.

Good views are also available from **Bangkok Aviation Centre** (222 Hanger 4414 Thanon Viphavadee Rangsit, Don Mueang, Bangkok; tel: 0-2535-7740; www.bangkokflying.com), who have sunset sightseeing tours in their four-seater Cessna planes. For a small surcharge you can sit in the co-pilot's seat. They also do training for a pilot's licence.

Tree Top Thrills

You tell yourself it will be fine. After all, you have an elasticated rope seurely strapped to your ankle, the platform isn't *that* high, and there's some water to break the fall if things go wrong. Right? **Jungle Bungy** (Thanon Vichitsongkram, Kathu, Phuket; tel: 0-7632-1351; www.phuketbungy.com) is fully licensed, with insurance and a good reputation for safety, but the heart still pounds. The idea is to keep your eyes open.

Alternatively, try touring the jungle like Tarzan on the **Flight of the Gibbon** (65 Sukhumvit Soi 1; tel: 08-9970-5511; www.treetopasia.com), which has 3km (2 miles) of zip lines interspersed with 26 platforms that stretch through the rainforest canopy.

They say any age can fly, from 5 to 90, with sightings of giant squirrels, monkeys and barking deer part of the thrill. Extra challenges for various skills and ages include suspended bridges, spider nets and flying swings. They have facilities in Chonburi and Chiang Mai, where rock climbing, mountain biking and whitewater rafting are options to add to the adventure. Overnight stays are possible in both centres.

A similar, though less extensive, experience with eight platforms on the zip line, is available in Ko Samui at **Canopy Adventures** (Best Beach Bungalow, Chaweng; tel: 0-7741-4150; www.canopyadventuresthailand.com).

Rock climbing

To dangle hands-free on a rope from a sheer cliff overhang surrounded by unearthly towers of rock that rise from tropical seas is a truly surreal

The sheer limestone cliffs of south Thailand attract climbers from all over the world

experience. You are hardly scared at all. Krabi attracts rock climbers to its 150 pegged routes both inland and offshore on the karsts of Phra Nang Bay. Most routes are challenging, but there are several for beginners, and operators can advise on courses to suit different ages, skills and fitness levels. Equipment rentals, instruction and guides are all available.

Hot Rock Climbing School (Bobo Plaza, Hat Railay West; tel: 0-7562-1771; www.railayadventure. com) also arranges speedboat and sailing trips. **Andaman Adventures** (23/8 Moo 2, Ao Nang, Krabi; tel: 08-4627-6779; www.andamanadventures.com) can advise on deep-water solo climbing areas around Ao Nang, Ko Phi Phi, Ko Lao Liang and Ko

Hong. **Chiang Mai Rock Climbing Adventures** (55/3 Thanon Ratchaphakhinai; tel: 0-5320-7102; www.thailandclimbing.com) offers guided rock climbs, caving and bouldering instruction at Crazy Horse Buttress limestone cliffs in Mae On district east of Chiang Mai.

Muay Thai

Before you step into the Muay Thai ring, be assured: this hurts. There's no preparation for that first kick to the ribs, but kicking with your own shins is just as bad, until you've practised so much that all the nerve ends go dead and the hairs on your legs fall out. Muay Thai training camps vary considerably. Some are set up for tourists with decent facilities, others are grittier, more authentic experiences, but with little more than a ring and skipping rope for equipment. Many will find fights for you if you like.

Well placed for the backpackers of Khao San Road is **Sor Vorapin** (13 Trok Kasab; tel: 0-2243-3651; www.thaiboxings.com), offering lessons from one day to a month.

In Chiang Mai, **Lanna Muay Thai** (161 Soi Chiang Khian, Chiang Mai; tel: 0-5389-2102; www.lannamuaythai.com) has a camp in town and another at Doi Modt (Ant Mountain), close to hill-tribe villages.

On Phuket, **Dragon Muay Thai** (10/14 Moo 5 Soi Ta-iead, Ao Chalong Muang, Phuket; tel: 0-7628-3611; www.muaythaitrainingthailand.com) has monthly courses run by ex-world champion Khun Thit, from B16,900, including accommodation.

Some Muay Thai training camps are open to tourists

Parasailing off Ko Hae (Coral island), Phuket

Watersports

With nearly 3,000 km (2,000 miles) of coastline, and fantastic weather, Thailand is a natural paradise for water-sports. Many beaches around the country have excellent facilities and conditions for things like diving, snorkelling and parasailing, and there's an increasingly well-equipped sailing community that hosts several regattas, year-round. For full details on water sports see *Beaches and Islands*, *(see p.28)*.

Birdwatching

With almost 1,000 species of birds – that's around one-tenth of the world's total – Thailand is a popular country in which to experience birding. As the habitat rolls down from the mountainous north to the mangrove swamps and rocky outcrops of the south, there's a terrific range of exotic names to spot, such as Thick-billed Flowerpeckers, Asian Paradise Flycatchers and the wondrous Javan Frogmouth.

If you choose to take an organised tour, you'll benefit from the guides' knowledge of the best spotting areas, and they can also fill you in about local lifestyles in the forests or fishing villages. Of course, they will also take care of accommodation in or near the national parks you visit, and any transport needed, such as kayaks for offshore exploring.

Thailand Bird Watching (www.thailandbirdwatching.com) has treks lasting from two, to a mammoth 35 days, taking in the full length of the country, including Doi Inthanon, Khao Yai, and Khao Sam Roi Yod Marine National Park, which on its own has around 300 species.

If you want to birdwatch independently, a good resource site is www.thaibirding.com, which has trip reports, photos and recommendations for sites to visit and travel details to each location.

Shopping

Thailand's shops and markets have so many hot bargains that choosing what not to buy is often the hardest decision. The country's developing blend of old and new means à la mode Paris fashions a few steps from ancient designs in tribal weave, and a gift idea on every corner.

Chatuchak Weekend Market

Thailand's exhilarating markets, mega-malls and local craft fairs mean a more than usually addictive experience for the unwary shopaholic. Markets offering a brush with colourful traders are both cheap and packed with local exotica from Siamese fighting fish to antique temple gongs. The enormous modern malls of downtown Bangkok are monuments to an Asian Tiger economy that bares its teeth in flagship stores of local and international

brands, whether you want Milanese gowns, funky New York denim, or locally designed silk suits.

Chiang Mai, the northern capital, is located on ancient trade routes, and renowned for ethnic handicrafts like Burmese silverware, hill-tribe textiles and fragile Thai ceramics. The northeast has swathes of expert silk weavers. All towns have markets, often several, and malls are found in most cities, particularly those on the tourist trail, such as Pattaya, Chiang Mai and Phuket.

Thailand is a rapidly changing country, with a surprisingly fluid mix of old and new, East and West, and has some beautiful finds for the alert shopper, often for small change.

Markets and Bazaars

Thailand's most famous shopping experience is **Chatuchak Weekend Market** (Thanon Paholyothin, Bangkok; Sat–Sun 8am–6pm), where some 250,000 shoppers swarm over nearly 10,000 stalls, making it the biggest flea market in the world. The maze-like alleys are filled with antiques, books, opium pipes, woven fabric, weird lamps and funky fashion. **Suan Lum Night Bazaar** (Thanon Rama IV, Bangkok; daily 5pm–midnight) is a well-organised, less frenetic alternative. Also popular after dark is **Patpong Night Market** (Thanon Silom, Bangkok; daily 6pm–midnight), located in the city's notorious red-light district. **China-town** (around Thanon Yaowarat) is the place for gold and traditional items used in dragon parades, while for sumptuous silks from the sub-continent, head to **Pahurat** (Thanon Chakkraphet), otherwise known as Little India.

Chiang Mai Night Bazaar (Thanon Chang Klan, Chiang Mai; daily 5–11pm) has quality silks, handicrafts, rugs and clothing, among many other items, as do Chiang Mai's walking street markets on Saturday evenings at Thanon Wualai and on Sundays from 2–10pm at Thanon Ratchadamnoen. **Warorot Market** (Thanon Chang Moi; daily 5am–6pm), Chiang Mai's oldest market, is housed in a huge ramshackle building stuffed with everything native to the area, from pre-served fruits to loom-woven textiles.

Shopping Malls

Monolith malls are mainly confined to wealthy cities with a tourist presence,

but such is their size and sheer variety, particularly in Bangkok, that spendthrifts are in credit-card heaven. Opening hours are 10am–9pm or 10pm daily. **Central World** (Thanon Ratchadamri, Bangkok; www.central-world.co.th) is a staggering 800,000 sq metres of chic fashion, beauty, home decor, electronics, and anything else you can imagine. **Siam Paragon** (991/1 Thanon Rama I; www.siam-paragon.co.th) is not much smaller, and adds Ferrari and Porsche to the mix, plus a walk-in aquarium, called Ocean World. Both have department stores, multiplex cinemas and scores of restaurants. **Mahboonkrong**, or MBK (444 Thanon Phayathai, Bangkok; tel: 0-2217-9119), is a crowded evocation of a Thai market, where stalls spill chaotically into the aisles and, unlike other

Chiang Mai Night Bazaar has three floors of shops

Bargaining

You can get amazing discounts with a little judicious bargaining.

- Don't bargain unless you really want to buy.
- Start by asking how much something is, then say it is too much and ask if there is a discount. The seller will ask you how much you want to pay.
- Don't be afraid to offer what you might consider a ludicrously low price – around one third of the original asking price is a good pointer towards what they might actually take. So start lower than that.
- From there only raise your offer in small increments.
- Good tips include watching locals to see what price they get. And if you walk away you may be called back with a better price. If not, you've at least established some groundwork for trying at another stall (many stock the same items).

malls, price bargaining is common. Popular around the country are **Central Festival Phuket** (74–75 Moo 5, Thanon Vichit; www.centralfestival-phuket.com) and its sister branch **Central Festival Pattaya** (78/54 Moo 9 Pattaya 2nd Rd; tel: 038-361-361). A further centre is scheduled to open in Chiang Mai in 2012.

Antiques

Antiques from around the region are available at **River City** (23 Trok Rong-namkaeng; tel: 0-2237-0077-8; www.rivercity.co.th; daily 10am–10pm), **Under the Bo** (22–24 Chiang Mai Night Bazaar, Thanon Changlan,

Chiang Mai; tel: 053-818-831; www.antique-arts-asia.com; daily 7–11pm) and **Chan's Antiques** (99/42 Moo 5, Thanon Chalermprakit; tel: 0-7626-1416; daily 10am–8pm). Common pieces are carved wood figurines from Nepal and Tibet; Indonesian face masks; Chinese and Indian furniture; temple drums and gongs from Burma; and tribal jewellery from Thailand and Laos. Beware, though; even people who know what they're doing get stung. Export permission is required to take genuine antiques out of the country, which the dealer should provide. For more details contact the National Museum, Bangkok (tel: 0-2224-1333).

Gems and Jewellery

Thailand is a conduit for stones from Burma and Cambodia and also has mines in **Chantaburi** and

Hill-tribe-influenced pendants are sold in Chiang Mai's vibrant night market

Kanchanaburi, where many stalls sell stones. Wherever you buy in Thailand, stick to shops endorsed by the Tourism Authority of Thailand and the Thai Gem and Jewellery Traders Association, which carry the Jewel Fest (www.jewelfest.com) logo, a certificate of authenticity and a money-back guarantee.

Bangkok is home to leading coloured gem cutters, and many shops cluster around the **Jewellery Trade Centre** (919/1 Thanon Silom; tel: 0-2630-0944; www.jewelrytradecenter. com; daily 10am–8pm), where you can have gemstones graded at the **Asian Institute of Gemological Sciences** (tel: 0-2267-4315; www.aigsthailand. com; Mon–Fri 8am–6pm). **SP Silver** (216/4 Thanon Khao San; tel: 0-629-3313; Mon–Sat 10am–7pm) is a popular Khao San shop and **Chatuchak Market** has stalls selling various beads, stones, chains and threads for making your own jewellery.

Traditional Crafts

Chiang Mai is known as the centre for Thai crafts, and there are many small workshops east of the city, where you can watch artisans toil, as well as buy products like lacquerware from **P Collection** (2 Moo 1, Thanon San Kamphaeng; tel: 0-5324-0222; daily 10am–10pm) and the area's famous bamboo umbrellas, with designs painted on *sa* (mulberry) paper, from **The Umbrella Making Centre** (111/2 Bo Sang, Chiang Mai; tel: 0-5333-8324; www.www.handmade-umbrella.com; daily 8am–5pm). **Sipsong Panna** (Nantawan Arcade, 6/19 Thanon Nimanhemin; tel: 0-5321-

Bamboo umbrellas from Chiang Mai

6096; daily 9.30am–6pm) is famous for high-quality detailed silverwork in tribal designs of hand-beaten serving bowls, jars and ornaments.

In Bangkok, **Narayana Phand** (127 Thanon Ratchadamri, Bangkok; tel: 0-2252-4670; daily 10am–9pm) is a popular one-stop shop with all sorts, from wooden carvings of mythical gods and bronze statues from classical drama, to natural fibre baskets and handbags, while **Asian Motifs** (3rd Floor, Gaysorn Plaza, Thanon Ploenchit, Bangkok; tel: 0-2656-1093; daily 10am–8pm) creates contemporary Thai designs by adding an elegant spin to traditional forms. **ThaiCraft** (242 Soi Akharn Songkroh; tel: 0-2676-0636; www.thaicraft. org) has no retail outlet, but holds regular Bangkok fairs with crafts from around Thailand that adhere to fair-trade practices. Check the website for events.

High-quality lacquerware is fashioned by skilled artists working mainly in north Thailand

Unique Experiences

In Phuket, there are lots of gift ideas at **Art and Gift Gallery** (Canal Village, Laguna Shopping Unit 16, 390/1 Moo 1, Thanon Srisoonthorn, Bang Thao, Phuket; tel: 0-7627-0616; daily 10am–8pm).

Ceramics

Pottery making dates back 5,000 years, and many ceramic designs are centuries old. Among the most well known are Sangkhaloke, from ancient Sukhothai, with its distinctive twin-fish design, and the five-coloured Bencharong (*bencha* is Sanskrit for 'five'; *rong* means 'colour'), from the Ayutthaya period. **Mengrai Kilns** (79/2 Thanon Arak; tel: 0-53-272-063; Mon–Sat 10am–7pm) have Celadon stoneware lamps, statuary and dinnerware finished with a jade-green or brown glaze.

Clothes and Fashion

Global labels like Versace and Jimmy Choo are common in malls, alongside domestic designers like Somchai Songwatana, who was lauded at British Designer 2000 and still looms large in Thai fashion. At his shop **Fly Now** (2/F, Gaysorn Plaza, Thanon Ploenchit, Bangkok; tel: 0-2656-1359; www.flynowbangkok.com; daily 10am–8pm) you can get accessories like bags, wallets and belts, or have a classic modern dress made to order. Off-the-peg clothes are usually in small (Thai) sizes, but they go up to XL at **Jaspal** (2nd Floor, Siam Centre, Thanon Rama I, Bangkok; tel: 0-2251-5918; www.jaspal.com; daily 10am–9pm), which is influenced by British and European trends and has branches in most malls.

Thailand's famed cheap tailors will accost you regularly in touristy sites like Phuket and Pattaya. Their trousers, dresses, suits and shirts 'made to order in 24 hours' sound great, but finish and fitting are usually poor at this pace. Give them several days to get a proper job. **Embassy**

Fashion House (29/1 Unico House Block A, Soi Langsuan, Bangkok; tel: 0-2251-2620; www.embassyfashion.com; daily 10am–6pm) caters to men and women and has a wide range of local and imported fabrics. Women's ready-to-wear shops often sell good cheap copies of current international fashions, and dressmakers will happily copy garments for you.

Thai Silk and Fabrics

Weavers produce colourful long-lasting Thai fabrics, from gossamer blouses to heavy bedspreads that are rightfully famous. Beautiful fashion and decor items, prized for printed fabrics by designers like Ed Tuttle and Ou Baholyodhin, are the domain of pioneer silk merchants Jim Thompson. The **Jim Thompson Factory Outlet** (153 Sukhumvit Soi 93; tel: 0-2332-6530; www.jimthompson.com; daily 9am–6pm) has lower prices than their numerous other stores around the country.

The royally initiated craft foundation **Mae Fah Luang Foundation** (4th Floor, Siam Discovery Centre, Thanon Rama I; tel: 02-658-0424-5; www.doitung.org; daily 10am–9pm) is acclaimed for its traditional weaves infused with contemporary designs.

Patricia Cheeseman, an expert on Southeast Asian textiles, has a Chiang Mai workshop-cum-gallery called **Studio Naenna** (138/8 Soi Chang Khian, Thanon Huay Kaew; tel: 0-5322 6042; www.studio-naenna.com; Mon–Sat 8.30am–5pm) that sells hill-tribe-inspired silk and cotton fabrics and clothing, and offers free

Shipping Items Home

If you're buying large items of furniture, expensive antiques or dealing with department stores, the seller may be able to arrange shipping for you. Otherwise, major post offices have packing facilities and are a cheaper, if less secure, option than going with a courier such as FedEx (hotline 1782; www.fedex.com). There's a selection of shippers at Section 7 of Chatuchak Weekend Market, beside the exit to Thanon Kamphaengphet 3.

weaving and dyeing demonstrations. And **Fai Thong** (39/2 Thanon Kuang Maen; tel: 0-5323-3419; Mon–Sat 9am–6pm) has an extensive collection of traditional northern Thai textiles that draw the city's boutiques and high-end seamstresses.

Silk items make excellent souvenirs

Spa Treatments

Whether you are looking to develop your spirituality, to learn alternative healing or just need a little pampering – Thailand has something for everyone, including spa treatments that include reiki, Thai massage, body scrubs and yoga, flower essence and hypnotherapy, many performed in beachside villas and romantic jungle hideaways.

A variety of traditional and modern treatments is available in Thai spas

The stunning weather and beautiful palm beaches are images that accompany ads proclaiming Thailand as Asia's top spa experience. But these exquisite trimmings paint only part of the picture. The country's historical and philosophical connections to elements of what the West might call 'alternative treatments' provide an emotional link that admen could only dream of.

Travelling monks arrived in Thailand in the 2nd or 3rd century AD, bearing not only Buddhism, but also *nuad paen boran* (ancient massage), which legend says was developed from Indian Vedic treatments by Shivakar Kumar Baccha, the Buddha's own medical adviser. Nearly 2,000 years after it entered the country, the world now calls it simply Thai massage.

This association with the country's religious philosophy means that the most dedicated masseurs still perform the service within the Buddhist concept of mindfulness. Before they start, true adherents will make a *wai* – a slight bow with hands clasped together – to pay respects to their teacher and focus on *metta* (loving kindness), which is thought to be the ideal state of mind in which to give massage.

For centuries throughout Thailand, temples were places of healing (many still have hospitals located next door), and they employed many of the treatments we now associate with modern spas, such as herbal compresses and herbal medicines.

Massage is such an inherent part of life in Thailand that you will see friends casually massage each other's backs and shoulders as easily as they might offer them a cup of coffee. It is these elements that make spa treatments such a natural part of the Thailand experience.

Thai Massage

Thai massage is the shining light in Thailand's spa spectrum, and many people head to a parlour straight from the plane. It's a quintessentially Thai experience that gets you quickly into the pulse of the country, as well as easing jet lag and soothing those aching limbs.

The most common operations are in small shophouses and consist of little more than mattresses on the floor, curtained-off from each other in the same room. Available on many streets, and numerous in tourist areas, they provide exquisite relaxation for as little as B200 an hour. In Bangkok, Sukhumvit has many shops, and also Silom, where a reliable option is **Arima Onsen** (37/10-14 Soi Surawong Plaza, Thanon Surawong; tel: 0-2235-2142; www.arimaonsenthailand.net; daily 9–1am). Unsurprisingly, Khao San Road is known for budget operations. **Tune Up Massage** (3rd floor, 193–195 Thanon Khao San, Bangkok; tel: 0-2629-1332; daily 10am–midnight) has a half-hour

starter at B100, which is cheap, but hardly worth disrobing for. But the place is smarter than most, and includes rooftop massage under the stars. The full hour at B180 is good value. The centre of Chiang Mai is packed with shops, with more around the Night Market. **Loi Kroh Massage** (1/2 Soi 3, Thanon Loi Kroh, Chiang

> ### Aromatherapy Ingredients
>
> Aromatherapists say you can treat ailments with essential oils extracted from plants. They are mainly used either inhaled, in massage, or added to baths. Each oil is believed to have properties that treat various ailments, such as:
>
> **Anxiety** bergamot, cedarwood
> **Colds and Flu** basil, eucalyptus, tea tree
> **Depression** jasmine, lavender, neroli
> **Headaches** chamomile, lavender, peppermint
> **Loneliness** marjoram

Treat yourself to a massage without leaving the beach

Spa Treatments

Mai; tel: 08-7920-0360; daily 10am–10pm) includes hot herbal compresses (where a hessian bag is filled with oil and herbs and heated before being used for massage) and hot stone massage, with heated stones covered in oil. They say one stroke with a stone is worth 10 by hand.

When you walk into a massage shop, there will be a menu to choose from, usually with Thai massage, oil massage and foot massage. For Thai massage you'll be given pyjamas to change into. Oil massage is customarily done naked, with strategically placed towels.

Before starting, the masseur (usually a woman) bathes your feet; then the massage proceeds in a standard sequence, from the feet, with you lying on your back. Legs, arms, hands, fingers, back, neck and head will all be treated.

Most shops outside red-light areas give only traditional Thai massage, but to avoid misunderstandings regarding the country's famous sexual services, it's best to steer away from 'soapy massage' or possible euphemisms like 'hot', 'teen', and 'pretty girl'.

The Technique

As it is based on ancient Indian teachings, Thai massage includes stretching elements of yoga alongside acupressure and reflexology. There should also be a meditative quality, although low-budget shops may have music playing or a television switched on which can spoil the mood.

The massage principle revolves around 10 energy lines, called *sip sen*, that are believed to carry physical,

Unique Experiences

Receiving treatment in a serene setting

emotional and spiritual energy between meridian points around the body. When the lines become blocked, it causes illness or emotional stress. It is the masseur's job to reopen these lines.

The experience is usually vigorous, employing push-and-pull stretching of tendons and joints and deep tissue kneading with elbows, knees and feet and fingers, so it is not a suitable treatment for people with back, neck or joint problems. *Bow bow, kap/ka* is a useful phrase, meaning 'softer please'. Sometimes an ointment is used on painful muscles – Tiger Balm is the most famous brand – but generally there are no oils or ointments involved.

If you've enjoyed the experience, depending on the length and quality of the massage, it is usual to give a tip of between B50 and B100.

Fish Foot Massage

A masseur's tired fingers are no problem for adherents of Thailand's latest treatment fad: Fish Foot Massage, in which you plunge your feet into a tank to have them nibbled by Turkish Garra Rufa, or Doctor Fish. This toothless predator apparently enjoys a dinner of dead skin, and the result, according to one owner, is shiny healthy feet. He also says Doctor Fish saliva contains 'a certain enzyme' that is good for skin problems, but agrees there is no scientific evidence for this. Rather, it's a fun addition – a faint scratching sensation – to Thailand's inventive spa menu. There are several shops in Bangkok's Suan Lum Night Bazaar. Just don't stumble into one that uses the Chinese lookalike Chin Chin fish. They have teeth.

Foot Massage

Foot massage is a fantastic comfort after a day dragging round the shops, and clears tension from the head as well as the feet. Usually lasting an hour, it is based on reflexology, focusing on pressure points in the feet and lower legs, normally with the application of oil or balm. It frequently takes place while sitting in chairs in the shop front, so you are visible through the window. But there's no need to feel embarrassed: it is such a common sight that no one takes any notice.

Oil Massage

For a smoother, less intense massage, try the oil option, based on Swedish massage. Available even in streetside shophouses, you usually get a private room, although sometimes they will just put a protective sheet on the existing mattress. The masseur may use aromatic oils, such as jasmine or lemongrass.

Massage Courses

An excellent memento of Thailand is to learn how to do Thai massage yourself. It is a very enjoyable experience that some people turn into a business opportunity when they get home. At the very least, your friends will love you all the more.

Some temples continue their ancient role by offering massage, often free of charge to the elderly. Wat Pho, in Bangkok, is known as the country's first university because of its traditional teaching facilities, and **Wat Pho Thai Traditional Massage School** (2 Thanon Sanam Chai; tel: 0-2622-3550; www.watpomassage. com; daily 10am–6pm) is regarded as the best place to learn in Bangkok. In Chiang Mai, the **International Training Massage School** (17/6-7 Hah Yak

53

Spa Treatments

Beachside massage menu

Santitham, Thanon Morakot, Chiang Mai; tel: 053-218-632; www.itmthai-massage.com; Mon–Fri 9am–4pm and some weekend classes) is well organised and accredited, with classes at several levels. They start each lesson with a little yoga or tai chi.

Yoga Retreats

Many yoga fans find a natural meditational quality in Thailand's tropical beach environment that is perfect for rewarding sessions. They travel to **Yoga Thailand** (55/23 Moo 4 Namuang, Bang Kao, Koh Samui; tel: 077-920-090; www.yoga-thailand.com) and **Agama Yoga** (Ananda Yoga Resort, 16/3, M-6, Ao Hin Kong, Ko Pha Ngan; tel: 089-233-0217; www.agamayoga.com) for a mix of classes at all levels. Yoga holidays satisfy people who want to improve general health or seek personal development, as much as dedicated students. Rooms are available at both centres, or you can stay elsewhere and visit for day classes.

Urban Spas

If you want to warm up the mood with candlelight and soothing music that help you drift away on the rhythmic flow of the massage, a good option without breaking the bank is an urban spa. These recent additions to the landscape are often in traditional teak houses, with private rooms and sympathetic decor of Asian objets d'art. They have more treatments on offer than mere massage, including beauty elements, such as body scrubs and facial treatments, bundled as 'half-day' and 'full-day' packages. A popular

Bangkok venue with several outlets is **Divana Spa** (8 Sukhumvit Soi 35; tel: 0-2261-4818; www.divana-dvn.com; Mon–Fri 11am–11pm, Sat–Sun 10am–11pm).

Resort Spas

Get a taste of how celebrity Thailand spa visitors such as Elle McPherson and Kate Moss approach life by treating yourself to a stay at one of the country's luxurious resort spas. It's the ultimate pampering reward. Beachside retreats are epitomised by **Six Senses Spa** (Evason Hua Hin & Six Senses Spa, 9 Moo 5 Paknampran Beach, Pranburi; tel: 032-632-111; www.sixsenses.com),

Tamarind Springs Spa, Ko Samui

with its palm-fringed setting that combines cute thatched-roof villas and infinity pools with massage, body scrubs, yoga and t'ai chi. **Anantara Spa** (Anantara Golden Triangle, 229 Moo 1, Chiang Saen, Chiang Rai; tel: 053-784-084; http://goldentriangle. anantara.com) offers a different take on romance, with massages, facials and body scrubs set in teak houses in the mountain jungles close to the Burmese border. **The Mandarin Oriental Spa** (Mandarin Oriental, 48 Oriental Avenue; tel: 0-2233-9630; www.mandarinoriental.com) is another traditional teak house, this time going back to the Indian origins of Thai treatments with its holistic menu of Ayurvedic therapies. Its Chiang Mai sister property **Dhara Dhevi** (51/4 Thanon Chiang Mai-Sankampaeng, Chiang Mai; tel: 053-888-888; www.mandarinoriental.com) is housed in a gorgeous reproduction of the ancient Burmese Palace at Mandalay, where the classic tumbling tiers of the roof represent the seven steps to Nirvana.

But perhaps the most impressive range of holistic treatments is at Thailand's pioneering resort spa **Chiva-Som** (73/4 Petchkasem Road, Hua Hin; tel: 032-536-536; www.chivasom.com), a beachside retreat where a full gamut of wellness options runs from massage to Traditional Chinese Medicine, reiki, meditation, spa cuisine, hypnotherapy and New Age options like crystals and flower essences. At Bangkok's **S Medical Spa** (2/2 Phakdi Building, Thanon Withayu, Bangkok;

tel: 0-2253-1010; www.smedspa.com) they have physicians, dermatologists, psychiatrists, cosmetic treatments and colonic irrigation alongside their jacuzzi and steam rooms.

Spa Terms

- **Colonic Irrigation** The removal of faecal matter from the colon.
- **Flower Essence** Made by immersing flowers in water and exposing to sunlight, the resulting liquid promotes awareness of emotional or spiritual imbalances.
- **Holistics** The practice of treating the whole person, physical, psychological and spiritual.
- **Qi** Spiritual energy that flows through the body. When it becomes blocked it causes illness.
- **Reiki** A Japanese laying on of hands that helps to guide *qi* through the body.

Culinary Experiences

The chilli hit of Thai food, the subtle lemongrass, galangal and smoky shrimp paste, draw people to the country by the thousand. The streets brim with tasty dishes at cheap prices, and cooking schools increasingly pass their secrets to home cooks and international chefs. There's now even a wine industry offering vineyard tours.

What's Cooking?

Food is hugely important in Thailand. Street vendors are everywhere, selling noodles and curries, grilled chicken and spicy soups from pushcarts, tables under parasols, or from pans merely scattered across the floor. People eat at all hours, snacking, and always sharing.

There are four regional food styles – Northern, Central, Northeastern and Southern – each influenced by its place in a landscape that runs for 1,800km (1,125 miles) from the foothills of the Tibetan Plateau to tropical islands just north of the equator.

The traditional migration patterns of the region have also left an impression. Northern cooking is influenced by Burma and Yunnan; the Northeast has strong ties with Laos; the royal kitchens have tempered the Central region, and the South has links with Malaysia and Indonesia. Chinese touches are everywhere, particularly in ubiquitous noodle dishes.

The best and cheapest meals are usually found at street stalls or in small *raan ahaan* (food shops), which use fresh ingredients and often pack up for the day when they run out. Consequently, hygiene problems are rare, particularly where food is freshly prepared in front of you, and a crowd of diners ensures high turnover.

People normally eat a single plate meal for lunch, but at dinner will share several dishes.

Markets and Streetfood

Markets are one of the cheapest and easiest ways to get a taste of a huge range of culinary experiences on offer in Thailand. There are lots of stalls around Bangkok's Chatuchak, for instance, and also at the Night Market in Chiang Mai, and the Fresh Market in Phuket Town. Tourist areas

Beachside restaurant, Phra Nang

around Thailand will all have dishes from the Central Plains, such as green curry and *tom yum goong*, which are famous overseas, and regional markets abound with local specialities. It's fun to hunt down items like the northern sausage *naem*; or the northeastern version of *somtam* (a spicy salad of green papaya with raw fish sauce, black field crabs and as many as ten chillis); or pungent *gaeng tai pla*, a fish stock.

Also in the south, the Phuket Vegetarian Festival, held according to the lunar calendar every September or October, is Thailand's most famous food event. It takes place near the six main Chinese temples around the island, the most important being Jui Tui Shrine, in Phuket Town. Along with religious rituals (see below), the streets teem with food stalls featuring 'mock meats', each with a yellow flag indicating their participation.

One of the best ways to cool down is to stop at a traditional fruit seller. Choose from their glass-fronted cart, perhaps pineapple, chopped, bagged and served with salt, ground chilli and a toothpick, so you can eat on the go. Another option is the notorious durian, a spiky, evil smelling no-go area for many Westerners, but known to Thais as the King of Fruit. Or try a fruit juice *naam phon-la-mai*, straight or blended with ice *(naam pan)*, sweetened with syrup, or salted.

Upmarket Experiences

Upmarket food in Thailand is still largely confined to hotels, with just a few independent restaurants in the main tourist centres. The food is often less spicy and sweeter in these places,

Satay is the perfect street snack

Culinary Experiences

and particularly in dinner theatre restaurants, where multi-course set meals are accompanied by ornately costumed classical dance drama. Each dance usually tells a story from the Thai classic fable *The Ramakien*, with scenes interspersed between courses. The classiest Bangkok venue is **Sala Rim Naam** (Mandarin Oriental Hotel, 48 Soi Burapa, Thanon Charoen Krung, Bangkok; www.mandarinoriental.com; daily 11.30am–2.30pm, 7–10.30pm). In the Chiang Mai version, called *khantoke*,

Spiceometer

Dishes here are rated from moderately spicy (✳) to red-hot (✳ ✳ ✳ ✳ ✳)

Gaeng Tai Pla (Fish Stomach Curry) ✳✳✳✳✳
Laab Gai (Chicken Salad) ✳✳✳✳
Gaeng Kiaw Waan (Green Curry) ✳✳✳
Yam Som-O (Pomelo Salad) ✳✳
Gaeng Mussaman (Muslim Curry) ✳

the food is served on bamboo trays, at places such as **Benjarong Khantoke** (101 Moo 15, Baan Sai Come, Suthep, Chiang Mai; www.benjarongkhantoke. com; daily 7–9.30pm).

For a good upmarket Thai food experience without cultural shows, try **Nahm** (Metropolitan Hotel, 27 Thanon Sathorn Tai; tel: 0-2625-3333; daily noon–2pm, 6.30–10.30pm), an outlet of Europe's only Michelin starred Thai restaurant, run by Australian chef David Thompson.

Cooking Schools

A great way to experience Thailand's delicious food is to learn how to cook it, and courses are available in most tourist centres. Some offer a hands-on experience, rather than a demonstration, and many have individual work stations and good equipment. The class might also include a trip to the market, such as Bangkok's Or Tor Kor, with its tangles of herbs and spices like coriander, galangal, lemongrass and chilli, and fat mounds of curry, shrimp and fish pastes that pinch your nose with deep and mysterious aromas.

When you get back to the kitchen you'll have your ingredients set before you, with recipe instructions to read as the chef explains the process. Toss your garlic into the wok, watch the hot oil sizzle, and you're off to culinary heaven. After the lesson you eat what you've cooked.

In Bangkok, the **Blue Elephant Cookery School** (233 Th. Sathorn; www.blueelephant.com; daily 8.45am–1pm, 1.15–4.30pm), part of a restaurant located in an old mansion, offers half-day, hands-on classes teaching four dishes in well-equipped kitchens. Morning classes begin with a market trip. At **Thai House** (32/4 Moo 8, Tambon Bangmaung, Nonthaburi; tel: 0-2903-9611; www.thaihouse.co.th; by appointment 10am–3.30pm) they have cookery lessons with or without accommodation in a handsome

Learning how to prepare it at a Thai cooking school in Bangkok

Wine Tours

Thailand has a fledgling wine industry, largely sparked in the early 1990s, and while growing conditions are far from ideal, some of these 'New Latitude' wines are surprisingly drinkable. The vineyards are settled in the cooler, hillier regions, and some are open for tours, with tastings and dining options.

After a look at the vines and harvesting techniques, you'll take a walk around the fermentation, bottling and barrique rooms, with someone on hand to explain the processes involved. To see If you want to see the grapes in full bloom, visit just before or during the harvest, in February.

One of the pioneers, **Chateau de Loei** (161 Moo 6, Tambon Rong Chik, Amphoe Phu Ruea, Loei; tel: 08-1729-9289; www.chateaudeloei.com; daily 8am–5pm; free) grows Syrah and Chenin Blanc grapes in northern Isaan. It has a vineyard tour, tastings and some accommodation, 12km (7½ miles) away.

Kaeng massaman, a Thai Muslim-style curry

traditional Thai house. One- to three-day courses are available, with market trips for overnight guests.

The **Chiang Mai Thai Cookery School** (Office: 47/2 Th. Moon Muang, Chiang Mai; tel: 0-5320-6388; www.thaicookeryschool.com; daily 10am–4pm), run by TV chef Sompon Nabnian from his home outside the city, has a long reputation. Its one- to five-day classes include market tours and an introduction to fruit carving. A recipe book is provided at the end.

Another professionally run school with hands-on courses is the **Samui Institute of Thai Culinary Arts** (SITCA; Hat Chaweng; www.sitca.net; daily 10am–1pm, 3–6pm). And, in Phuket, **Mom Tri's Boathouse** (Hat Kata; www.boathousephuket.com; Sat–Sun 10am–1pm) has courses taught by the executive chef of the acclaimed Boathouse restaurant.

Culinary Experiences

Vegetarian Festival

The Phuket Vegetarian Festival is a Taoist religious celebration, in which devotees abstain from meat and stimulants such as alcohol, garlic and sex. Most appealing to visitors, though, are acts of self-mortification, in which people enter a trance and walk barefoot on hot coals or drive sharp objects into their bodies. The festival happens in Bangkok, too, but without the mutilation. Both include cultural shows, such as Chinese opera.

PLACES

Bangkok and Surroundings – *p.64* **Central Thailand** – *p.92*
Eastern Seaboard – *p.106* **The Gulf Coast** – *p.122*
Northern Andaman Coast – *p.142* **The Deep South** – *p.170*

Chiang Mai and Around – *p.182* **Northern Thailand** – *p.198*
Northeast Thailand – *p.222*

Getting Your Bearings

Because of cultural and linguistic traits, Thailand is usually divided into four regions – North, Northeast, Central Plains and the South. It is an 1,800km (1,100-mile) trek from the foothills of the Tibetan Plateau in the north to tropical islands in the south, but the transport system is very good, with decent roads, and cheap buses, trains and flights to all areas. There are literally hundreds of islands off the Andaman coast and in the Gulf of Thailand, and most are not reachable by scheduled ferry. But there are longtail boats readily for hire to hop around between them.

For easy reference when using this guide, the regions have

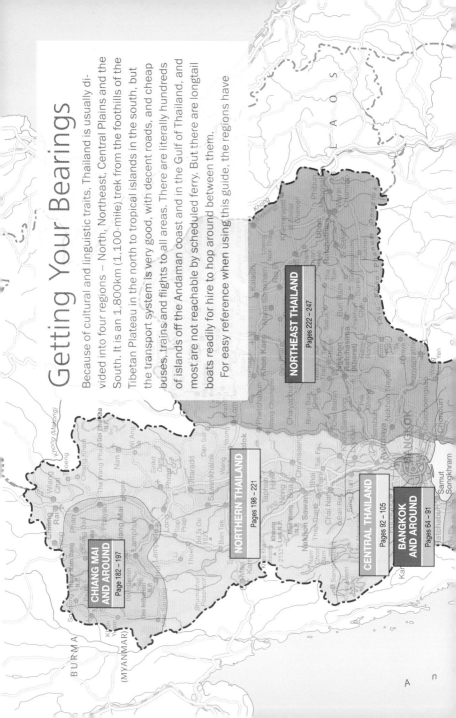

NORTHEAST THAILAND
Pages 222 – 247

NORTHERN THAILAND
Pages 198 – 221

CHIANG MAI AND AROUND
Page 182 – 197

CENTRAL THAILAND
Pages 92 – 105

BANGKOK AND AROUND
Pages 64 – 91

LAOS

BURMA
(MYANMAR)

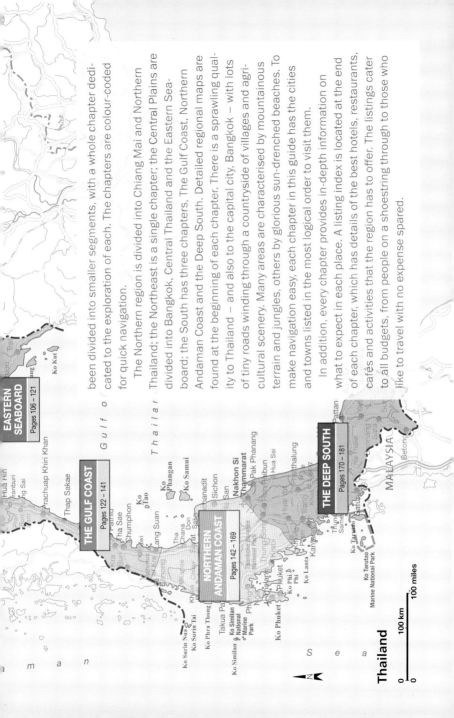

been divided into smaller segments, with a whole chapter dedicated to the exploration of each. The chapters are colour-coded for quick navigation.

The Northern region is divided into Chiang Mai and Northern Thailand; the Northeast is a single chapter; the Central Plains are divided into Bangkok, Central Thailand and the Eastern Seaboard; the South has three chapters, The Gulf Coast, Northern Andaman Coast and the Deep South. Detailed regional maps are found at the beginning of each chapter. There is a sprawling quality to Thailand – and also to the capital city, Bangkok – with lots of tiny roads winding through a countryside of villages and agricultural scenery. Many areas are characterised by mountainous terrain and jungles, others by glorious sun-drenched beaches. To make navigation easy, each chapter in this guide has the cities and towns listed in the most logical order to visit them.

In addition, every chapter provides in-depth information on what to expect in each place. A listing index is located at the end of each chapter, which has details of the best hotels, restaurants, cafés and activities that the region has to offer. The listings cater to all budgets, from people on a shoestring through to those who like to travel with no expense spared.

EASTERN SEABOARD
Pages 106 – 121

THE GULF COAST
Pages 122 – 141

NORTHERN ANDAMAN COAST
Pages 142 – 169

THE DEEP SOUTH
Pages 170 – 181

Gulf of Thailand

Hua Hin
Pranburi
Prachuap Khiri Khan
Thap Sakae
Chumphon
Lang Suan
Ko Tao
Ko Phangan
Ko Samui
Chanadit
Sichon
Pak Phanang
Nakhon Si Thammarat
Hua Sai

Ko Surin Nua
Ko Surin Tai
Ko Phra Thong
Ko Similan
Ko Similan National Park
Marine Park
Takua Pa
Ko Phuket
Ko Phi Phi
Ko Lanta

MALAYSIA

Ko Tarutao
Ko Tarutao National Park
Marine National Park

Andaman Sea

Thailand

0   100 km
0   100 miles

N

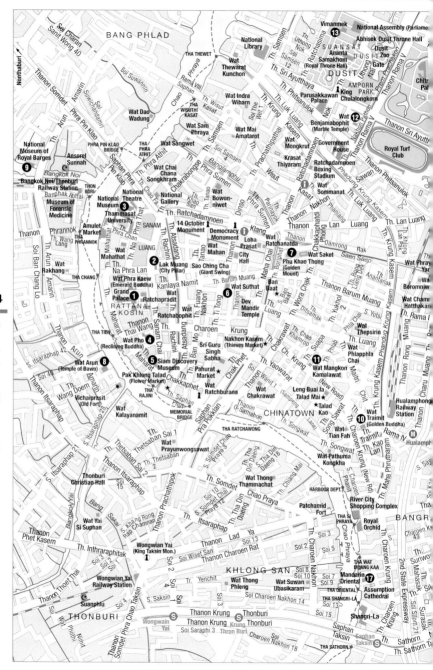

Bangkok and Surroundings

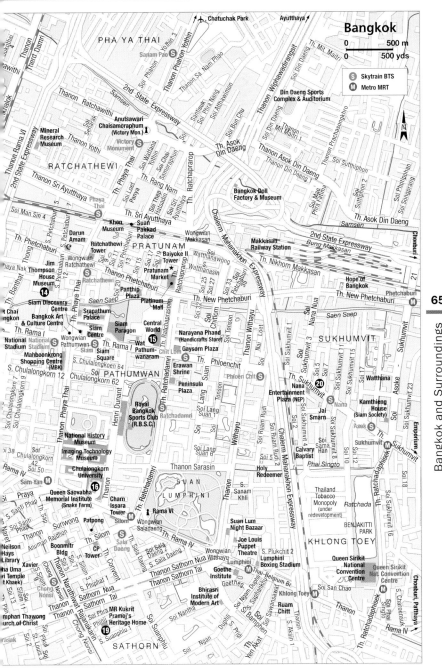

Bangkok

0		500 m
0		500 yds

Skytrain BTS
Metro MRT

Chatuchak Park
Ayutthaya
PHA YA THAI
Sanam Pao S
Thanon Phahon Yothin
Th. Mit Maitri
Din Daeng Sports Complex & Auditorium

2nd State Expressway
Thanon Ratchawithi
Thanon Sa Nam Phao
Thanon Wiphawadirangsit
Soi Din Daeng
Thanon Prachasongkhro

Mineral Research Museum
Thanon Yothi
Anutsawari Chaisamoraphum (Victory Mon.)
Victory Monument
Th. Asok Din Daeng
Thanon Asok Din Daeng
Thanon Din Daeng 1
Soi Sutthiphon
Soi Phetphan
Soi Photiphan

RATCHATHEWI
Thanon Sri Ayutthaya
Th. Phaya Thai
Th. Rang Nam
Bangkok Doll Factory & Museum
Soi Mae Phra Fatima
Th. Asok Din Daeng
Soi Songprang

Soi Man Sin 4
Th. Phetchaburi
Phaya Thai S
Khen Museum
Suan Pakkad Palace
Wongwian Makkasan
Makkasan Railway Station
2nd State Expressway
Bung Makkasan
Chonburi

Darun Amam
Ratchathewi Tower
PRATUNAM
Baiyoke II Tower
Soi Watthanawong
Th. Nikhom Makkasan
Chalerm Mahanakhon Expressway

Jim Thompson House Museum 14
Th. Phetchaburi
Wongwian Ratchathewi
Ratchathewi S
Thanon Phetchaburi
Pratunam Market
Ratchaprarop
Soi 25
Soi 27
Th. New Phetchaburi
Hope of Bangkok
Phetchaburi M

Siam Discovery Centre
Panthip Plaza
Platinum Mall
Saen Saep
Th. New Phetchaburi
Saen Saep

Bangkok Art & Culture Centre
Srapathum Palace
Siam Centre
Siam Paragon 15
Central World
Narayana Phand (Handicrafts Store)
SUKHUMVIT
Soi Sukhumvit 3
Soi Sukhumvit 11
Soi Sukhumvit 15
Sukhumvit

National Stadium S
National Stadium
Siam S
Siam Square
Wat Pathumwanaram
Gaysorn Plaza
Th. Phloenchit
Soi 5
Soi 7
Watthana
Asoke

Mahboonkrong Shopping Centre (MBK)
Th. Rama I
Soi PATHUMWAN
Erawan Shrine
Phloen Chit S
Nana Entertainment Plaza (NEP)
Nana S
Kamthieng House (Siam Society)
Soi Sukhumvit 23

National History Museum
Henri Dunant
Royal Bangkok Sports Club (R.B.S.C.)
Peninsula Plaza
Soi Lang Suan 1
Jai Smarn
Asok S
Soi Sukhumvit 8
Soi Sama Han

Imaging Technology Museum
Chulalongkorn University
Ratchadamri
Withayu
Soi Ruam Rudi 2
Calvary Baptist
Phai Singto

Sam Yan M
16
Thanon Sarasin
SUAN LUMPHINI
Soi Sanam Khli
Holy Redeemer
Thailand Tobacco Monopoly (under redevelopment)
Ratchada
Soi Sukhumvit 16
BENJAKITTI PARK
KHLONG TOEY

Queen Saovabha Memorial Institute (Snake Farm)
Charn Issara Tower
Rama VI
Suan Lum Night Bazaar
Ratchadaphisek

Praya
Patpong
Th. Silom
Sala Daeng S
Joe Louis Puppet Theatre
Lumphini Boxing Stadium
Queen Sirikit National Convention Centre
Queen Sirikit Nat. Convention Centre

Neilson Hays Library
Boonmitr Bldg
CP Tower
Soi Convent
Thanon Sathorn Nua
Goethe Institute
Thai-Belgium Br.
Khlong Toey M
Chonburi, Pattaya

Xavier
Uma Temple (Khaek)
Chong Nonsi S
Thanon Narathiwat Rajanakarin
Thanon Sathorn Tai
Bhirasri Institute of Modern Art
Ruam Chitt

SATHORN
MR Kukrit Pramoj's Heritage Home 19
Thanon
Rama IV

65

Bangkok and Surroundings

Bangkok and Surroundings

Thailand's capital might be a shock to the senses, but there is plenty to see for anyone prepared to put up with the heat and confusion. From its huge shopping malls, shady temples and bustling markets, to its restaurants, sleepy canals and brazen nightlife, Bangkok offers endless surprises.

Bangkok

Population: 5,705,000

Local dialling code: 2

Local tourist office: Thanon New Petchaburi; tel: 0-2250-5500; www.tourismthailand.org

Main police station: 139 Thanon Whitayu; tel: 0-2255-5993. **Tourist Police** anywhere in Thailand call 1155.

Main post office: 1156 Thanon Charoen Krung

Hospitals: Bumrungrad International 33 Sukhumvit Soi 3; tel: 0-2667-1000; www.bumrungrad.com. BNH Hospital, 9/1 Th. Vonvent, Silom, tel: 0-2686-2700; www.bnhhospital.com

Local newspapers/listings magazines: *Bangkok Post; Nation; BK*

King Rama I launched Bangkok as Thailand's capital city in 1782, building a stunning Grand Palace complex, crisscrossed canals and magnificent temples, originally modelled on the old capital of Ayutthaya. The king also gave Bangkok the longest place name in the world, which locals shorten to *Krung Thep*, or 'City of Angels'.

Much of the old town and Chinatown, in sites such as Wat Pho, the Golden Mount and pungent 200-year-old street markets, are evocative of Bangkok's distant past, and although the heat and humidity are oppressive, these areas are the most walkable. To the north, the wide boulevards of Dusit – home to regal buildings from the late 19th century – have an almost European feel.

Elsewhere, Bangkok has hurtled into the 21st century, with the huge shopping malls and luxury hotels of Pathumwan and Pratunam, the business district of Silom and nightclubs along Sukhumvit.

When the bustle gets too much, there are bucolic pastures and countryside temples less than an hour away from the city by boat along the river and canals.

Bangkok

The key to touring Bangkok is not to take on too much in one go. The heat is immensely draining – one of the reasons Thais like sleeping so much (it's often listed as their favourite activity). Carry water, take lots of breaks and walk in the shade where possible.

Rattanakosin and Old City

A short walk east of Tha Chang pier, along Thanon Na Phra Lan, the **Grand Palace ①** and **Wat Phra Kaew** (daily 8.30am–3.30pm; charge) stand in a white-walled complex. Beyond the ticket booths and the **Coins and Decorations Museum** are the stunning buildings of **Wat Phra Kaew**. On the left, the gold mosaic **Phra Si Rattana Chedi ④** is believed to enshrine a piece of the Buddha's breastbone. Further on are the **Phra Mondop ⑤** (Library), containing the Tripitaka

The city at night viewed from the rooftop restaurant, Sirocco

(holy Buddhist scriptures) inscribed on palm leaves, and the **Prasat Phra Thep Bidom ⑥** (Royal Pantheon) and its statues of the first eight Chakri kings.

Behind the library is a detailed sandstone model of Angkor Wat, in Cambodia. Along its northern edge are the **Ho Phra Nak** (Royal Mausoleum), **Viharn Yot** (Prayer Hall) and **Ho Phra Montien Tham** (Auxiliary Libray). Opposite Viharn Yot is the first of the wat's 178 murals recounting the Thai epic the *Ramakien*.

The main draw of Wat Phra Kaew is the **Emerald Buddha ⑦** located in the *bot* (ordination hall). The 66cm

Bot of the Emerald Buddha

Bangkok and Surroundings

Entering the Grand Palace

At the Grand Palace main gate, a sign proclaims 'Do Not Trust Wily Strangers'. Take the advice and ignore the touts hovering outside, who will tell you the palace is closed but they know the perfect alternative. This ruse ends with a visit to a gem shop where you may get ripped off. Note that shorts are forbidden within the grounds, but you can hire trousers for a small fee at the gate.

Airports: Suvarnabhumi (BKK), **www.bangkokairportonline.com**, is 30km (19 miles) east of the city centre. The Suvarnabhumi Airport Rail Link (SARL) has two services: the City Line, calling at eight stations en route to Phaya Thai (fare: B15–40 for 30-minute journey, 24-hour service), and the Express Line direct to Bangkok City Air Terminal (fare: B150, 15-minute journey, operates 6am–1am). The Airport Express Bus to the city; fare B150 for 60–90-minute journey, hourly 5am–midnight, from Arrivals on 1st floor. Metered taxis are on the ground floor outside the terminal. Don Muang (DMK), **www.donmuangairportonline.com**, lies 30km (19 miles) north of the centre. Trains into the city depart 2.45am–7.27pm from the station opposite the airport. Fare: B21; journey time 50 minutes. Public taxis and buses depart for the city centre from outside the airport. Metered taxi fare around B250–300 to town centre including B50 airport surcharge and expressway fees; journey time 35–45 minutes. Bus tickets B18.

 Public bus: Bangkok Mass Transit Authority (BMTA), **www.bmta.co.th**. *Bus Routes and Map guide* (B50) gives route details. Green bus: flat fare B6.50; red bus: B7, blue air-con bus: B11–18; orange bus B13–22.

 Metro: Bangkok has two rapid transit systems. **Bangkok Metro (MRT)** tel: 0-2624-5200, **www.bangkokmetro.co.th**, which runs from Hua Lamphong railway station to Bang Sue, connecting with the Skytrain at Silom/Sala Daeng, Sukhumvit/Asok and Chatuchak/Mo Chit; tickets (B16–41) are sold in kiosks or station vending machines; and **Sky Train (BTS)**, tel: 0-2617-7340, **www.bts.co.th**. The BTS Sukhumvit line runs from On Nut, on Thanon Sukhumvit, to Mo Chit in the north of the city; the Silom line runs from Wong Wien Yai, across the river, to National Stadium. Fares: B15–40; day pass: B120.

 Taxi: metered taxis start from B35. Passenger pays motorway tolls. Easily available 24 hours.
Motorcycle taxi: drivers cluster at junctions wearing coloured waistcoats. Passenger rides on the back (pick one with helmets available). Short rides B10–20; B80–100 should get you across town.

 Tuk-tuk: available 24 hours. No meter, so you need to bargain. Expect to pay B30–50 for a short journey (under 15 minutes); B50–100 for longer journeys. A B100 ride should get you across most parts of downtown.

(26in) statue, which is actually made of jade, not emerald, is Thailand's most revered religious artefact. It sits on a golden throne, overseen by a nine-tiered umbrella and representations of the sun and moon. Kings Rama I and III made robes for the Buddha to wear, one for each season. They were replaced in 1996 to celebrate the current king's Golden Jubilee. He personally presides over robe-changing ceremonies: a golden, diamond-studded tunic for the hot season, a gilded robe flecked with blue for the rainy season, and one of enamel coated with solid gold for the cool.

Grand Palace
South of Wat Phra Kaew is the **Grand Palace** (building interiors are closed

Sat–Sun). until the overthrow of absolute monarchy in 1932, this was a veritable city within a city, including the king's and king's wives' quarters, ceremonial buildings, military and civil wings, and a prison.

The buildings are roughly arranged in four clusters. On the left, the Borombhiman Hall, built in 1903, is used as a guesthouse for visiting heads of state. Behind is the Buddha Ratana Starn (Chapel of the Crystal Buddha). To the right, the Phra Maha Montien Group is dominated by three structures: the Amarin Vinitchai Throne Hall, built in 1785; the Paisal Taksin Hall, where new monarchs are crowned; and the Chakraphat Phiman Hall, the royal residence for the first three kings. To the right, the centrepiece of the Chakri Group is the **Chakri Maha Prasat ⓔ**, an Italianate structure with three spires on a Thai-style roof. It was completed in 1882 to commemorate Bangkok's first centenary.

Further right, the **Dusit Maha Prasat ⓕ**, heading the Dusit Group, is the final resting place of royal family members before they are cremated in Sanam Luang.

To the north, **Wat Phra Kaew Museum ⓖ** has beautiful Buddha statues of crystal, silver, ivory and gold, and scale models of the Grand Palace as it looked a century ago and as it looks today.

Another 100 m/yds further, across Thanon Sanam Chai, is the **Lak Muang ❷** (City Pillar; daily 5am–7pm), which is believed to hold the spirit of Bangkok. Diagonally opposite to the north is the green expanse of **Sanam Luang**, which holds royal ceremonies.

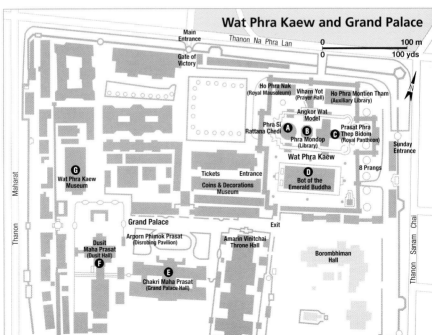

Rattanakosin makes a good day's walking tour, with sights that include the magnificent Grand Palace, the largest museum collection in Southeast Asia, and a shrine that holds the city's spirit.

Start the tour at Tha Chang pier which leads to a little market square of 19th-century shophouses, and beyond, 100m/yds ahead along Thanon Na Phra Lan, the Grand Palace and Wat Phra Kaew – the former royal residence and Thailand's principal temple. Opposite the gate, the café Ch Phrathumthong is a handy refreshment break.

The ticket booth is 100m/yds beyond the gate. Inside are the gold and twinkling glass facades of **Wat Phra Kaew**, including the **Phra Si Rattana Chedi** and **Prasat Phra Thep Bidon** (Royal Pantheon). Pride of

place in the wat goes to the **Emerald Buddha**, which at a mere 66cm (26ins) tall is Thailand's most revered religious artefact.

South, within the compound, is the **Grand Palace**. The royal family lived here until 1946, when it included the king's and king's wives' quarters, ceremonial buildings, military and civil wings, and a prison.

Leave the complex via the main entrance and turn right. At the end cross Thanon Sanam Chai to the white prang (Khmer-style tower) that holds the **Lak Muang** (City Pillar), which Thais believe contains the spirit of the city itself. The compound has several shrines, and a traditional theatre group near the far gate. Turn left at the gate into Thanon Na Hap Phoei.

Re-cross the main road, enter the large park and walk through it diagonally to the opposite corner. This expanse is **Sanam Luang**, where royal

The Emerald Buddha is protected by a nine-tiered umbrella

Tips

- Distance: 3.5km (2¼ miles)
- Time: A full day
- From downtown, start the tour with an express boat to Tha Chang pier
- Set aside a couple of hours for the Grand Palace and Wat Phra Kaew alone
- Admission to the Grand Palace and Wat Phra Kaew also includes access to Vimanmek Mansion and other Dusit sights (*see p.75*)
- This tour is best tackled Wed–Fri, when both the interior of the Grand Palace and the National Museum are open

ceremonies and cremations are carried out. It is likely to be closed in 2011 for a year's renovations, so you may need to walk back down Thanon Na Phra Lan and turn right at Thanon Na Phra That.

Towards the end on the left, the **National Museum** claims the largest collection in Southeast Asia, including beautiful murals and the bronze Phra Buddha Sihing, Thailand's second-most sacred religious image.

Walk back along Thanon Na Phra That, then right into Thanon Phra Chan, and then through the market at the end to Tha Phra Chan. At the pier go left into the Amulet Market, where people bargain for religious items, from large Buddhas to tiny carvings. The lane leads eventually to Thanon Maharat.

Across the road on Thanon Maharat is **Wat Mahathat**, Thailand's major Buddhist university, where King Rama IV lived as a monk before ascending

Temple exteriors are often very ornate, such as that of the Bot of the Emerald Buddha

the throne in 1851. The temple interior is closed to the public.

Heading south along Thanon Maharat, passing the next street on the right, Trok Thawiphan, there is a large sign saying Maharat Pier. You can only catch expensive tourist boats from here, but if you are feeling hungry, the **S & P** café is a good place to stop for a meal. Otherwise continue past yet more street vendors for 200m/yds to reach Tha Chang, from where you can catch the express boat home.

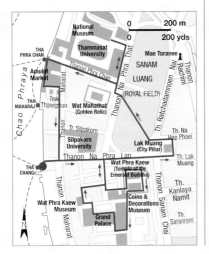

A small pagoda in the grounds of the National Museum

The road west of Sanam Luang is Thanon Na Phra That, where, towards the end on the left, the **National Museum** ❸ (www.thailandmuseum. com; Wed–Sun 9am–4pm; charge, guided tours available at 9.30am in English) has the best collection of artefacts in the country. Thanon Phra Chan, south of the museum, leads 150m/yrds to the river. South of here, along Thanon Maharat, are Wat Mahathat (closed to the public), on the left, and the **Amulet Market** (daily 9am–6pm) opposite.

Continuing south, passing the Grand Palace, Bangkok's oldest surviving temple **Wat Pho** ❹ (daily 8am–5pm; charge) is on Thanon Thai Wang. It is home to the Reclining Buddha. Further south, the road bends east into Thanon Chakkaphet, where the 24-hour **Pak Khlong Talad Flower Market** – liveliest at night – supplies the old town temples with wreaths.

North of the turn to Chakkaphet, on the corner of Thanon Sanam Chai, the interactive displays at the **Siam Discovery Museum** ❺ (Tue–Sun 10am–6pm; charge 🏛) explain the history of Thai people.

A kilometre (⅔ mile) northeast of the museum, on Thanon Fuang Nakhon, is **Wat Ratchabophit** (daily 5am–8pm; free), a mix of local and European architecture. A hundred metres/yards northeast on Thanon Bamrung Muang, **Wat Suthat** ❻ (daily 8.30am–9pm; charge) has a Sukhothai-era Buddha. Opposite is the **Giant Swing** (Ching Cha), once used for Brahman ceremonies.

A kilometre (⅔ mile) northeast,

off Thanon Chakkapathdi Phong, the **Golden Mount** ❼ (Phu Khao Thong; daily 7.30am–5.30pm; charge) is named after the golden chedi standing at the top. Directly west off Thanon Maha Chai, the **Loha Prasat** (Metal Palace) shares grounds with **Wat Ratchanatda** (both daily 9am–5pm; charge).

The main road north of here is the royal avenue of Thanon Ratchadamnoen, where 100m/yrds to the west, **Democracy Monument** celebrates Thailand's 1932 transition to constitutional monarchy. A short walk west is the **14 October Monument**, honouring people killed by the army in 1973 demonstrations.

The giant Reclining Buddha at Wat Pho

The great Khmer-style *prang* of Wat Arun represents the Hindu-Buddhist Mount Meru, home of the gods with its 33 heavens

Moving north, Thanon Tanao passes the famous backpacker hangout of **Khao San Road**, before reaching Thanon Phra Sumen, where **Wat Bowonniwet** (daily 8am–5pm; free) is famous for murals painted by Khrua In Khon.

Thonburi

Across the river is Thonburi, which was Thailand's capital immediately prior to Bangkok. The ferry from Tha Tien pier, close to Wat Pho, leads directly to **Wat Arun** ➑ (daily 8.30am–5.30pm; charge). Its alternative name, The Temple of Dawn, derives from the arrival of King Taksin, who, following the fall of Ayutthaya, first viewed Wat Arun at dawn, and chose the area as the new capital of Siam. Porcelain fragments cover the temple exterior, and the main Khmer-style prang (spire) stands at 79m (259ft).

Just 1.5km (1 mile) north, the **Museum of Forensic Medicine** (Mon–Fri 9am–4.30pm; charge) on Thanon Phrannok is also reachable from Tha Wang Lang pier. The stomach-churning exhibits include mummified corpses of Thailand's most notorious criminals, deformed foetuses and postmortem photographs.

Most piers have longtail boats for hire to tour **Khlong Bangkok Noi**, which bears west from the river, slightly north of Tha Wang Lang. The first sight along the canal is the **National Museum of Royal Barges** ➒ (daily 9am–5pm; charge), which has spectacular golden boats only used on rare royal occasions. A few minutes west, beyond a small pier, is the village of **Ban Bu**, where craftsmen have made bronzeware bowls called *khan long hin* for 200 years.

A short sail further are two waterside temples. **Wat Suwannaram** (daily 5am–9 pm; free) was formerly an execution site for Burmese prisoners of war, while **Wat Sisudaram** (daily 6am–8pm; free) has Buddhist and Hindu deities, as well as a small shrine to Thailand's greatest poet, Sunthorn Phu (1786–1855), who studied here.

One of the brightly coloured three-wheeled *tuk-tuk* taxis whose name comes from the incessant noise their two-stroke engine makes

Chinatown

The beginnings of Chinatown were formed when King Rama I relocated Chinese labourers and merchants downstream in order to build the Grand Palace in 1872. Today, it still thrives as one of the most colourful market centres of the capital. Near its eastern edge, on Thanon Charoen Krung, **Wat Traimit** ❿ (daily 8.30am–5pm; charge) contains the world's largest solid gold Buddha, and is consequently also known as The Temple of the Golden Buddha. Just west, on Thanon Yaowarat, **Wat Tian Fah** has a 2.5m (8ft) golden statue of Guan Yin, the Goddess of Mercy, to whom people pray for recovery from illness. Northwest of here, the old market lane of Soi Issaranuphap leads south to Thanon Charoen Krung, where **Wat Mangkon Kamalawat** ⓫ (daily 6am–5pm; charge) is the main focus of the Vegetarian Festival in October (see *Listings*). Issaranuphap continues south, passing **Leng Buai Ia**, the oldest Chinese shrine in Bangkok, on its way to rejoin Thanon Yaowarat. Across the street in Yaowarat Soi 11,

Corridors of Power

Some of Thailand's most powerful people are Chinese. During the Ayutthaya period, Chinese merchants acquired influential business positions and many of their daughters became royal concubines. In the Rattanakosin era businessmen gained concessions as tax collectors, and used the ensuing riches to buy into rice mills, taking advantage of Thailand's greatest export. Modern examples of powerful Chinese include ex-prime minister Thaksin Shinawatra, formally Thailand's richest man, and Chin Sophonpanich, a one-time labourer who founded Bangkok Bank.

Talad Kao (**Old Market**) has operated nonstop for 200 years.

At the soi's end, **Sampeng Lane** (also called Wanit Soi 1) was Chinatown's original thoroughfare in the late 18th century. It is still full of stalls selling eclectic goods. Turning west, it passes **Tang Toh Kang** (daily 9.30am–4.30pm), Bangkok's oldest goldsmith, before reaching Thanon Chakrawat, which, to the south, hosts **Wat Chakrawat** (daily 8am–4.30pm; free). Sampeng Lane continues west to the Indian enclave at **Pahurat Market**.

Dusit

North of the Old City, on Thanon Rama V, **Wat Benjamabophit** ⓬ (daily 8am–5.30pm; charge), completed in 1911, was the last major temple built in central Bangkok. It was designed by King Chulalongkorn's half-brother Prince Naris and Italian architect Hercules Manfredi, and has dramatic Western elements, notably walls of Carrara marble and stained-glass windows. A gallery to the rear has originals and copies of significant Buddha images from around Asia.

About 200m/yrds north-west is Royal Plaza, with its bronze equestrian **Statue of King Chulalongkorn** (Rama V). Behind it, the Italian-Renaissance-style **Ananta Samakhom Throne Hall** (daily 8.30am–4.30pm; charge or free with Grand Palace entrance ticket) is the tallest building in Dusit Park, a network of former royal gardens with canals, fountains and several small museums.

Also in the park, to the north, is the **Abhisek Dusit** (Royal Throne Hall; daily 9.30am–4pm; charge, or free with Grand Palace entrance ticket). The ornate building, melding Victorian and Moorish styles, is now a museum of traditional arts and crafts, with examples of jewellery, woodcarving and silk products. A shop sells village handiwork.

Beyond the throne hall, **Vimanmek Mansion** ⓭ (www.thai.palaces.net; daily 9.30am–4pm; charge, or free with Grand Palace entrance ticket) is billed as the world's largest golden teak building. The gingerbread fretwork and octagonal tower look more Victorian than period Thai. King Chulalongkorn and his large family lived here for five years, during which time no other males were allowed entry. A guided tour takes in Thailand's first bathtub and flushing toilet and the first typewriter with Thai

Keeping watch at Dusit Zoo

Concerts by the Lake

Lumphini Park (daily 4.30am–9pm; free) is Bangkok's biggest green space, easily recognisable by the statue of King Rama VI at the gates. The park, named after the Buddha's birthplace in Nepal, has lakes (with pedal boats for hire) and is full of t'ai chi, aerobics and bodybuilders lifting weights at the open-air gym. In the cool season from November to February, there are open-air concerts by the Bangkok Symphony Orchestra every Sunday evening.

characters. In the east of the park, across a small road, **Dusit Zoo** (daily 8am–6pm; charge) was originally the king's private botanical gardens. It now has 300 mammal species and a lake, on which you can hire pedaloes.

Pathumwan and Pratunam

A short walk west of National Stadium Skytrain station, the **Jim Thompson House Museum ⑭** (www.jimthompsonhouse.com; daily 9am–5pm; charge for compulsory guided tour) is at the end of Soi Kasemsan 2. This is one of the finest traditional houses in the city, built by the Thai silk entrepreneur Jim Thompson in 1959 from other houses relocated from around the country. Inside is Thompson's collection of Asian art and antiquities. There is also a café, a gallery and a gift shop.

Turning east along Thanon Rama I, the **Bangkok Art and Culture Centre** (www.bacc.or.th; Tue–Sun 10am–9pm; free) has some of the city's best exhibitions and art markets on the concourse.

Across Thanon Rama I, **Mahboonkrong** (MBK) shopping centre retains a market place ambience, with tiny shops and stalls selling goods from cosmetics and cameras to clothes and copies of master artworks.

Further east, along Thanon Rama I,

A visit to the Jim Thompson House Museum offers respite from the cacophony of the city

Placing offerings at the Erawan Shrine

filled with 30,000 marine creatures. Visitors can ride in a glass-bottomed boat and dive with the sharks.

Across Thanon Rama I, a grid of sois called **Siam Square** has a strong youth culture, its own radio station with street speakers that drown out the traffic, and boutique shops with eccentric names like It's Happened to Be a Closet. East of Siam Paragon, **Central World** (www.centralworld.co.th) is Bangkok's largest mall. It includes the department store Isetan, along with a staggering array of shops and restaurants. Another department store here, Zen, was burnt to the ground during the 2010 Red Shirt protests.

Diagonally opposite, at the corner of Thanon Ratchadamri and Thanon Ploenchit, is **Erawan Shrine** (daily 8am–10pm), where people buy garlands and incense as spirit offerings in return for good fortune.

South, at the end of Thanon Ratchadamri, is **Lumphini Park** *(see Box, opposite)*. To its west on Thanon Rama IV, the **Snake Farm** Mon–Fri 8.30am–4.30pm, Sat–Sun 8.30am–noon; charge) has venom-milking sessions (Mon–Fri 11am and 2.30pm, Sat–Sun 11am), when the audience can handle snakes.

East of Lumphini Park, along Thanon Rama IV, is **Suan Lum Night Bazaar** (daily 3pm–midnight), an open-air bazaar of souvenirs, clothing, handicrafts and home decor.

Thanon Ratchadamri, running north from Central World, leads to Pratunam, where turning left at Thanon Petchaburi the new,

Bangkok and Surroundings

there is a line of up-market shopping malls linked by an overhead 'Skywalk,' so people can skip between them without negotiating the noisy streets. All are open from 10am to 9pm. They begin with **Siam Discovery Centre** and **Siam Centre**, the former is scheduled to re-open by early 2011 following a revamp. including the opening of a Madame Tussaud's waxworks museum. Siam Centre attracts teens, with local designer wear and sports clothes.

Across the concourse east of Siam Centre is **Siam Paragon** (www.siam-paragon.co.th), full of chichi labels, from Apple to Ferrari, plus restaurants and an impressive aquarium, **Siam Ocean World** (www.siamoceanworld.com; daily 9am–10pm; charge),

Cinemas, cafés restaurants and boutiques populate the low-rise grid of Siam Square

five-storey **Platinum Mall** (daily 10am–9pm) sells mainly clothes. In the narrow lanes on the other side of Petchaburi is **Pratunam Market** (daily 9am–midnight), with cheap clothes, fabrics and shoes. Some 200 m/yds west, on Thanon Petchaburi, **Panthip Plaza** (daily 10am–9pm) is Bangkok's most famous IT mall.

North, on the parallel Thanon Sri Ayutthaya, **Suan Pakkad Palace** (www.suanpakkad.com; daily 9am–4pm; charge, includes a guided tour) Set amid a lush garden and lotus pond, the palace comprises five teak houses converted into a museum displaying antiques and artefacts. Also here, the **Khon Museum** has details on the classic dance-theatre *khon*.

Bangrak and Sathorn

The district of Bangrak was an early centre for Western merchants in the 19th century. It still has a few grand period buildings at its river end, where the **Mandarin Oriental hotel** ⓱ (www.mandarinoriental.com), founded in the 1870s, serves popular afternoon tea in its Author's Lounge. Behind the sadly neglected 19th-century buildings opposite the hotel on Charoen Krung Soi 40, a small tree-lined square contains **Assumption Cathedral** (daily 6am–9pm; free), which has a rococo interior with stained-glass windows and gilded pillars topped with a domed ceiling.

Bangrak continues east up Thanon Silom, where, on the corner of Thanon Pan, the vibrantly coloured Hindu **Maha Uma Devi Temple** ⓲ (daily 6am–8pm; free) is named after Shiva's consort, Uma Devi. Established in the 1860s by the Tamil community, whose presence is still strong in the area, on holy days the temple is busy with a lively spectrum of worshippers, including Indian, Thai and Chinese. The structure has a 6m (20ft) -high facade, with an ornate diorama of religious statuary.

The upper, eastern, end of Thanon

Silom is a nightlife area that contains the famous go-go bars of **Patpong** (Soi 1 and Soi 2) and their notorious ping-pong acrobatics. There is also a busy night market here 5pm–1am, in Patpong Soi 1 and between Silom Sois 2–8. It sells fake name-brand watches, bags and clothes, plus CDs and DVDs.

Off Thanon Sathorn, which runs parallel, south of Silom, **MR Kukrit Pramoj's Heritage Home** (www.kukritshousefund.com; daily 10am–4pm; charge) is on Narathiwat Soi 7. Kukrit was of royal descent, a prime minister, author and cultural preservationist. His former home is now a museum of five traditional stilt buildings containing antique pottery, memorabilia and photos.

Kukrit Pramoj's Heritage Home is a good example of traditional Thai architecture

Sukhumvit

About 100 m/yds from the expressway where **Thanon Sukhumvit** ㉒ begins, to the south is Soi 4, and the go-go bars of Nana Entertainment Plaza, and opposite is Soi 3, known as 'Soi Arab' for its lanes of Lebanese cafés and shisha pipes. These sois mark the start of Sukhumvit's tailors, bars and hotels. Along these early blocks a night market sells souvenirs, bags, T-shirts and watches.

Two of the city's best clubs are found on Soi 11, where **Q Bar** (www.qbarbangkok.com; daily 8pm–2am; charge) and **Bed Supperclub** (www.bedsupperclub.com; daily 7.30pm–1am; charge) are pick-up spots for all manner of people who like hip-hop with their vodka shots. Further along, Soi 21 (Soi Asoke), running north, has another pole-dancing neon strip at Soi Cowboy, and, 100m/yrds further on, the more genteel ambience of the **Siam Society** (www.siam-society.org; Tue–Sat 9am–5pm), where **Kamthieng House** (charge) serves as an ethnological museum.

On the corner of Sukhumvit Soi 24, beside Phrom Phong Skytrain station, is Sukhumvit's premier shopping mall, **Emporium** (www.emporiumthailand.com; daily 10am–9pm), where on the top floor the **Thailand Creative & Design Centre** (www.tcdc.or.th; Tue–Sun, 10.30am–9pm; free) has exhibitions.

Half a kilometre (1/3 mile) east, Sukhumvit Soi 55, or Soi Thonglor has many shops, clubs, bars and restaurants, and a boutique, out-of-town-ambience that appeals both to Thais and expats.

TOUR OF CHINATOWN

This long full-day's walk through evocative Chinatown includes a 200-year-old market, Taoist temples, and a 5-tonne solid-gold Buddha at Wat Traimit.

Begin the tour at **Wat Traimit**, which contains the world's largest solid-gold Buddha, a 5.5-tonne, 3m (10ft) Sukhothai-era statue, and is consequently known also as the Temple of the Golden Buddha.

Leaving the temple, turn right on Thanon Traimit and walk to the Chinatown ceremonial arch. Turn right, cross Thanon Charoen Krung, and go northwest along **Thanon Yaowarat**. On the left is Wat Tian Fah, and further on the large gold shops that give Yaowarat its alternative name of 'Gold Street'. Cross Thanon Phadung Dao (where two famous seafood stalls, Rut & Lek and T & K, open at 6pm daily), and then turn

right at Thanon Plaeng Nam.

At the top, cross Thanon Charoen Krung into **Thanon Phlapphlachai** and follow the bend left. This street serves the many temples with red-and-gold displays of paper temple banners, 3m (10ft)-tall incense sticks and funeral offerings.

At the end of the bend, turn left into Thanon Yommaratkhum and left again, immediately, into **Trok Itsaranuphap**. This has more the feel of the original Chinatown, of hectic alleys and shops selling food, clothes, crockery, trinkets and more funerary items.

Turn right at Thanon Charoen Krung to reach **Wat Mangkon Kamalawat**, Chinatown's biggest temple, and after 100m/yds the bustling Hua Seng Hong Yaowaraj, on the left, a good place to eat. Continuing south along Trok Itsaranuphap, which from here is also named Charoen Krung Soi 16, a short way down is Hong Kong Noodle, an alternative lunch stop.

Another 30m/yds on the left brings you to the small courtyard of **Leng Buai Ia**. Coming to Thanon Yaowarat, cross the street into Yaowarat Soi 11. The tangy smells here herald the entrance on the left of Talad Kao (Old Market), which has been in business for 200 years.

Tips

- Distance: 2.75km (1¾ miles)
- Time: A full day
- You can get to Wat Traimit either by taxi or by metro to Hualamphong Station and then a taxi

Bright banners span a busy Chinatown street

The venerable Talad Kao (Old Market) has a reputation for high-quality produce

The alley crossing 150m/yds ahead is **Sampeng Lane**. Turning right here takes you through a market selling everything from dresses and toys, to Chinese dice and semiprecious stones. At the junction of Soi Mangkon is the gold shop Tang Toh Kang, which has a museum upstairs.

Moving on along Sampeng, at Thanon Chakrawat turn left for 100m/yds to the stone gates beside the old Chinese herbalist and turn into **Wat Chakrawat**. After 70m/yds go through the ornate gate on your left. Climb the small wall overlooking the pond on the left and see if you can spot the crocodile.

Retrace your steps, and turn left into Sampeng Lane, which climbs a small humpbacked bridge over Khlong Ong Ang. If you go left into the alley immediately after it you'll find Punjab Sweets and Restaurant, after 150m/yds. The aromas are distinctly different here at the edge of Pahurat, Bangkok's Little India.

At the end of Sampeng Lane, cross the road into Thanon Pahurat. After 100m/yds duck into **Pahurat Market** and root around in a two-floor emporium of all things Indian.

Catch a taxi home or go past the market and turn left at Thanon Tri Phet. After 15 minutes you will come to Memorial Bridge express boat pier.

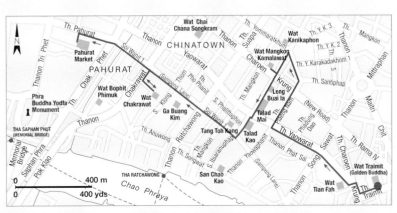

Around Bangkok

There are plenty of attractions for day trips less than an hour from the city centre. A boat trip to bucolic Ko Kret leaves the fumes far behind, and, for culture, try an eccentric museum housed in a giant elephant.

Nonthaburi and Ko Kret

The provincial riverside town of **Nonthaburi** **Ⓐ**, some 10km (6 miles) north of Bangkok, is best reached by express boat to the end of the line at Tha Nonthaburi pier (around 45 mins). Spend some time here exploring the streets and markets, or visit the beautifully restored 19th-century temple **Wat Chalerm Phra Kiet** (daily 8.30am–5pm; free), five minutes upriver in Bang Sri Muang.

From Nonthaburi, private longtail boats leave for the car-free island of Ko Kret **Ⓑ**, where tourists soak up a relaxed pace among the mainly ethnic Mon villagers, known for their pottery workshops. The island can be walked around in less than two hours, but there are bicycles, motorcycle taxis and boats for hire.

Chatuchak and North Bangkok

Next to both Kamphaeng Phet MRT station and the northernmost Skytrain stop at Mo Chit, is the sprawling **Chatuchak Weekend Market** **Ⓒ** (Sat–Sun 7am–6pm; *see Box, opposite*). Some 10km (6 miles) northeast, on Thanon Rangsit Nakornnayok, **Dream World** **Ⓓ** (www.dreamworld-th.com; Mon–Fri 10am–5pm, Sat–Sun 10am–7pm; charge **Ⓜ**) has roller-coasters and attractions like Snow Town, where locals get to experience frosty weather,

Bangkok's Skytrain is efficient and affordable

Around Bangkok

0   5 km
0   5 miles

Souvenir shopping par excellence at the well-stocked Chatuchak weekend market

with sled rides down artificial snow.

About 5km (3 miles) southeast, **Safari World** (www.safariworld. com; daily 9am–5pm; charge) is on Thanon Ramindra. There is both a safari park and a marine park. You can drive a car around or take an organised minibus tour with English-speaking guide.

Southeast Bangkok

About 6km (3½ miles) east of down-town Bangkok, at Thanon Krung-thep Kreetha Soi 4, **Prasart Museum** (tel: 0-2379-3601; Thur–Sun 10am–3pm; charge) takes visits by appointment only. Its antique Thai artefacts, belonging to the private collector Prasart Vongsakul, are in several magnificent buildings inspired by architectural classics, including a European-style mansion, a Khmer shrine, and Thai and Chinese temples.

Some 7km (4 miles) south, on Sukhumvit at Soi 101, **Wat Tham-mamongkhon** (daily 6am–6pm; free) has the tallest chedi in Bangkok,

at 95m (312ft), and a 14-tonne jade Buddha image. Around 5km (3 miles) south, at Sukhumvit Soi 119, in Samut Prakan, the **Erawan Museum** (www.erawan-museum.com; daily 8am–3pm; charge) is housed in an extraordinary 43m (141ft) -high, three-headed elephant. It has Chinese and Thai antiques; crafts, from ceramics to stucco work; and antique Buddha statues dating to the Dvaravati period, 1,200 years ago.

Bangkok and Surroundings

The World's Biggest Market

Chatuchak is said to be the world's biggest flea market, drawing 400,000 visitors every weekend. Although the sheer size makes navigation confusing, it has logic, and maps are available at the gates. The stalls sell pretty much anything imaginable, from handmade jewellery, pop T-shirts and vintage Thai film posters, to snakes and tribal fabrics, Chinese antiques and Stetson hats. It is fun to just follow your nose and see what turns up.

ACCOMMODATION

Bangkok's accommodation options run the full gamut, from riverside glamour to cheap but oh-so-stylish side-street lodgings, at a price-to-comfort ratio that must represent some of the best deals on the planet. Facilities, too, are impressive, with pools and restaurants included even at the lowest end.

Arun Residence
38 Soi Pratoo Nok Yoong, Thanon Maharat, Rattanakosin
Tel: 0-2221-9158
www.arunresidence.com
A small riverbank hotel housed in an old Sino-Portuguese mansion with views of Wat Arun, and just a short walk from Wat Pho and 100-year-old Chinese shophouses. Its French-Thai restaurant, The Deck, is an atmospheric spot for cocktails and dinner. **$$$**

Baan Saladaeng
69/2 Saladaeng Soi 3, Bangrak
Tel: 0-2636-3038
www.baansaladaeng.com
A very tasteful budget operation with just nine themed-decor rooms with names like Neo Siam, Moroccan Suite and Pop Art Mania. Each has air conditioning, TV and wireless internet. There's a small coffee bar, and it's a great location for transport, restaurants and nightlife. **$$**

Rooftop pool Le Bua at State Tower

The Eugenia
267 Sukhumvit Soi 31
Tel: 0-2259-9011
www.theeugenia.com
This 12-suite accommodation in a deliciously renovatetd 19th-century manor has old-world colonial charm. All rooms have antique furnishings and many have four-poster beds. There is no lift, of course, but plenty of staff on hand to help with luggage. The hotel's limousines are a fleet of vintage Jaguars and Mercedes Benz. **$$$$**

JW Marriott
4 Thanon Sukhumvit Soi 2
Tel: 0-2656-7700
www.marriott.com
Close to Sukhumvit's nightlife, this place has a huge fitness centre, efficient business facilities and spacious, well-appointed rooms. Some of the city's best dining is at Tsunami Japanese restaurant and the New York Steakhouse. **$$$$**

Khao San Palace
139 Thanon Khao San, Banglamphu
Tel: 0-2282-0578
www.khaosanpalace.com
Among the better Banglamphu guesthouses, this is just off Khao San down a small alley. The newer rooms are very smart, with en-suite showers, air conditioning and TV. Good views from the small rooftop pool. **$**

Le Bua at State Tower
1055/111 Thanon Silom
Tel: 0-2624-9999
www.lebua.com
Contemporary Asian-style rooms and suites

Teatime at the Mandarin Oriental.

in the 64-storey State Tower, with river- or city-view balconies. The rooftop outlets, collectively called The Dome, feature the top restaurants Sirocco, Mezzaluna and Breeze, and the sophisticated Distil Bar. **$$$**

Mandarin Oriental
48 Oriental Avenue
Tel: 0-2659-9000
www.mandarinoriental.com
Bangkok's riverside 'Grand Dame' has hosted guests since 1876 in its original Authors' Wing, which still has period suites and a delightful tearoom. It also has the excellent Le Normandie French restaurant and Ayurvedic pleasures in the Oriental Spa. **$$$$$**

Novotel Bangkok
Siam Square Soi 6
Tel: 0-2255-6888
www.accorhotels-asia.com
Tucked in the buzzy Siam Square, a short walk to shopping malls and the Siam Skytrain station, location is a big draw here. Its large basement entertainment complex, Concept CM2, is a frequently packed local nightspot. **$$$**

Old Bangkok Inn
609 Thanon Phra Sumen
Tel: 0-2629-1785
www.oldbangkokinn.com
Situated in the heart of the historic district, this is one of Bangkok's newest boutiques. With teak furniture and fittings, this 10-room hotel is a gem of traditional Thai character, set in a late 19th-century royal home. Some rooms have split-level accommodation, and each has satellite TV, DVD players, broadband and even computers. **$$$**

Sukhumvit 11 Hostel
1/33 Thanon Sukhumvit Soi 11
Tel: 0-2253-5927
www.suk11.com
Non-smoking, bare rooms with no TV or fridge, but lots of wood and rustic decor at this family-run guesthouse. There is internet access in the lobby, plus a common room with TV and DVDs. A short walk from the Skytrain. **$**

Take a Nap
920–926 Thanon Rama 4
Tel: 0-2637-0015
www.takeanaphotel.com
Basic but cutely attired rooms, each with an artistic theme, such as Japanese waves, Pop Art, and the child-like Happy Forest. There is air conditioning and a few TV stations, but no fridge or wardrobe. Close to the Patpong and Skytrain and subway stations. **$$**

RESTAURANTS

Bangkok's legendary streetfood offers a tantalising array of flavours from around the country, available at stalls on any corner of the city for a dollar a plate. And when you need a little more comfort (or cooling air conditioning), the capital is bursting with international restaurants of every type.

Bangkok

Bo.lan
42 Soi Pichai Ronnarong, Sukhumvit Soi 26
Tel: 0-2260-2962
www.bo.lan.com
Cute townhouse operation run by alumni of London's Michelin-starred Thai restaurant Nahm. Very traditional recipes run through mysterious regional flavours in dishes like sweet cured pork in coconut cream and deep-fried fish with an eye-watering spicy-sour dipping sauce. **$$$**

Krua Apsorn
Thanon Samsen, Dusit
Tel: 0-2241-8528
A plastic-table café owned by former royal cook Paa Daeng (Auntie Red). You won't go wrong with anything here, but the yellow curry with lotus shoots is legendary. There's no street number; find it just north of the National Library. **$**

Le Bouchon
37/17 Patpong Soi 2
Tel: 0-2234-9109
Atmospheric seven-table bistro that gains frisson from its Patpong location – slightly naughty, like a Marseille dockyard diner. Popular with local French for its simple home cooking and friendly banter at the small bar where diners sip Pastis. **$$–$$$**

Chote Chitr
Thanon Praengphutorn, Phra Nakorn
Tel: 0-2221-4082
Five-table shophouse opened 100 years ago by a doctor of traditional medicine. They've served excellent food (and medicines) ever since. Try the dark, pungent wing bean salad, *mee krob*, or wonderful, sour and peppery 'old-fashioned soup'. **$**

Ch Prathumthong
11 Thanon Na Phra Lan, Rattanakosin
Tel: 0-2221-3556
There are just six tables inside and out, but the large menu here encompasses fried rice, noodles, curries and salads. At night it is a bar hang-out for Thammasat and Silpa-korn students. **$**

The Deck
Arun Residence, 36–38 Soi Pratoo Nok Yoong, Rattanakosin
Tel: 0-2221-9158
Just two minutes' walk from Wat Pho, this cute place has outdoor seating, river views of Wat Arun and a bar, Amorosa, on the third floor. A mixed Thai and Euro fusion menu features plates such as carpaccio of tea-smoked duck. **$$–$$$**

Hong Kong Noodle
136/4 Trok Issaranuphap, Chinatown
Tel: 0-2623-1992
You will probably have to wait for a seat at this jammed alley shophouse, where cooks in constant motion ladle duck and pork on noodles. For dessert grab a custard tart next door at Hong Kong Dim Sum (no relation). **$**

Hua Seng Hong Yaowaraj
438 Charoen Krung Soi 14, Chinatown
Tel: 0-2627-5030
A busy air-conditioned café that sells all-day dim sum from an outside counter and all manner of congee, hot and sour soup,

barbecued pork, fish maw and braised goose-web dishes inside. **$–$$**

Nahm
Metropolitan Hotel, 27 Thanon Sathorn Tai
Tel: 0-2625-3333
This 2010 newcomer is an outlet of Europe's only Michelin-starred Thai restaurant, run by Australian chef David Thompson. The ultra-traditional menu includes intriguing flavours in dishes like jungle curry with snakehead fish that are becoming harder to find in modern Thai cooking. **$$$$**

Punjab Sweets And Restaurant
436/5 Thanon Chak Phet, Pahurat
Tel: 0-2623-7606
This small vegetarian café (also with dairy-free options) features South Indian curries, great-value thalis (a bit of everything), dosas (rice-flour pancakes) and Punjabi sweets wrapped in edible silver foil. **$**

Sirirat Market
Thanon Phrannok, Thonburi
Rough-and-ready food stalls in this general goods market offer tasty local fare: spicy sausages, satay, deep-fried chicken, stir-fries and noodles. A small shop called Paa Sidaa, next to a sign reading Wienna, is one of Bangkok's most famous *somtam* sellers. **$**

Sirocco
Fl 63 Lebua at State Tower, 1055 Thanon Silom
Tel: 0-2624-9555
www.thedomebkk.com
Spectacular 200m (656ft) -high outdoor rooftop restaurant with magnificent views over the river. Greco-Roman architecture and a jazz band add to the sense of occasion. In the same complex, there's the classy Distil Bar, the Italian Mezzaluna, and the alfresco pan-Asian restaurant Breeze. **$$$–$$$$**

Rut & Lek
Thanon Padung Dao, Chinatown
One of Bangkok's most famous foodstalls sells great curried crab, plus seafood charcoal grilled or fried with garlic and chilli.

There's another operation opposite, T & K, that's just as good. Bangkokians refer to them collectively as 'Soi Texas seafood'. **$$**

S & P
222 Maharaj Pier, Rattanakosin
Tel: 0-2222-7026
This riverfront branch of a restaurant chain does a dependable Thai spectrum, including chicken in coconut soup and sea bass in mango and chilli dressing. Choose from an air-conditioned interior or outside seating. It also serves decent coffee. **$**

Around Bangkok
Funtalop
Section 26, Chatuchak Market
No phone
Low tables jammed with diners feasting on chicken deep-fried with soy sauce, tamarind and pepper, and *somtam* (a spicy green papaya salad). Tables are communal; if there's a space, just smile and sit down. **$**

Rim Fung
235/2 Thanon Pracharat, Nonthaburi
Tel: 0-2525-1742
Wooden-plank floating restaurant with a menu that includes marinated hot-plate chicken, whole catfish and fried frogs, served with spicy salads. **$**

Street-corner restaurant in Chinatown

NIGHTLIFE

Bangkok is a nightlife city, whether you want cheap beers and jamming blues, custom cocktails in a stylish lounge or design-conscious clubs full of house and hip-hop. There are official closing times of 1–2am, but keep your ear to the ground and you can party all night.

808
RCA Block C
Tel: 0-2203-1043
www.808bangkok.com
Brick and steel innards, an ace sound system and a regular influx of international DJs like Grandmaster Flash.

Ad Here the 13th
13 Thanon Samsen, Banglamphu
Tel: 08-9769-4613
Musicians jamming blues in a bar the size of a guitar case. You sometimes get surprises like Charlie Musselwhite playing when they're in town.

Balcony
86–88 Silom Soi 4, Bangrak
Tel: 0-2235-5891
www.balconypub.com
Lively, long-standing bar with a party crowd who spill out onto this gay-friendly street.

Bed Supperclub
26 Sukhumvit Soi 11
Tel: 0-2651-3537
www.bedsupperclub.com
This striking elliptically shaped building hides a pumping bar-club. Laid-back music is played by a monthly roster of imported DJs while diners mull over their meals. There's a cool fusion-y restaurant attached, where you lie on beds to eat.

Club Culture
Ratchadamnoen Klang, Banglamphu
Tel: 08-9497-8422
www.club-culture-bkk.com
A firm favourite on Bangkok's ever-evolving club scene. This refurbished old Thai theatre venue has three floors with a capacity of over 1,000 people for some hot visiting and local DJs, plus an art space.

The Living Room
Sheraton Grande Sukhumvit
205 Thanon Sukhumvit
Tel: 0-2653-0333
www.starwood.com/bangkok
There's a very good house band at this open-plan jazz venue, plus overseas visitors like The Preservation Hall Jazz Band.

Q Bar
34 Sukhumvit Soi 11
Tel: 0-2252-3274
www.qbarbangkok.com
Stylishly dark two-floor venue with cool dance music from locals and imports. The impressive drinks list includes 50 brands of vodka.

Saxophone Pub
3/8 Thanon Phaya Thai
Tel: 0-2246-5472
www.saxophonepub.com
This lively two-floor bar hosts good resident bands (at least two a night), playing pop-jazz, R&B, soul and funk.

New York style comes to Bangkok at Q Bar

ENTERTAINMENT

Theatre has an understated presence in the capital. Some up-market Thai restaurants have traditional shows, and there are a couple of venues where you can see the real thing. The contemporary art scene grew in 2008 with the opening of a huge downtown gallery, and there are many smaller galleries around town. Show details are at www.rama9art.com.

Art Galleries

Bangkok Art and Culture Centre
939 Thanon Rama 1
Tel: 0-2214-6630
www.bacc.or.th
This huge 11-storey space stages some of Bangkok's best art and multimedia shows. The retail outlets on its lower floors are occupied by small independent galleries or organisations like the Thai Film Foundation. Has art markets on the concourse.

Culture Shows

Siam Niramit
19 Thanon Tiamruammit
Tel: 0-2649-9222
www.siamniramit.com
A beautifully costumed extravaganza that traverses the country's history and diverse cultures in three acts, nightly shows at 8pm.

Theatre

Aksra Theatre
8/1 Soi Rangnam
Tel: 0-2677-8888
www.aksratheatre.com
Thai and other Asian puppetry with cultural performances themed around events like cock fighting and Muay Thai.

Patravadi Theatre
69/1 Soi Wat Rakhang
Tel: 0-2412-7287
www.patravaditheatre.com
The nucleus of the Thai contemporary theatre scene melds traditional and modern dance and drama either in this theatre or in Studio 9, which is adjacent on the river.

Sala Chalerm Krung
66 Thanon Charoen Krung
Tel: 0-2222-1854
A rare space to hear some Thai classical music, as it hosts *Khon* masked drama performances every Friday and Saturday evening from 7pm.

Thailand Cultural Centre
Thanon Ratchadaphisek
Tel: 0-2247-0028
www.thaiculturalcenter.com
Stages everything from pop concerts to works by the Bangkok Symphony Orchestra and Bangkok Opera (www.bangkokopera.com).

SPORTS AND ACTIVITIES

Fitness buffs and sports fanatics won't go far wrong in Bangkok – there is a wide choice of facilities, with a smattering listed below. There are many top-class golf courses within an hour of the capital. Kids love the fun of go-karting, while many people come to Thailand specifically to train in Muay Thai.

Go-Karting

Easykart.Net
2nd Floor, RCA Plaza, Royal City Avenue, Thanon Rama IX
Tel: 0-2203-1205

www.easykart.net
A 600m (1,968ft) race circuit with fast, light karts reaching speeds around 60kph (37mph). 🍴

Bangkok Golf Club

Golf
Bangkok Golf Club
99 Moo 2 Thanon Tivanond
Tel: 0-2501-2828
www.golf.th.com
An attractive club with courses modelled on famous holes from around the world. About 40 minutes from Central Bangkok.

Gyms
True Fitness
Exchange Tower, 388 Thanon Sukhumvit

Tel: 0-2663-4999
www.truefitness.co.th
Well-equipped growing chain with a good choice of weights, running and biking facilities, and classes in yoga, dance and Pilates.

Muay Thai Training
Sor Vorapin
13 Trok Kasab, near Thanon Khao San
Tel: 0-2243-3651
A simple gym offering Muay Thai lessons. If you turn out to be any good they might even find you fights at local stadiums.

Yoga
Yoga Elements Studio
Vanissa Building, 29 Soi Chidlom
Tel: 0-2391-9919
www.yogaelements.com
Popular classes based on Ashtanga Vinyasa that teach elemental procedures like breath control as well as advanced techniques.

TOURS

There is an awful lot to see around hectic Bangkok, and sometimes the best way to cut through the confusion is to let a tour company make arrangements for you. The choice of sights includes ancient ruins, floating markets, dinner-theatre shows and canal communities, while the modes of transport take in boats, bikes and planes.

Sightseeing
Bangkok Aviation Centre
222 Hanger 4414 Thanon Viphavadee Rangsit, Don Mueang
Tel: 0-2535-7740
www.bangkokflying.com
Arranges sunset tours over Bangkok and Ayutthaya in four-seater Cessna planes.

Grand Pearl Cruises
Tel: 0-2861-0255
123–125 Charoen Nakhon Soi 13
www.grandpearlcruise.com
This company operates day trips to Bang Pa-In and Ayutthaya. Depart by coach at 7.30am and return by boat on board the *Grand Pearl*, arriving in Bangkok by 4pm.

Oriental Escape
187 Ratchawithi Soi 21
Tel: 0-2883-1219
www.orientalescape.com
Offers a wide range of tours, including Thai boxing, floating markets and Thai dance and dinner shows. In Bangkok and around Thailand.

Real Asia
10/5–7 Soi Aree, Sukhumvit Soi 26
Tel: 0-2665-6364
www.realasia.net
Day-long cycling tours into the capital's more scenic and traffic-free countryside. Also has walking and canal boat tours and a train tour into Samut Sakhon.

FESTIVALS AND EVENTS

In addition to its wide entertainment profile, Bangkok has the biggest annual event calendar in the country. The red carpet comes out for the Bangkok International Film Festival; carnivals of dance and theatre draw eclectic performers from around the world and the year is rounded out with sports tournaments and celebrations of traditional Thai culture.

May
Royal Ploughing Ceremony
Sanam Luang

A Brahman festival in which a pair of sacred cows are led to a choice of foodstuffs, such as rice, green beans and liquor. Whichever they consume first prophesises the coming harvest.

June
La Fete
Various venues
www.lafete-bangkok.com

A month-long French multicultural festival at various venues around the city. It takes in film, fashion, art, music, street theatre and all points between.

September
Bangkok International Festival of Dance and Music
Thailand Cultural Centre
www.bangkokfestivals.com

A month of mainly classical music and ballet performances by companies from around the world, with smatterings of jazz, folk and cultural variations thrown in.

Bangkok International Film Festival
Various venues
www.bangkokfilm.org

Usually close to 100 films from a variety of countries, many entered in competition. Plus seminars and workshops on film-making.

September–October
Thailand Open Tennis Tournament
Impact Arena

Thailand's major men's tennis competition usually attracts a few top players, such as Rafael Nadal and Jo-Wilfried Tsonga.

October
Vegetarian Festival
Chinatown

A Taoist religious festival, during which people abstain from meat and stimulants such as sex. The Chinatown streets are full of parades and performances of Chinese opera.

December
The King's Birthday
5 December
Ratchadamnoen and Sanam Luang

The king's birthday is celebrated in Bangkok with an elaborate parade on Ratchadamnoen Klang Avenue and cultural shows at Sanam Luang.

Monks at The King's Birthday celebration

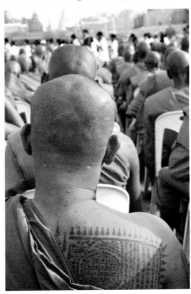

Central Thailand

When Bangkok overwhelms, easy escapes within a few hours' drive from the city provide welcome relief. The flat, fertile Central Plains, known as the country's Rice Bowl, contain the ruins of former kingdoms that ruled these lands from as long ago as the 6th century AD. For adventurous types there are several national parks with trekking opportunities and shoppers can explore the floating markets.

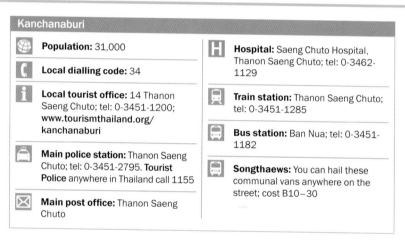

Kanchanaburi

Population: 31,000

Local dialling code: 34

Local tourist office: 14 Thanon Saeng Chuto; tel: 0-3451-1200; www.tourismthailand.org/kanchanaburi

Main police station: Thanon Saeng Chuto; tel: 0-3451-2795. **Tourist Police** anywhere in Thailand call 1155

Main post office: Thanon Saeng Chuto

Hospital: Saeng Chuto Hospital, Thanon Saeng Chuto; tel: 0-3462-1129

Train station: Thanon Saeng Chuto; tel: 0-3451-1285

Bus station: Ban Nua; tel: 0-3451-1182

Songthaews: You can hail these communal vans anywhere on the street; cost B10–30

Many people make Bangkok their base for separate trips to surrounding destinations in easy reach of the capital. To the north, Thailand's former capital Ayutthaya was an important Asian city with an 18th-century population greater than London's. Invading Burmese armies destroyed it in 1767, and the ruins are preserved in Ayutthaya Historical Park. Prior to Ayutthayan power, the surrounding lands were ruled by the Khmer Empire, of which there are remnants in Lopburi.

Even earlier, artefacts found at Nakhon Pathom, west of Bangkok, date the site to around 150BC. Nakhon Pathom was an important centre of Mon culture from the 6th century AD, and is thought to be Thailand's oldest continuously functioning city. Further west, Kanchanaburi, home to the Bridge on the River Kwai and the infamous World War II 'Death Railway', also has endless possibilities for river rafting and jungle treks.

South of Bangkok is the country's best-known floating market, which provides a fascinating glimpse into Thailand's past, when many people shopped on water.

West of Bangkok

The road west leads to Nakhon Pathom and the world's tallest Buddhist monument, before reaching Kanchanaburi, the gateway to the western national parks and home of the famous Bridge on the River Kwai. Then, there is a beautiful drive towards the Burma (Myanmar) border and the multiethnic lakeside community of Sangkhlaburi.

The Bridge on the River Kwai

Nakhon Pathom

An hour's drive west of Bangkok on Route 4 is Nakhon Pathom, where the main attraction is **Phra Pathom Chedi** ❶ (tel: 0-3424-2143; daily 6am–6pm; charge) on Thanon Khwa Phra. It is claimed to be the tallest Buddhist monument in the world, and possibly the oldest Buddhist site in Thailand, dating to 3BC.

Kanchanaburi

About 90 minutes west of Nakhon Pathom, the town of **Kanchanaburi** ❷ is known for the **Bridge on the River Kwai**, built by Allied and Asian prisoners in World War II. South of the bridge on Thanon Mae Nam Kwai, the **World War II Museum** (tel: 0-3451-2596; daily 7am–6pm; charge)

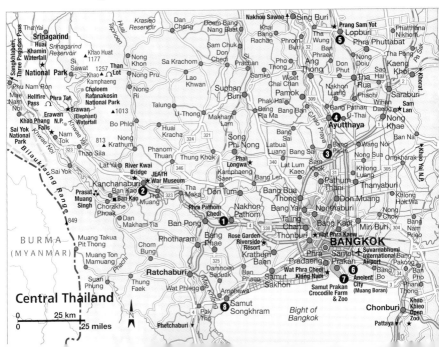

Central Thailand

| 0 | 25 km |
| 0 | 25 miles |

Erawan National Park

Local guide shops on Thanon Mae Nam Kwai in Kanchanaburi have various itineraries from day trips to week-long jungle treks, including rafting, elephant rides and visits to tribal villages in the national parks surrounding Kanchanaburi. Erawan National Park, at Km 44, on Route 3199 (www.dnp.go.th; daily 8am–4.30pm; charge), is one of the most popular destinations. The main attraction is the Erawan Waterfall, which is a two-hour trek to the top, passing seven tiers with pools to swim in.

has an odd mix of war exhibits and murals of Miss Thailand winners. Further south, after around 2km (1 mile), left on Thanon Jaokunnen, is the Thailand–Burma Railway Centre and its **Death Railway Museum** (www.tbrconline.com; daily 9am–5pm; charge). It has eight galleries on the railway and the life of the prisoners

building it. Opposite is the **Kanchanaburi Allied War Cemetery** (daily 7am–6pm; free), the last resting place of 6,982 Allied soldiers.

At the south end of town, five minutes' drive from the cemetery, the informative **JEATH War Museum** (Wat Chaichumpol; tel: 0-3451-5203; daily 8am–6pm; charge) is on Thanon Chaichumpol. It has photographs, sketches and paintings made by prisoners.

Sangkhlaburi

A beautiful 230km (140-mile) drive west of Kanchanaburi is the small town of Sangkhlaburi, on a man-made lake. The population includes Karen, Mon and Burmese, as well as Thai, so Burmese dishes and goods are sold in local cafés and at the dry market. Thailand's longest wooden bridge links to a Mon village across the lake. Guesthouses can arrange boating, fishing and trekking trips to

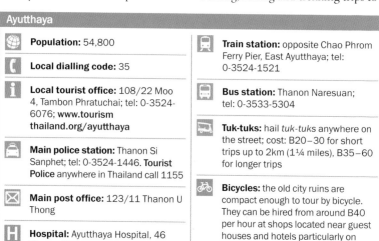

Ayutthaya

Population: 54,800

Local dialling code: 35

Local tourist office: 108/22 Moo 4, Tambon Phratuchai; tel: 0-3524-6076; www.tourism thailand.org/ayutthaya

Main police station: Thanon Si Sanphet; tel: 0-3524-1446. **Tourist Police** anywhere in Thailand call 1155

Main post office: 123/11 Thanon U Thong

Hospital: Ayutthaya Hospital, 46 Thanon U Thong; tel: 0-3524-1888

Train station: opposite Chao Phrom Ferry Pier, East Ayutthaya; tel: 0-3524-1521

Bus station: Thanon Naresuan; tel: 0-3533-5304

Tuk-tuks: hail *tuk-tuk*s anywhere on the street; cost: B20–30 for short trips up to 2km (1¼ miles), B35–60 for longer trips

Bicycles: the old city ruins are compact enough to tour by bicycle. They can be hired from around B40 per hour at shops located near guest houses and hotels particularly on Naresuan Soi 2.

The old palaces of Bang Pa-In are an interesting hybrid of East-West design

national parks, and day passes into Burma are available at the Three Pagodas Pass border post, nearby.

North of Bangkok

The regions north of Bangkok are some of the most historically rich in the land. The ruins of the old capital Ayutthaya contain hints of the 18th century when this was one of the most important trading cities in Asia. And to the north are the Khmer-influenced temples of Lopburi, complete with their current-day monkey inhabitants.

Bang Pa-In

About 55km (33 miles) north of Bangkok, **Bang Pa-In ❸** (www. palaces.thai.net; daily 8am–3.30pm; charge 🅜) was a royal summer palace from the 17th century. It has series of

buildings in Thai, Chinese, Gothic and Neoclassical styles around a man-made lake. Most were built during the reigns of Rama IV (1851–68) and Rama V (1868–1910), with the highlight being **Phra Thinang Aisawan Tippaya-Art** (The Divine Seat of Personal Freedom), a Thai-style pavilion in the middle of the lake. The grounds are walkable, but there are also buggies for hire.

Ayutthaya

The old Thai capital, **Ayutthaya ❹**, 20km (12½ miles) north of Bang Pa-In, is a Unesco World Heritage Site containing the ruins of buildings destroyed in 1767 by the invading Burmese army. The major attractions begin with an overview at the **Ayutthaya Historical Study Centre** (Thanon Rotchana; tel: 0-3524-5124; Wed–Sun 9am–4.30pm; charge) and the **Chao Sam Phraya Museum** (Thanon Rotchana; tel: 0-3524-1587; Wed–Sun 9am–4pm; charge). Among the main temples are the new **Viharn Phra Monkhon Bophit** and the ruins of **Wat Phra Sri Sanphet** (charge), which lies nearby, opposite the foundations of the old **Grand Palace**. Three minutes' walk southeast is **Wat Phra Ram** (charge), near **Khun Paen's House**, an example of traditional Thai housing. It is located beside the **Ayutthaya Elephant Palace and Kraal** (🅜). A 10-minute walk away are **Wat Phra Mahathat** (Thanon Maharat; daily 7.30am–6.30pm; charge) and **Wat Ratchaburana** (Thanon Maharat; daily 7.30am–6.30pm; charge). For more details, *see the Tour, pp.96–7.*

🚶 TOUR OF AYUTTHAYA

Take a full-day trip into Thailand's glorious past, when its ancient capital Ayutthaya had 2,000 golden temples. The tour is mainly walkable, but bicycles and *tuk tuks* are available everywhere for hire.

Entering Ayutthaya along Thanon Rotchana, turn left into the **Ayutthaya Historical Study Centre**, which has five sections covering traditions and village life. Turning left from the centre, near the junction on the right, the **Chao Sam Phraya Museum** has relics discovered in the city.

Turn right at the top of the road into Thanon Si Sanphet, and go left at the roundabout into Thanon Pha Thon. Turn right before the bridge over the canal, and turn into the car park on the right. A **market** (daily 7am–6pm)

Buddha head entwined within the gnarled roots of a banyan tree at Wat Mahathat

here sells crafts and souvenirs. It also has lots of food stalls, so is a good spot for lunch. Beyond is **Viharn Phra Mongkhon Bophit**, a new building, but highly venerated for its massive 15th-century bronze Buddha, which lay unsheltered amid the ruins here for two centuries until the *viharn* was built to house it in 1956.

A path on the left leads to the walled **Wat Phra Sri Sanphet**, built in 1491 to honour three kings, whose remains are in the trio of much-photographed *chedis* standing in a line. The Burmese melted the gold off the main standing Buddha image here, which was a full 16m (52½ feet) high. The remains were later removed by King Rama I and concealed inside Chedi Sri Sanphet at Bangkok's Wat Pho. Beyond the wall opposite are the foundations of the **Grand Palace**.

Outside Wat Phra Sri Sanphet, beside the palace, turn right along the wall and turn right at the end. Ahead to

Tips

- Distance: 3km (1¾ miles)
- Time: A full day
- There are regular buses and trains from Bangkok to Ayutthaya. By car it takes around one hour.
- Several operators and hotels arrange overnight boat trips to Ayutthaya at various levels of price and comfort. Try www.manohracruises.com or www.asian-oasis.com. They are romantic, but you will see less of the city.
- To arrive when all sites are open travel Wednesday through Sunday.

Take a ride on an elephant

the left is **Wat Phra Ram**, constructed in 1369, and one of the city's oldest temples. Elephant gates punctuate the old walls, and the central terrace is dominated by a crumbling *prang* with a gallery of stucco naga serpents, garudas and Buddha statues.

In the park opposite, walk along the right of the lake and cross the first wooden bridge to **Khun Paen's House**, which, though empty of furnishings, is a good example of a traditional Thai abode, showing the three separate dwellings of the extended family arranged around a communal verandah for socialising and dining.

Leave the house by the kitchen stairs, turn left, and follow the path to the right to the **Ayutthaya Elephant Palace and Kraal** for shows and elephant rides (charge). Leave the entrance gate, turn right over the footbridge, then left through the car park. Go over the footbridge on the right and pass the lake. Cross the next bridge, turn left, then right and you are back into the market.

Reclaim your car (or take a *tuk tuk*). Turn left from the car park and take the first left into Thanon Pha Thon. At the second roundabout, turn left into Thanon Maharat, then left again into the car park at **Wat Phra Mahathat**, one of the most visited (and most atmospheric) temples. From the entrance, walk to the right to find a stone Buddha head on the ground trapped in the roots of a bodhi tree – one of Thailand's iconic images. The complex dates from the late 14th-century reign of King Ramesuan, though it was largely restored around 1663.

Turn left from Wat Mahathat to the corner, where King Borom Ratchathirat II built **Wat Ratchaburana** in 1424 as a memorial to his elder brothers who killed each other here in an elephant-back duel for the throne. Some murals still exist, while other artworks found here are now kept in the Chao Sam Phraya Museum.

Do a U-turn from Wat Ratchaburana and turn left by **Ruean Rojjana** into Thanon Naresuan. At the end turn right, then right again before the bridge. Ahead, 200m/yds on the left, **Pae Krung Kao Ayudthaya**, a well-regarded riverside restaurant with rural views and good food, makes a fitting and tasty end to the tour.

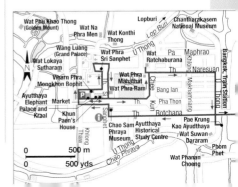

⭐ THAI BOXING

Thailand's national sport of Muay Thai, or Thai boxing, has been a tourist attraction for decades. Burly Westerners climbing into the ring in places like Phuket to fight Thai fighters half their size have become one of the iconic images for the more macho visitor to these shores. It should be no surprise that they often lose. Muay Thai is a centuries-old discipline that was used to choose elite palace guards, and even today young boys begin their ring careers from the age of seven.

The earliest records of Muay Thai date to 1411, when two young Chiang Mai princes reportedly fought 'to the first blood' for the crown after their father King Sen Muang Ma died. Royalty has always had a strong connection with the martial art, and it is known as the Sport of Kings. Palaces traditionally had boxing grounds outside, both for public entertainment and to choose elite palace guards. Sanam Luang performed the function for Bangkok

and still has boxing matches today on special occasions such as the King's birthday.

Every soldier during the Ayutthaya period trained in Muay Thai, a practice that continues, and its importance is seen in the attempts of some Ayutthaya kings to be champions. Naturally, as it was forbidden to hit – or in fact touch – the king, this was in some cases fairly straightforward. King Sanpet VIII (known as the 'Tiger King'),

Thai boxing combines punching and kicking

Muay Thai, Thailand's wildly popular national sport, is a must-see for visitors

however, is legendary for fighting in disguise at a local temple fair and, so the story goes, beating the national champion.

Young boys still have their first fights at temple fairs, usually in impoverished Isaan, sometimes as young as seven. They may win prize money of a few hundred baht; the good ones will be snapped up by promoters and soon become the family's main breadwinner.

Despite prosaic names for the moves, such as 'Bird Peeping Through the Nest', this is a brutal way to earn a living. Fists, feet, elbows and knees are all used to inflict damage. But there is also a strict ritual element to the sport. Before the fight starts, the boxers perform a *wai kru ram muay* dance around the ring to display respect to their trainers and appease the ring spirits.

The fights themselves are a popular, raucous spectacle, with a traditional Thai *pipat* band accompanying the action in a wailing of pipe and reed instruments. The crowd becomes increasingly animated as the punches rain and the betting action is a whirlwind of arms, signalling odds and wagers across the arena. Thai boxing is one of only two sports, along with horse racing, that are exempt from laws prohibiting gambling in Thailand.

Most towns where tourists congregate will have facilities to learn Muay Thai, sometimes with accommodation included. The gyms may even arrange fights if you're good enough.

Thai Boxing

Training for this punishing and brutal martial art begins as early as age seven

Lopburi

Another important settlement, about 75km (50 miles) north of Ayutthaya, is **Lopburi ❺**. The town was significant in the Mon Dvaravati kingdom (6th–10th centuries), and was later an outpost of the Angkor empire. Lopburi was also a mid-17th-century summer retreat from Ayutthaya for King Narai.

Opposite the train station, on Thanon Na Phrakan, is **Wat Phra Si Rattana Mahathat** (daily 8am–6pm; charge), with a few intact elements of its Khmer heritage. North, at the corner of Thanon Wichayen, **Prang Sam Yot** (daily 8am–6pm; charge) has Brahman, Khmer and Buddhist elements, often dubbed the Lopburi style. It is famous for its resident monkeys.

Southwest, on Thanon Sorasak, **Phra Narai Ratchanivet** (daily 8am–6pm; charge) was King Narai's palace. The buildings include the **Narai National Museum** (www.thailandmuseum.com; Wed–Sun 9am–4pm; charge).

South of Bangkok

A few hours south of the capital there are some fascinating sites that illuminate both living culture – in the form of floating markets and contemporary makers of traditional crafts – and ancient heritage, as seen in the near life-size reproductions of some of Thailand's most important long-vanished temples and palaces.

Ancient City

About 33km (20 miles) southeast of Bangkok, the **Ancient City ❻** (www.ancientcity.com; daily 8am–5pm; charge) is loosely laid out in the shape of Thailand, with over 100 monuments, palaces and houses. Some are relocated original buildings, others near life-size reproductions of existing and lost structures, notably royal palaces from Ayutthaya.

Crocodile Farm and Zoo

Some 5km (3 miles) west of Ancient City is **Samut Prakan Crocodile Farm & Zoo ❼** (tel: 0-2703-4891; open daily 7am– 6pm; charge 🅼). It claims to have over 60,000 crocs, including the world's largest in captivity, the 6m (20ft) -long and 1,114kg (2,456lbs) Chai Yai.

Samut Sakhon

The port of Samut Sakhon, 28km (17 miles) southwest of Bangkok, has the area's main fish market, located at Mahachai pier, where boats are available for a round trip to the principal temple, Wat Chong Lom, at the mouth of the Tachin River.

The three Khmer-style *prang* of Prang Sam Yot at Lopburi

Sample the fresh produce at Damnoen Saduak Floating Market

Samut Songkram

Around 46km (27 miles) southwest, **Samut Songkhram** ❽ is the gateway to the canal zone and the floating markets. A tasty diversion is **Don Hoi Lot**, 15 minutes' drive away at the mouth of the river, where seafood restaurants serve the *hoi lot* (similar to razor clams) that give the area its name.

Amphawa

Travelling 10km (6 miles) west on Route 325 leads to Amphawa, where there is a floating market each Friday, Saturday and Sunday. Close by, the **Rama II Memorial Park** (tel: 0-3475-1666; daily 6.30am–5pm; charge) has arts and crafts from the early Rattana-kosin period in traditional teak stilted houses. Leaving Amphawa, just off Route 325 on the left is a turn to **Ban Pinsuwan Benjarong** (tel: 0-3475-1322; Mon–Sat 8am–5pm; free), a small family workshop that produces various traditional pottery styles and has a modest museum.

Damnoen Saduak

Another 15km (9 miles) west on Route 325 is the famous **Damnoen Saduak Floating Market** (daily 7am–1pm). It is best to arrive before 9am to miss the coachloads arriving from Bangkok. The market runs in three sections and mainly consists of women in broad-brimmed hats selling vegetables the traditional way from flat-bottomed boats. Less traditional are the stalls on shore selling tourist souvenirs.

Get an Early Start

It is best to get to the Floating Market at Damnoen Saduak as early as possible in the morning. To avoid a 6am departure from Bangkok, consider staying overnight at Baan Sukchoke, which, as well as having decent rooms and a restaurant, performs five daily cobra shows (charge). Other animals that get in on the act are pythons and a mongoose, and the climax sees a handler catch a snake in his mouth.

ACCOMMODATION

Outside of Kanchanaburi, the historic old towns of Central Thailand are geared more towards day-trippers, and the choice of accommodation reflects that custom. But while there are no resorts of the five-star variety you might expect on the islands, the comfort levels are surprisingly high for the low cost of rooms.

West of Bangkok

Apple Guest House
52 Th. Saengchuto, Kanchanaburi
Tel: 0-3451-5061
www.applenoi-kanchanaburi.com
This friendly and well-run place has quiet bungalows just a stone's throw from the river, and is locally famous for its outstanding food and Thai cooking courses. **$**

Felix River Kwai Kanchanaburi Resort
9/1 Moo 3 Thamakham, Kanchanaburi
Tel: 0-3451-5061
www.felixriverkwai.co.th
Comfortable resort-style riverside hotel in a pretty garden setting near the bridge. The Felix has been around for a long time but it well-maintained. The de luxe rooms facing the river are worth the premium rates. The free-form pool is perfect for lounging. **$$$**

P Guest House
81/2 Moo 1, Tambon Nongloo, Sangkhlaburi

Tel: 0-3459-5061
www.pguesthouseresort.com
Mainly fan rooms with a shared bathroom on a slope leading down to the lake. The few air-conditioned chalets with private bathroom cost not much extra. The decent and very friendly outdoor restaurant has Thai, Burmese and Western dishes. **$**

River Kwai Jungle Rafts
Baan Tahsao, Amphur Saiyoke, Kanchanaburi
Tel: 08-1734-0667, or Tel: 0-2642-5497 (Bangkok office)
www.serenatahotels.com
Sleep in the quaint raft rooms and eat and drink on the adjoining floating restaurant and bar. You can swim or fish in the river, ride elephants and visit nearby ethnic tribal villages. **$$**

River Kwai Resotel
55 Moo 5 Tambol Wangkrajae, Amphur Saiyoke, Kanchanaburi
Tel: 08-1734-5238
www.riverkwairesotel.net
Good riverside location with basic but clean rooms in rustic thatched-roof bungalows, with a lovely pool area. Offers plenty of activities (rafting, canoeing, hiking, village excursions, etc), although the buffet food is a little boring. **$$$**

North of Bangkok

Krungsri River Hotel
27/2 Moo 11, Thanon Rojchana, Ayutthaya
Tel: 0-3524-4333
www.krungsririver.com

Bungalow at River Kwai Resotel

A decent provincial hotel in a town with few options (mainly because most people visit Aytthaya on day trips from Bangkok). Modern facilities but not much character. The rooms have air conditioning and cable TV, and there's a pool, fitness centre, sauna, restaurant and bar. **$$**

Lopburi Inn Resort
144 Thanon Paholyothin, Lopburi
Tel: 0-3642-0777
www.lopburiinnresort.com
Probably the poshest hotel in town, which doesn't say very much for it. There is a range of rooms, all with air conditioning, and a restaurant serving a mix of Thai and Western dishes. There is a decent-sized swimming pool. **$**

River View Place Hotel
35 Thanon U-Thong, Ayutthaya
Tel: 0-3524-1444
www.riverviewplacehotel.com
One of Ayutthaya's better options, with large rooms, kitchenettes and spacious balconies. Feels more like a condo than a hotel because it was originally built as apartments. **$$$**

South of Bangkok
Baan Sukchoke Country Resort
103 Moo 5, Damnoen Saduak
Tel: 0-3225-4301
Simple, clean wooden bungalows arranged around a canal, with traditional boats and farming equipment scattered around as decor. **$**

RESTAURANTS

Hotels and guesthouses at towns in the Central region will have a selection of Western dishes, but the best food in this area is overwhelmingly Thai. Luckily there is lots of it, from market stalls and quaint riverside terraces, selling the delicious specialities of the region, such as the famous *tom yum goong*.

Restaurant Price Categories
Prices are for a three course meal without drinks
$ = below B300
$$ = B300–800
$$$ = B800–1,600
$$$$ = over B1,600

103

Listings

West of Bangkok
Chedi Square Foodstalls
Thanon Khwa Phra, Nakhon Pathom
A variety of stalls opposite the *chedi*, where, along with regular Thai dishes, you'll find local specialities such as pink pomelo and *khao lam* (black beans, palm sugar and sticky rice grilled in hollow bamboo). **$**

Inn Chan
Rose Garden Riverside Resort, Km 32, Thanon Phetkasem, Sampran, Nakhon Pathom
Tel: 0-3432-2544
There are a number of eateries at Rose Garden, but Inn Chan offers the most authentic Thai food, priding itself on the use of ingredients from the surrounding villages. **$**

Keereetara Restaurant
43/1 Thanon Mae Nam Kwai, Kanchanaburi
Tel: 0-3462-4093
Stylish, boutique-style restaurant with mock Sukhothai-era pillars and detailing. Best to sit on the atmospheric riverside terraces to enjoy a range of dishes including the speciality snakefish with spicy salad. **$-$$**

Old Town Market
Viharn Phra Mongkhon Bophit, Ayutthaya
Diners sit at communal tables ringed by individual vendors selling dishes like Thai omelettes, curries and noodle soups. **$**

Tara Buree
48 Thanon Song Kwai, Kanchanaburi
Tel: 0-3451-2944

Floating restaurant jutting into the river on several pontoons. The view compensates for the basic standard of dishes such as deep-fried prawns with garlic and steamed sea bass with lemon sauce. $–$$

Ya Jai
301/1 Thanon Mae Nam Kwai, Kanchanaburi
Tel: 0-3462-4848
Delightful garden restaurant known for its excellent Isaan specialities and classic Central Thai dishes. Most evenings young musicians perform Thai ballads and northeastern country music. $

North of Bangkok
Pae Krung Kao Ayudthaya
Km 4, Moo 2, Thanon Authong, Ayutthaya
Tel: 0-3524-1555
This large but cosy restaurant on the riverbank is a picturesque spot for one of Ayutthaya's oldest floating restaurants. Dishes include curries and spicy salads, or a whole fried fish eaten with dipping sauces. $–$$

Ruean Rojjana
22/13 Thanon Maharat, Ayutthaya
Tel: 0-3532-3765
Offering some outside tables and traditional triangular cushion seating with temple views, this spot serves tourist favourites like fried chicken with cashew nuts. $–$$

White House Garden
18 Thanon Phraya Kamjat, Lopburi
Tel: 0-3641-3085
A pleasant spot opposite the Lopburi tourist office. Locals come here for the excellent Central Thai food and to listen to the resident guitarist play some Thai folk classics. $

South of Bangkok
Khun Pao Restaurant
1/3 Moo 4, Don Hoi Lod, Samut Songkram
Tel: 0-3472-3703
Rustic wooden planks overlooking the Mae Khlong River delta. Speciality seafood dishes include the celebrated *hoi lod* (razor clams), unappetisingly referred to as 'worm shells' on the menu. Delicious. $–$$

NIGHTLIFE AND ENTERTAINMENT

Nightlife options are at a premium in the Central region, with most people doing their drinking by staying on at the restaurant after dining. What stand-alone bars there are offer little more than TV and a pool table as extras. Good areas to check out are Naresuan Soi 1, in Ayutthaya and Thanon Mae Nam Kwai in Kanchanaburi.

West of Bangkok
Jazz Bar
Thanon Naresuan, Soi 1, Ayutthaya
No phone
Run by the Chaikawiphan Jazz Band, this is a relaxed place to enjoy a few beers accompanied by live music.

No Name Bar
Thanon Mae Nam Kwai, Kanchanaburi
No phone
This stretch of road is the best place to find nightlife in Kanchanaburi, and this bar has the typical cheap beers and sport-on-TV theme.

A popular Kanchanaburi bar

SPORTS, TOURS AND ACTIVITIES

Kanchanaburi is one of the most visited centres of adventure tours in Thailand, yet retains a sense of serenity. Trips from there include rafting, jungle treks and visits to Karen villages. Thai cooking courses are also popular. Numerous tours of the region are organised out of Bangkok, which many people use as a centre for visiting all these destinations.

Adventure

Good Times Travel
63/1 Thanon River Kwai,
Kanchanaburi
Tel: 0-3462-4441
www.good-times-travel.com
Experienced, English-speaking guides lead tours to surrounding national parks, including rafting, jungle treks and visits to Karen villages. Also handles fishing and golf trips.

RSP Jumbo Travel
3/13 Thanon Chao Kun Nen
Tel: 0-3451-4906
www.jumboriverkwai.com
Trips include rainforest walks, elephant riding and off-road adventure, plus tours of local sites.

Cooking

Apple's Retreat & Guesthouse
153/4 Moo 4, Sutjai Bridge
Tel: 0-3451-2017
www.applenoi-kanchanaburi.com
Hands-on cooking school that includes a market trip and recipe book. Apple also runs adventure tours and has a guesthouse.

Heritage Tours

Oriental Escape
187 Ratchawithi Soi 21
Tel: 0-2883-1219
www.orientalescape.com
This Bangkok-based company runs river trips to Ayutthaya with tours of the old city sites. It also has trips to Damnoen Saduak and Kanchanaburi.

Listings

FESTIVALS AND EVENTS

In one of the main events of the Central Plains, the people of Lopburi prepare a large monkey feast to thank the resident primates of the town for the tourist dollars they attract. The feast is, of course, a prime tourist attraction in itself. Other festivals celebrate the ancient heritage of Ayutthaya and the more recent history of Kanchanaburi.

November

Monkey Buffet
Lopburi
Chefs travel from Bangkok to help prepare a buffet costing around half-a-million baht to feed the monkeys at Prang Sam Yot.

River Kwai Festival
Kanchanaburi
The Bridge on the River Kwai is the focal point for folk entertainment and a sound-and-light presentation recapturing the dark period of recent history, when thousands of Asians and Europeans died at the hands of the Japanese while building the infamous Death Railway during World War II.

December

Ayutthaya World Heritage Fair
Ayutthaya
Parades, sound-and-light shows, folk performances and handicrafts commemo-rate the city's status as a Unesco World Heritage Site.

Eastern Seaboard

Although the this is Thailand's industrial centre, it has miles of sandy beaches, particularly around Pattaya and dozens of beautiful islands such as Ko Samet and Ko Chang. There are relatively calm seas all year, and Pattaya is full of activities such as diving, sailing and golf to pull in the weekend crowd. All these await on Thailand's easily accessible Eastern Seaboard.

Pattaya

Population: 104,200

Local dialling code: 38

Local tourist office: 609 Moo 10, Thanon Pratamnak; tel: 0-3842-7667; **www.tourismthailand.org/pattaya**

Main police station: Pattaya 2nd Rd; tel: 0-3842-9371. **Tourist Police** anywhere in Thailand call 1155

Main post office: Soi Post Office

Hospitals: Bangkok Pattaya Hospital, 301 Moo 6, Th. Sukhumvit km143; tel: 0-3842-7777. Pattaya International Hospital, Pattaya Soi 4; tel: 0-3842-8374/5; **www.pih-inter. com**

Local newspapers: *Pattaya Mail*

Pattaya, the principal tourist town of the region, rose to prominence in the 1960s, when American servicemen arrived on 'R&R' from the Vietnam War. At the time, this primarily equated to go-go bars and prostitution, and the city has lost little of its taste for the oldest profession. Despite this, surprisingly, it is also a popular destination for family holidays. There are some decent hotels along with the cheap digs and lots of things to do for all the family, whether it is cultural shows, bungy jumping or top-notch golf courses. And there are water sports galore to distract you from the less than pristine beach. You need a tolerance for the seedier things in life to enjoy Pattaya, no doubt, but it has

many pleasures not-of-the-flesh to keep you amused. Further east are the islands of Ko Samet and Ko Chang, where there are white sands and beach BBQs in abundance.

Bang Saen to Pattaya

The stretch of coast nearest Bangkok begins in earnest at Bang Saen, a weekend getaway for local families. The road then passes through Siracha, famous for its Si Racha Sauce, and tiger zoo. Before reaching Pattaya, there's a detour offshore to Ko Si Chang and King Chulalongkorn's summer palace.

Bang Saen

Just beyond Chonburi, on the road from Bangkok, weekenders hit Bang

Saen, the nearest beach to the capital. It is covered with beach umbrellas and inflatable inner tubes, and the surf is a mass of bobbing bodies, fully dressed to avoid the sun (as Westerners want to be tanned, Thais want to be lighter).

Si Racha

About 10km (6 miles) further on is Si Racha, where people head to water-front restaurants for seafood with the town's famous sauce *nam prik si racha*. Nearby, **Sriracha Tiger Zoo** ❶ (tel: 0-3829-6556; daily 8am–6pm; charge 🍴) has over 200 Bengal tigers. You can feed the cubs. They also have elephant and bear shows, pig racing and ostrich riding.

Ko Si Chang

A 45-minute boat ride from Siracha, the island of Ko Si Chang (different

Feed a cub at Siracha Tiger Zoo

from Ko Chang, further east) is known primarily for the late King Chulalongkorn's retreat at **Judhad-hut Palace** (daily 8am–6pm; free). Recently restored, the grounds double as an oceanfront public park. The

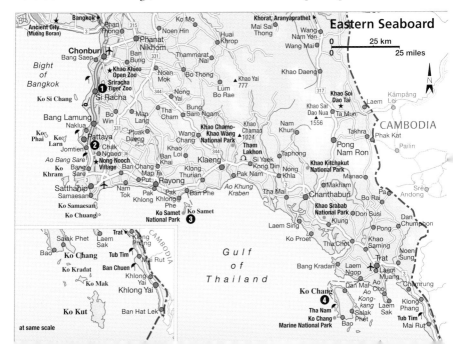

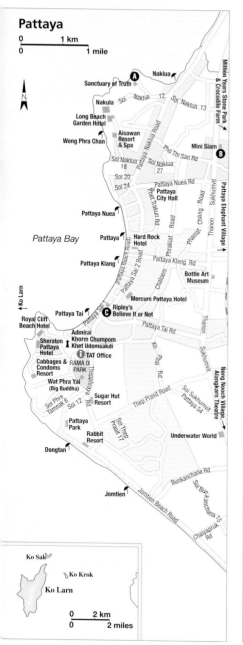

Pattaya

teak palace here was dismantled and rebuilt in Bangkok as the Vimanmek Mansion (see p.75), but several other structures have been remodelled.

Pattaya

Another 40km (25 miles) south from Siracha, the road arrives at **Pattaya** ❷, a town with a reputation for sex services stretching back to the 1960s, when it was a playground for American troops on R&R from the Vietnam War.

North of the city is the small fishing village of Naklua, and, on Naklua Soi 12, **The Sanctuary of Truth** Ⓐ (www.sanctuaryoftruth.com; daily 8am–5pm; charge). This extraordinary building, like a fairy-tale castle on the edge of the sea, is over 100m (330ft) high and made entirely of hard-woods. Its intricately carved figures of gods and spirits are representations of Asian religions. They also offer horse riding and dolphin shows here.

Back on the main Sukhumvit

Pattaya Transport

 Train station: Soi 45, Thanon Sukhumvit; tel: 0-3842-9285

 Bus station: North Pattaya Rd; tel: 0-3842-9877

 Taxis: Image; tel: 0-3825-1755; www.imagelimo.com. PT Taxi Service; tel: 08-5444-9035; www.pttaxiservice.com

 Songthaew: Hail these communal vans anywhere on the street; cost B10–50

 Car hire: Budget; tel: 0-3872-6185; www.budget.co.th. VIA; tel: 0-3842-6242
Motorcycle hire: motorcycle taxis are available on street corners; cost from B20

Road, heading south, are **Mini Siam** **B** (www.minisiam.com; daily 8am–10pm; charge 🏋), where you can step around tiny scale models of many of the world's architectural landmarks, and **Pattaya Elephant Village** (www.elephant-village-pattaya.com; daily 8.30am–7pm; charge 🏋), with its daily elephant shows and rides into the countryside.

At the waterfront, Pattaya has an umbrella-crammed wisp of yellow sand and a narrow Beach Road jumble of bars, restaurants, souvenir shops, hotels, and **Ripley's Believe It or Not** **C** (www.ripleysthailand.com; daily 11am–11pm; charge 🏋) at the Royal Garden Plaza.

Due south, Hat Jomtien has a marginally better beach. But the two have plenty of options for kite-boarding, windsurfing and diving at nearby

109

Eastern Seaboard

The fantastical teak Sanctuary of Truth is dramatically perched on on the seafront at Pattaya

wreck sites. The further-flung islands of **Ko Rin** and **Ko Man Wichai** are the best dive spots, with marine life including sharks and turtles. The most popular with day-trippers for soft sand and waterside seafood is **Ko Larn**. The area surrounding Pattaya and Jomtien is full of recreational facilities, such as golf, go-karting and bungy jumping.

Pattaya's nightlife around Beach Road and Walking Street is a range of Irish pubs, German brew houses, go-go bars and massage parlours. Vegas-style transsexual or 'lady-boy' cabaret shows are also popular **Alangkarn Theatre** (www.alangkarn-thailand.com; Tue–Sun shows at 7pm and 8.45pm; charge 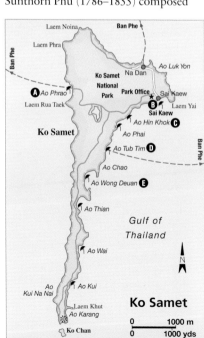) at Km 155 along Thanon Sukhumvit is themed on Thai history, with elephant battles, lasers and pyrotechnics.

Travelling south, at Sukhumvit Km 163, **Nong Nooch Village** (www.nongnoochtropicalgarden.com; daily 8am–6pm; charge) is a 243-hectare (600-acre) residential landscaped parkland with flower gardens, mini-zoo, butterfly garden and cultural shows.

Ko Samet

Following the coastline as it turns east leads to **Ko Samet**, a weekend retreat for Bangkok residents. The white sands and clear waters are part of a national marine park, and most accommodation is fairly restrained. The island is best avoided on public holidays, when visitors outnumber beds, and tents appear everywhere.

Three hours by road from Bangkok, plus a short boat trip from the harbour of Ban Phe, Ko Samet has a laid-back vibe, exceptionally fine white sand and clear turquoise waters. It is well known among Thais as the place where the romantic court poet Sunthorn Phu (1786–1855) composed

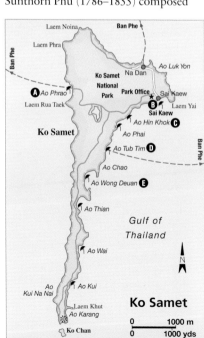

some of his works. Sunthorn called the island Ko Kaew Phisadan, or 'island with sand like crushed crystal', and it was here that he set his best-known poem, *Phra Aphaimani* – a tale about a prince and a mermaid.

Ko Samet is part of a national marine park, so technically most of the resorts constitute illegal development. Perhaps because of this they are in the main fairly unobtrusive single-storey huts and bungalows. A few new boutique resorts have opened on the quieter beaches, while other establishments are upgrading their facilities.

Almost all the island's sandy beaches run down the east coast, gradually getting more isolated as the island narrows to the southern bay of Ao Karang. Most of the island's infrastructure – school, clinic, temple, market and a few shops – is located near Na Dan pier and along the paved road to Hat Sai Kaew.

The island is only 6km (4 miles) long and 3km (2 miles) wide, so a hike from end to end, passing the east-coast beaches, can be completed in a few hours, though the coastal track cuts across several rocky headlands. There is a single road running down the centre of the island, which turns into a bumpy dirt track along its outer reaches.

Ao Phrao Ⓐ, the only beach on the west coast, is the most exclusive, with two up-market hotels nestled into the small scenic bay. On the east coast, **Hat Sai Kaew Ⓑ**, a short walk from Na Dan pier, is the most developed and one of the most congested. This is where most Thais and package-tour visitors stay, as there are more air-conditioned hotels, bars and seafood restaurants.

Further down the coast, the bay of **Ao Hin Khok Ⓒ** is separated from Hat Sai Kaew by a promontory marked by a weathered statue of a mermaid, inspired by Sunthorn Phu's

Eastern Seaboard

Beach vendors on Ko Samet – once a quiet poetic retreat, now a popular resort island

Beach bungalows on Hat Sai Khao – an idyllic Ko Chang beach with a swathe of powdery sands framed by a backdrop of casuarina trees

famous poem. Foreigners tend to stay here or at the next bay, **Ao Phai**, with its equally fine white sands.

The next bay, the intimate **Ao Tub Tim ⓓ**, has only two places to stay, but the noisier attractions of Ao Phai are just a short walk away. There are two more quiet bays, Ao Nuan and Ao Chao, before you hit the picturesque, crescent-shaped **Ao Wong Deuan ⓔ**, which is becoming increasingly marred by boats and noisy jet-skis. It has a clutter of bars and mostly mid- to upper-price-range accommodation, in addition to minimarts, motorcycle rental and internet cafés.

After Ao Wong Deuan, the bays are very peaceful. Scenic **Ao Thian** (Candlelight Beach) is actually a series of small beaches separated by rocky outcrops, while the southern **Ao Kui** is little more than a beach,

and the location of the island's most expensive resort. Several resorts on Ko Samet offer snorkelling trips.

Ko Chang

Near the Cambodian border, Thailand's second-largest island, **Ko Chang ❹** (Elephant Island) dominates the 52 isles that make up the national marine park of the same name. While a development drive transforms the hilly island from backpacker bungalows to higher-end boutique resorts, it remains one of the more unspoilt islands in the Gulf of Thailand.

Verdant Ko Chang is a five-hour drive from Bangkok, or 45 minutes by air to Trat, then a 45-minute transfer by boat from the mainland pier of Laem Ngop. Located near the Cambodian border, for years Ko Chang escaped the rapid development seen elsewhere on the coast, remaining a firm favourite with backpackers. Things began to change from the early 2000s with plans to make it a playground for the rich. Resort construction and infrastructure increased, including an upgrade of the road system, and the opening of a domestic airport in Trat.

The availability of quality and stylish accommodation is drawing in a greater number of vacationers, who, with the increase of car ferries from the mainland, seem intent on bringing their vehicles over to explore the island's single road.

Despite the development, the island retains its relatively untouched interior, areas of mangrove forest and lovely beaches, of which the foremost are along the west coast. The fine sands of **Hat Sai Khao** Ⓐ (White Sand Beach) form the most developed and longest stretch, and host the main action in Ko Chang's subdued nightlife, with live music at many bars.

Moving south, canals divide the picturesque and quiet **Hat Khlong Phrao** Ⓑ into north, central and southern sections. Beyond that, and the fast-developing **Hat Kai Bae**, is the last vestige of Ko Chang's hippie traveller scene, the lovely stretch of **Hat Tha Nam** Ⓒ, or Lonely Beach. The fine sand here gets a little coarser towards the south, but is the island's best beach for swimming. Next is **Ao Bai Lan**, a bay with rocks and reef but no beach.

At the southern end of the west coast, the fishing village of **Ban Bang Bao** Ⓓ has accommodation over the waves on a pier, plus seafood restaurants, dive shops, souvenir shops and

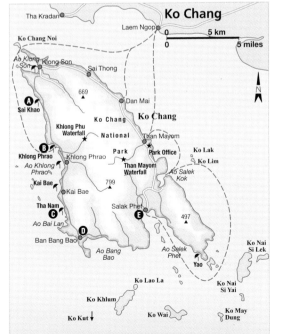

Hat Tha Nam – the 'Lonely Beach'

⭐ LADY-BOY CULTURE

High on the list of many people's must-see spectacles when they visit Thailand are transsexual cabaret shows, such as Tiffany, in Pattaya, or Bangkok's Mambo. The lip-synching routines, with source material based on anything from Hollywood musicals to traditional Thai theatre, are packaged Las Vegas-style with troupes of glamorous, long-legged dancers in feather boas, headdresses and sequinned costumes. Except, of course, these dancers are all transsexual, popularly referred to as *kathoey*, or internationally as lady-boys.

There is no direct Western equivalent to the term *kathoey*, and its meaning changes according to circumstance, so it is difficult to translate accurately as a single word. It is used to describe a wide range of people, from men who merely dress as women to transgenders who have undergone complete sex-change surgery, and even to describe a completely new third sex.

But one thing is certain, *kathoeys* are highly visible throughout Thailand. They are a mainstay of TV, the equivalent of Western pantomime dames, acting the crazy sidekick of soap opera stars, and presenting game shows. *Kathoey* Vegas-style cabaret is a tourism staple, with some revues appearing internationally at events such as the Edinburgh Festival. And they are a flamboyant presence around red-light districts, as many a male visitor fooled by their feminine charms might testify.

But it is also common to find *kathoey*

An elaborately dressed lady-boy performing a Vegas-style song-and-dance routine

pursuing more mundane careers, from waitressing and shop assistants to corporate business and advertising. Famous sporting *kathoeys* include Parinya 'Nong Tum' Charoenphon, who was a male kick-boxing champion undergoing hormone therapy. She wore make-up in the ring and would give her defeated opponents a kiss.

Thailand's famous *kathoey* shows have become an international staple

Many *kathoey* are apparent from a very young age. Nalada Thamthana-korn, the 2010 winner of Miss Tiffany Universe, says she knew she was different from the age of seven, and any high school in Thailand will have a coterie of *kathoey* students. Although they are not allowed to wear women's clothes, they are unashamed in extravagantly feminine gestures from early teens. Some will already be taking hormones to help form more shapely hips and the beginnings of breasts, although implants will probably come later. One school poll found 10 percent of students identified as transgender, and more than one educational establishment has installed a third set of toilets to accommodate them. They are seldom bullied. One student says: 'Nobody messes with them. They have sharp tongues.'

However, while *kathoey* are generally much better represented and accepted in Thailand than transsexuals are in the West, they still suffer prejudice (even those who have undergone full gender reassignment are still legally regarded as men). However, recent debates in parliament about legally recognising a third sex seem set to address such issues.

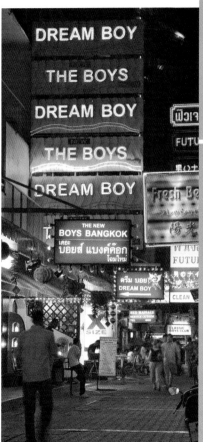

Neon signs outside *kathoey* cabaret revue bars on a street in Bangkok

guesthouses. It is the departure point for dive and snorkel trips to surrounding islands.

The next bay along the south coast, **Salak Phet** Ⓔ fishing village, has a more authentic, less developed feel. It is accessed from the east coast, which has few beaches and is largely ignored by most visitors. This makes the leisurely drive along the hills and plantations a real pleasure, with few vehicles and the reward of a seafood lunch at Salak Phet. An alternative route runs east of Salak Phet, where a winding road continues all the way to **Hat Yao**, or Long Beach, on the southern tip.

Several companies, such as **Ban Kwan Chang** (book through Jungleway; www.jungleway.com), operate elephant treks into the interior. Other popular activities include kayaking and treks to waterfalls. Snorkelling and diving trips usually head to the outlying islands south of Ko Chang. The best sites include the pinnacles off Ko Rang, reefs around Ko Wai, and shallow dives off Ko Khlum and Hin Luk Bat. The Thonburi Wreck, off Ko Chang's southeastern tip, is another highlight.

KO CHANG ARCHIPELAGO

Staying offshore is an option for some. The tiny island of **Ko Wai**, around 10km (6 miles) out, has limited and basic accommodation, but the views of surrounding islands are spectacular and there's a good coral reef a short swim from the main beach. **Ko Mak**, an hour by speedboat from Laem Ngop, is dense with coconut trees and has two beautiful quiet beaches, Ao Kao and Ao Suan Yai, with basic accommodation and restaurants.

The southernmost island is **Ko Kut**, 2½ hours away by speedboat. Its attractions include several fine beaches, Khlong Chao Waterfall and the fishing village at Ao Sa Lad. Due to its remote location, development has been low-key, and it draws mainly tour groups.

Walking along the pier at Ko Mak with a tree lined beach as a backdrop

ACCOMMODATION

There is a good range of accommodation in Pattaya, from cheap guesthouses located centrally near bars and restaurants to resort complexes with more isolation and luxury facilities. Ko Samet has many mid-range beach bungalows, while rapidly developing Ko Chang has some increasingly up-market options that belie its recent backpacker heritage.

Bang Saen to Pattaya

Mercure Pattaya
484 Soi 15, Moo 10, Thanon Pattaya 2
Tel: 0-3842-5050
www.mercurepattaya.com
Large elegant outlet in the heart of down-town. The rooms are equipped with modern conveniences, and there is a large swimming pool and four restaurants. **$$**

The Siam Guest House
528/26 Moo 10, Soi 12, Pattaya 2nd Road
Tel: 0-3842-4245
www.siam-guesthouse.com
Close to the bars and shops off Beach Road, but far enough away for peace when you need to sleep. The simple clean rooms with Wi-fi access and satellite TV are a bargain. **$**

Sheraton Pattaya
437 Thanon Phra Tamnak
Tel: 0-3825-9888
www.sheraton.com/pattaya
Located on the Phra Tamnak headland, this beautifully landscaped resort has calming water features and its own beach. Many rooms have ocean-facing pavilions. **$$$$**

Ko Samet

Samed Villa
89 Moo 4, Ao Phai
Tel: 0-3864-4094
www.samedvilla.com
Located at the end of Ao Phai beach on a headland with good sea views. The bungalows here have air conditioning, and TV, and the restaurant does great Thai and international food. Book ahead. **$$–$$$**

Ko Chang

Barali Beach Resort
77 Moo 4, Ao Khlong Phrao
Tel: 0-3955-7238
www.baraliresort.com
These contemporary Asian-style villas are representative of the recent up-market development on Ko Chang. The cosy, private villas come with TV, CD system and safe; some have beautiful sunken bathtubs. The infinity pool is a perfect spot to relax. **$$$$**

Koh Chang Kacha Resort & Spa
88–89 Moo 4, Hat Sai Khao
Tel: 0-3955-1421
www.kohchangkacha.com
The Koh Chang Kacha is one of Hat Sai Khao's best hotels in this price range. The new extension includes a lovely pool and spa with the main hotel building and sea-view villas, while the older section has more verdant gardens and some large split-level family bungalows located right on the beach. **$$$**

Sunset over the water, Ko Chang

RESTAURANTS

With miles of coastal waters, it's no surprise that seafood plays a large part in the dining pleasures of the region. Numerous resorts on the islands hold beach barbecues that are great fun and often better than the local restaurants. In Pattaya, many international cuisines feature alongside Thai.

Bang Saen to Pattaya
Bruno's
306/63 Chateau Dale Plaza, Thanon Thappraya, Pattaya
Tel: 0-3836-4600
www.brunos-pattaya.com
One of Pattaya's most popular expat-friendly bistros, Bruno's offers fine dining at afford-able prices and a warm, welcoming vibe. Expect well-presented French-European dishes and an extensive wine list. **$$$**

Mumaroi
83/4 Naklua Banglamung, Pattaya
Tel: 0-3823-4352
Fantastic deep-fried sea bass, curried crab and spicy seafood salad with a view of fish-ing boats, old sea barges and the bamboo stakes of mussel farms out in the bay. **$–$$**

Ko Samet
Naga Bungalows
Ao Hin Khok
Tel: 0-3864-4034
This restaurant-bar run by an Englishwoman sits up a hill overlooking the beach and is a long-time favourite with backpackers. Known for its bakery and late-night revelry, it also serves decent Western breakfasts, sandwiches, pizzas, burgers and Thai dishes. **$–$$**

Sea View Restaurant
Ao Prao Resort, Ao Phrao
Tel: 0-3864-4101
www.samedresorts.com
If you're hungering for an elegant dining experience away from beach barbies, then this selection of well-presented Thai food,

A plate of seafood noodles

steaks and international dishes is as good as it gets on the island. Decent, but not gourmet. **$$$**

Ko Chang
Hungry Elephant
Opp Sky Bar, between Hat Sai Khao and Hat Khai Muk
Tel: 08-9985-8433
Few tourists venture to this unassuming streetside restaurant, but it is well known among Bangkok expats. Run by a friendly Thai couple, the menu has Thai staples and some good French dishes. **$$**

Salak Phet Seafood
43 Moo 2, Salak Phet
Tel: 0-3955-3099
www.kohchangsalakphet.com
Considered by many the best seafood on the island, this restaurant and resort on stilts is part of the fishing village of the same name. Great for crab, squid, shrimp and fish that you choose from the sunken nets below the pier. **$–$$**

NIGHTLIFE AND ENTERTAINMENT

The raucous Pattaya nightlife is legendary, mainly for its full-on go-go bars catering to gays and straights alike, and these places are easy to find if you want them. Alternatively, there are bars and clubs aplenty to suit most tastes, from live blues to lady-boy cabaret and German beers. The islands, while less brash, still have beer and boogie on offer.

Bang Saen to Pattaya

The Blues Factory
131/3 Moo 10, Soi Lucky Star (off Walking Street), Pattaya
No phone
www.thebluesfactorypattaya.com
One of Pattaya's best music venues and suitable for all. It features live blues and rock by resident bands.

Hopf Brew House
219 Thanon Hat Pattaya (Beach Road), Pattaya
Tel: 0-3871-0653
Popular microbrewery for its wood-fired pizzas and Italian and European dishes. An in-house band livens things up.

Lucifer
Thanon Hat Pattaya (Walking Street), Pattaya
Tel: 0-3871-0216
The Latin bar opening onto Walking Street attracts a slightly older clientele, while inside in the back is the pumped up, hell-themed club playing mainstream R&B and hip-hop.

Tiffany's
464 Moo 9, Thanon, Pattaya 2
Tel: 0-3842-1700
www.tiffany-show.co.th
Pattaya's most famous *Kathoey* or 'lady-boy' cabaret routine with three nightly shows (6pm, 7.30pm and 9pm).

Ko Samet

Silver Sand
Ao Phai
Tel: 08-1996-5720
This beach bar is usually crammed for its decibels cranked to the hilt and fire juggling.

Ko Chang

Lek Bar
Kai Bae Beach Resort, Hat Kai Bae
Tel: 0-7065-4231
Run by a Brit and his Thai partner, this has a rustic look with a garden and live music.

Sabay Bar
7/10 Moo 4, Hat Sai Khao
Tel: 0-3955-1098
Easily the busiest bar on Hai Sai Khao, whether for sundowners or live bands.

Beach restaurant on Ko Samet at dusk

SPORTS AND ACTIVITIES

The Eastern Seaboard is well served for sports and activities for all the family. The countryside around Pattaya has many top-class golf courses, while close to the centre of town are go-karting and bungy jumping parks. In addition, the area is full of water-sports operators, and Ko Chang has treks to the interior of the island.

Bungy Jumping

Jungle Bungy Jump
Thanon Boonkanjana Soi 5,
Jomtien
Tel: 0-6378-3880
www.thaibungy.com
Claiming to operate the original and safest bungee jump in Thailand, this company offers a 50m (165ft) launch over a fishing lake behind the beach. A jump costs B1,900 (inclusive of insurance, insurance, 24 photos, souvenir cap and a 'courage' certificate. Additional jumps are progressively cheaper and the fourth jump is free.

Diving

Aquanauts Dive Centre
437/17 Moo 9, Thanon Hat Pattaya (Beach Road), Soi 6
Tel: 0-3836-1724
www.aquanautsdive.com
British-owned, with over a decade's experience in Pattaya, they offer basic and speciality courses, as well as wreck and cave dives for more experienced divers.

Water World Diving
Ko Chang Plaza, 17/3 Moo 4,
Hat Chai Chet
Tel: 08-6139-1117
www.waterworldkohchang.com
Professional and well equipped, with a comfortable boat to get to the dive sites. Competitive prices and multilingual courses.

Go-karting

K.R. Go-Kart Grand Prix
62/125 Moo 12, Thanon Thepprasit
Tel: 0-3830-0347
Burn some rubber at this 1,100m (1,200yd) track. Engine sizes (80–110cc) suit novice and experienced drivers. A 10-minute ride costs B300 to B700. 〽

Golf

Laem Chabang International Country Club
106/8 Moo 4, Si Racha
Tel: 0-3837-2273
www.laemchabanggolf.com
Rated one of the region's best, this 27-hole course (par 72) was designed by Jack Nicklaus and has mountain scenery and good water features.

Sailing

Ocean Marina Yacht Club
74/1–9 Moo 4, Thanon Sukhumvit Km 157, Pattaya
Tel: 0-3823-7310
www.oceanmarinayachtclub.com
A range of yachts or catamarans for a half-day, overnight and longer cruises to the islands in the Gulf.

Sea Adventures
Hat Sai Khao, Ko Chang
Tel: 08-4728-6387
Day-long tours of Ko Chang and the islands on a 13m (40ft) British-owned catamaran. English-speaking crew, snorkel and mask, beach barbecue lunch, and hotel pick-up included.

Trekking

Trekkers of Ko Chang
Tel: 0-3952-5029
Full-day treks into Ko Chang's jungled interior, all led by experienced guides.

Wind and Kite Surfing

Blue Lagoon Water Sports Club
24/20 Moo 2, Na Jomtien Soi 14, Sattahip
Tel: 0-3825-5115/6
This is one of Thailand's few professional kite-surfing schools. They also rent out kayaks and windsurfing boards.

TOURS

With each destination on the Eastern Seaboard having developed facilities and being relatively small, exploring independently is not difficult. But some companies offer all-in-one packages that take away the strain, whether you want land-based treks, adventuresome fishing and diving, or the thrills of offshore wakeboarding, away from the crowds.

Boat Trips

Vision Marine
Blue Lagoon, 23/4 Moo 2, Najomtien Soi 14, Pattaya
Tel: 08-9607-1414
www.speedboatforhirepattaya.com
Speedboat trips leave from Pattaya for the outlying islands, where you can feed the monkeys (above and below water) at Monkey Island. They also offer wakeboarding, water-skiing, deep-sea fishing and seafood BBQs.

General

i-site Koh Chang
23/9 Moo 4, Klong Prao, Ko Chang
Tel: 08-1773-4221
www.i-sitekohchang.com
This all-purpose company organises tours and activities on Ko Chang, the islands and the region. They offer jungle treks to Mount Salek Phet and around Bang Bao, one- and two-hour elephant treks, all-terrain vehicles, cooking tours, snorkelling, and fishing excursions.

FESTIVALS AND EVENTS

There are three big events in the area that locals and visitors alike eagerly anticipate each year. Competitions held on both land and sea – centuries-old buffalo racing and state-of-the-art yachting – celebrate the best of Thailand old and new, while the Pattaya Music Festival, likewise, combines traditional and modern.

March

Pattaya Music Festival
Various Pattaya venues
A mix of music styles, modern and traditional, with occasional visiting acts from overseas.

May

Top of the Gulf Regatta
Ocean Marina
Thanon Sukhumvit, Jomtien
Local and foreign sailors compete in several classes of yacht racing over several days. It is sometimes possible to pick up crewing opportunities at these events.

October

Buffalo Races
Chonburi

The festival atmosphere at this centuries-old event includes traditional music, parades and sideshows to accompany the bareback racing. The buffaloes are fed beer beforehand to ensure a lively performance.

Don't miss the Chonburi Buffalo Races

The Gulf Coast

There are charming towns in the Northern Gulf that are accessible from Bangkok in a few hours, whether it is historic Phetchaburi, the royal seaside retreat of Hua Hin, the popular beach getaway of Cha-am or the celebrity-friendly Pranburi. Further south, the islands offer idyllic palm-covered beaches, some of the best diving in the country and notorious Full Moon Parties.

Hua Hin

Population: 42,000

Local dialling code: 032

Local tourist office: 114 Thanon Phetchkasem; tel: 0-3253-2433

Main police station: Thanon Damnoen Kasem; tel: 0-3251-1027. **Tourist Police** anywhere in Thailand call 1155

Main post office: Thanon Damnoen Kasem

Hospital: San Pau Lo Hospital Thanon Phetchkasem; tel: 0-3252-0371

Local listings magazine: *Hua Hin Observer*

Train station: Thanon Damnernkasem; tel: 0-3251-1073

Bus station: Thanon Chomsin; tel: 0-3251-1230

Taxis: Hua Hin Limousine Service; tel: 0-3253-1073; www.huahin-limousine.com. HuaHin Taxi; tel: 08-6375-6972; www.huahintaxi.com

Tuk-tuks: hail *tuk-tuks* anywhere on the street; cost: B20–40

Car hire: Car Rent Hua Hin; tel: 08-1384-4731; www.carrenthuahin.com. Hua Hin Car Rental; tel: 08-6006-2924; www.huahincarrental.com
Motorcycle hire: available on street corners and intersections; cost from around B20

Just a two-hour drive from Bangkok, Phetchaburi is a peaceful historical town with temples dating to the Ayut-thaya period over 200 years ago. It is a very easy place to walk around and makes a pleasing stop-off or overnight stay on the way to the beach attractions of Cha-am and Hua Hin, an hour further south. Cha-am is a very Thai-style weekend getaway, only recently

attracting tourism development, while Hua Hin was the country's first resort destination, a high-society recreation spot since the 1920s.

Out in the Gulf of Thailand there are three of the country's most famous islands: Ko Samui, Ko Phan-gan and Ko Tao, known for three of its most popular activities: spa treat-ments, beach parties and diving. Ko

Samui has many high-end resorts, while the other two are still happily geared more towards the budget traveller. All have idyllic beaches and crystal-clear waters.

Northern Gulf Coast

The towns south of Bangkok have been a favourite summer retreat of several kings. Both Phetchaburi and Cha-am have old summer palaces to visit, while the current king has a residence in Hua Hin. Close by are national parks, spas and golf courses that provide a break from the beach.

Phetchaburi

Historically rich **Phetchaburi** ❶ is one of Thailand's oldest towns and has been an important trade and cultural centre since the 11th century. Of several temples around the town, four are particularly notable. The 17th-century **Wat Yai Suwannaram** (daily 8am–4pm; free) is best known for its murals of Hindu gods that date back to the 18th century. Its ample grounds also have a lovely teak pavilion. To the south, the former Hindu **Wat Kamphaeng Laeng** (daily 8am–4pm; free) has five laterite Khmer *prang*. It is one of Phetchaburi's key religious sites, and is thought to have marked the southernmost point of the Khmer kingdom.

Southwest of here are the fading but beautiful murals of **Wat Ko Keo Sutharam** (daily 8am–4pm; free), which date from 1734, and then northwest are the five white stucco-covered *prang* of **Wat Mahathat** (daily 8am–4pm; free). The temple is known for intricate depictions of angels and other mythical creatures

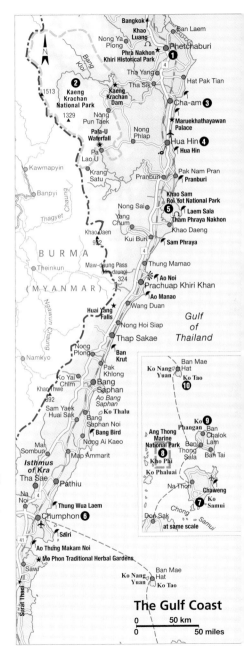

The Gulf Coast

0   50 km

0   50 miles

Detail from one of the exquisite murals at Wat Yai Suwannaram

in low-relief stucco. To the east, the **Day Market** has lots of food stalls with local specialities, and on the western edge of town, **Phra Nakhon Khiri Historical Park** (daily 8.30am–4.30; charge) has the summer residence of King Rama IV (King Mongkut) perched on the top of Khao Wang. Phetchaburi is

Silks, Crafts and Seafood

Just north of Sofitel Centara, the narrow Naresdamri Road is Hua Hin's tourist shopping street, full of Thai massage outlets and Indian tailors, plus bars and restaurants, including tasty fresh seafood at wooden deck restaurants on several piers. Hua Hin Soi 57, on the left, leads across two main roads into Dechanuchit Road, where Hua Hin Night Market (daily 5–11pm) is good for Thai silks, crafts, artworks, clothes and jewellery. There is lots of streetfood here, too.

pleasant and easy to walk around *(see Tour p.128)*.

Kaeng Krachan National Park

About 60km (37 miles) southwest of Phetchaburi, the 3,000-sq-km (1,158-sq-mile) **Kaeng Krachan National Park ❷** (www.dnp.go.th; daily 6am–6pm; charge) is the largest in Thailand. It contains mammals such as elephants, leopards and bears, and is a prime birdwatching spot. Trekking guides are available at the park's headquarters, along with basic lodgings, but a tour organised by Hua Hin hotels is easier. Boating in the vast reservoir, climbing the 1,207m (3,960ft) **Phanoen Tung**, and visiting the 18-tier **Tho Thip Waterfall**, are popular activities.

Cha-am

The beach town of **Cha-am ❸**, 40km (25 miles) south of Phetchaburi, is a popular weekend trip from Bangkok, but is quiet during the week. It has plenty of cheap waterfront restaurants and seafood stalls. Some 10km (6 miles) south towards Hua Hin, the teak **Maruekhathaiyawan Palace** (tel: 0-3250-8039; daily 8am–4pm; charge) has three wings interconnected by covered walkways. It was a seaside retreat for King Vajiravudh in the years before his death in 1925.

Hua Hin

About 25km (18 miles) south of Cha-am, the relaxed town of **Hua Hin ❹** is famous for the royal summer residence Klai Kangwon ('Far from Worry') Palace (closed to the public). The town has been a retreat for Bangkok's upper classes

Hua Hin Railway Station

> **Going to the Park**
>
> Most Hua Hin and Pranburi hotels organise day trips to Khao Sam Roi Yot National Park, but travellers can also catch a train or bus to Pranburi, and from there take a songthaew to the fishing village of Bang Pu. Then it's a short boat ride to the park checkpoint on Hat Laem Sala beach. The Forestry Department runs accommodation here, but a better option is to stay at a hotel, such as the **Dolphin Bay Resort** (tel: 0-3255-9333; www.dolphinbayresort.com).

since the 1920s, and train travellers still arrive at the beautiful **Hua Hin Railway Station** that brought the original tourists. Thanon Damnoen Kasem leads from the station to the beach and another historic landmark, the 1923 colonial-style **Sofitel Centara Hua Hin Resort**, the country's first resort hotel, originally called the Railway Hotel.

South of town, **Khao Takiab** has a 20m (66ft)-tall Buddha image at the top, some monkeys to feed and panoramas of the sea and sands.

Khao Sam Roi Yot National Park

The road south continues through Pranburi, and some of Thailand's most exclusive beachfront hideaways, on the way to **Khao Sam Roi Yot National Park ❺** (www.dnp.go.th; daily 6am–6pm; charge), 63km (39 miles) away. The name, meaning 'Three Hundred Mountain Peaks,' refers to dramatic limestone pinnacles that jut from the mangrove swamps. The 98-sq-km (38-sq-mile) park has beaches, marshes and brackish lagoons, forests, caves and offshore islands, with wildlife that includes migratory birds, crab-eating macaques and a rare mountain antelope, called a serow.

The most famous attraction is **Tham Phraya Nakhon**, a huge cave with a large sinkhole that allows light to illuminate a grand pavilion built in the 1890s for a visit by King Chulalongkorn.

South to Chumphon

Heading south, most foreign visitors go directly to Chumphon or Surat Thani for ferries to Ko Tao, Ko Samui or Ko Phangan, bypassing less tourist-oriented places on the way. But **Chumphon 6** has several good beaches, including **Thung Wua Laem** and **Ao Thung Makam Noi**, while, 20km (12 miles) offshore, the islands of Ko Ngam Yai and Ko Ngam Noi are popular with divers.

Ko Samui

Around 80km (50 miles) from the mainland town of Surat Thani, **Ko Samui 7** is the biggest of 80 islands in the Samui Archipelago, and easily its most popular. With multi-million-dollar resorts appearing almost weekly, for some, Ko Samui is a victim of its own stunning beauty. For others it remains a palm-fringed paradise.

Laem Yai and Hat Maenam

Travelling north from the pier at Na Thon, the secluded Laem Yai marks the turn eastwards along the north coast, where the first beach of note is **Hat Maenam Ⓐ**. The 4km (2½-mile) stretch is fairly isolated and quiet. The golden sand underfoot is a little coarse and the beach is pleasant but quite narrow. Numerous budget hotels here take advantage of the relative isolation and quiet nights.

The vast cave, Tham Phraya Nakhon, is Kao Sam Roi's most famous attraction

Hat Lamai beach

Hat Chaweng

Around the headland, the east coast leads to Ko Samui's busiest beach, the 6km (4-mile) -long **Hat Chaweng ⊙**. The stunning powdery white-sand faces clear turquoise waters from the northern headland near the island of Ko Matlang, all the way to the curving bay and rocky end point of South Chaweng. A coral reef shelters the north beach, so the sea is often as still as a millpond. It is also less crowded than Central Chaweng, which is the most built-up. Chaweng Beach Road, behind the cramped line of beach resorts, is a sprawl of restaurants, bars and shopping arcades. Beyond a tiny spit of land the relatively quiet South Chaweng is thinner on accommodation and restaurants.

Hat Lamai

Continuing down the east coast, Samui's second-most populous beach, **Hat Lamai ⊙**, is far less hectic and has better accommodation choices for budget travellers, along with several boutique resorts. A little past the southern tip are two rock formations known as **Grandfather Rock** (Hin Ta) and **Grandmother Rock** (Hin Yai), which resemble male and female genitalia, and are hence a popular photo spot. Probably unconnected is Lamai's slightly lascivious nightlife scene, and its stretch of girlie bars.

South and West Coasts

Barring a few beautiful resorts, the south and west coasts are the least

Hat Bophut

East of Maenam is **Hat Bophut ⊙**, which has a nice beach and a quaint fishermen's village. This is one of the more attractive places on the island to wander around. Nearby, **Samui Monkey Theatre** (tel: 0-7724-5140; daily 10.30am, 2pm, 4pm; charge 🅜) has 'monkey work coconut' shows, revealing how simian labour traditionally assists in harvesting coconuts.

Hat Bangrak

On the headland to the northeast of Bophut, Hat Bangrak is better known locally as Big Buddha Beach owing to the presence of **Wat Phra Yai** (daily 8am–5pm; free) on a small islet across the bay. A causeway links to its 12m (39ft) golden Buddha image.

Spend a day walking around 18th-century Ayutthaya-period temples or hopping between sights on bicycle rickshaw in an old-fashioned Siamese town that also has the summer palace of King Rama IV.

Local Temples

Phetchaburi – usually pronounced Petburi – was once a significant port, from where goods were ferried by river and canal to the old Siam capital of Ayutthaya. Of its many temples four are of particular interest. Start at **Wat Yai Suwannaram** on Phongsuriya Road. It has many ornately tiled buildings within a low-walled complex, and fine murals that are among the country's oldest. The stucco work predates the symmetric Ayutthaya style. The old library building on stilts in the middle of the pond illustrates an early method of protecting manuscripts from termites.

Turn right out of the wat and right again onto Phokarong Road, to **Wat Kamphaeng Laeng**, 800m/yds on the right. The sandstone compound wall is partly original, as are four Khmer-style *prangs*, one of which contains a Buddha footprint relic. Next, turn right down Phra Song Road for about 1km (²/₃ mile), then left at the crossroads at Matayawong Road. After 800m/yds turn right at the clock tower to find **Wat Ko Keo Sutharam**, 50m/yds on the left. The fading but beautiful murals here date from 1734.

On leaving, turn left on to Phanit Charoen Road. After 800m/yds turn left at Phra Song Road and follow it to the large white tower of **Wat Mahathat**, which contains many murals and a statue of five integrated Buddhas.

Day Market

Retrace your steps on Phra Song Road and turn left into Phanit Charoen Road,

Hindu gods are represented in the ancient, fading murals at Wat Yai Suwannaram

Tips

- Distance: 5.5km (3½ miles)
- Time: A full day
- You may prefer to get around town by hiring a *pok pok* (a squat open-sided minivan), a *samlor* (a three-wheeled bicycle rickshaw) or a motorcycle taxi. Find them at the train and bus stations or the Day Market, or flag one down on the road. It should cost around B20 for each hop, but bargain a price before you set off and be sure to ask the driver to wait while you tour each site.

Phra Nakhon Khiri Historical Park is a curious mélange of Thai, Chinese and Western architectural styles taking the form of shrines, temples, pagodas and other structures

where the **Day Market** is 150m/yds on the right. Phetchaburi is reputed to have Thailand's finest palm sugar, so visiting locals usually leave with a souvenir bag of the famous local desserts. Also look out for another speciality called *khao chae*, a dish of cold rice in chilled, jasmine-infused water, accompanied by titbits like stuffed chillis and fresh fruit.

King's Retreat

Stay on Phanit Charoen Road and then turn left after 100m/yds onto Chisa-In Road, which almost immediately crosses the river. Take the next right, then left at Ratchawithi Road, for 1.5km (1 mile) to the end, keeping an eye out on the way for the blue Thai-language sign in the window of **Krua Thai café** on the left at number 57. The cafe is air-conditioned and serves decent rice meals, stir-fries and soups so is an ideal place to break for lunch. Approximately 150m/yds directly ahead of the café is the ascent on foot to **Phra Nakhon Khiri Historical Park**. If you don't fancy the

climb, turn right, then immediately left at the traffic lights. Just after the green overhead signs to Bangkok, go left at the road marked 'cable car'. After 200m/yds a white building marks cable-car access that costs B70, including entry to the park.

Amid the trees at the top are several temples and a **summer palace** of King Rama IV (1851–68), who was the subject of several books and the film *The King & I*, based on the memoirs of Anna Leonowens. All are regarded in Thailand as disrespectful to the monarchy and are banned. Do not take food with you: the hillside is populated by potentially aggressive wild monkeys.

pretty on Samui. **Hat Laem Set** is a secluded option with ample choice of accommodation and a nearby **Butterfly Garden** (tel: 0-7742-4020; daily 8.30am–5.30pm; charge 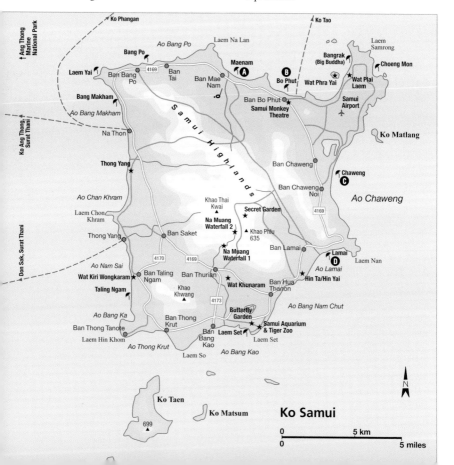).

Samui Interior

Taking Route 4169 inland from Hat Lamai leads to **Wat Khunaram** (daily 8am–5pm; free), home of the mummified monk Luang Phor Daeng, his body seated in the meditating position he held when he died over two decades ago.

Continuing past the village of Ban Thurian, in the wet season, **Na Muang Waterfall 1** has a 20m (66ft) cascade of water that plunges into a large pool. From there, a fairly strenuous 1.5km (1-mile) trek, or an elephant ride, leads to a second waterfall, **Na Muang Waterfall 2**.

At the **Samui Aquarium & Tiger Zoo** (www.samuiorchid.com; daily 9am–6pm, show at 1pm; charge) in south Lamai, the bird and Bengal tiger shows are better than the aquarium.

Ang Thong National Marine Park is encircled by sheer limestone walls covered in vegetation

Samui Activities

Samui's surrounding waters are not particularly good for diving or snorkelling, and most trips head to the nearby Ang Thong Marine National Park, Hin Bai and Ko Tao. But there are plentiful other water-sport options, including kayaking, windsurfing, deep-sea fishing and sailing. For land-based action, jeeps and mountain bikes are available to explore the dirt trails.

Ang Thong National Marine Park

Although Ko Phi Phi's Maya Bay (see p.156) was the chosen location for the 2000 film The Beach, it was the dra-matic scenery of **Ang Thong Marine National Park ❽** that inspired Alex Garland's bestselling novel. Lying over a 100-sq-km (39-sq-mile) area, 31km (19 miles) west of Ko Samui, these 42 islands are virtually uninhab-ited. They contain lagoons, beautiful beaches and sheer limestone cliffs, a habitat for wildlife such as macaques, langurs and monitor lizards. Dolphins shelter here late in the year.

Several operators run day trips from Ko Samui, which usually include a 400m (1,300ft) climb up to a lookout point on **Ko Wua Talab** and a visit to **Tham Bua Bok**, or Waving Lotus Cave. Diving and snorkelling at Ang Thong are usually best at the northern tip, around **Ko Yippon**. The shallow makes it easy to view the colourful coral beds, inhabited by sea snakes, fusiliers and stingrays, and there are caves and archways to swim through.

Ko Phangan

The second-largest island in the Samui Archipelago, **Ko Phangan ❾** is blessed with numerous white-sand beaches and richly forested moun-tains. Its international reputation stems almost exclusively from the infamous Full Moon Party (*see feature, Backpacking, p.26*). Consequently, the island remains a destination favoured mainly by budget travellers for its cheap guesthouses, cafés, bars and nightlife.

Ban Tai and Ban Khai

East of the arrival port of Thong Sala, the south coast has continuous beaches all the way to the Hat Rin cape, although shallow reefs make the water difficult for swimming. Basic but comfortable family-run bungalows operate between the most popular beaches from **Ban Tai** to **Ban Khai**, the only spot that offers night-time activity.

Hat Rin

East of Ban Khai, Hat Rin has all the action on two beaches with sensational sunrise and sunset views. The wider, more popular, **Hat Rin Nok** 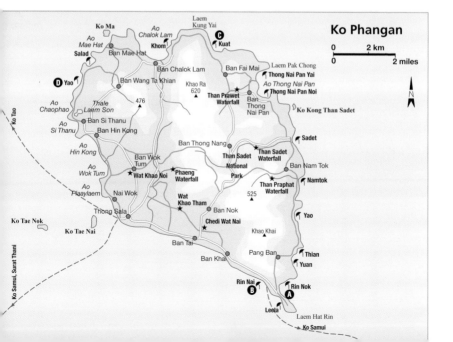, or Sunrise Beach, holds the main nightlife, including the monthly **Full Moon Parties**. The walk across a flat headland to the less attractive **Sunset Beach** or **Hat Rin Nai** is packed with accommodation, shops, restaurants, internet cafés and travel agents. A 15-minute walk south, the pretty **Hat Leela** is more peaceful.

East Coast

The small bays immediately up the east coast from Hat Rin are only accessible by boat. They include **Hat Yuan**, **Hat Yao** (not to be confused with Hat Yao on the west coast) and **Hat Thian**, and are relatively isolated. At the northern end of the east coast are the increasingly popular, and beautiful, **Ao Thong Nai Pan**

Than Sadet beach on Ko Phangan

considered the island's best snorkelling and dive site.

Further down the coast there's more good snorkelling at **Hat Salad**, before reaching **Hat Yao O**, or Long Beach, which is rivalling Hat Rin for accommodation, bars and restaurants. There are also more decent facilities further south at **Ao Chaophao**.

Phangan Interior

Of several waterfalls in Phangan's thickly forested interior, one in particular, **Than Sadet Waterfall**, was a favourite spot of King Chulalongkorn's when he used to visit the island. It flows out to Hat Sadet beach on the east coast, near Ao Thong Nai Pan Yai.

Phangan Activities

At night, Phangan is party central, with a mix of trance, techno and drum 'n' bass. See *Listings (p.139)* or keep up to date with a copy of *Phangan Info* (www.phangan.info).

Noi and **Ao Thong Nai Pan Yai**. There is good cheap accommodation at both.

North Coast

Reaching the north coast, **Hat Kuat O**, or Bottle Beach, is accessible by boat from Ao Chalok Lam *(see below)*. The splendid white sands backed by steep hills mark one of Ko Phangan's best bays, but, as usual, accommodation is at the budget end. A second bay to the west, **Ao Chalok Lam**, has a large fishing village, the island's second port, and a small cove, **Hat Khom**, with a coral reef offshore.

West Coast

Moving south, the attractive west-coast beaches see fewer visitors than those in the southeast. Low tide at **Ao Mae Hat** reveals a sandbank connected to **Ko Ma** and a reef

The Gulf Coast

> **Phangan Below the Waves**
>
> Although Ko Tao is the best diving destination in the Gulf, there are several sites accessible from Ko Phangan. **Hin Bai**, halfway to Ko Tao, is one of the best sites around, and suitable for all levels. The granite pinnacle has schools of pelagic fish, and a dramatic vertical chimney with entrances 6m (20ft) and 19m (62ft) underwater. The best snorkelling and diving actually on Phangan are at the northwestern reefs, particularly around Ko Ma.

Ko Tao

You don't have to be a diver to enjoy **Ko Tao ⑩** (Turtle Island), but it helps. It is the northernmost inhabited island in the Samui Archipelago, around 40km (25 miles) northwest of Ko Phangan and 60km (37 miles) from Ko Samui. The remote and tiny 21-sq-km (8-sq-mile) isle is topped with tropical forest and fringed with some secluded bays. Ka Tao is a laid-back outpost of affordable dive schools that operate expeditions to coral-abundant waters, making this one of the world's best places to learn diving.

West Coast

Ko Tao is accessed from the mainland port of Chumphon, as well as from Ko Samui, Ko Phangan or Surat Thani to the south. Boats arrive at the lively village of **Ban Mae Hat** on the west coast. North of here, beyond the shallow bay of Ao Hat Mae, is the 2km (1½-mile)-long **Hat Sai Ree Ⓐ**, the island's longest and most popular beach. It has hotels to suit most budgets. Further on, the road inclines upwards to cliff-top resorts with stunning sunset views.

North Coast

A short boat ride off the island's northern tip are the three picture-perfect islets of **Ko Nang Yuan Ⓑ**, joined by slivers of sand. The setting, both above and below sea level, is such that dive trips and boat tours from all over the region converge here. Only the **Nangyuan Island Dive Resort** (www.nangyuan.com), with its simple bungalows, has the rights to operate here, and outside visitors must pay B100 merely to land on the island.

One of the many speed-boat ferries to Ko Tao

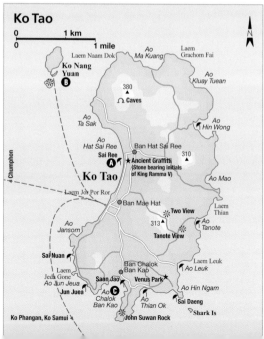

The islets of Ko Nang Yuan are joined by wisps of sand that can be walked across at low tide

East Coast

The east coast has several isolated inlets with scant sleeping options and no outstanding beaches. But there are plenty of good snorkelling and dive spots. The dirt trails can be treacherous (the only other access is by boat), and, once there, it can be difficult and expensive to return. Heading south, the bays include the scenic horseshoe of **Ao Tanote** and the lovely **Ao Leuk**.

South Coast

The island's second-busiest beach, **Ao Chalok Ban Kao ⊝**, is on the southern shores. It is a well-protected bay jammed with resorts, dive shops, eateries and bars. **John Suwan Rock**, a large headland at the eastern end, has incredible views.

Ko Tao Activities

Ko Tao as a dive destination suffers through the sheer number of divers, but visibility is sometimes over 30m (100ft) and there are over 25 sites less than 30 minutes away. Sightings of giant groupers and turtles are not uncommon, while whale shark and manta ray are a special event. Most dive schools offer PADI open-water certification.

Ko Tao is also ideal for walking, and longtail boat operators at most beaches offer day-long boat trips around the island. Water sports such as kayaking, wakeboarding and water-skiing can be enjoyed on Ao Tanote or Hat Sai Ree beaches. Nightlife is limited to beach bars and fire juggling.

ACCOMMODATION

The Gulf Coast has been going steadily up-market, as even destinations like Cha'am that were previously low on the tourist radar gain more stylish beach resorts. The island of Samui is a glut of spas and resorts, and today, even on the traditional backpacker haven of Ko Phangan, it is harder to find genuine budget prices.

Northern Gulf Coast

Alila Cha-am
115 Moo 7, Tambon Bangkao, Cha-am
Tel: 0-3270-9555
www.alilahotels.com
Ch-am's first truly de luxe resort is an expression of tasteful design. Using natural materials, its clean minimalist design manages to feel both contemporary and tropical at the same time. Rooms and villas are capacious, with oversized bathrooms and rain showers. Two restaurants, a stunning lap pool, spa and fitness centre complete the scene. **$$$–$$$$**

Rabieng Rim Nam Guesthouse
1 Thanon Chisa-In, Petchaburi
Tel: 0-3242-5707
Located on the beach at Hat Chao Samran, this popular backpacker haunt is centrally located beside a busy bridge over the river. Cheap, but with small, box-like rooms and shared bathrooms. It does have one of the best diners in town. **$**

Lobby of the Sofitel Central Hua Hin

Sofitel Central Hua Hin
1 Thanon Damnoen Kasem, Hua Hin
Tel: 0-3251-2021
www.sofitel.com
Historic colonial-style hotel nestled in a tropical garden. Although in the heart of Hua Hin beach, it feels very private. As well as six swimming pools, there's a spa and fitness centre, plus several international dining options. **$$$**

Ko Samui

The Lodge
Moo 1, Hat Bophut
Tel: 0-7742-5377
In the Fishermen's Village, this place has cosy rooms, hardwood floors and balconies with sea views. The upper-floor Pent Hut rooms are more expensive. The beachfront bar does great breakfasts and evening cocktails. **$$**

Poppies Samui
Chaweng Beach
Tel: 0-7742-2419
www.poppiessamui.com
At the quieter end of Chaweng, these private cottages have Thai silk and teak floors and furniture. The bathrooms feature sunken baths opening onto private gardens, and there's an outstanding beachside restaurant. **$$$$**

Ko Phangan

Cocohut Village
Ban Tai (Leela Beach)
Tel: 0-7737-5368
www.cocohut.com

Located on quieter Leela beach, yet within walking distance of Hat Rin, this popular resort sprawls over prime beachfront. Rooms range from the simple guesthouses with shared bathrooms to pool-facing executive suites. **$$–$$$$$**

Haad Son Resort
Hat Son
Tel: 0-7734-9103
www.haadson.net
Occupying a rocky headland at the end of an uninhabited pristine white-sand beach, this is one of the best resorts on the west coast. There is a variety of rooms here, including thatch-roof huts, air-conditioned poolside villas and penthouse suites with private pools. The sunset views are gorgeous. **$$–$$$**

Ko Tao
Ko Tao Grand Coral Resort
Hat Sai Ree
Tel: 0-7745-6431
www.kohtaocoral.com
These salmon-pink cottages are clustered

Big, beautiful pool at a Ko Samui resort

around a free-form swimming pool and located on the far end of Sai Ree beach. All have nice wooden interiors and private terraces. Small restaurant on-site. **$$$**

RESTAURANTS

The long Gulf coast means netfuls of briny fresh seafood, and most of these destinations have waterfront restaurants where the food is so fresh all you need is a bottle of wine to make perfection. There's a good choice of international cuisines here too.

Restaurant Price Categories
Prices are for a three-course meal without drinks
$ = below B300
$$ = B300–800
$$$ = B800–1,600
$$$$ = over B1,600

Northern Gulf Coast
Krua Thai
57 Thanon Ratchavitee,
Petchaburi
Tel: 0-3242-6941
A blue Thai language sign on the window marks this air-conditioned café serving decent rice meals, stir-fries and soups. It's on the left, 150m/yds before Phra Nakhon Khiri Historical Park. **$**

Poom
274/1 Thanon Ruamchit,
Cha-am
Tel: 0-3247-1036
This simple outdoor restaurant with a sea-view patio has been serving some of Cha'am's best Thai-style seafood, freshly caught in the bay, for over a decade. It's so popular with locals it's best to book ahead, especially at weekends. **$$**

Ocean-view dining, Chaweng Beach

Ko-Seng
95/1 Moo 1, Maenam Beach
Tel: 0-7742-5365
Excellent Thai food in a very simple, family-run dining room. They have delicious coconut fish and, among several types of Thai curry, a tasty fresh crab with curry and chilli sauce. **$**

Ko Phangan
A's Coffee Shop
Buakao Inn Guest House, Thong Sala
Tel: 0-7737-7226
A long-time favourite, A's has great variety, from Thai to Pacific Rim, with pizza baguettes, English, German and American breakfasts, and excellent pastas, washed down with espresso, cappuccino and large margaritas. **$–$$**

The Village Green Restaurant & Bar
Ao Chaophao
Tel: 0-1078-1670
www.villagegreen.phangan.info
One of the west coast's best eateries, serving hearty international and Thai dishes. Full English-style breakfasts, as well as pastas, pizzas, steaks and seafood for lunch and dinner. **$$**

Ko Tao
Café del Sol
Mae Hat
Tel: 0-7745-6578
A pleasant eatery with French, Italian and other international fare cooked by a Gallic chef. Big breakfasts, tender steaks, smoked salmon, home-made pastas and bruschettas. They have good wines and coffee too. **$–$$**

New Heaven Restaurant & Bakery
New Heaven Bungalows, Ao Thian Ok
Tel: 0-7745-6462
www.newheavenkohtao.com
This family-run restaurant, bakery and bungalows is famous for its hilltop location that overlooks a beautiful bay. Large menu of simple international and Thai fare, with an emphasis on seafood. **$–$$**

Brasserie de Paris
3 Thanon Naresdamri
Tel: 0-3253-0637
Sit upstairs at this wooden pier restaurant for views of fishing boats bobbing on the waves. It has delicious, freshly caught seafood served French style, such as rock lobster *au beurre blanc*. **$$$**

Chao Lay
15 Thanon Naresdamri, Hua Hin
Tel: 0-3251-3436
One of the most popular of several Thai restaurants on stilts over the sea. All kinds of seafood, grilled, deep-fried and steamed, either freshly caught or live from tanks downstairs. **$$–$$$**

Ko Samui
Betelnut
46/27 Chaweng Boulevard
Tel: 0-7741-3370
Small, elegant restaurant serving a fusion of Californian and Thai cuisine. Specialities include sea scallops with Pernod cream and salmon with a tamarind glaze. The home-made desserts are exquisite. **$$$**

NIGHTLIFE AND ENTERTAINMENT

Nothing beats the beach atmosphere at night, whether lying romantically on a mat with a beer and a hookah pipe, or full-on raving under the stars at Ko Phangan's famous Full Moon Parties. And if all you want is a game of pool and sport on TV, there's plenty of that, too.

Northern Gulf Coast

Jungle Juice Bar & Restaurant
19/1 Thanon Selakam, Hua Hin
Tel: 0-6167-7120
A friendly low-key place with lots of locals and a menu of Brit-style pub grub.

Monsoon
62 Thanon Naresdamri, Hua Hin
Tel: 0-6877-7808
This charming wooden bar is good for tapas and cocktails. There is also an upstairs restaurant.

Ko Samui

Christy's Cabaret
Chaweng
Tel: 0-7741-3244
Packing them in every night for the 11pm free show, Christy's is Ko Samui's most popular *kathoey*, or transsexual, cabaret act.

Gecko Village
Bophut
Tel: 0-7724-5554
www.geckosamui.com.
This beach bar features some of Ko Samui's best DJ dance beats, with international names making guest appearances.

Green Mango
Soi Green Mango, Chaweng
Tel: 0-7742-2148
Ko Samui's best-known club, this huge barn of a venue is crammed on most nights.

Ko Phangan

Outback Bar
Hat Rin
Tel: 0-7737-5126
This watering hole has a friendly vibe and attracts a regular crowd for pool tables, sports on the big-screen TV, and pub grub.

Pirate's Bar
Ao Chaophao
This bar takes the form of a boat built into the rock face at the end of the beach. Pirate's Bar hosts the monthly Moon-Set Party a few days before the Full Moon Party starts.

Sheesha Bar
Ao Chalok Lam
Tel: 0-7737-4161
www.sheesha-bar.com
Modern Asian design sets the scene for a relaxing night out with beachfront daybeds and hookah pipes to puff away on.

Ko Tao

AC Bar
Hat Sai Ree
Tel: 0-7745-6197
Loud pumped-up dance bar that is one of the island's original night-time hang-outs.

Dragon Bar
Mae Hat Centre
Tel: 0-7745-6423
DJs play great music at one of the island's hippest hang-outs. Serves inventive cocktails and has a pool table.

A beach bar on Ko Samui

SPORTS AND ACTIVITIES

Whether you like your action on the waves or off, there's a good choice of sports in the Gulf. Ko Tao is rated one of the best sites in the world to learn to dive, while, on land, Hua Hin has top-class golf courses nearby. There is also sailing and wakeboarding, plus go-karting and jungle zip rides for the kids.

Cable Rides

Canopy Adventures
Best Beach Bungalow, Chaweng, Ko Samui
Tel: 0-7741-4150
www.canopyadventuresthailand.com
Glide through the forest canopy on a zip line in Ko Samui's lush interior. The 2- to 3-hour trip includes six treetop rides, a swim in a waterfall and a drink at the jungle bar.

Diving and Watersports

Black Tip Diving & Watersports
Ao Tanote
Tel: 0-7745-6488
www.blacktipdiving.com
Operating from a small east coast resort, in addition to dive trips, it has wakeboarding and water-skiing lessons, and hires out kayaks and banana boats.

Discovery Dive Centre
Amari Palm Reef Resort, Chaweng, Samui
Tel: 0-7741-3196
www.discoverydivers.com
A small but well-equipped dive centre with its own speedboat. As well as offering courses and fun dives, it rents out underwater video and photography equipment.

Making ready at a Ko Tao dive centre.

Hat Yao Divers
Sandy Bay Bungalows, Hat Yao,
Ko Phangan
Tel: 08-6279-3085
www.haadyaodivers.com
Reputable European-run outfit has its main office at Hat Yao beach, another branch on Ao Chaophao and a retail centre in Thong Sala. It offers PADI and speciality courses.

Hua Hin Kite Centre
Hua Hin Soi 75/1
Tel: 08-1591-4593
www.kiteboardingasia.com
IKO licensed operation offering 1- to 3-day kite-board training and also rents and sells kites and boards.

Samui Boat Charters
Tel: 08-7276-7598
www.samuiboatcharter.com
Has a fleet of speedboats and yachts for trips to the islands, deep-sea fishing or diving. Professionally crewed and full waiter service if you need it.

Go-karting

Samui Go-Kart
101/2 Moo 1, Bophut
Tel: 0-7742-7194
Open from 9am till late, this jungle-fringed track has three types of karts, the slowest of which are suitable for kids.

Golf

Royal Hua Hin Golf Club
Thanon Damnoen Kasem, Hua Hin
Tel: 0-3251-2475
Opened in 1924, this is Thailand's oldest golf course. It was designed by a Scottish railway engineer and is located opposite the railway station. Large mature trees fringe the undulating topography.

TOURS

The Gulf Coast has an abundance of coastline and activities to match, from deep-sea fishing to kayaking and pleasure cruising. But landlubbers are well catered for, too, as the national parks and forests attract nature-lovers for trekking and camping. Golfers, meanwhile, head for the manicured greens.

Adventure Tours

Hua Hin Adventure Tour
69/8 Thanon Petchkasem
Tel: 0-3235-0314
www.huahinadventuretour.com
Offers a wide variety of tours into Kaeng Krachan and Sam Roi Yot National Parks, lasting from 1-day to 3-days with camping, trekking, kayaking and rock climbing.

Mr Ung's Magical Safari
Moo 3, Chaweng, Ko Samui
Tel: 0-7723-0114
www.ungsafari.com
Mr Ung runs half- and full-day safaris, including elephant rides, four-wheel-drive jungle climb, and a waterfall swim. Packages include lunch, soft drinks and hotel transfers. Deep-sea fishing excursions are also offered.

Boat Cruises and Fishing

Mermaid Cruises
77/5 Moo 1, Pak Nam Pran, Pranburi
Tel: 08-4800-7400
www.huahincruises.com
A teakwood pleasure boat, the *Peacock*, embarks on all-day fishing, evening squid fishing trips, or cruises to Monkey Island and Sam Roi Yot National Park.

Kayaking

Blue Stars
Chaweng, Ko Samui
Tel: 0-7741-3231
www.bluestars.info
This outfit runs 1- and 2-day kayak trips around Ang Thong Marine National Park. The 2-night trips feature a barbecue dinner and overnight camping on a desolate beach. The departure point on Ko Samui is Na Thon pier.

Listings

FESTIVALS AND EVENTS

As the rest of Thailand hits the low season the Gulf Coast get a second bite of the cherry – their second 'high season'. This is when sailors and music-lovers head for the beach, as the Samui and Hua Hin Regattas and the Hua Hin Jazz Festival draw people from around the country.

May–June

Samui Regatta
Chaweng Beach
www.samuiregatta.com
There are good winds aplenty off Chaweng Beach for this annual regatta that draws a decent crowd of international sailors, and much beach revelry.

June

Hua Hin Jazz Festival
Various locations, Hua Hin
www.jazzfestivalhuahin.com

With a very liberal interpretation of 'jazz', this will likely not satisfy purists, but occasional top-class international acts do crop up. Otherwise it's a fun beach party with lots of live music.

July–Aug

Hua Hin Regatta
This annual sailing event takes place in a less raucous location than Samui, but the sailing is generally good, often with lively winds and a good variety of classes to compete in.

Northern Andaman Coast

The beautiful Northern Andaman Coast is one of the world's prime holiday destinations. It forms the proverbial tropical paradise of TV and film, covered with fine white-sand beaches and palm-fringed islands. There are top-class diving sites offshore, spectacular limestone karsts offering prime viewpoints for climbers, and jungle treks.

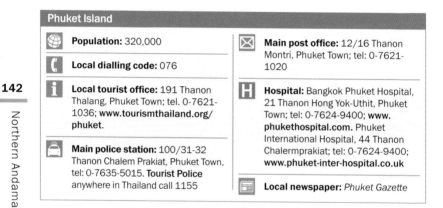

Phuket Island

Population: 320,000

Local dialling code: 076

Local tourist office: 191 Thanon Thalang, Phuket Town; tel. 0-7621-1036; www.tourismthailand.org/phuket.

Main police station: 100/31-32 Thanon Chalem Prakiat, Phuket Town, tel: 0-7635-5015. **Tourist Police** anywhere in Thailand call 1155

Main post office: 12/16 Thanon Montri, Phuket Town; tel: 0-7621-1020

Hospital: Bangkok Phuket Hospital, 21 Thanon Hong Yok-Uthit, Phuket Town; tel: 0-7624-9400; www.phukethospital.com. Phuket International Hospital, 44 Thanon Chalermprakiat; tel: 0-7624-9400; www.phuket-inter-hospital.co.uk

Local newspaper: *Phuket Gazette*

The Northern Andaman Coast is dominated by the island of Phuket (pronounced 'poo-ket'), which has sun-kissed beaches and is the main launch site for some of the best diving in the world. Some 4 million tourists arrive every year, around 12 times more than the island's total population, primarily for the glorious bays along the west coast, which include both luxury seclusion at the north end and raunchy nightlife at busy Patong. The island's pristine waters are ideal for snorkelling, while water sports include paragliding, windsurfing and sailing. Meal breaks are taken at beachfront seafood stalls, which sell the famous Phuket lobster, eaten grilled with a dash of lime.

Along the mainland coast to the east and south of Phuket, the famous karsts of Phang Nga and Krabi form a fantasy backdrop to gorgeous sunsets. And to the north are quieter beach locations, such as Kao Lak, and other alternative departure points for the islands of Similan and Surin and the Burma Banks, where clownfish, turtles and whale shark are common underwater companions.

Ranong to Khao Lak

The less developed northern coast, running south from Ranong, has some tranquil islands offshore, many of which comprise the best diving in Thailand – and Burma (Myanmar). The area has its fair share of paradise beaches, with the attraction of cheaper accommodation before reaching the more salubrious shores of Phuket and beyond.

Ranong and Surrounds

Ranong Town is a large port with few nearby beach facilities – divers use it mainly as a launch point for trips to the Burma Banks *(see box p.145)* – and its most famous attraction is about 2km (1½ miles) southeast of town. **Raksawarin Park Hot Springs** ❶ (daily 8am–5pm; free) are actually too hot to bathe in at around

Ranong's public mineral baths

65°C (150°F), but there are concrete pools where people from Ranong sit to inhale the reviving steam. Water is also piped directly from here to **Jansom Hot Spa Ranong** (www.jansomhotsparanong.net; charge) at Thanon Petchakasem.

The quiet island of **Ko Chang** ❷ is accessible by boat from Ranong in 2½ hours (Nov–Apr). Most of its beaches are on the west coast, the longest being **Ao Yai**, which has most of the island's basic beach huts. There are no cars on Ko Chang and two concrete tracks lead to its only village, which has a single shop and a restaurant.

Surin Islands Marine National Park

Around 55km (34 miles) from Ranong, the five islands of **Surin Islands Marine National Park** ❸ (Nov–May; charge) are renowned

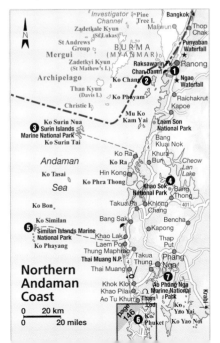

Investigator Channel · Pine Tree I. · Bangkok

Zadetkale Kyun (St Lukas')

St Andrews Group

Zadetkyi Kyun (St Mathew's I.)

Mergui

BURMA (MYANMAR)

Maliwun · Thop Chak

Punyaban Waterfall

Raksawarin P.K. · Ranong

Chan Damri ❶

Ngao Waterfall

Archipelago

Ko Chang ❷

Than Kyun (Davis I.)

Ko Phayam

Raichakrut

Kapoe

Christie I.

Mu Ko Kam Yai

Laem Son National Park

Ko Surin Nua

❸ Surin Islands Marine National Park

Ko Surin Tai

Bang Kluai Nok

Andaman

Ko Ra

Ko Ra · Bur

Khura

Cheow Lan Lake

Hin Kong

Ko Tasai

Ko Phra Thong

Khao Sok National Park ❹

Bang Thong

Sea

Takua Pa · Khlong Chang

401

Ko Bon

Bang Sak

Bencha

Ko Similan

❺ Similan Islands Marine National Park

Khao Lak

Kapong

Ko Phayang

Laem Pol

Thap Put

Thung Maphrao

Thai Muang N.P.

Takua Thung

Phang Nga

Northern Andaman Coast

Thai Muang

Khok Kloi

Ao Phang Nga Marine National Park

Khao Pilai

Ao Tu Khun

Tham Pann

Krabi

0   20 km

0   20 miles

Ko Phuket

Ko Yao Noi

Ko Yao Yai

Phuket Island Transport

 Airport: Phuket International Airport; **www.airportthai.co.th**. Metered red and yellow taxis run from the airport to Phuket Town. Fares will be around B350 to Phuket Town for the 30-minute journey. Buses run every 30 minutes from 6.30am–9.30pm to Phuket Town only. Tickets are B70 and the journey takes 1 hour.

 Bus station: Thanon Ranong, Phuket Town; tel: 0-3251-1230

 Taxis: Phuket Airport Taxi; tel: 0-7637-9571; **www.phuket airporttaxi.com**

 Songthaew: run between the bus station in Phuket Town and the beaches from 6am–6pm. Return journeys end at 4pm; cost: B30–40.

 Tuk-tuks: hail *tuk-tuks* anywhere on the street; a journey to the beach fom Phuket Town will cost upwards of B300.

 Car hire: Phuket Car Rent; tel: 0-7620-5190; **www.phuketcarrent. com**; P ure Car Rent; tel: 0-7621-1002; **www.purecarrent.com**

for superlative diving and snorkelling. The scenery above water is equally spectacular, with numerous sandy bays backed by verdant jungle. Because of the distance, they are mainly visited by divers on live-aboard boats. The two main islands, **Ko Surin Nua**, which has the park's headquarters and the island's only accommodation, and **Ko Surin Tai**, are separated by a narrow channel of small beaches and mangroves that can be forded at low tide. The most popular dive site, **Richelieu Rock**, is one of the world's top locations for sighting whale sharks.

The man-made reservoir Chiao Lan Lake at Khao Sok National Park

Bang Niang beach, Khao Lak

Khao Sok National Park

Further south on the mainland, **Khao Sok National Park** ❹ (www. dnp.go.th; daily 6am–6pm; charge) is home to one of the world's oldest evergreen rainforests, at 160 million years, and is the wettest area in Thailand. The world's second-largest flower, the *Rafflesia Kerrii*, grows here, up to 80cm (31ins) in diameter when in bloom, and cobras, tarantulas and scorpions are common. There are several waterfalls to visit, and **Cheow Lan Lake**, which has over 100 small islands and facilities for boat trips, fishing and canoeing.

Khao Lak

Around 160km (100 miles) south of the park headquarters, sleepy Khao Lak is a less commercialised alternative to Phuket, with a string of attractive beaches divided from each other by rocky outcrops. It is also the closest access point to the marine-life paradise of the Similan Islands, some 60km (37 miles) offshore.

Similan Islands Marine National Park

The beautiful **Similan Islands Marine National Park** ❺ (www. dnp.go.th; Nov–May; charge), 100km (62 miles) northwest of Phuket has nine islands, all uninhabited, except for **Ko Ba Ngu** and **Ko Miang**. Over 20 dive locations here include the popular sites of **Christmas Point** and **Breakfast Bend**, both at Ko Ba Ngu, where soft coral growth and colourful sea fans are among the largest found

in Thailand. The Napoleon Wrasse, a rare sight in Thailand, is occasionally glimpsed at Breakfast Bend, along with leopard sharks resting on the

Diving in Burma

Ranong gives access to one of the best dive sites in the world, the Burma Banks, without having to travel down to Khao Lak or Phuket. Hiring a live-aboard dive boat from one of these three places is the only way to access this renowned site. The Burma Banks are around 150km (90 miles) west of Ranong. There are no islands there, but three submerged peaks, Silvertip, Roe and Rainbow, which rise to within 15m (50ft) of the surface water. Encounters with silvertip, nurse and, occasionally, grey reef sharks are almost guaranteed.

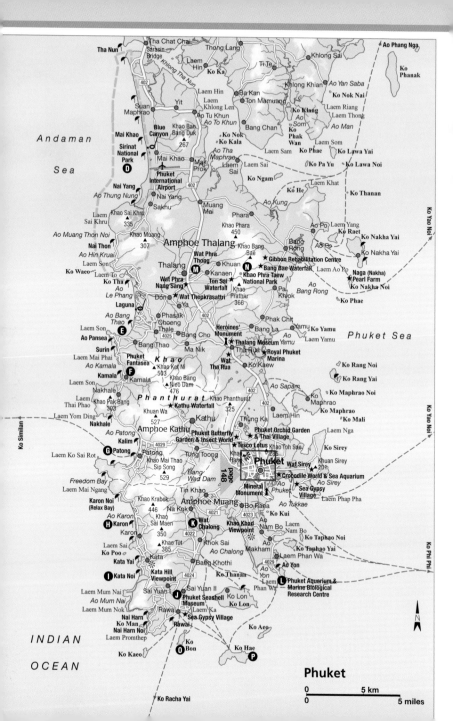

Phuket

Offerings on the altar at Wat Jui Tui

sands beneath. The western side of the archipelago offers more exhilarating diving, with currents swirling around granite boulder formations, with dramatic holes, overhangs and colourful soft coral so thick the rock is no longer visible. Popular areas are **Fantasy Reef** and **Elephant Head**, with clownfish, lionfish and turtles. As navigation can be tricky, most west-coast sites are best done with a guide.

Phuket

Phuket ❻, Thailand's largest and most expensive island resort and second-richest province, caters to a broad range of holiday-makers, with bars and beaches, diving and offshore islands, and a cultural diversity that includes large Chinese and Muslim populations. There are hotels to suit most budgets and shopping complexes second only to Bangkok.

Phuket Town

Unsurprisingly, many people head straight for the beaches and give Phuket Town a miss. But it is worth at least a day trip for sights and shops and a sprinkling of good bars and restaurants. In the heart of town, between Thanon Thalang and Thanon Deebuk, old colonial houses and Sino-Portuguese mansions dominate **Chinatown ❹**. West of here, on Thanon Krabi, the Taoist temple **Sanjao Sam San ❸** (daily 8am–6pm; free) was built in 1853 in dedication to Tien Sang Sung Moo, the Goddess of the Sea, and Patron Saint of Sailors. Parallel to the south, Thanon Ranong hosts **Wat Put Jaw ❻** (daily 8am–6pm; free). It is dedicated to Kwan Im, the Chinese Goddess of Mercy, and, at over 200 years old, is the oldest Chinese Taoist temple in Phuket. Next door, **Wat Jui Tui** (daily 8am–6pm; free) is the main location

Shopping in Phuket

Slightly at odds with the image of a laid-back tropical island, Phuket is gaining a plethora of shopping facilities that are as good as any in Thailand outside Bangkok. In Phuket Town, **Central Festival Phuket** (74–75 Moo 5, Thanon Vichit; www.centralfestivalphuket.com) has three storeys, including a department store, a supermarket and brand name shops with items like perfume, watches, jewellery and clothes. Even beach locations have increasing facilities for bargain hunters, such as **Jungceylon** (www.jungceylon.com), in Patong, and **Turtle Village** (www.royalgardenplaza.co.th) at Hat Mai Khao.

for the annual October Vegetarian Festival, when devotees perform acts of self-mutilation. East along Thanon Ranong, **Central Market** has piles of vegetables, fruit and fish.

About 2.5km (1½ miles) north along Thanon Thepkrassatri, **Phuket Orchid Garden and Thai Village** (daily 8am–9pm; charge 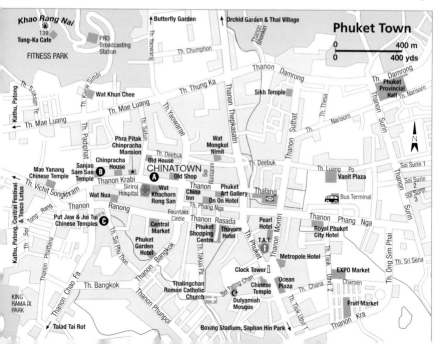) has traditional dances, elephant shows and a handicraft centre. Parallel, to the west, on Thanon Yaowaraj, **Phuket Butterfly Garden and Insect World** (www.phuketbutterfly.com; daily 9am–5.30pm; charge) includes native birds in its collection. Insect World has stick insects, tarantulas and scorpions.

The beautiful west-coast bays are Phuket's main claim to fame. A significant part of the northwest cape consists of **Sirinat National Park** (www.dnp.go.th; daily 6am–6pm; charge), which incorporates beaches at **Hat Nai Yang** and **Hat Nai Thon**, the mangroves of **Hat Mai Khao**, and a large chunk of sea with coral reefs. Sea turtles lay eggs at Hat Mai Khao between November and February each year. Despite being a protected area, the national park has a few hotels and beach huts, but is still very laid-back compared to beaches further down the coast.

South of the park, the 8km (5-mile) **Ao Bang Thao** is one of the loveliest beaches on the island, and dominated by luxury hotels. It is followed by Thai-style pavilions at the short **Ao Pansea**, and then a beach popular with locals at **Hat Surin**. Vendors here often have makeshift stalls selling

Longtail boats moored off Hat Nai Thon beach

grilled seafood at the beach car park. Next is relaxed **Hat Kamala**, where **Phuket Fantasea** (www.phuket-fantasea.com; Fri–Wed 5.30–11.30pm, showtime 9pm) has shows combining acrobatics, pyrotechnics and a vast menagerie of performing animals.

A few minutes' drive south is **Hat Patong** , Phuket's busiest beach, with a multitude of shops, restaurants, street stalls, flashy bars and clubs. The beach is crowded, but the location is naturally beautiful and it's good for swimming and snorkelling despite the jet-skis whizzing by. The nightlife includes a fair share of prostitution and sex shows, notably along Thanon Bangla. Heading south on Thanon Sirirat, **Phuket Simon Cabaret** (www.phuket-simoncabaret.com; daily, showtime 7.30pm and 9.30pm; charge) has *kathoey*, or 'lady-boy', shows *(see p.114)*.

Leaving Patong, and beyond the private beach at Hat Karon Noi, is Phuket's second most popular beach,

Hat Karon . Surfers like the rainy season waves here. Just past the headland is **Hat Kata Yai**, overlooking tiny Ko Poo (Crab Island). Kata's lovely beach is good for swimming and snorkelling, but can get quite busy. At night, people dine at seafood restaurants lit by fairy lights beside the shore. Separated from here by a rocky headland, **Hat Kata Noi** is even prettier and more peaceful, with some decent coral for snorkelling. There is a breathtaking panorama from **Kata Hill Viewpoint**, which has some bars jutting out of the hillside along the road.

South of Kata, the stunning white-sand **Hat Nai Harn** is a quiet haven with just a few small bars, restaurants and shops.

South Coast

The south-coast beaches are largely mediocre and mainly visited as a departure point for the islands. But there is a popular viewpoint above

Nai Harn, called Laem Promthep, that is packed most evenings with tourists scanning the horizon.

Further east, Hat Rawai is picturesque, with its rows of fishing boats, but exposed rocks at low tide make it unsuitable for swimming. Lots of stalls here serve fresh seafood day and night. To the south of the beach is a small sea gypsy village, and, on Thanon Viset, the **Phuket Seashell Museum ❶** (www.phuketseashell.com; daily 8am–6pm; charge 🅼) has over 2,000 species of shells and fossils. Some are over 380 million years old.

Further along the coast, dive expeditions and boat trips leave from **Ao Chalong**, and, inland from Rawai on Route 4021, **Wat Chalong ❷** (daily 8am–6pm; free) is Phuket's most important Buddhist temple.

East Coast

Moving to the east coast, the only decent beach is **Laem Phan Wa**, 10km (6 miles) southeast of Phuket Town. This quiet cape is frequently filled with yachts sailing the unspoilt bay of Ao Yon. **Khao Khad Viewpoint**, along Thanon Sakdidej, has vistas of the Phuket and out towards Ko Phi Phi. On the southernmost tip of Laem Phan Wa, **Phuket Aquarium and Marine Biological Research Centre ❸** (daily 8.30am–4pm; charge 🅼) has an impressive display of sharks, tropical fish, reefs and a touch pool with starfish and sea cucumbers.

Towards the north of the east coast, about 20km (12 miles) from Phuket Town, **Ao Po** is the departure point for the 30-minute boat ride to **Ko Nakha Noi** and the **Naga Pearl Farm** (daily

9am–3.30pm; charge), where full-sized South Sea pearls worth thousands of dollars are cultivated. Visitors can view the various stages of cultivation.

Phuket's Interior

About 12km (7 miles) north of Phuket Town along Thanon Thepkrasattri (Route 402), **The Heroines' Monument** honours Lady Chan and Lady Muk. They were the widow of the governor of Phuket and her sister, who led the successful defence of the island against the invading Burmese in 1785. A short distance northeast, Phuket's history from prehistoric cave dwellers to the present day is recounted at **Thalang Museum** (www.thailandmuseum.com; daily 9am–4pm; charge).

Bang Pae Waterfall

Further along Route 402 is Thalang Town, where **Wat Phra Thong**  (daily 8am–6pm; free) contains a golden Buddha half-buried in the ground, which, from the chest up, measures about 2m (7ft). A curse associated with the image is said to have caused the death of people trying to dig it up to claim the gold. In fact, the statue is made of brick and plaster, with just a thin gold veneer.

East of Thalang Town is **Khao Phra Taew National Park** (www.dnp.go.th; daily 6am–6pm; charge), Phuket's largest tract of virgin rainforest. It has monkeys, civets and other small animals and a couple of waterfalls that are good for lunch and a swim. A 15 to 20-minute walk from **Bang Pae Waterfall**, the **Gibbon Rehabilitation Centre** (http://gibbonproject.org; daily 9am–4pm; free) is a non-profit organisation working against the poaching of gibbons for use as tourist attractions and for sale in the pet trade. Although located within the national park, the Gibbon Rehabilitation Centre receives none of the money from park fees and relies solely on donations from visitors.

Islands

The waters off south Phuket are dotted with islands, all of which can be reached via longtail boats at Hat Rawai or Ao Chalong pier. Nearest to shore is the small but pretty **Ko Bon**, which has no fresh water, electricity or accommodation, so is just a day-trip destination. The Evason Resort owns one side of the island, and food and drink prices at its clubhouse are steep. Most people head for the other

Just 10 minutes by boat from Phuket is Ko Kaeo, marked by numerous Buddha statues

side, where a small Thai and seafood restaurant caters for customers on the sandy beachfront. There is some coral offshore for snorkelling.

About 20 minutes from Phuket, and often combined on a day trip with Ko Bon, is **Ko Hae** (Coral Island), which has several restaurants, a few small shops and some water sports. Overnight stays are possible at **Coral Island Resort** (www.coral-islandresort.com), the island's only accommodation. The beach is fine for both swimming and snorkelling, with a shallow coral reef within easy swimming distance.

Approximately 20km (12 miles) off Rawai are **Ko Racha Noi**, a small uninhabited island with more rocks than beaches, and the larger **Ko Racha Yai**, which is a high-season hotspot, with day-trippers arriving

The geological oddity Ko Tapu, meaning Nail Island, viewed from Phang Nga bay

on longtail boats and filling out the sands. These islands have some of the best diving in the Phuket area and are often compared to the Similans. On Ko Racha Yai, the Bungalow Bay reef offshore of **Ao Batok** has clear waters and soft coral gardens, with good visibility and currents that allow gentle drift diving along sloping reefs.

Prehistoric Cave Paintings

Travelling by road towards Krabi, about 35km (21 miles) southeast of Phan Nga on Highway 4, **Thanboke Koranee National Park** (www.dnp.go.th; daily 8am–6pm; charge) is famous for **Tham Pee Huakalok**, a cave with hundreds of wall paintings and prehistoric drawings, estimated to be 2,000–3,000 years old. The cave, deep in a hill surrounded by water and mangroves, is accessed by boat from **Bor Tor Pier**, 7km (4 miles) south of nearby Ao Luk.

On the east coast is **Ao Kon Kare** and, within swimming distance of the small sandy beach, Lucy's Reef, a nickname given to the staghorn coral found here. Further up the east coast, a submerged wreck lies off **Ao Ter** at depths of 25 to 35m (80 to 115ft).

The smaller Ko Racha Noi, where depths are generally greater and currents stronger, has good dive sites for experienced divers. Lots of reef fish are drawn to a 27m (88ft) shipwreck on the southwest side, while a large pinnacle at the northern tip attracts stingrays and reef sharks. Phuket's dive shops are also the prime operators for major sites scattered around the Andaman Coast (*see above*).

Ao Phang Nga

Less than an hour by road from Phuket airport, the mainland town of Phang Nga has boats leaving for Thailand's most striking islands of jungle-clad limestone rock, in the waters of **Ao Phang Nga Marine National Park** ❼ (www.dnp.go.th). Impressive by day, these towering limstone rock formations known as karsts are especially captivating on moonlit nights, when the silvery light casts haunting shadows onto the watery depths. Trips to the bay are mostly arranged from either Phuket or Krabi, but they can also be booked in Phang Nga Town itself. A good way of exploring is by sea canoe, which, at low tide, can slip through sea tunnels under the limestone karsts to hidden lagoons, or *hong*.

The karsts support their own mini ecosystems, including troupes of monkeys that reportedly swim from island to island. The best trips are to the more remote areas in late afternoon and evening, when there are fewer boats around.

Krabi

Krabi's stunning mainland beaches and idyllic islands, some of them blissfully isolated, are surrounded by marvellous sheer-sided karsts. These outcrops are a magnet for both rock climbers and camera crews shooting commercials, TV shows and films, and provide a spectacular sunset backdrop for tourists enjoying the clear waters.

Krabi Town

About 80km (50 miles) from Phan Nga, **Krabi Town** ❽ is the main jump-off en route to the beaches and islands of Krabi Province. Thanon Maharat hosts the main market and most restaurants and shops, while there are guesthouses and hotels on Thanon Chao Fa, a just a few minutes' walk from Chao Fa Pier.

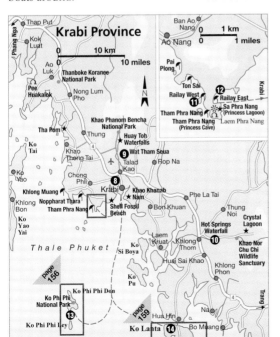

Eggs for sale on Krabi

There are boats for hire at the pier to mangroves on the opposite bank of the Krabi River, where a small fishing community lives in wooden huts raised on stilts. The trips include two 100m (328ft) limestone pinnacles that rise beside the river, called **Khao Khanab Nam**. One peak has a series of caves with impressive stalactites and stalagmites.

Krabi Interior

Set into forests and cliffs, 9km (6 miles) north of Krabi Town, **Wat Tham Seua** ❾ (daily 8am–6pm; charge) has 1,272 steps leading to a 600m (1,970ft) peak. It has fantastic views and a small shrine with a Buddha footprint in the rock.

Heading southeast of Krabi Town on Highway 4, after 55km (34 miles) is the **Hot Springs Waterfall** ❿ (daily 8am–5pm; charge), where people first bathe in the hot water as it cascades down the boulders, before dipping into a cool stream.

Rock Climbing in Krabi

Most of Krabi's 600-plus climbing routes are located on Railay Bay peninsula, which has dramatic sheer limestone cliffs facing the sea. The climbs involve crags, steep pocketed walls, overhangs and hanging stalactites, and are suitable for beginners through to professionals. Among the most popular is the phenomenal, and challenging, Thaiwand Wall at the southern end.

Any of the Railay climbing operations will advise on the best routes, some of which are accessed by a combination of boat and jungle hike.

A 10-minute drive east of the waterfall, the **Khao Nor Chu Chi Wildlife Sanctuary** (daily 8am–5pm; charge) is said to be the last patch of lowland rainforest in Thailand. It's also one of the few habitats of an endangered bird called Gurneys Pitta.

Krabi Beaches

Three Krabi beaches are accessible by road, starting with the secluded **Hat Khlong Muang**, 30-minutes' drive from Krabi Town. A finger of land separates it from **Hat Noppharat Thara** and then **Ao Nang**, the most commercial and developed bay. Both have views of limestone islands.

But most visitors head to one of the outlying beaches for which Krabi is most famous. Laem Phra Nang, better known as **Railay Bay**, which surrounded on three sides by sheer limestone cliffs and only accessible by boat, feels like an island, but is actually a peninsula with four beaches.

Most boats go to **Hat Railay West** ⓫, on the western side of the peninsula, where the absence of a pier means a short wade to shore. On the opposite side of the peninsula **Hat Railay East** ⓬, which is backed by dense mangroves, is less scenic and not great for swimming. Accordingly, the bungalows here are lower priced, but get their fair share of trade, as there's only a 5-minute walk from one beach to the other. The same people appreciating sunsets on Railay West are often seen a few hours later enjoying fire juggling and all-night parties at Railay East.

The prettiest beach, **Hat Tham Phra Nang**, has a single

Wooden huts on stilts in a Muslim village across the river from Thara

accommodation option, Rayavadee Resort (www.rayavadee.com), amid coconut groves, surrounded by limestone cliffs. Day-trippers flock here from Railay West and Railay East to sunbathe, swim and snorkel.

At the beach's eastern end **Tham Phra Nang** has a collection of wooden phalluses left as offerings to a princess who was believed to bestow fertility to the area. A map here points the way towards a viewpoint and **Sa Phra Nang**. The route is straightforward but involves clinging to ropes to clamber up a fairly steep incline at the start. It is not suitable for the very young, elderly or unfit, and good footwear is essential. The lagoon is suitable for swimming.

Another beach, **Hat Ton Sai**, is popular with budget travellers for its cheaper accommodation and vibrant nightlife. Longtail boats can be hired to make the 5-minute journey from Hat Railay West, but if you are feeling energetic it is also possible to walk at low tide, or even swim. Beach bars are open until the early hours and host monthly full-moon parties. The sea view is beautiful, but the sand is less white, and at low tide gets muddy.

Ko Phi Phi

The twin islands of **Ko Phi Phi** ⑬ are in the Andaman Sea just two hours from the main hubs of Phuket and Krabi. While heavy development on Ko Phi Phi Don and the crowds on Ko Phi Phi Ley means they are no longer the idyll of old, these islands remain among Thailand's most popular diving locations.

Ko Phi Phi Don

Ko Phi Phi Don is actually two islands, with most development on the bays Ao Ton Sai and Ao Lo Dalam, along each side of the isthmus that joins them.

Boats to the island dock at **Ao Ton Sai Ⓐ**, where restaurants, bars, dive shops, internet cafés and stalls sell everything from sarongs and beaded jewellery to sandwiches and banana pancakes. A few minutes' walk opposite, **Ao Lo Dalam Ⓑ** is a quieter and

Massage with a view on Ko Lanta

prettier bay with a lovely curve of white sand and clear blue waters.

South of Ao Ton Sai, on the west coast of the larger island, are **Hat Hin Khom** and scenic **Hat Yao**, which can be reached by longtail boat or walked in 40 minutes. The path east from Hat Hin Khom forks right to breathtaking sunrise and sunset views from bluff at the southern end of **Ao Lo Dalam**. Running north up the east coast are the low-key **Hat Ran Ti** and **Hat Pak Nam**, before reaching **Hat Laem Thong ⓒ**, which has the best snorkelling and the most exclusive resorts, and is home to a sea gypsy community (*see Beaches and Islands, p.33*).

Ko Phi Phi Ley

About 4km (2 miles) south of Ko Phi Phi Don, the uninhabited Ko Phi Phi Ley is formed entirely from limestone and circled by steep karsts rising from the sea. Most famous of the picturesque bays is **Ao Maya ⓓ**, on the west coast, which was the prime location for the film *The Beach*,

starring Leonardo Di Caprio. To avoid the crowds, it's best to get here very early in the morning or late in the afternoon. Another major draw, in the northeastern of the island, is the **Viking Cave ⓔ**, where coloured drawings of boats on the walls are believed to have been chalked hundreds of years ago by pirates who sheltered here. Today, villagers climb rickety ladders to collect swifts' nests built by the hundred in crevices high up on the cave walls. Their booty goes to Chinese restaurants and herbalists for bird's nest soup and traditional remedies. The swifts build every year between January and April, using their saliva as bonding material.

The best diving and snorkelling sites off Phi Phi Ley are **Hin Bida** (Phi

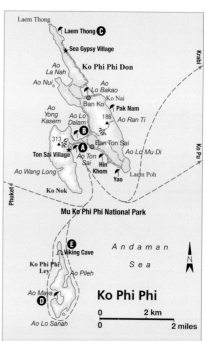

Ko Phi Phi

Phi Shark Point), **Ko Pai** (Bamboo Island), **Ko Yung** (Mosquito Island) and Ao Maya. The **King Cruiser Wreck**, between Phuket and Ko Phi Phi, is another favourite.

Ko Lanta Yai

Ko Lanta Yai is the most remote and perhaps most pleasant part of Krabi province. It is one of only three inhabited islands in an archipelago of over 50, and is usually referred to simply as **Ko Lanta** ⑭. A single main road gives access to white sand beaches, sea gypsy settlements and spectacular sunsets.

Ban Sala Dan

The Ko Lanta ferry drops visitors at **Ban Sala Dan** Ⓐ, a small village with police post, clinic, convenience stores, tour agents and internet facilities, but not much charm. So people usually transfer quickly to their beach accommodation, perhaps after a break at one of the island's seafood restaurants.

Hat Khlong Dao

A few kilometres south, **Hat Khlong Dao** Ⓑ is the first beach on the western shore, where the most development has taken place. This is a good choice for families for its shallow waters and safe swimming conditions, and there are plenty of mid-range accommodation options. It's also popular with divers for its closeness to Ban Sala Dan and access to nearby dive sites. Despite the picturesque hilly backdrop and dramatic sunsets, Khlong Dao is rarely crowded.

Cruising Ko Phi Phi Ley's magnificent Maya Bay by longtail boat

Diving around Ko Lanta

The waters off Ko Lanta have some of Thailand's finest snorkelling and dive spots. **Ko Rok**, about 47km (29 miles) south, is most visited for snorkelling. There are actually two islands, Ko Rok Nai and Ko Rok Nok, separated by an extensive patch of coloured coral with good visibility and interesting fish.

Approximately 20km (12 miles) further out, the twin peaks of **Hin Daeng** and **Hin Muang** pierce the water's surface. With an incredible variety of marine life, including pelagics, large tuna and barracuda, they are frequently rated in the world's top 10 dive locations. Grey reef sharks often approach divers and whale shark sightings are among the most common in the world.

Ao Phra Ae

Neighbouring to the south, **Ao Phra Ae ❸** is shaded by tall coconut and pine trees, and is fine for swimmers, although the sea bed is steep in places, so it's not suitable for small children. There is plenty of accommodation here and a variety of restaurants.

Hat Khlong Khong

Next is laid-back **Hat Khlong Khong ❹**, which, though not great for swimming, is one of the island's best beaches for snorkelling; at low tide the rocky underlay reveals an assortment of fish and other marine life in the rocks at low tide. Accommodation is generally cheaper here, with the clean but basic beachfront bungalows mostly having restaurants and beach bars.

Hat Khlong Nin and Hat Khlong Hin

Continuing south, the road leads to **Hat Khlong Nin ❺**, a lovely beach with a relaxed small-village atmosphere. The sands stretch about 2km (1 mile) and the calm waters are excellent for swimming. Stylish resorts cluster here, along with lots of buzzing beach bars. At the southern end, beyond a clump of trees, is the smaller, more secluded **Hat Khlong Hin**.

Ao Kantiang

About 6km (4 miles) further on, **Ao Kantiang ❻**, framed on three sides by jungle-covered hills, has a private feel. To the north, high on the hill, small stilted bungalows offer lovely views, but demand a stiff walk.

Ao Khlong Chak and Ao Mai Phai

A short drive south by dirt track are some of the most scenic and underdeveloped beaches on the island. **Ao Khlong Chak ❼**, one of the smallest at just 400m (1,310ft) long, has a handful of budget to mid-range resorts. A waterfall, 1.5km (1 mile) inland, is impressive during the monsoon season. A bumpy drive south finds **Ao Mai Phai** (Bamboo Bay), surrounded by mountains, and with just a few resorts.

Mu Ko Lanta National Marine Park

Mu Ko Lanta National Marine Park comprises 15 small islands and two beaches: **Laem Tanode** and the rocky **Hat Hin Ngam** on the southern tip of Ko Lanta. The latter hosts the park headquarters. A 2.5km (1½-mile) hiking trail starting along the cliff provides rewards with fauna such as fruit bats, deer, wild pigs and reptiles.

Ko Lanta Interior

Among the few attractions in Ko Lanta's interior are the caves at **Tham Mai Kaeo** , best reached on organised trip from one of the resorts. They can be found with some difficulty by following the road south from Hat Khlong Khong and forking left to the east coast. A turn-off at the 3km (2-mile) mark to the right leads to the caves. The clamber up a steep hill, slippery paths, bamboo ladders and confined spaces make this a trip for the reasonably fit, but the expedition leads through a labyrinth of winding tunnels and caverns, past dramatic rock formations to a deep pool, where you can cool off.

Further on the road east, **Viewpoint Hill** is worth the morning effort for a sunrise breakfast with panoramic views at the hilltop Khao Yai Restaurant.

Ko Bubu and Ko Jum

Located 7km (4 miles) off the east coast of Ko Lanta, tiny **Ko Bubu** takes just 30 minutes to circumnavigate on foot. The uninhabited isle has only a basic restaurant and a few simple rooms on its stunning west-coast beach, at **Bubu Bungalows** (tel: 0-7561-2536), the only resort on the island. They arrange boat transfers, or longtail boats can be hired at Krabi and Ko Lanta.

Larger, but still pleasantly undeveloped, is **Ko Jum** to the northwest. The island has good beaches and clear waters with plenty of healthy coral reefs, but accommodation is limited, and most people visit only for the day.

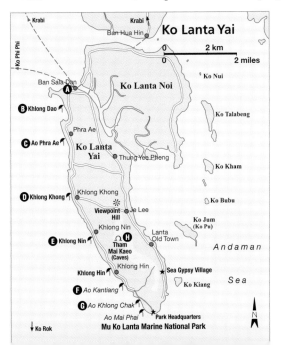

There is plenty to do on Hat Khlong Dao

ACCOMMODATION

The coasts around the North Andaman contain some of Thailand's most valuable real estate and its top-end resorts rival any in the world for setting and sheer opulence. But the region also retains pockets of chump-change beach huts and the back-to-nature ambience that first attracted backpackers in the 1970s.

Ranong to Khao Lak

Bamboo Bungalows
Ko Phayam, Ko Phayam
Tel: 0-7782-0012
www.bamboo-bungalows.com
This popular cluster of bungalows, open year-round, is one of the livelier places in the evenings, when guests from nearby resorts come to enjoy the music on the beach. **$–$$**

Cashew Resort
Ao Yai, Ko Chang
Tel: 0-7782-0116
Ko Chang's largest resort has 25 sea-view bungalows made of wood, bamboo and stone. Facilities include a dive school and a beach bar with pool table. Open only from mid-October to May. **$**

Jai Restaurant and Bungalows
5/1 Moo 7, Khao Lak
Tel: 0-7642-0390
This is about ten minutes' walk from the

Bungalows on Ko Chang

beach, which is about normal for this price range in Khao Lak. The bungalows are clean, with small private terraces, and are set just behind Jai Restaurant. **$**

Phang Nga Guest House
99/1 Th. Petchkasem, Ao Phang Nga
Tel: 0-7641-1358
Basic, but comfortable, clean rooms with choice of fan or air conditioning. This is one of the better budget options in town, conveniently situated and with friendly staff. **$**

The Sarojin
60 Moo 2, Khuk Khak
Tel: 0-7642-7900
www.thesarojin.com
Arguably Khao Lak's most luxurious resort, with direct access to a secluded private beach. Rooms are situated in low-rise buildings and decorated with strong Thai accents. Facilities include two restaurants, a bar, spa and infinity pool. **$$$$$**

Six Senses Hideaway
Ko Yao Noi, Ao Phang Nga
Tel: 0-7641-8500
www.sixsenses.com
Stunning property with gorgeous views of Ao Phang Nga from villas complete with private infinity-edge pools and a personal butler. Also on-site are a spa, gym and two restaurants. The resort arranges dive trips and tours of Ao Phang Nga. **$$$$$**

Tinidee Hotel@Ranong
41/144 Thanon Tamuang, Ranong
Tel: 0-7783-5240

Formerly the Royal Princess Ranong, the Tinidee has clean and decently appointed rooms and friendly staff. Hot spring water is provided in all guest rooms as well as in the swimming pool and jacuzzi areas. **$$**

Phuket

Amanpuri
Pansea Beach
Tel: 0-7632-4333
www.amanpuri.com
These ocean-view, wood-floor pavilions amid the palm trees have the perfect ambience for the film stars who visit each year. There is a private beach with water sports, a beautiful pool and a fleet of yachts on hand for cruises. **$$$$$**

Banyan Tree
33 Moo 4, Thanon Srisoonthorn, Amphoe Talang
Tel: 0-7632-4374
www.banyantree.com
The epitome of luxury in manicured grounds at Bang Tao Bay. All the villas have teak floors, tasteful decor and private outdoor jacuzzis. Some have private pools. There are tennis courts, water sports, a spa and three good restaurants. **$$$$$**

Kaya House
52/24 Thanon Rat-U-Thit
Tel: 0-7629-0088
www.kayaphuket.com
Just five minutes' walk from the beach, these are tiny, basic rooms, but have TV, air conditioning, refrigerator and en-suite shower, making them a good deal at this price. Kaya also organises tours. **$**

Thavorn Beach Village and Spa
6/2 Moo 6, Nakalay Bay, Patong
Tel: 0-7629-0334
www.thavornbeachvillage.com
Close to the bustle of Patong, yet tranquil enough, with its own private beach. A cable car transports guests from the open-air main lobby to the comfortable rooms built high on a hill. There is a large pool, a spa and a Thai restaurant. **$$**

The pool at Amanpuri

Krabi

Krabi Mountain View Resort
Ao Ton Sai
Tel: 0-7562-2610
www.krabimountainviewresort.com
Pleasant bungalow-style huts situated between the cliffs and waters of Ton Sai Beach. Railay West is just a 10-minute walk away at low tide. Rooms are clean and modern, and good value for money. **$$**

Railay Village Resort
Hat Railay West
Tel: 0-7562-2578
www.railayvillagekrabi.com
Perfectly situated for sunsets on scenic Railay West, this recently refurbished hotel has bungalows among coconut groves close to the beach. Facilities include a swimming pool, restaurant and tour desk. **$$$$**

Rayavadee
Hat Tham Phra Nang
Tel: 0-7562-0740
www.rayavadee.com
Idyllic two-storey pavilions set in coconut groves next to huge cliffs and bordering three beaches. Full range of restaurants, bars, tennis, spa and water sports. **$$$$$**

Sand Sea Resort
Hat Railay West
Tel: 0-7562-2574
www.krabisandsea.com
A pleasant hotel with a variety of room styles and prices. There is a beachfront swimming pool, minimart and internet facilities on-site, and a restaurant serving Thai and Western food. **$$–$$$**

Ko Phi Phi
Phi Phi Andaman Resort
1 Moo 7, Hat Hin Khom
Tel: 0-7560-1111
www.phiphiandamanresort.com
Mix of bungalows with fan or air conditioning set in a tropical garden a few minutes' stroll from Ton Sai pier. There is a bar and restaurant on the beach. **$$**

Phi Phi Banyan Villa
Ao Ton Sai
Tel: 0-7561-1233
www.ppbanyanvilla.com
If location is everything, then this place, right in the centre of Ao Ton Sai, wins hands down. The beach, restaurants, shops and pier are just 5 minutes' walk away. Comfortable air-conditioned rooms with cable TV and hot water. **$$**

Phi Phi Island Village Resort & Spa
Ao Lo Bakao
Tel: 0-7623-6616
www.ppisland.com
This attractive resort is on 800m (870yds) of private beach. Rooms are tastefully appointed but it is the idyllic location above all else that keeps guests coming back. Three restaurants, two bars and a spa. **$$$$–$$$$$**

Ko Lanta
Lanta Sand Resort & Spa
Ao Phra Ae
Tel: 0-7568-4633
www.lantasand.com
Everything spells tropical at this lovely resort, with its swimming pool, spa and guest rooms tucked in between luscious greenery and coconut palms. All rooms have open-air, natural garden bathrooms. **$$$–$$$$$**

Rawi Warin Resort & Spa
Hat Khlong Nin
Tel: 0-7560-7400
www.rawiwarin.com
Situated at the base of hills overlooking a lovely beach, this has four swimming pools, including one built into the sea and a kids' pool. Complete range of facilities and even a mini cinema. **$$$–$$$$$**

Southern Lanta Resort
Hat Khlong Dao
Tel: 0-7568-4174
www.southernlanta.com
Largest of the resorts on Hat Khlong Dao. Each bungalow has its own private balcony and garden area. Not the most modern compared to some of the island's other developments, but prices are keen and it has a range of facilities including two restaurants and a spa. **$$**

Accommodation at Waterfall Bay, Ko Lanta

RESTAURANTS

Good Thai food is available in all destinations and it is a good idea to follow your eyes and nose, particularly with fresh seafood displayed at beachfront diners. Just buy what looks good on the day. There are lots of up-market restaurants on Phuket, covering many nationalities, while dining options on other islands and beaches such as Krabi's Hat Railay will often be at resorts, and will invariably offer Thai dishes with a few Western favourites.

Khao Lak Seafood
19/1 Moo 7, Khuk Khak, Khao Lak
Tel: 0-7642-0318
Favoured by residents and widely said to serve the best fresh seafood in Khao Lak, this little restaurant is busy throughout the year and well worth a visit. **$–$$**

Pizzeria Spaghetteria Italica
5/3 Moo 7, Khuk Khak, Khao Lak
Tel: 0-7642-0271
It has basic decor, but this homely Italian-managed restaurant makes fresh pasta and sauces right on the premises. The restaurant also has a wide selection of pizza and decent home-made gnocchi. End the meal with real Italian coffee or liqueur. **$–$$**

Ranong to Kao Lak

Sophon's Hideaway Bar and Restaurant
Thanon Ruangrat, Ranong Town
Tel: 0-7783-2730
Very popular Australian-owned restaurant serving everything from Thai to Italian. Look out for the Aussie-inspired daily specials. The pleasant attitude of the wait staff makes up for the often slow delivery. **$–$$**

Phuket

Baan Rim Pa
100/7 Thanon Hat Kalim, Patong
Tel: 0-7634-0789
Exquisitely prepared Thai food from a restaurant on a cliff overlooking the ocean. It includes specialities such as steamed fish in pickled-plum sauce and hot-and-sour soup with fish and vegetables. Good selection of vegetarian dishes. **$$$$**

The Boathouse Wine & Grill
Mom Tri's Boathouse, 12 Kata Noi Road, Hat Kata
Tel: 0-7633-0015
Offering fine views of the Andaman Sea, this beachfront restaurant features refined Thai and European dining as well as seafood specialities. There is also a large wine selection. Indoor and outdoor seating available. **$$$**

Las Margaritas Grill
528/7 Thanon Patak, Hat Karon
Tel: 0-7628-6400
www.las-margaritas.net
Cuisine from Mexico, India, Hawaii, the Mediterranean and of course Thailand. The Mexican offerings are the best, with sizzling chicken fajitas going well with a ice-cold bottle of Corona. **$$**

Red Onion
486 Thanon Patak, Hat Karon
Tel: 0-7639-6827
Open-air eatery with mostly mediocre Western options, but excellent Thai classics such as *gaeng keow waan gai* (green chicken curry), washed down with Thailand's favourite Chang beer. **$**

The Red Room
293/25–6 Thanon Srisoonthorn, Ao Bang Thao
Tel: 0-7627-1136
Red candles and walls create a seductive

ambience for plates such as fillet of salmon drizzled with champagne lemon dill sauce, or the tuna with capsicum and garlic sauce. Features live jazz on Friday evenings. **$$–$$$**

Rockfish
33/6 Hat Kamala
Tel: 0-7627-9732
This three-storey open-sided house has a casual atmosphere and lovely sunset beach views to match a flashy menu including kingfish wrapped in spinach leaves served with red curry sauce. Trendy food at reasonable prices. **$$$–$$$$**

Salvatore's
15–17 Thanon Rasada, Phuket Town
Tel: 0-7622-5958
www.salvatoresrestaurant.com
The tables in this rustic interior are fully booked most nights so reservations are recommended to enjoy meals such as gnocchi with lamb sauce, home-made ice cream and rounded off with Italian coffee. **$$–$$$**

Savoey Seafood
136 Thanon Thawiwong, Hat Patong
Tel: 0-7634-1171
www.savoeyseafood.com
Impossible to miss with its prime beachfront location and displays of fresh fish and huge Phuket lobsters. Select your seafood and choose your cooking method, whether deep-fried, grilled or steamed with Thai herbs. **$$**

Tung-Ka Hill Top Restaurant
Rang Hill, Th. Korsimbi, Phuket Town
Tel: 0-7621-1500
This popular restaurant on the peak of Rang Hill serves *pla nueng manao* (steamed lemon fish) and similar dishes. The wine list is limited, but there is no corkage fee if you take your own. Good night-time views of the town. **$**

Krabi
Chanaya's Thai-Dutch Restaurant
Ao Nang (opp. Krabi Seaview Resort)
Tel: 08-9993-3716
Quirky rainforest setting with an interior

Quench the fire with a cool fresh salad

overflowing with plants and colourful birds in wooden cages hanging from the ceiling. Choices include salmon, steak and even ostrich. Delicious baguette sandwiches at lunch time. **$**

Flametree Restaurant and Bar
Hat Railay West
No phone
Good location for sunset views, so this is a favourite for dinner. There is a tempting mix of Thai and international dishes, plus snacks and Western breakfasts. Also serves good coffee. **$$**

Ruen Mai
Thanon Maharat, Krabi Town
No phone
Vegetarians love this place as staff can prepare on request meat-free versions of any dish on the menu. Strong flavours and lashings of chilli are not sacrificed to protect sensitive palates. **$–$$**

Ko Phi Phi
Pum's Restaurant
Ton Sai Village
Tel: 08-1521-8904
Pum serves a large selection of well-presented Thai dishes, including green and red curries, spicy salads and seafood specials. And if you get a taste for it, try one of her cooking classes, too. **$$**

Restaurant H.C. Andersen
Ton Sai Village
Tel: 08-4846-9010
www.phiphisteakhouse.com
Long-standing steak house with a casual and welcoming feel aided by the cheerful Matts, from Denmark, who runs it. Has a wide selection of international food, including Greek and Mexican. **$$**

Ko Lanta
Red Snapper
Ao Phra Ae
Tel: 0-7885-6965
www.redsnapper-lanta.com

This alfresco garden restaurant with beach access has an interesting East-West fusion menu that changes every two months but is dependably delicious. There is also a bar here and good-value rooms. **$$**

Same Same But Different
85 Moo 5, Ao Kan Tiang
Tel: 08-1787-8670
Location is key to the popularity of this laid-back beach restaurant, with many customers strolling in from the neighbouring Pimalai resort. The dishes are standard Thai fare but there's a great sunset view. **$–$$**

NIGHTLIFE AND ENTERTAINMENT

Much of the region's nightlife is enjoyed in the open air, lying on idyllic beaches with cocktail or beer in hand watching fire jugglers light the night sky. More raucous revelry is found on Phuket, especially at Patong, on Phi Phi Don, and at the tiny beach bars of Krabi.

Phuket
Angus O'Toole
516/20 Thanon Patak, Hat Karon
Tel: 0-7639-8262
www.otools-phuket.com
Popular Irish bar located at the end of a plaza, slightly off the main road. Shows live sports matches on TV and serves decent pub grub to go with your Guinness.

Kathoey revue at Simon Cabaret

Banana Disco
Thanon Thawiwong, Patong
Tel: 0-7634-0301
This busy venue plays Top 40 hits and has a large dance floor.

Molly Malone's
68 Thanon Thawiwong, Patong
Tel: 0-7629-2774
www.mollymalonesphuket.com
Popular Irish pub at the centre of Patong with both indoor and outside drinking and dining areas. Features live music nightly.

Safari Pub and Disco
28 Thanon Sirirat, Patong
Tel: 0-7634-1079
Outdoor safari-themed disco surrounded by trees, waterfalls and jungle vines. Several dance floors and doesn't shut until daylight.

Simon Cabaret
8 Thanon Sirirat, Patong
Tel: 0-7634-2114
www.phuket-simoncabaret.com

Draws in the crowds with sequinned *kathoey* or 'lady-boy' cabaret shows.

Krabi

Bobo's
Bobo Plaza, Hat Railay West
No phone
This quiet beach bar with candlelit tables is the only purpose-built bar on Railay West to watch the setting sun.

Irish Rover Bar and Grill
247/8 Moo 2, Ao Nang
Tel: 0-7563-7607
Irish-style pub with a convivial atmosphere, Guinness and sport on overhead TVs.

Ko Phi Phi

Reggae Bar
Ao Ton Sai
No phone
The island's biggest party venue plays dance music and has choreographed fights in a Thai boxing ring. The open-air upper is good for cooling off. One of many bars on this stretch.

Ko Lanta

Funky Fish
Ao Phra Ae
There are several bars on this beach, of which Funky Fish has a nice ambience and a waterfront setting.

SPORTS, TOURS AND ACTIVITIES

Activities and tours around the Andaman are largely sea based, with most of the diving and boat tours leaving from Phuket and Krabi for the surrounding islands. Most notable are the Similan and Surin Islands and the Phang Nga Archipelago. Krabi also has world-class rock climbing, including beginner lessons for novices and kids, and there are several golf courses for landlubbers.

Adventure Tours

Siam Safari
45 Thanon Chaofa, Chalong, Phuket
Tel: 0-7628-0116
www.siamsafari.com
One of Phuket's longest-running tour companies, offering a land-based tours incorporating jeep safaris, elephant trekking, canoeing and visits to villages and national parks.

Canoeing in Phang Nga Bay

Deep-sea Fishing

Aloha Tours
44/1 Thanon Visit, Chalong, Phuket
Tel: 0-7638-1215
www.thai-boat.com
The experienced crew takes boats out daily in search of the massive tuna, marlin and king mackerel that thrive in Phuket's waters.

Ao Nang Fishing and Snorkelling
31/4 Moo 2, Ao Nang, Krabi
Tel: 0-7569-5408
Arranges fishing day-trips aboard longtail boats off the coast of Krabi.

Diving

Blue Planet Divers
Ban Sala Dan, Ko Lanta
Tel: 0-7568-4165
www.blueplanetdivers.net
A PADI five-star centre with extensive courses and dive trips aboard a modern air-conditioned boat. Multilingual staff.

Dive Asia
24 Thanon Karon, Kata, Phuket
Tel: 0-7633-0598
www.diveasia.com
Offers numerous training programmes in
different languages as well as dive day trips
and all-inclusive live-aboards.

Divers Land
4/56 Moo 7, Khuk Kak, Khao Lak
Tel: 0-7642-3710
www.diversland.com
An integrated diving resort, with accommodation, restaurant, fitness and training
centres, as well as equipment sales and
service centres. Organises diving and snorkelling trips.

Island Divers
157 Moo 7, Ko Phi Phi
Tel: 0-7560-1082
www.islanddiverspp.com
Friendly and professional staff offer PADI
dive courses, day trips and live-aboard
diving, as well as snorkelling and kayaking
tours.

Scuba Cat Diving
94 Thanon Thawiwong, Patong, Phuket
Tel: 0-7629-3120
www.scubacat.com
This Canadian-owned, English-managed
centre is the most prominent on Patong due
to its central location and outdoor training
pool.

Sub Aqua Diver Centre
5/21 Moo 7, Khao Lak
Tel: 0-7642-0165
www.subaqua-divecenter.com
Professional and well-established multilingual dive outfit offering daily excursions to
the Similan Islands on board one of three
modern speedboats. Offers a range of PADI
courses.

Viking Divers
Moo 7, Ko Phi Phi
Tel: 08-1719-3375
www.vikingdiversthailand.com

Several companies offer PADI scuba courses

Provides training for all PADI courses, as
well as trips to local dive sites.

Go-karting
Patong Go Kart Speedway
118/5 Thanon Vichitsongkram
Tel: 0-7632-1949
www.gokartthailand.com
This 750m (2,460ft) racetrack has go-karts
capable of speeds up to 110kph (70 mph).
Open daily and floodlit to enable night rides.
Situated at the foot of Patong Hill in the
Kathu district, next to Jungle Bungee.

Golf
Blue Canyon Country Club
165 Moo 1, Thanon Thepkasattri, Phuket
Tel: 0-7632-8088
www.bluecanyonclub.com
Beautifully landscaped on a 290-hectare
(720-acre) green with two award-winning
18-hole courses. First golf course to ever
hold the Johnnie Walker Classic twice and
has played host to such greats as Nick Faldo
and Tiger Woods.

Laguna Phuket Golf Club
34 Moo 4, Thanon Srisoonthorn,
Bang Thao, Phuket
Tel: 0-7627-0991
www.lagunaphuket.com/golfclub
An 18-hole course that trails around scenic

Listings

lagoons, coconut groves and rolling fairways. Water features loom over 13 holes, making this one of Phuket's more challenging golf courses.

Pakasai Country Club
Ban Lik Nai, Nua Klong, Krabi
Tel: 0-7561-1984
www.pakasaicountryclub.com
This 9-hole course with lake views is currently Krabi's only golf facility.

Thai Muang Beach Golf and Marina
157/12 Moo 9, Thanon Limdul, Khao Lak
Tel: 0-7657-1533
An 18-hole course just a 30-minute drive from Khao Lak or Phuket. Has an interesting placement of bunkers and water hazards, but is most popular for its scenic beachside location.

Rock Climbing

Hot Rock Climbing School
Bobo Plaza, Hat Railay West
Tel: 0-7562-1771
www.railayadventure.com
Courses are from half- to three-day, with routes chosen to suit the climber's grade. The Kids and Family climbs have child-size equipment.

King Climbers
Hat Railay East
Tel: 0-7563-7125
www.railay.com
Reputable outfit with many years' experience, and run by authors of the well-regarded *Kings Climbers Route Guide Book*.

Sailing

Meroja
86 Thanon Patak, Kata, Phuket
Tel: 0-7633-0087
www.meroja.com
A well-equipped 26m (85ft) ketch for charter into the waters of the Andaman Sea. The boat, manned by a European skipper, a Thai chef and two deck hands, sleeps 11 people.

Kicking and punching in Patong

SY Stressbreaker
Phuket
Tel: 08-1894-3966
www.thailand-sail.com
Adventure sailing in the Mergui Archipelago aboard a choice of four boats that sleep up to 10. They can arrange diving, deep-sea fishing and kayaking and supply food and drinks on board.

Sea Canoeing

John Gray Sea Canoe
124 Soi 1 Thanon Yaowarat, Phuket Town
Tel: 0-7625-4505
www.johngray-seacanoe.com
The original and best sea canoe operation, run by the charismatic John Gray who organises trips around the region, including Krabi, the sea caves at Phang Nga and even as far as Ko Tarutao *(see Deep South, p.176)*.

Sea Canoe Thailand
367/4 Thanon Yaowarat, Phuket Town
Tel: 0-7621-2252
www.seacanoe.net
Runs expeditions around the Phuket coast, as well as to Phang Nga, Krabi and further afield.

Sea Kayak Krabi
40 Thanon Maharat, Krabi Town
Tel: 0-7563-0270
www.seakayak-krabi.com

Offers both half- and full-day guided canoeing excursions to Ao Thalane, Ao Luk and Ko Hong. Lunch is provided on the full-day tours.

Shooting
Phuket Shooting Range
82/2 Thanon Patak, Phuket
Tel: 0-7638-1667
www.phuket-shooting.com.
Indoor and outdoor ranges with choice of rifles, handguns and shotguns. Price depends on the calibre and quantity of ammunition purchased.

Thai Boxing
Muay Thai Stadium
Saphan Hin, Phuket Town
Tel: 0-7639-6591
Muay Thai Stadium hosts several Thai boxing matches every Friday night. Tickets can be purchased at the door or from any travel agency.

Patong Boxing Stadium
Soi Kebsap 2, Thanon Sai Nam Yen, Patong, Phuket
Tel: 0-7634-5578
Fights, including Thai and foreign boxers, are at 8pm every Monday, Thursday and Saturday.

Trekking
Mr Anong
Ko Chang
Mobile tel: 08-6152-5271
A one-man trekking outfit. Led by the knowledgeable Mr Anong, full-day treks cost B1,200 per person.

Trekkers of Ko Chang
Ko Chang
Tel: 0-3952-5029
Mobile tel: 08-1578-7513
Selling itself as an eco-friendly company, it has several full-day treks into Ko Chang's jungled interior, led by experienced guides.

FESTIVALS AND EVENTS

Two of Thailand's best-known annual events happen on Phuket towards the end of the year, as the seasonal monsoons ease off. The Phuket Vegetarian Festival sees a spectacular series of street parades that reflect the island's large Chinese population, and the King's Cup Regatta makes best use of the region's ideal sailing conditions.

October
Phuket Vegetarian Festival
A Chinese Taoist festival in which adherents abstain from meat and sex and perform religious rituals that involve walking on coals and driving sharp objects through their bodies.

December
Phuket King's Cup Regatta
Dec 5–11
Kata Beach, Phuket
www.kingscup.com
Thailand's best-known regatta is held in honour of the King's birthday. It attracts sailors from around the region and beyond.

Phuket Vegetarian Festival devotee

The Deep South

The large Chinese and Muslim communities in the south of Thailand lend a different cultural texture to the rest of the country. Historic Nakhon Si Thammarat was once capital of an ancient kingdom and the area also boasts some of the most idyllic and isolated beaches in the land, where diving, snorkelling and kayaking through caves provide countless days of pleasure.

The Deep South

 Population: Nakhon Si Thammarat 108,300, **Songkhla** 73,170, **Hat Yai** 157,600, **Satun** 21,498, **Trang** 61,300

 Local dialling codes: Nakhon Si Thammarat 75, **Hat Yai** 74, **Trang** 75

 Local tourist offices: Nakhon Si Thammarat Sanamnamueang, Thanon Ratchadamnoen; tel: 0-7534-6515; www.tourismthailand.org/nakhonsithammarat. **Hat Yai** 1/1 Soi 2 Thanon Niphatuthit 3; tel: 0-7423-1055; www.tourismthailand.org/hatyai. **Trang** 199/2 Thanon Wisetkul; tel: 0-7521-5867; www.tourismthailand.org/trang

 Main police station: Nakhon Si Thammarat Thanon Phaniad;
tel: 0-7535-6500. **Hat Yai** 1/1 Soi 2 Thanon Niphatuthit 3; tel: 0-7424-6733. **Trang** Thanon Ratchadamnoen; tel: 0-7521-8633. **Tourist Police** anywhere in Thailand call 1155

 Main post offices: Nakhon Si Thammarat Thanon Ratchadamnoen; **Hat Yai** Thanon Niphat Songkhro; **Trang** Thanon Phra Rama VI

 Hospitals: Nakhon Si Thammarat Maharat Nakhon Si Thammarat Hospital, Thanon Ratchadamnoen; tel: 0-7534-0250. **Hat Yai** Hat Yai Hospital, Thanon Rattakarn; tel: 0-7424-3016. **Trang** Watanapat Hospital; 247 Thanon Pattalung; tel: 0-7521-8018

Thailand's southernmost provinces are among the poorest in the country and have been plagued in the last decade by Muslim separatist violence. Consequently, comparatively few outsiders, either foreign or Thai, visit the area, and there is scant tourist infrastructure. But there are many interesting sites, and, of course, relative isolation is what numerous visitors crave.

At the time of writing, most governments warn against visiting the provinces of Narathiwat, Yala, Pattani and Songkhla, where incidents such as bomb attacks, shootings and even beheadings have occurred on an almost daily basis. Schools and prominent locations such as Hat Yai airport have been among the targets.

Nakhon Si Thammarat Province, north of Songkhla, along the Gulf of

Thailand, is technically speaking not part of the Deep South, and is spared the troubles. Trang and Satun are also considered safe to travel. All three have pristine desolate beaches and a genuine local Thai flavour.

Nakhon Si Thammarat

The mainly mountainous Nakhon Si Thammarat Province is home to an excellent national park and has some nice beaches to the north. The main town, Nakhon Si Thammarat, is known for excellent southern food, important Buddhist temples and the art of leather shadow puppets, called *nang thalung*.

Nakhon Si Thammarat Town

Nakhon Si Thammarat Town ❶ was the 2nd-century capital, Ligor, of the ancient Tambralinga kingdom,

Wat Phra Mahathat

and later a significant port and centre of the Sumatra-based Srivijaya empire, until at least the 10th century.

Today, it has one of Thailand's most important historical collections outside Bangkok, at the **National Museum** (Thanon Ratchadamnoen;

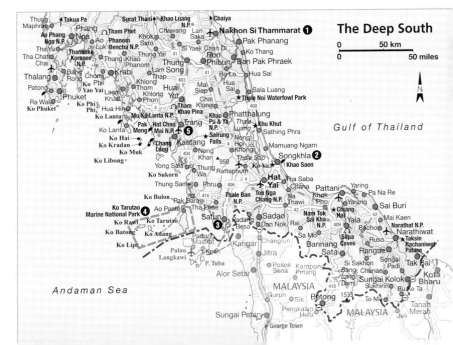

Nakhon Si Thammarat

 Airport: Thanon Ratchadamnoen; tel: 0-7531-2500; **www.airportthai. co.th**. Minivans from the airport cost B300 for the vehicle, not per person; distance 20km (13 miles); journey time is approximately 40 minutes

 Train station: Thanon Yommarat; tel: 0-7535-6364

 Bus station: Thanon Phaniant; tel: 0-7534-1125

 Songthaews: run from 6am–8pm on several routes; from B10
Motorcycle taxis: available on street corners; from B20–50 for trips around town

Hat Yai

 Airport: Thanon Sanambin Panij; tel: 0-7422-7130; **www.airportthai. co.th**. Songthaew run to the city from the airport; cost B10; distance 15km (9 miles); journey time 30 minutes

 Train station: Thanon Na Sathani; tel: 0-7426-1290

 Bus station: Thanon Sripoowanart

 Songthaews: run from 6am–8pm on several routes; cost from B8
Motorcycle taxis: available on street corners; cost from B20–40 for short trips around town

 Car hire: Avis; tel: 0-7422-7259; **www.avisthailand.com**. Budget; tel: 1 800 283 438 (toll free); **www.budget.co.th**

Trang

 Airport: Thanon Visetkul; tel: 0-7521-8224; **www.airportthai. co.th**. Tuk-tuks are available in the airport concourse. Bargain for a price (around B150). Journey into Trang Town takes around 15 minutes.

 Train station: Thanon Phraram 6, tel: 0-7521-8012

 Bus station: Thanon Huay Yod; tel: 0-7521-0455

 Tuk-tuks: can be hailed anywhere in Trang Town

tel: 0-7534-1075; Wed–Sun 9am–4pm; charge). A kilometre (²/₃ mile) southeast is **Suchart Subsin's Shadow Puppet Workshop** (10/18 Thanon Si Thammasok Soi 3; tel: 0-7534-6394; daily 8am–4pm; free). Subsin is Thailand's most famous maker and performer of *nang thalung* leather shadow puppets. He sells puppets, and for a small donation will stage a show (*see p.175*). To the southwest, **Wat Phra Mahathat** (Thanon Ratchadamnoen; daily 8am–4.30pm; charge) is one of Thailand's six royally sanctioned temples.

Songkhla

Currently, governments warn against travel to **Songkhla** ❷, due to the violence surrounding the Muslim separatist movement. If you do visit, the border city of Hat Yai offers great food and bargain shopping, and the southern pastime of bullfighting. The tiny provincial capital, Songkhla town, is a melting pot of southern Thai culture.

Songkhla Town

Songkhla's old enclave between Than-ons Nakhorn Nok and Nang Ngaam has Chinese restaurants, old coffee shops and Sino-Portuguese buildings, one of which houses the **Songkhla National Museum** (Thanon Watchi-anchom; tel: 0-7431-1728; Wed–Sun 9am–4pm; charge), with local archae-ological finds, artworks and furniture.

South of the museum, Songkhla's most famous temple, **Wat Matchi-mawat** (Thanon Saiburi; daily 8am–6pm; free), has 200-year-old paintings, and north is the hilltop temple com-pound of **Khao Tang Kuan** (Thanon Sukhum; daily 8am–7pm; charge). The quasi-European complex, accessi-ble by air-conditioned tram, has views over Songkhla Town and Ko Yo.

Around Songkhla

West of Songkhla, in the saltwater lagoon Thale Sap, Ko Yo is known for hand-loomed weaving called *phaa kaw yaw*, which sells at the market. In the north of the island, **Thaksin Folklore Museum** (tel: 0-7433-1184; daily 8.30am–5pm; charge) displays architecture and handicrafts.

Hat Yai

Southwest of Songkhla, Hat Yai's 'massage' parlours and nightclubs are a magnet for Malaysians and Singaporeans, and, on the first Satur-day of the month, bulls lock horns at **Noen Khum Thong Stadium** (Thanon Phetkasem; Sat 9am–4pm; charge), about 10km (6 miles) west of Hat Yai.

Satun

Remote and mountainous Satun Province shares a border with Malay-sia, and culturally is in many ways more Malay than Thai. Despite this, it has successfully avoided the conflicts

The Deep South

Traditional hand-painted fishing boat at Songkhla

★ PERFORMANCE ART

While touring the south keep your eyes open and you may be lucky to experience colourful performances of increasingly rare art forms that are unique to the region. The puppet theatre called *nang thalung* and the traditional dance form *Nora* are believed to have arrived in Thailand with Muslim traders around five centuries ago, but such was their impact that they influenced performance culture across the country.

The deep south is famous for two forms of traditional performance art, *nang thalung* shadow-puppet theatre and a dance theatre called *Nora*, which appears in slightly different forms throughout the region.

Nora mainly recounts the stories of the *Ramakien*, the Thai version of the Indian epic the *Ramayana*, but often with a contemporary theme added. The name is a derivative of Manohra, who was a *Kinnaree* (a half-woman, half-bird character) kidnapped in the *Ramakien*.

The dance employs graceful movements with the kind of intricate hand positions that are common to many dance styles throughout Southeast Asia. Performances are usually accompanied by improvised lyrics spoken by 'rappers', who frequently compete to determine the best in the locality. They might portray moral tales with sometimes spiritual or ritualistic overtones, but often have a comical dimension, too, played out through a masked lead male character called *pran*, or the

Shadow puppet performance at the Suchart Subsin Museum, Nakhon Si Thammarat

hunter. In one version the *pran* runs through the forest chasing a group of *Kinnaree* in a graceful routine akin to slapstick ballet.

Nora is the forerunner of *Likay*, a costumed dance form popular in the Central region incorporating melodrama, slapstick and comedy. Performers also indulge in rapping, often with bawdy lyrics. *Likay* had a surge in popularity after a Muslim troupe of *Nora* players gave a performance for King Rama V in 1880.

The puppet theatre of *nang thalung* is 500 years old in Thailand, but it is fast disappearing, as new generations more interested in modern pursuits decline to learn the skills. This form of puppetry has its origins in the Middle East and was originally brought to Southeast Asia by Muslim traders. Versions of it are still found in Malaysia and Indonesia. *Nang thalung* performances recount tales mainly from the *Ramakien*, with puppeteers using buffalo horn handles to manipulate figures made from *nang* (dried buffalo hide). They act out the scenes from behind a translucent screen between it and a light source. The movements are accompanied by singing or commentary and music.

Thailand's most famous exponent is Suchart Subsin, whose workshop in Nakhon Si Thammarat is open to the public *(see p.172)*. Otherwise performances are mainly seen as nighttime theatre at temple fairs or other festivals. Another regional form, known as *nang yai*, uses life-size puppets, but is even harder to find.

Colouring a translucent, intricately perforated *nang thalung* puppet

Nang thalung shadow-puppets are fashioned from buffalo hide and horn

Where Mermaids Come From

Dugongs are among the strangest ocean mammals: related to the elephant, and dubbed the 'sea cow', yet thought to be the origin of legends about seductive mermaids. They are found from Australia to East Africa, staying underwater for up to six minutes, grazing on grasses, before coming up for air. Dugongs are now legally protected, but their populations remain endangered, and hunters target them for meat, oil, skin, bones and teeth. Sighting one in Thailand's southern waters is to be transported to prehistoric times.

of its neighbours to the east, and is a safe area to travel. It has one of the country's best marine national parks.

Satun Town

Although set in a lovely green valley, the only real attraction in **Satun Town ❸** is **Satun National Museum** (Sathun Thani Soi 5; tel: 0-7572-3140; Wed–Sun 9am–4pm; charge), with its exhibits on Muslim lifestyles. The Sino-Portuguese building – the Kuden Mansion – was built for an unfulfilled visit by King Rama V. In 1902 it became the governor's mansion, and was the headquarters for Japanese forces in World War II.

Ko Tarutao Marine National Park

Sixty kilometres (40 miles) north is Pak Bara fishing village, where boats leave for **Ko Tarutao Marine National Park ❹** (mid-Nov–mid-May; charge), 30km (20 miles) into the Andaman Sea. The park has 51 islands and over 1,400 sq km (541 sq miles) of forests

and seas, with Thailand's best coral reefs, said to harbour 25 percent of the world's tropical fish species. Only three islands are inhabited, mainly by *chao lay* (sea gypsies). The wildlife includes whales, dolphins and dugongs.

The largest island, Ko Tarutao, has excellent hiking, cave exploring, and powdery white western sands, known as Ao Phante Malacca. Just behind are the park headquarters and views from the summit of Toe Boo Cliff. A two-hour walk south, sea turtles lay their eggs every January on Ao Sone beach.

Thai prisoners in the 1930s and 40s were sent into exile at Ao Taloh Wow, on the east coast, south of Ao Rusi, the 2002 location for the American reality TV show *Survivor*.

Ko Lipe and Ko Adang

About 50km (30 miles) west of **Ko Tarutao** is Adang-Rawi Archipelago, with good dive spots and the park's most popular island, Ko Lipe, home to sea gypsies. It has easy access to dive sites like Ko Rawi, Ko Yang and Ko Hin Sorn. Ao Pattaya, on the south coast, is Lipe's most popular beach, with a long sandy bay, clear waters and most accommodation. Sunset Beach, north of Hat Na Ko, where boats arrive from Pak Bara, is the most beautiful. It has a few small resorts and wonderful views of neighbouring islands.

Trang

Trang holds probably the greatest variety of attractions of the deep south provinces, with pretty beaches to the north, plus islands with ample accommodation, a wealth of outdoor activities and good food. To the south, the isolated beaches and islands have fascinating wildlife and the chance to observe rural island ways.

Trang Town

An overnight stay in the predominantly Chinese **Trang Town** ❺ is notable for good southern food, Chinese-style coffee shops, and seafood stalls that line the streets behind the Ko Teng Hotel. The nearby Thanon Ruenrom night market is one of Thailand's best.

Trang's Beaches

South of Hat Pak Meng, where boats depart for the islands, is the isolated **Hat Chang Lang**, with walkable sand banks and spectacular sunsets, bathing the islands and limestone crags in an orange glow. Inland from Hat Yao, further south, Tham Lod caves are best reached by kayak, drifting through a tiny gap. A 10-minute paddle in darkness leads to a lagoon

Buying dinner at a Trang Town food stall

The Deep South

circled by mangroves and limestone walls. At Ban Chao Mai, more boats leave for the islands.

Trang's Islands

16km (10 miles) southeast of Hat Pak Meng, coral surrounds **Ko Hai**, which has several low-key resorts and near-perfect swimming on its eastern side. At Ko Muk, 8km (5 miles) south, the finest beach is the west-coast Hat Farang, but the highlight is the partially submerged Tham Morakot (Emerald Cave), in the north. You can swim through it at low tide, the last few metres in complete darkness, to emerge at a hidden beach banked by limestone cliffs.

Ko Kradan, about 6km (4 miles) southwest, is touted as the most beautiful island, with white beaches and good reefs. Ramshackle accommodation means it is used mainly by day-trippers. Further southwest is **Ko Libong**, where Libong Nature Beach Resort offers snorkelling trips to see dugongs.

Singing Stars

The streets of many towns in the deep south are lined with elaborate wooden birdcages holding *merbok*, also known as zebra doves. These birds are famous for their singing voice, and regional competitions can attract over 1,000 entries, even from Indonesia, Singapore and Malaysia. Although prizes usually consist only of domestic appliances, there are fortunes to be made in breeding. Top performers are valued in excess of one million baht, and people pay B20,000 merely for the egg of a champion bird.

ACCOMMODATION

As the Deep South is one of the areas least visited by tourists, the accommodation options are not as varied as they are in the rest of the country, and in some cases are very uninspired. Nevertheless, the landscape is also gloriously undeveloped and the small-scale

rooms and bungalows are, for many, entirely appropriate. And there are a few choices that will suit travellers who need a little more comfort.

Nakhon Si Thammarat

Grand Park Hotel
1204/79 Thanon Phanakorn, Nakhon Si Thammarat
Tel: 0-7531-7666
The pickings are slim in this town so this is as good as it gets. A bit sterile but clean and comfortable and located just outside the heart of downtown Nakhon Si Thammarat. Rooms in the new building are slightly more expensive but are larger and more modern. **$**

Twin Lotus Hotel
97/8 Thanon Pattanakarn-Kukwang, Nakhon Si Thammarat
Tel: 0-7532-3777
www.twinlotushotel.net
Although it is located away from the town centre, many people head here for the smart and comfortable rooms and facilities such as sauna, jacuzzi and fitness centre. There's a restaurant and bar on-site and a supermarket opposite if you run short of supplies. **$$**

Songkhla

BP Samila Beach Hotel & Resort
8 Thanon Ratchadamnoen, Songkhla Town
Tel: 0-7444-0222
www.bphotelsgroup.com
This grand-looking hotel is located at the end of Hat Samila, near the mermaid statue. It offers clean, comfy rooms, the more expensive of which have views over the Gulf of Thailand. There's a pool, fitness centre, spa and restaurants. **$$$**

Novotel Hat Yai Centara
Thanon Sanehanusorn, Hat Yai
Tel: 0-7435-2222
www.novotel.com
Located in the heart of Hat Yai, above the Central Department Store, this imposing hotel, easily the best in town, has comfortable rooms plus the usual four-star facilities. **$$$**

New Season Hotel
106 Thanon Prachathipat, Hat Yai
Tel: 0-7435-2888
Relatively small but clean and well-designed budget hotel. Excellent location in downtown Hat Yai. Good value for money. **$**

Pavilion Songkhla Hotel
17 Thanon Platha, Songkhla Town
Tel: 0-7444-1850
www.pavilionhotels.com
One of the taller buildings in Songkhla, the Pavilion is one of only two higher-end hotels in the town. It has the amenities one would expect in a hotel of this category, as well as a snooker room and Thai massage. **$$$$**

Satun

Ko Tarutao National Park
Ao Phante Malacca and Ao Taloh Wow
Tel: 0-7478-3485
http://web2.dnp.go.th
Very basic lodgings are available from November to May. Book with the park authorities on the island or online. Electricity is available only from 6pm to 6am. **$**

Lee Pae Resort
Ao Pattaya, Ko Lipe
Tel: 0-7472-4336
Located in the middle of Pattaya beach, this operation is one of the biggest on the island and offers several comfy bungalows in a shady wooded area. **$**

Pinnacle Tarutao Hotel
43 Thanon Satun Thani, Satun Town
Tel: 0-7471-1607
www.pinnaclehotels.com
Satun's only 'up-market' hotel lies slightly outside the town centre, but is a comfortable place to stay, and a far better choice than lodging downtown. **$**

Trang
Anantara Si Kao Resort & Spa
198–9 Moo 5, Thanon Changlang, Sikao
Tel: 0-7520-5888
http://sikao.anantara.com
The only international-class hotel in the area, the Anantara took over from Amari (which ran this property for many years) and added its own distinctive gloss. Expect excellent design, superb food and facilities, and service that is good even by Thai standards. The programme of activities includes Thai cooking classes. **$$$$**

CoCo Cottage
Ko Hai
Tel: 0-7521-2375
www.coco-cottage.com
Balinese-style wooden bungalows with open-air bathrooms, just steps from the beach. Rooms with both air conditioning and fan are available. **$$$**

Koh Mook Charlie Beach Resort
Hat Farang, Ko Muk
Tel: 0-7520-3281
www.kohmook.com
This immensely popular resort, the largest on Hat Farang, has nice rooms at a range of prices, Internet access, film screenings, and a wonderful location among the cliffs and coconut trees. Good restaurant on-site. **$$**

Thumrin Thana Hotel
69/8 Thanon Trang Thana
Tel: 0-7521-1211
www.thumrin.co.th
Largely oriented towards business travellers, this is Trang's poshest hotel. It has a convenient downtown location and all the amenities one would expect from a hotel of this size. Internet bookings are a steal and can dip into the budget range. **$**

RESTAURANTS

The Deep South is filled with Thai-Chinese food shops that are terrific for local favourites, often involving seafood freshly caught from the area's abundant coastline. Trang is well known for old-world Chinese coffee shops, known as *raan kopi*.

Restaurant Price Categories
Prices are for a three-course meal without drinks **$** = below B300 **$$** = B300–800 **$$$** = B800–1,600 **$$$$** = over B1,600

Nakhon Si Thammarat
Krour Nakorn
Bovorn Bazaar, Thanon Ratchadamnoen
Tel: 0-7531-7197
This is a well-known restaurant where locals come to eat authentic southern Thai food in a clean and comfortable environment. **$**

Tempting treats at a road-side restaurant

Songkhla

Ginger
Novotel Centara Hat Yai, 3 Thanon Sanehanusorn
Tel: 0-7435-2222
www.centarahotelsresorts.com
For a splash out, head to this smart modern hotel restaurant with dishes such as *tom yum goong*, dim sum and sushi from a mixed menu of Thai, Chinese and Japanese. **$$$**

Hat Yai Night Market
Thanon Montri 1
Hat Yai's night market is a great place to sample local food, such as the Muslim-influenced *khao mok kai*, or rice cooked with chicken and spices. There are lots of sea-food dishes here. **$**

Raan Tae Hiang Iw
85 Thanon Nang Ngam, Songkhla Town
Tel: 0-7431-1505
The legendary Chinese-Thai eatery known to locals as 'Tae' has earned its reputation. Highly recommended are *yam mamuang*, a spicy sour mango and dried shrimp salad, and *tom yam haeng*, a dry version of the famous *tom yum* soup. **$**

Songkhla Night Market
Th. Wachira
Probably the largest night market in the region has Chinese, Thai and Muslim food all at very low prices. **$**

Satun

Ko Uan
43/6-7 Thanon Surat Thani
Tel: 0-7471-2103
This cheap and tasty Chinese diner is a good place to get out of the searing southern heat – it has air conditioning. The duck and chicken noodle dishes are popular picks. **$**

Time
43/1-2 Satun Thani Road
Tel: 0-7471-2286
Smart restaurant with air conditioning, located next to the Pinnacle hotel. There is a huge menu of Thai dishes to choose

Freshly caught lobsters on ice lure diners into a seafood restaurant

from, including curries, single-plate rice dishes and spicy salads. **$**

Trang

Acqua
Anantara Si Kao Resort & Spa, 198–9 Moo 5, Thanon Changlang, Sikao
Tel: 0-7520-5888
http://sikao.anantara.com
Impressive Italian with indoor and outdoor seating, the latter beside an on-site river. The kitchens make great use of the local freshly caught seafood. **$$$**

Raan Khao Tom Phui
Thanon Phraram IV, Trang Town
Tel: 0-7521-0127
This unpretentious restaurant, popular with locals and open only in the evenings, is an excellent place to fill up on spicy Chinese-Thai favourites such as *khanaa fai daeng* (Chinese kale fried with chillies and garlic), or *hoi lay phat phrik phao* (clams fried with chilli paste). **$**

Trang Thana
Thumrin Thana Hotel, 69/8 Thanon Trang Thana
Tel: 0-7521 1211
Basic hotel coffee shop with a good selection of Thai food, as well as some Western dishes. The breakfast and lunch buffets are good value. **$$**

TOURS

Most of the attractions for visitors to the Deep South involve the natural beauty of the beaches and islands. There are many good spots for snorkelling and diving amid the clear waters and coral reefs. There are also hidden underwater caves to explore. An easy way to find the best sites is to travel with a professional tour company.

Kayaking

PaddleAsia

Satun, Songkhla & Trang

Tel: 0-7624-1519

www.paddleasia.com

This Phuket-based company has kayak tours of Trang and Tarutao islands. It can be strenuous if you actually paddle between the islands, but it is great fun. The less fit can hop between islands on a motorboat and just kayak on-site. The company also organises birdwatching trips around Songkhla.

Explore the coast by sea kayak

FESTIVALS AND EVENTS

Communities in the Deep South celebrate national festivals like Songkran and Loy Krathong, and many villages organise fairs to raise money for the temples of the area. The two festivals of particular interest described below are local variations of national religious days or events.

February & May

Hae Pha Khun That

Wat Phra Mahathat, Nakhon Si Thammarat

Twice a year, on Makha Bucha Day (February) and Visakha Bucha Day (May). Buddhists make a procession to wrap the Phra Borom That Chedi in a sacred painted cloth.

Retreat. Buddha images from temples in the region parade along the streets, where there are also cultural performances, such as *nang thalung* shadow puppets.

Decorated altar at Wat Phra Mahathat

September/October

Boon Duan Sip

Nakhon Si Thammarat

Marked by a procession through the streets bearing food offerings to pacify and nourish the souls of the dead.

October/November

Chak Phra Pak Tai

Nakhon Si Thammarat and Songkhla

This festival hails monks leaving the temple at the end of the 3-month annual Rains

Chiang Mai and Around

Chiang Mai, the capital of the north, with its beautiful, historically important old city, is thought by many to be the cultural centre of Thailand. The mountainous surrounding countryside is rich with old towns and villages where traditional lifestyles remain largely unscathed, filled with lovely Lanna-style temples, markets and museums.

Chiang Mai

Population: 147,500

Local dialling code: 053

Local tourist office: 105/1 Thanon Chiang Mai-Lamphun; tel: 0-5324-8604; www.tourismthailand.org/chiangmai

Main police station: Thanon Fa Ham; tel: 1699. **Tourist Police** anywhere in Thailand call 1155

Main post office: Thanon Charoen Muang

Hospital: Chiang Mai Ram I Hospital, 9 Thanon Boonruang Rit; tel: 0-5326-2200

Local newspaper/listings magazine: *Citylife*; *Welcome to Chiang Mai and Chiang Rai*

Chiang Mai ❶, on the banks of the Ping River, has grown into a tourist magnet of luxury rooms, cheap guesthouses, European restaurants and tours to mountain hill tribes. Around the old city, streets have red-brick cobbles; the city walls have been restored and the moat populated by fish and turtles.

Historically, Chiang Mai was a major trading post along caravan routes from China to the seaports of Burma, when in the 13th century it emerged under King Mengrai as the capital of the kingdom of Lanna (Million Rice Fields). The mountainous terrain ensured sufficient isolation from the Central Plains to develop a separate culture, characterised by unique architecture and crafts like woodcarving, ceramics and lacquerware.

The ethnic mix extends to Northern Thai cuisine, with its enticing blend of Thai, Lao, Shan and Yunnanese elements, and Chiang Mai is famous for its cookery courses. More restrained facets of Northern culture are found in the ancient towns of Lamphun and Lampang, south of Chiang Mai.

The more temperate climate is also a change from the rest of Thailand.

Pack a sweater if you come between October and January or plan to go hill-tribe trekking in the mountains, where it is much cooler at night.

Chiang Mai City

The old city quadrangle, bounded by moats and brick city walls, is filled with historic temples, shops, hotels and guesthouses. Away from the main avenues and tourist districts, the narrow, winding lanes draw the visitor into an atmospheric world populated by cobblers and other trades people, noodle shops, and over 30 Lanna-style temples.

Wat Phra Singh

The Old City

Chiang Mai's oldest temple, the 13th-century **Wat Chiang Man** 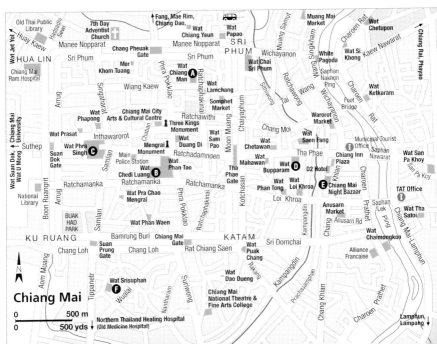(Thanon Ratchaphakinai; daily 9am–5pm; free), is in the northeastern quarter of the

old city. It contains two important ancient religious statues. The first, Phra Satang Man, is a 10cm (4ins)-tall crystal Buddha that King Mengrai brought from Lamphun, where it had reputedly been for 600 years. The statue is paraded through the city streets during the Songkran festival in April. The second image, a stone Phra

Chiang Mai

0   500 m
0   500 yds

Sila Buddha in bas-relief, is believed to have originated in 8th-century India. Both are said to bring rain and to protect the city from fire. A short walk southwest, the **Chiang Mai City**

Arts and Cultural Centre (Thanon Phra Pokklao; Tue–Sun 8.30am–5pm; charge) has interactive displays.

Further south, King Mengrai was reportedly killed by lightning near the 15th-century **Wat Chedi Luang** (Thanon Phra Pokklao; daily 8am–6pm; free). The large *chedi* in the central courtyard housed Thailand's most revered image, the Emerald Buddha, for 84 years from 1475. It is now in Bangkok's Wat Phra Kaew. A local legend says that when the gigantic gum tree in the temple grounds falls, so will Chiang Mai. The *lak muang*, or city pillar, believed to hold the spirit of the city, stands near its base.

To the west, **Wat Phra Singh** (Thanon Ratchadamnoen; daily 8am–6pm; free) is Chiang Mai's most important temple. Founded in 1345, it contains an elaborate wooden Buddhist library, raised on a high brick-and-stucco base decorated with bas-relief deities. The small but beautiful **Phra Viharn Lai Kham**, fronted by a wall with *lai kham* (gold leaf) flowers on red lacquer, has intricately carved wooden door frames that lead to an interior of Burmese-influenced murals.

Outside the City Walls

About 500m (1,640ft) travelling east from the Tha Phae Gate, **Wat Bupparam ⓓ** (Thanon Tha Phae; daily 8am–6pm; free) contains a Lanna-style ordination hall of carved teak, a larger, modern *viharn* and a Shan-style *chedi*. Deity sculptures surrounding the complex are guardians in animal form, such as the mythical *mom*, part-lizard and part-dog.

Half a kilometre further, to the right, is **Chiang Mai Night Bazaar ⓔ** (Thanon Chang Khlan; daily 5–11pm ⓜ), covering several blocks, with a good selection of stalls selling items from woodcarvings and inexpensive silk and cotton clothing to elaborate Thai or hill tribe-inspired home accessories.

Travelling south of the old city walls, **Wat Srisuphan ⓕ** (Thanon Wualai; daily 8am–6pm; free) was founded in the early 16th century by migrant silversmiths from Burma. There are still silver workshops along Thanon Wualai. A striking unique *ubosot* in the grounds is built of pure silver, tin, and silver mixed with aluminium. Wat Srisuphan is known for the Shan-style Poy Sang Long Festival, every March, when boys dressed in princely regalia don the saffron robes of monkhood in a group ordination.

Continuing southwest, the **Northern Thailand Healing Hospital**

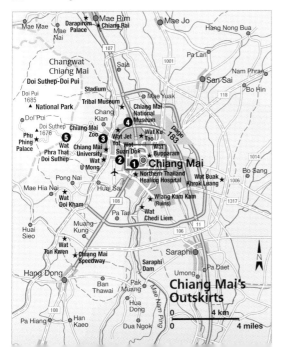

Paintings on offer at Chiang Mai's Night Bazaar.

⭐ ELEPHANTS

Elephants – the official symbol of Thailand, and for centuries so entwined in the fabric of life – are having a rough time as the country charges into the modern age. They remain a symbol of endurance and power, used to promote products from extra-strong lager to herbal cures for impotence, and are still greatly revered, in theory. In practice, their numbers decline rapidly in the wild, and in captivity they are widely abused.

Elephants are highly esteemed in Thailand owing to their historical importance as gigantic cavalry steeds-cum-battering rams in warfare, and as beasts of burden in forests and farms. Rare white elephants are regarded as sacred, as the Buddha's mother is said to have dreamt of one the night before his birth. It gave her a lotus flower, the symbol of purity and knowledge. Until 1917 the flag of Siam was a white elephant on a red background, designed by King Rama IV, and any white elephants found in the wild to this day immediately become the property of the king.

Historically, the gift of a white elephant from a monarch was a highly prized reward, but one that could be ruinously expensive to maintain. For this reason they are said to be the origin of the English term 'white elephant', for something less desirable than it originally seems.

Performing at the Elephant Conservation Centre on the outskirts of Lampang

One of the main traditional roles of elephants was logging, and when the government declared a ban in 1989, many elephants and their handlers (mahouts) became unemployed. Mahouts started coming to the cities, charging tourists to feed their elephants sugar cane. As the problem increased – some fell into manholes, others were hit by vehicles – the government enacted regulations to protect the animals, like the wearing of reflective stripes as they ambled down the roads. Elephants were eventually banned from cities altogether, but they are still a common sight, poking their trunks into bars and cafés.

Elephants being washed in the river near Chiang Mai

Elephant camps, some set up to care for the animals, buy the elephants and give the mahouts a job. This in turn brings its own problems. The revenue for these places comes from tourism, and tourism is big business. As elephant camps increase, so does the demand for elephants. Many bought now come from the wild.

The Wildlife Conservation Division estimates the number of wild elephants in Thailand has fallen to around 2,000, and hunting them is illegal. All domestic elephants must be registered and given an identity certificate, and most are implanted with a chip. But registration is not needed until an elephant is eight years old. Consequently, hunters capture younger elephants, train them, then claim they were born in captivity. Corruption is rife, and identity certificates are easy to get. Conservation groups want the registration age of elephants lowered to 30 days old.

Elephants

Exploring the northern hills on an elephant-back trek near Chiang Rai

(78/1 Soi Siwaka Komarat; www.
thaimassageschool.ac.th) is Thailand's
main centre for *nuat phaen bohraan*
(traditional northern Thai massage
therapy and herbal medicine). Many
foreigners enrol here for two-week
massage courses.

Around 1km (²/₃ mile) from the old
city western gate lies one of Chiang
Mai's most impressive temple complexes, **Wat Suan Dok ➋** (Thanon
Suthep; daily 8am–6pm; free), built in
1373 by the sixth Lanna king, Phyaa
Keu Na. At its northwest corner is
a whitewashed *chedi* with the ashes
of Chiang Mai's royal family, and a
larger central *chedi*, said to hold eight
Buddha relics.

Fierce architectural detail at Wat Suan Dok

Running from the northwest
corner of the old city, Thanon Huay
Kaew leads after 4 km (2½ miles) to
Chiang Mai Zoo and Arboretum ➌

Going Underground

About 3km (2 miles) west of the old
city, turning left from Thanon Suthep,
is the 15th-century **Wat U Mong** (Soi
Wat Umong; daily 8am–6pm; free),
located on a hill with honeycombs of
underground tunnels and meditation
cells. There is a large Lanna-style
chedi here and a lake surrounded
by rustic *guti* (monastic huts). Wat U
Mong had been all but abandoned,
but was revived in the 1960s by a
famous reformer monk, the late Than
Ajahn Buddhadasa. The restored site,
amid grand teak trees, is one of the
few truly quiet spots left in Chiang
Mai. Resident foreign monks give free
English-language talks on Buddhism on
Wednesdays and Sundays.

(Thanon Huay Kaew; www.chiang-
maizoo.com; daily 8am–5pm; charge;
additional fee for panda viewing 🄜),
which houses a wide range of mammals (including two giant pandas),
reptiles, over 5,000 birds representing
150 species, and a large aquarium,
plus local and imported flora.

Departing the old city from the
northern gate, Thanon Chang Puak
arrives at the Superhighway after
2km (1¼ miles), where, turning left,
Chiang Mai National Museum ➍
(Superhighway; www.thailandmu-
seum.com; Wed–Sun 9am–4pm;
charge) has a collection of almost
one million artefacts, and, continuing north, the **Tribal Museum** (Suan
Ratchamangkhala, Thanon Chotana;
www.tribalmuseumchiangmai.com;
Mon–Fri 9am–4pm; charge) displays
a fascinating hill-tribe jewellery, costumes, handicrafts, tools and musical
instruments.

Around Chiang Mai

The Chiang Mai surrounds have many day-trip pleasures. Northwest is the steep escarpment of Doi Suthep and Doi Pui; southwest stands Thailand's highest peak, Doi Inthanon; and north are the craggy mountain ranges around Doi Chiang Dao. And in the plains to the south two of north Thailand's most historic towns, tranquil Lamphun and Lampang, have Lanna-period temples.

Doi Suthep

Hairpin curves climb the 1,676m (5,497ft) Doi Suthep, 15km (9 miles) along Thanon Huay Kaew, northwest of Chiang Mai, to **Wat Phra That Doi Suthep ❺** (daily 8am–6pm; charge). A 290-step stairway (or cable car; charge) leads to the temple, where there are great views over Chiang Mai and a 24m (80ft) -high gilded *chedi*. A road from the parking area ascends first to **Phu Phing Palace** (gardens only: Sat–Sun and holidays 8.30am–4pm when the royal family is absent; charge), a royal winter residence with beautiful gardens, and then to the

commercialised Hmong hill-tribe village of Doi Pui, and its **Opium Museum** (daily 9am–5pm; charge) with multimedia displays and implements relating to the history, cultivation and trade of the opium poppy.

North of Chiang Mai

Travelling north on Route 107, branching left at Mae Rim leads to **Mae Sa Elephant Camp ❻** (119/9 Thanon Mae Rim-Samoeng; www.maesaelephantcamp.com; shows at 8am, 9.40am and 1.30pm daily; charge ), where visitors can watch elephants performing various feats. About 2km (1½ miles) further on, the **Queen Sirikit Botanic Gardens** (Thanon Mae Rim-Samoeng; daily 8am–5.30pm; charge ) were developed with the help of Britain's Kew Gardens.

Continuing north on Route 107, at the 56km marker is **Chiang Dao Elephant Training Centre ❼** (108/1 Moo 9, Thanon Intakhin; www.chiangdaoelephantcamp.com; daily 8am–5pm; charge ), where visitors watch elephants bathe, then take an elephant ride, and a river raft trip.

The cloister at Wat Phra That Doi Suthep is lined with Buddha statues

A few kilometres north, Route 107 passes a dirt road, left, to Thailand's third-highest peak, Chiang Dao, and the **Doi Chiang Dao Wildlife Sanctuary**, before entering Chiang Dao, where close by guides lead visitors into the caves of **Tham Chiang Dao** (daily 8am–5pm; charge), filled with Buddha statues.

East of Chiang Mai

About 4km (3 miles) east of Chiang Mai along route 1006, the 19th-century **Wat Buak Khrok Luang** (daily 8am–6pm; free) has well-preserved Shan and Lanna murals. It is a charming stop en route to **Bo Sang** ❽, known as the 'Umbrella Village'. Much of the community here crafts painted *saa* paper umbrellas, made from mulberry tree bark, but the shops also sell other crafts.

Located off Route 1317, a scenic country road parallel to Route 1006, is **Tham Muang On**, a sacred Buddhist cave in a limestone cliff, where Buddhist visitors worship a large stalactite. Not far from here is Crazy Horse Buttress, a set of steep cliffs with over 100 climbing routes.

South of Chiang Mai

Some 58km (34 miles) south on Route 108, the elegant **Wat Phra That Si Chom Thong** (daily 8am–6pm; charge) has beautiful bronze Buddhas, a gilded *chedi*, dated 1451, and a large **Meditation Centre** (tel: 0-5382-6869) that offers courses.

The town here is the gateway to **Doi Inthanon National Park** ❾ (daily 8am–6pm; charge), leading 47km (28 miles) to Thailand's highest peak, at 2,596m (8,516ft). Hmong and

Buddha statues inside Tham Chiang Dao caves

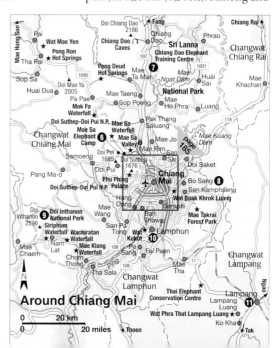

Around Chiang Mai

The elegant Wat Phra That Si Chom Thong displays a Shan/Burmese penchant for elaboration

Karen villages remain in the reserve. Park authorities allow three- to five-day treks up the mountain on foot or by pony by prior arrangement, with several campsites (B40) and bunga-lows (B800–1,000) providing simple accommodation (tel: 0-5328-6730).

Beyond, the town of Mae Chaem is famous for the distinctive weaving of the northern *pha sin* skirt. A few kilo-metres south is **Wat Pa Daet** (daily 8am–6pm; free), known for its rare post-Lanna murals.

Lamphun

Peaceful **Lamphun ⑩**, 25km (15 miles) south of Chiang Mai, was a centre of Mon culture until King Mengrai overran the city in 1281. Today, it has many attractions apart from its legendary 'most beautiful women in Thailand'. The historic temples are among the most famous in the country, and the delicious local fruit is known throughout the land.

In the town centre, mythical lions guard the riverside portals to **Wat Phra That Hariphunchai** (Thanon Inthayongyot; daily 8.30am–4pm; charge). Its buildings, dating to the 11th century, include an open-air pavilion with one of the world's largest bronze gongs, and a museum of old Buddhist art. Standing oppo-site, the **Hariphunchai National Museum** (Thanon Inthayongyot; Wed–Sun 9am–4pm; charge) has

Shopping for Crafts

On the route south of Chiang Mai there are three crafts communities that are good for shopping and watching artisans at work. About 15km (9 miles) on Route 108, **Hang Dong** is a centre for ceramics, antiques, wooden furniture and crafts made from woven bamboo, cane and rattan. Just east are **Ban Wan**, with a selection of antique and furniture shops, and then **Ban Thawai**, which deals in woodcarvings and made-to-order furniture.

artefacts from the Hariphunchai, Dvaravati and Lanna kingdoms.

A kilometre (²/₃ mile) west of the old town moat, **Wat Chama Thewi** (Thanon Chama Thewi; daily 8am–6pm; free) was originally an 8th- or 9th-century Dvaravati Mon site, rebuilt by the Hariphunchai Mon in 1218. Its stepped Chedi Kukut has five tiers, each with three niches containing Buddha statues. A pedal taxi is a satisfying way to travel there, passing orchards of lamyai, a fruit for which the region is famous.

Lampang

Lampang 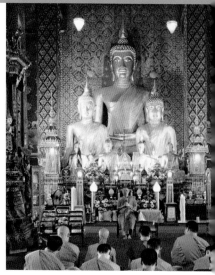 is best explored by horse and carriage, a common sight in this beautiful old town, 100km (62 miles) southeast of Chiang Mai. Three temples deserve special mention: Wat Phra Fang, with its golden *chedi*; the Burmese-influenced Wat Phra Kaew Don Tao; and Wat Phra That Lampang Luang, considered by many to be the most attractive in northern Thailand.

Thirty-seven kilometres (34 miles) before Lampang on the main road from Lamphun, the **Thai Elephant Conservation Centre** (Km 37, Highway 11; www.changthai.com; daily 8am–3.30pm; charge 🅼) promotes elephant welfare. Twice-daily shows include elephants playing music together on gigantic instruments and painting artworks. For an additional fee, visitors take elephant rides through the grounds.

On reaching Lampang, **Wat Phra Kaew Don Tao** (Thanon Phra Kaew; daily 8am–6pm; free) is a striking fusion of Burmese and Lanna architecture near the banks of the Wang

Chiang Mai and Around

Wat Phra That Haripunchai

River. On the ceiling of the mondop, inlaid enamel, mother-of-pearl and cut glass form a kaleidoscope of mythical animals.

Surrounded by rice fields 6km (4 miles) north, **Wat Chedi Sao** (Thanon Pratuma; daily 8am–6pm; free) has 20 chalk-white *chedi* in lovely grounds landscaped with casuarinas and bougainvillea. A 1,507kg (3,311lb) 15th-century solid gold Buddha sits in a glass-encased room built over a pond.

Southeast of town, 18km (11 miles) along the Asia 1 Highway, **Wat Phra That Lampang Luang** (daily 8am–6pm; free), a masterpiece of northern Thai temple architecture, is all that remains of a fortress city that flourished over 1,000 years ago. The open-sided Viharn Luang, built in 1476, is the oldest wooden building in Thailand. It displays a 16th-century bronze Buddha image.

ACCOMMODATION

Chiang Mai has an excellent range of accommodation, from cheap and cheerful guesthouses to extraordinary luxury. Most places will have at least a small café to eat in and at the top end multiple restaurants, bars and spas. The beautiful mountain countryside, meanwhile, is home to spectacular resorts just an hour away.

Accommodation Price Categories

Prices are for one night in a standard double room without breakfast and taxes

$ = below B1,000
$$ = B1,000–2,000
$$$ = B2,000–4,000
$$$$ = B4,000–8,000
$$$$$ = over B8,000

Chiang Mai City

Chiang Mai Plaza Hotel
92 Thanon Si Donchai
Tel: 0-5390-3161
www.cnxplaza.com
Five minutes' walk from the Chiang Mai Night Bazaar, this hotel has a relaxing ambience. Thai and Chinese restaurants, a lobby bar, large swimming pool and fitness centre. $$$

Galare Guest House
7/1 Soi 2, Thanon Charoen Prathet
Tel: 0-5381-8887
www.galare.com
A well-managed place that has spacious rooms around a garden courtyard. With en-suite air-conditioned rooms, cable TV and a riverside restaurant, the Galare is good value. Close to the Night Bazaar. $

Karinthip Village
50/2 Thanon Chang Moi Kao
Tel: 0-5323-5414
www.karinthipvillage.com
Located just outside the old city, Karinthip Village occupies a quiet landscaped corner opposite Wat Chomphu. The three guest wings contain rooms decorated in different themes: Chinese, Thai or colonial. Facilities include a Thai-Western restaurant, large pool and a spa. $$

Mandarin Oriental Dhara Dhevi
51/4 Thanon Chiang Mai-San Kamphaeng
Tel: 0-5388-8888
www.mandarinoriental.com
A stunning complex in extensive grounds with villas modelled on local Lanna architecture. In communal areas are replicas of famous buildings such as the ancient Palace of Mandalay, in Burma. Top-class restaurants include the French Farang Ses and Fujian Chinese. $$$$$

The Rachamankha
6 Thanon Rachamankha
Tel: 0-5390-4111
www.rachamankha.com
A lovely boutique property modelled on a Beijing Ming-dynasty noble house. The rooms resemble monks' cells. $$$$

Around Chiang Mai

Four Seasons Chiang Mai
Thanon Mae Rim-Samoeng Kao
Tel: 0-5329-8181
www.fourseasons.com
Capacious suites and 2- and 3-bedroom residences surrounded by rice terraces and gardens and a spa that is a masterpiece of contemporary Lanna architecture. Also has a highly regarded cookery school. $$$$$

The magnificent Mandarin Oriental

Listings

RESTAURANTS

Chiang Mai has a good selection of restaurants, including Thai, Chinese and Western. Further away from Chiang Mai the options will be mainly Thai, but still with many small shop houses and street stalls serving excellent examples of northern cuisine, which is the least spicy in the country.

Chiang Mai City

Baan Rai Yam Yen
Soi Wat Lanka 3, Thanon Fa Ham
Tel: 0-5324-7999
Long-running establishment with a cult following for its excellent Northern and Central Thai food. If you're feeling adventurous, try the steamed beehive *(rang pheung)*. Not easy to find but any *tuk-tuk* driver will know it. **$**

Huen Phen
112 Thanon Rachamankha
Tel: 0-5327-7103
This old wooden house decorated with local antiques is said to serve some of the best northern Thai dishes in Chiang Mai. Good picks are *laap khua* (spicy minced-pork salad) and *kaeng hang-leh* (savoury, Burmese-influenced curry). **$$**

The Gallery
25–29 Thanon Charoenrat
Tel: 0-5324-8601
Lovely riverbank restaurant in an old teak house that doubles as an art gallery. It has a

wide variety of northern Thai dishes, a selection of vegetarian specialities and a small wine list. **$$**

Giorgio Italian Restaurant
2/6 Thanon Prachasamphan
Tel: 0-5381 8236
A short walk from the Chiang Mai Night Bazaar, this is one of Chiang Mai's best Italian restaurants. Good for tasty home-made pasta in a formal but pleasing ambience. **$$$**

Around Chiang Mai

Chiang Dao Nest
144/4 Moo 5, Chiang Dao
Tel: 0-5345-6242
Daily-changing Western menu includes items like pork tenderloin in blue cheese sauce, thin-crust pizzas baked in a stone oven, and warm chocolate soufflés. **$$**

Huay Kaew Restaurant
Thanon Huay Kaew, Doi Suthep
No phone
The wood-and-bamboo pavilions overlooking Huay Kaew Falls are perfect for a sunset beer or toothsome Northern and Northeastern fare on the way back from Doi Suthep. **$–$$**

Khao Mao Khao Fang
Thanon Ratchapreuk, Hang Dong
Tel: 0-5383-8444
Heading south from Chiang Mai, on the right before the turn-off to Ban Thawai, this lovely Thai garden restaurant is a good place to relax after a shopping spree in the village. **$$**

Long Krathin market, Chiang Mai

Lamphun
Kuaytiaw Kai Jaw
Thanon Wangsai
No Phone
This corner spot offers a unique dish of rice noodles, steamed chicken sausage, carrots and seaweed. It is an energy-booster and a good way to begin a day among Lamphun's temples. **$**

Lamphang
The Riverside
328 Thanon Tipchang
Tel: 0-5422-7005
A collection of old teak houses, teetering on the Wang River bank, packs in locals and tourists alike for Thai, Western and vegetarian fare, with live music. **$$**

Dining at dusk at a riverside restaurant in Chiang Mai

NIGHTLIFE

While Chiang Mai could never be described as a nightlife paradise, there are a number of bars and pubs, including some atmospheric places beside the river that have nightly live music. There's also a blues place run by one of Thailand's best guitarists, a top venue for Thai country rock, and even a couple of joints for those who prefer their music spun by DJs.

Chiang Mai City
Chai Blues House
Thanon Suthep Soi 4
Tel: 0-5332-8296
www.chaiblueshouse.com
Opened in 2009 by Chai, one of Thailand's best blues guitar players, they have bands every night, including early-week jazz.

Club 54
179 Thanon Mahidol
Tel: 0-5326-7389
DJs at this new club, opened in 2010, intersperse hip-hop, house and techno with live bands.

Riverside Bar & Restaurant
9–11 Thanon Charoenrat
Tel: 0-5324-3239
Sprawling complex on the Ping River with two stages and three bands playing rock, funk and R&B.

Sudsanan
Thanon Huay Kaew
Tel: 08-5038-0764
This large wooden bar is one of Thailand's best venues for Thai country rock, called 'Songs for Life'. Also has blues and reggae.

Thailand's most popular beer

ENTERTAINMENT

One of the most popular activities for visitors to Chiang Mai is to take in a dance and drama dinner show, where local delicacies are enjoyed with various forms of traditional theatre. Art galleries, too, are increasingly common, with a mix of local and regional artists showing regularly.

Art Galleries

La Luna Gallery
190 Thanon Charoenrat
Tel: 0-5330-6678
www.lalunagallery.com
At this relatively new commercial gallery near the east bank of the Ping River, the collection includes paintings, sculptures, prints, photographs and designer works from all over Southeast Asia, as well as by artists living in Chiang Mai.

Cultural Shows

Old Chiang Mai Cultural Centre
185/3 Thanon Wualai
Tel: 0-5327-5097
www.oldchiangmai.com
Diners sit on the floor in traditional style for a *khantoke* dinner of various Northern dishes served on a bamboo tray. Hill-tribe and Lanna dances, backed by a classical Northern orchestra, accompany the meal. Nightly from 6.45–9.30pm.

SPORTS AND ACTIVITIES

Much of the physical activity in the areas around Chiang Mai involves donning a sturdy pair of shoes and heading to the hills for strenuous hill-tribe treks *(see Tours p.197)*. There are few spectator sports in the area, although Muay Thai is popular and there are also facilities available to learn a few moves.

Bicycle Hire

Cacti Bike
94/1 Thanon Singharat, Chiang Mai
Tel: 0-5321-2979
Chiang Mai is an easy place to cycle around, particularly within the old city walls. Cacti Bike has good-quality mountain bikes to rent that will suit more challenging trips around the countryside. Many guesthouses also rent bikes.

Rock Climbing

Chiang Mai Rock Climbing Adventures
55/3 Thanon Ratcha-phakhinai
Tel: 0-5320-7102
www.thailandclimbing.com
This outfit offers guided rock climbs, caving and bouldering instruction around Crazy Horse Buttress, the limestone cliffs in Mae On district east of Chiang Mai.

Cooking Schools

Chiang Mai Thai Cookery School
47/2 Thanon Moon Muang
Tel: 0-5320-6388
www.thaicookeryschool.com
This most famous of the many cooking schools around the city is run by TV chef Sompon Nabnian. Courses last one to five days, and include market tours and a recipe book to take away.

Thai Boxing

Lanna Muay Thai
161 Soi Chiang Khian
Tel: 0-5389-2102
www.lannamuaythai.com
Northern Thailand's best-known Thai kickboxing training camp offers instructions on a daily, weekly and monthly basis. They also have a training camp in the hills outside town.

TOURS

Chiang Mai is well set up for tours to the surrounding countryside, where you can go trekking into the mountains and stay overnight in hill-tribe villages. These facilities are widely available at guesthouses and hotels and on the street, and will include options such as elephant riding and rafting. Specialist companies organise ballooning, whitewater rafting and off-road biking *(see Adventures, p.36 for more details)*.

Cycling Tours
Click and Travel
158/40-41 Thanon Chiang Mai-Hod
Tel: 0-5328-1553
www.clickandtravelonline.com
Arranges cycling tours around Chiang Mai and northern Thailand lasting from half a day to two weeks. Trailer bikes, tandems and child seats are available for families.

River Cruises
Mae Ping River Cruises
Thanon Charoen Prathet
Tel: 0-5327-4822
www.maepingrivercruise.com
Located at a pier directly behind Wat Chai-mongkhon, the boat runs either 2-hour day cruises of the Ping River or dinner cruises from 7–9.15pm.

Trekking
Eagle House
16 Thanon Changmoi Gao, Soi 3
Tel: 0-5387-4126
www.eaglehouse.com
A reputable outfit owned by a Thai and Irish husband-and-wife team, Pon and Annette, who organise hill-tribe treks in north Thailand.

FESTIVALS AND EVENTS

In addition to the big national festivals like Songkran and Loy Krathong, Chiang Mai has a decent selection of its own cultural events that draw locals and visitors alike. Many of them are fairs dedicated to local crafts or a celebration of the natural beauty of the area.

January
Bo Sang Umbrella Festival
Bo Sang
The famous umbrella-making village of Bo Sang shows off it's wares annually with with demonstrations, cultural shows and competitions.

February
Flower Festival
Chiang Mai
This annual event features flower displays, floral floats and beauty contests. It coincides with the period when the province's flowers are in full bloom.

April
Chiang Mai Art & Culture Festival
Chiang Mai
Events around the city include music and dance, art shows, food stalls and workshops.

A floral float at the Chiang Mai flower festival

Northern Thailand

Some of Thailand's wildest regions lie in the far north, where the country meets Myanmar and Laos in the Golden Triangle. The ragtag ethnic markets in the frontier towns have an electric atmosphere, while the hinterland offers remote mountain and jungle treks. Later, wind down with ancient culture in the ruins of Sukhothai, Thailand's first capital.

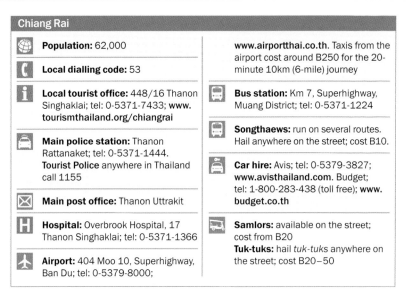

Chiang Rai

Population: 62,000

Local dialling code: 53

Local tourist office: 448/16 Thanon Singhaklai; tel: 0-5371-7433; www.tourismthailand.org/chiangrai

Main police station: Thanon Rattanaket; tel: 0-5371-1444. **Tourist Police** anywhere in Thailand call 1155

Main post office: Thanon Uttrakit

Hospital: Overbrook Hospital, 17 Thanon Singhaklai; tel: 0-5371-1366

Airport: 404 Moo 10, Superhighway, Ban Du; tel: 0-5379-8000;

www.airportthai.co.th. Taxis from the airport cost around B250 for the 20-minute 10km (6-mile) journey

Bus station: Km 7, Superhighway, Muang District; tel: 0-5371-1224

Songthaews: run on several routes. Hail anywhere on the street; cost B10.

Car hire: Avis; tel: 0-5379-3827; www.avisthailand.com. Budget; tel: 1-800-283-438 (toll free); www.budget.co.th

Samlors: available on the street; cost from B20
Tuk-tuks: hail *tuk-tuks* anywhere on the street; cost B20–50

Much of the far north is defined by its borders with Laos and Myanmar, where towns like Mae Sai and Mae Sot have an ethnic mix of Thai, Burmese, Lao, Shan and various hill-tribes, and there is an easy flow of people and trade. Sop Ruak is at the heart of the Golden Triangle and its notorious crop of opium poppy. Thailand's output has shrunk, but tension still breaks out occasionally as drug warlords across the border flex their muscles.

The small communities nestled in perfect mountain countryside, such as Nan, include some of the most untrammelled lands in Thailand, and are idyllic retreats for hill-tribe treks and rafting. In the lower north is Sukhothai, which was Thailand's original capital city in the 13th century. Together with the satellite towns of Si Satchanalai and Kham-paeng Phet, it has many impressive temple ruins, while Phitsanulok has

one of Thailand's most important
Buddha images – Wat Phra Si Rattana
Mahathat.

Chiang Rai and East
The far north's largest city, Chiang
Rai, is the gateway to many rewarding
sights, both historical and natural. To
the north, the once notorious 'Golden
Triangle', where Thailand, Laos and
Myanma evokes images of uncertain
frontiers and illicit smuggling, while
to the east, the provinces of Phrae and
Nan reveal a Thai culture that few
tourists ever encounter.

Chiang Mai to Chiang Rai
Visitors travel north from Chiang Mai
on one of two major roads, Route
118 *(see p.201)* or Route 107, via
Fang, 150km (94 miles) away. During

Tea plantation in Mae Salong

the 1950s, the district had a minor
oil rush, and 'nodding donkeys' still
groan in the fields.

Some 40km (25 miles) west, the
1,935m (6,348ft) **Doi Ang Khang**
has an agricultural station to research
temperate crops and a few accommodation options. The most luxurious
is **Angkhang Nature Resort** (www.
oamhotels.com/angkhang), an excellent base for excursions.

A few kilometres south of Fang,
Route 109 cuts east towards Chiang
Rai. Alternatively, north from Fang, a
rough road leads 25km (15 miles) to
Thaton, where you can rent a boat for
an exciting three-hour journey through
the Kok River rapids to Chiang Rai.

North of Thaton, the town of **Mae
Salong ❶** clings to the hillside near
the Myanmar border. Its houses are
decorated with red banners and gold
Chinese characters, and everyone
speaks Chinese. Many are descended
from Kuomintang soldiers, given
refuge in Thailand after China's
Communist takeover. Many became
involved in the opium trade, led by
infamous warlords like the Shan-
Chinese Khun Sa. Under Royal Project

Hill-tribe Akha man playing a wooden flute at
Ban Ruammit near Chiang Rai

Northern Thailand

Northern Thailand

0 — 50 km
0 — 50 miles

BURMA (MYANMAR)

LAOS

BURMA (MYANMAR)

Tachilek
Mae Sai ⑤
Sop Ruak
Chiang Saen ④
Chiang Khong
Houei Sai
Nam Hkok
Nam Ngam
Khong (Mekong)
Doi Sam Sao Noi
Doi Pha Hom Phok 2285
Tham Luang
Mae Salong
①
Chiang Chan
Wiang Kaen ▲803
Doi Luang Tam
Phaya Mengrai
Fang
Thaton
Hot Springs 107
Doi Ang Khang 1935
110
Mae Ai
Chiang Rai ③
Wiang Chai
109
Mae Suai
Mae Lana
Tham Lot ⑨
Doi Li Ki 1843
Soppong
Huay Nam Dang N.P.
Doi Wiang Pa 1695
Phan
Pa Daet
Chiang Kham
1739
Thung Chang
Huay Kon
Ton Tong Waterfall
Pang Tong Royal Palace
Tham Pla ⑩
Doi Kong Mu
Mae Hong Son ⑩
1995
Doi Mae Yen
⑧ Pai
Doi Chiang Dao 2186
Chiang Dao
Sri Lanna Elephant Training Camp N.P.
Wiang Pa Pao
Wat Kaew Falls
Wat Kalong
Mae Chai
Dok Kham Tai
Pong
Lao Ri
Chiang Klang
Pua
Doi Phu Kha N.P.
Doi Phu Kha 1985
Doi Mae Ya 2005
Mae Taeng
Mae Malai
San Sai
Doi Saket
Wang Nua
② **Phayao**
Tha Wang Pha
Nan ⑥
Doi Kang
Doi Luang 1250
Mae Rim
Doi Pui N.P.
Doi Suthep
Samoeng
Doi Inthanon 2596
Hang Dong
San Pa Tong
Chiang Mai
Doi Ang Tho 2031
Chae Hom
Muang Pan
Ngao
Chiang Muan
Pa Thum
Doi Phu Kha N.P.
Santi Suk
Wat Phra That Chae Haeng
1652
Doi Charim
Doi Long
1770
Lamphun
Khun Tan N.P.
Tham Pha Thai
Kiew Lom Dam
Ban Luang
Wi Ang
Sa
Doi Khun
Nam Tok Mae Surin N.P.
⑪
Khun Yuam
1818
Doi Inthanon
Mae Chaem
Khao Om Phai 1563
Chom Thong
Sang
The
Thai Elephant Conservation Centre
Hang Chat
Lampang
Mae Chang Dam
Song
Hom Chom
Na Noi
Rong Kwang
▲1728
Sao Din
Na Mun
Bah Khok
1061
page 190
Hot
Wang Luang
Doi Tao
Li
Lampang Luang
Mae Tha
Ko Kha
Mae Mo
Phrae ⑦
Long
Den Chai
Doi Phaya Fa 1465
Sak Yai N.P.
Fak Tha
Sirikit Dam
1061
Mae Sariang 108
Kong Loi
Ob Luang Gorge
Phra That
Soem Ngam
Sop Prap
Wang Chin
Tha Pla
Sung Men
Mae La Noi
Mae Tub Yai
Om Koi
Doi Thae Yi Chao 1764
Mae Ping Mae Hat Mae Kor N.P.
Doi Khun Mae Ap
Thoen
Doi Ta Chi
Thung Saliam
Si
1027
Lap Lae
102
Nam Pat
Khao Mun Ram 1564
Na Haew
Phu Kat 1468
Dan Sai
1820
Khao Khun Mae Tun 1081 ▲
1240
Sam Ngao
Doi Chom Phu ▲1285
101
Si Satchanalai ⑮
Si Satchanalai
Tron
Nakhon Thong
Phichai
Saen Khan
Chat Trakan
Nakhon Thai
Lom Sak
Tha Song Yang
Bhumibol Dam
Ban Tak
Ban Dan Lan Hoi
Si Samrong
Sukhothai
Phrom Phiram
Wang Tong
Yaong
203
Mae Ramat
Doi Luang 1182
Tak
12
Rama Khamhaeng N.P.
K. Luang 1185
Kong Krailat ⑭
Bang Rakam
Phitsanulok ⑯
Wang Kratum
Thung Salaeng N.P.
Khao Kho
1350
Khon Kaen
⑫ **Mae Sot**
Lan Sang N.P.
105
104
Phran Kratai
Lan Krabu
Khiri Mat
Bang Ngam
Sam Ngam
Wang Sai Phun
Noen Maprang
Phw
Kawkareik
Phop Phra
Wang Chao
Khao Son N.P. ⑰
Kamphaeng Phet
Sai Ngam
Phichit
Pho Prathap Chang
Taphan Hin
113
Chon Daen
Nong Phai
Pa Sak
Phetchabun
Wang Pong
Chaiyaphum
BURMA (MYANMAR)
Mudon
Wagaru
Thanbyuzayat
Khlong Lan N.P.
2152
Khun Kha Khaeng
Khato Mamuang 1432
⑬ Um Phang
Um Phang Wildlife Sanctuary
1960
Khao Mokochu
Khlong Lan
Khlong Klung Reservoir
Khanuworalak
Pho Thale
Thap Khlo
Wang Sai Phun
Wang Pong
Ban Mun Nak
Nong Bua
Khlong
Buri
Khlong Lan
Khwae Noi
Mae Wong Reservoir
Mae Wong N.P.
Lat Yao
Kao Liao
Chumsaeng
Tha Tako
Bung Sam Phan
Nai
Wichian Buri
Si Thep
Ye
Tavoy
Sangkhlaburi
Kanchanaburi
1811
Klong Pho Reservoir
Thap Salao Dam
Nam Chon Reservoir
Khao Yai 1554
Huai Kha Khaeng Wildlife Preservation Centre
1530
Huai Khot
Sawang Arom
Lan Sak
Uthai Thani
Manorom
Nong Chang
Ta Khli
Tak Fa
Chai Nat
Bangkok
Chai Badan
21
Nakhon Sawan
Bung Boraphet
Phaisali
225
Sawang Arom

incentives, the farmers converted to other crops, and many now tend tea plantations and brew rice wine.

Route 118 via Phayao

After 80km (50 miles) on Route 118, heading north from Chiang Mai, Route 120 turns right to **Phayao ❷**, where an ancient site may predate the Bronze Age. On the southern edge of Kwan Phayao Lake, **Wat Si Khom Kham** (daily 8am–6pm; free) has a 400-year-old 16m (55ft) Buddha image, Phra Chao Ton Luang. Modern Thai artist Angkarn Kalayanapongsa has cleverly reinterpreted traditional mural themes in a new *bot* (ordination hall) on the lake's edge.

Next door, the **Phayao Cultural Exhibition Hall** (Wed–Sun 9am–4pm; charge) has historic sandstone sculptures from pre-Lanna Phayao cultures, along with lacquerware, ceramics, textiles and other handicrafts.

Chiang Rai Town

From Phayao, Highway 1 continues for 100km (62 miles) to **Chiang Rai ❸**, capital of Thailand's northernmost province. King Mangrai founded the city in 1292, and is commemorated by a much-venerated statue in the northeast of the city on Thanon Uttrakit.

About 500m (yds) southwest is the **Hill Tribe Museum and Education Centre** (www.pda.or.th/chiangrai; Mon–Fri 9am–6pm, Sat–Sun 10am–6pm; charge) on Thanon Tanalai. It provides a useful overview of hill-tribe community life and sells ethnic handicrafts at its gift shop. All proceeds go towards supporting hill-tribe community projects.

The Golden Triangle: Thailand (foreground), Myanmar (middle), Laos (across the river)

Two kilometres (1¼ miles) west of here, on Thanon Trairat, **Wat Phra Kaew** (daily 8am–6pm; free) once contained the Emerald Buddha, Thailand's holiest image, now housed in Wat Phra Kaew in Bangkok (*see p.67*). Local chronicles say the *chedi* was struck by lightning in 1434, revealing the jadeite Buddha image. A close copy, the Phra Yok Chiang Rai (Chiang Rai Jade Buddha), remains on the temple grounds.

The Golden Triangle

Some 60km (37 miles) northeast of Chiang Rai, off Route 110, the ancient city of **Chiang Saen ❹** sits near the point where Myanmar, Laos and Thailand meet, called the Golden Triangle, and known for its opium production. The trade continues in Laos and especially Myanmar, but Thailand's output has dropped greatly in the last three decades.

Crossing to Laos

A longtail boat trip is possible from Chiang Saen down the Mekong to Chiang Khong, where ferries cross to Houei Sai, a Lao town where visas are available on arrival. Chiang Khong is known for the giant Mekong catfish, the world's largest freshwater fish, at up to 3m (10ft) and 300kg (660lbs). The fish is on the brink of extinction and anglers are only permitted to catch it during two weeks of May each year.

Scholars believe Chiang Saen was founded at the end of the 13th century, and today it is a thriving river port for goods from China. Passengers with a visa, obtainable in Chiang Mai or Bangkok, can travel to the Chinese town of Jinghong.

Just west of town, the ruins of **Wat Pa Sak** (daily 8am–6pm; charge) contain Srivijaya, Dvaravati and Sukhothai influences. On a hill 1km (^{2}/3 mile) north, **Wat Phra That Chom Kitti** (daily 8am–6pm; free) has a good view of Chiang Saen. Inside the western old city gate, on Thanon Pahonyothin, **Chiang Saen National Museum** (www.thailand-museum.com; Wed–Sun 9am–4pm; charge) has prehistoric and hill-tribe artefacts, along with Lanna-period Buddha images and northern Thai ceramics. Immediately east are the ruins of **Wat Chedi Luang**.

Around 9km (6 miles) north of Chiang Saen, **Sop Ruak** enjoys a boom of resorts and souvenir shops based on its position as the 'Heart of the Golden Triangle.' Boat trips are possible from here to Chiang Saen, Chiang Khong (*see box, above*) and along the Mekong. In the southwest of town a small, well-designed museum, **The Hall of Opium** (tel: 0-5378-4444; Tue–Sun 10am–3.30pm; charge),

Monuments beside the Mekong in Sop Ruak

records local life surrounding cultivation of the *Papaver somniferum* poppy.

Some 35km (22 miles) northeast, the road reaches Thailand's most northerly town, **Mae Sai** ❺, on the border with Tachilek, which is clearly visible in Myanmar across the small Sai River. At shops and stalls in Mae Sai, Burmese, Thai, Shan and hill-tribe traders sell gems, lacquerware, antiques, imported whisky, cigarettes and medicinal herbs.

To the west of the main street, a flight of steps ascends to Wat Phra That Doi Wao, constructed in memory of Burmese soldiers who died fighting the Kuomintang army, who opposed Mao Zedong's Communists for control of southern China.

The grounds have views over Mae Sai and Myanmar. Visitors can cross for the day to **Tachilek**, though there is not much to see.

About 6km (4 miles) south of Mae Sai, the cave of **Tham Luang** (daily 8am–5pm; charge) burrows several kilometres into the hills. Gas lanterns can be hired at the entrance.

Nan Province

A drive of 300km (180 miles) south-east of Chiang Rai on Route 1, the town of **Nan** ❻ is the capital of the province of the same name. It may be Thailand's last great undiscovered tourist territory. Beyond the modern concrete, the old wooden houses are built in three distinct styles, which are detailed at the **Nan National Museum** (www.thailandmuseum. com; Mon–Sat 9am–4pm; charge;) on Thanon Pha Kong. There is also information on hill tribes, crafts and the history of the region.

Across the street, **Wat Phra That Chang Kham** (daily 8am–6pm; free) has some 15th-century Suk-hothai styling, while next door the even older **Wat Hua Khuang** (daily 8am–6pm; free) has a northern Lao wooden veranda. The two are good examples of Nan's differing influences over 600 years.

A short walk south, **Wat Phumin** (daily 8am–6pm; free), constructed in 1596, has a *bot* with a rare cruciform layout and some famous 19th-century murals. They depict the usual episodes from the Buddha's life, but also rowing boats with bearded Western

203

⭐ BUDDHISM

The image of Thailand is often wrapped in pictures of Buddhist monks in saffron robes, and Buddhism plays an important role in the daily life and philosophy of the people. King Ramkamhaeng declared Buddhism to be the official religion during the ascendancy of Sukhothai in the 13th century, and nearly 95 percent of people in the country are now devotees.

Most Thais adhere to Theravada Buddhism, which is a mixture of Buddhist, Hindu and animist beliefs. It is the oldest of all branches of Buddhist faith, tracing its origins to the teachings of Siddhartha Gautama in the 6th century BC. Gautama was an Indian prince who gave up his royal privileges to follow an ascetic life.

Adherents believe he lived 500 lives, before he reached Enlightenment, or Nirvana, and became the Buddha. The belief is that followers will also be repeatedly reincarnated (an idea adopted from Hinduism) and finally, if they live a good cycle of lives, will also reach Nirvana.

To do this, Gautama advocated living life the 'Middle Way', along an Eightfold Path. The central doctrines are based on *dukkha* (stress, misery), *anicca* (impermanence) and *anatta* (the absence of self). The Buddha taught that it is craving for self-worth and possessions that creates misery. But, as everything is impermanent, nothing

Seated images of Buddha at Wat Suthat in Bangkok

can be possessed, and the exercise is futile. Therefore, if we suppress desire and practise detachment we will cease to be unhappy.

For Buddhists, living a good cycle of lives requires rightful and mindful actions and thoughts. In practice this is aided by *tham boon* (making merit). Tradition requires that every Buddhist male enter the monkhood for a brief period before marriage. This is a way of making merit both for himself and his parents. Employers customarily grant paid leave to do this. Unlike other Buddhist countries, women cannot be ordained in Thailand.

Working monks, in Trang Province

Other ways of making merit include donating food to monks, or money to a worthy cause. People can also release birds or fish into the wild, which market stalls sell for the purpose.

Buddhism is a philosophy rather than a religion, and the Buddha image and the Buddha himself are inspiration for right thought and deed rather than objects to be worshipped. Yet, for many people the images are very powerful and amulet markets thrive, selling Buddha idols and other items blessed by monks. Some monks have cult followings, and totems associated with a particular monk or temple can be very lucrative. New houses and businesses or those having undergone misfortune will be blessed by monks for good luck, and many have photos of famous monks alongside Buddha images.

While they are idealised views, the postcards are not far wrong: in day-to-day life Buddhism defines Thailand and its people to a significant degree.

A Buddhist monk visiting Ayutthaya's Wat Phanan Choeng

Detail from one of the beautifully rendered 19th-century murals at Wat Phumin

About 60km (37 miles) south of Nan, the strange **Sao Din** earth pillars have been carved by the wind to form desolate canyons. The easiest way to get there is to rent a motorbike.

Southwest to Phrae

Travelling southwest from Nan, at 135km (82 miles) Route 101 arrives in the old walled city of **Phrae** ❼, a sleepy provincial capital full of old teak mansions and historic temples. Founded in the 15th century, it was later an important centre of the teak trade in the 19th and early 20th centuries.

Perched on a low hill 9km (5 miles) southeast of town off Route 1022 is Phrae's best-known temple, **Wat Phra That Cho Hae**, with its 33m (108ft) gilded *chedi* at its centre. It is an important pilgrimage site. Just outside the old city, to the northeast on Thanon Ban Mai, the towering wooden roofs of 19th-century **Wat Chom Sawan** demonstrate Burmese Shan influence, a legacy of the once-thriving teak merchants, most of whom hailed from Burma.

The best surviving example of local teak architecture is **Vongburi House** (daily 8am–5pm; charge), inside the city wall on Thanon Phra Non Tai. The two-storey mansion, completed in 1907, originally housed Phrae's last monarch, Luang Phongphibun. It is now a museum filled with his antique furniture and personal effects.

The Northwest

Tucked beside the Thailand-Myanmar border, Mae Hong Son is one of Thailand's least populous provinces,

men in naval caps smoking pipe, and heavily dressed European women.

On a hill across the Nan River, about 3km (2 miles) southeast of town, **Wat Phra That Chae Haeng** (daily 8am–6pm; free) has a 55m (180ft) classic Lanna gilded *chedi* and a lengthy plaster *naga* serpent snaking down the hill. Interestingly, the *bot* has a sweeping five-layered wooden roof, low ceilings and a *naga* carved in stucco over the entrance – all influences of the minority Thai Lü, who settled in the Nan Valley about 150 years ago.

Hill treks are available from Nan, or on the 80km (50-mile) journey northeast to **Doi Phu Kha National Park** (www.dnp.go.th; daily 8am–6pm; charge), where rangers can direct you to scenic spots like the 1,300m (4,300ft) mountain Don Khao and Ton Tong Waterfall.

where a sense of separateness is compounded by shared cultures and economy, both legal and illegal, with neighbouring Myanmar. For visitors, there are many off-the-beaten-track experiences exploring the mountains, rivers and forests.

To Mae Hong Son

A favourite stop for many travellers going west on Route 1095, known as the Mae Hong Son Loop, is the picturesque town of **Pai ❽**, on an elevated plateau about four hours' drive from Chiang Mai. Although still a firm favourite on the backpacking trail, it now has resorts and restaurants that appeal to a wider clientele within its colourful selection of cafés, bars, and galleries. The population is a blend of Shan, northern Thai, Chinese Muslim, Lisu and Western expats.

Nearby attractions include the mountain-top **Wat Mae Yen**, painted

by local Thai artists, and **Tha Pai Hotsprings** (daily 7am–6pm; charge), which are perfect for soaking year-round. Rafting trips on the Pai River are popular *(see Listings, p.220)*.

Around 40km (25 miles) northwest on Route 1095, the Shan market town of **Soppong** (also known as Pang-mapha) is a jump-off point for visits

Northern Thailand

Motor biking in Mae Hong Son Town with Wat Chong Klang in the background

to **Tham Lot** ❾ (daily 8am–5.30pm; charge), some 8km (5 miles) away. This is the most famous limestone cavern complex in northern Thailand and one of the longest in Southeast Asia. The caves contain ancient teak coffins suspended on wooden scaffolds, suggesting it had been a prehistoric burial site. Guides carrying gas lanterns are mandatory, and included in the entry fee. When the water is high, visitors travel by bamboo raft on a stream that runs through the caves.

A winding 70km (44-mile) drive southwest leads to **Mae Hong Son** ❿, capital of a province that is 75 percent forests and mountains, and central to border smuggling routes. The combined population of Karen, Hmong, Lawa, Shan, Lisu and Lahu tribespeople outnumbers ethnic Thai.

In the south of town, two Burmese-Shan temples, **Wat Chong Klang** (daily 8am–6pm; free) and **Wat**

Chong Kham (daily 8am–6pm; free), are reflected in Nong Chong Kham Lake. The latter is famous for its painted glass panels and carved wooden figures that illustrate episodes from the Buddhist Jataka tales.

Tour agencies, hotels and guesthouses in Mae Hong Son all arrange two- to seven-day treks to mountain valleys, caves and hill-tribe villages in the vicinity, including the 'longneck villages' *(see Box, p.207)*.

Towards Mae Sot

South of Mae Hong Son, Route 108 runs along the border through breathtaking mountain scenery, and after 80km (50 miles) passes the village of **Khun Yuam** ⓫, which has one of the most charming Shan Buddhist monasteries in the province. Inside **Wat To Pae** (daily 8am–5pm; free), hidden behind curtains is a 150-year-old antique Burmese *kalaga*

Young Lisu girls in Mae Hong Son Province

Burmese style pagoda, Mae Sot

(embroidered tapestry). A modest **World War II Museum** (daily 8am–4pm; charge), also in Khun Yuam, contains artefacts left by Japanese troops retreating from Burma along the Skeleton Road (named for the many who died en route).

Around 90km (56 miles) further on, Route 108 reaches **Mae Sariang** on the banks of its namesake river and hemmed in by high mountains that contain a number of Shan, Karen and Hmong villages. In town, **Wat Uthayarom** (also called Wat Jong Sung) is worth a brief stop for its Shan-style tin-trimmed teak architecture and 19th-century *chedi*. Mae Sariang has pleasant riverside guesthouses and a few shops selling Karen handicrafts.

Mae Sot

Another 226km (136 miles) south, the road reaches **Mae Sot** ⑫, a boisterous border junction, whose diverse ethnic groups mostly have family ties and/or business links in Myanmar, across the Moei River. In a confusion of bicycles and excited shoppers, businesses in the narrow streets bear signs in Thai, Chinese, Burmese and English.

Along with a vigorous smuggling trade (especially in Burmese teak, since a 1989 Thai ban on logging), refugee camps on the outskirts of town provide much of Mae Sot's livelihood and contribute to its 'not-quite-Thailand' ambience. The town is also the centre of the region's gem trade, specialising in precious and semiprecious stones from Myanmar, particularly jade and rubies.

On the 5km (3-mile) drive from Mae Sot to the border crossing, **Wat Wattanaram** (daily 8am–6pm; free) is an ornate Burmese-style temple with tiers of red-tiled rectangular roofs forming a tower fringed with intricate silverwork. Inside, one of its four Buddha images has heavy gold jewellery distending its earlobes.

The Thai-Myanmar Friendship Bridge spans the Moei River to **Myawadi**, a typical Burmese town of dusty streets and glittering pagodas. A riverbank casino here entertains Thai gamblers at weekends. Visitors can tour Myawadi on a day pass (charge) from 8am to 5pm.

Um Phang

Continuing south, the steep and winding Route 1090 meanders through the mountains. It passes two scenic falls, **Pha Charoen** and **Thararak**, after 26km (15 miles) and 41km (24 miles) respectively, before

Sukhothai

 Population: 36,000

 Local dialling code: 55

 Local tourist office: 130, Thanon Jarot Wittithong; tel: 0-5561-6228; www.tourismthailand.org/sukhothai

 Main police station: Thanon Singhawat; tel: 0-7424-6733. **Tourist Police** anywhere in Thailand call 1155

 Main post office: Thanon Nikhon Kasem

 Hospital: Sukhothai Hospital, 2/1 Thanon Jarot Wittithong; tel: 0-5561-0280

 Airport: Km27, Route 1195; tel: 0-5561-2448; www.airportthai.co.th. Taxis from the airport cost around B250 for the 10km (6-mile) journey into the city which takes around 20 minutes.

 Bus station: Thanon Prawet Nakhon; tel: 0-5561-3296

 Songthaews: Hail these communal vans anywhere on the street; cost B10 around the new city. Regular songthaew trips from New Sukhothai to Sukhothai Historical Park run from 6.30am–6pm; cost B20 for the 30-minute journey.

 Samlors: Available on the street; cost from B20

reaching the sleepy town of **Um Phang** ⓭, in a remote rural district 150km (90 miles) from Mae Sot.

Um Phang is a centre for elephant

View of the Um Phang valley

treks and whitewater rafting. One of the most popular trips follows the Klong River to the lofty 400m (1,312ft) **Thilawsu**, the largest waterfalls in Thailand. The falls are found in **Um Phang Wildlife Sanctuary**, a Unesco World Heritage Site that forms part of Thailand's largest wildlife corridor, along with the adjacent Thung Yai Naresuan Reserve, Huay Kha Kaeng Reserve, Khlong Lan National Park and Mae Wong National Park. The sanctuary is part of one of the most pristine natural forest zones in Southeast Asia.

Following a trail along the Myanmar border, it is possible to hike all the way from Um Phang to **Sangkhlaburi** *(see p.94)* in Kanchanaburi Province. Experienced guides for the seven-day trekking expedition can be hired through any Um Phang guesthouse.

Tin- and thatched-roof dwellings at a Sangkhlaburi Mon settlement

Lower North

The lower north is notable for Sukhothai, which was the centre of the first independent Thai kingdom, considered to be the golden era of Thai history. Its magnificent temples and palaces vie for attention with the nearby monuments at the ancient satellite towns of Si Satchanalai, Phitsanulok and Kamphaeng Phet.

Sukhothai

About 150km (90 miles) east of Mae Sot, off Route 105, the ancient city of **Sukhothai** ⓮ is widely regarded as Thailand's first capital city. It was the centre of the Sukhothai kingdom, founded in 1238 following King Intharathit's assertion of independence from the Khmer empire. At one time Sukhothai included most of modern Thailand and parts of the

Malay Peninsula and Burma, and is synonymous with some of the finest artistic endeavours in the history of Thailand, including the most exquisite Buddha images.

The most notable of the Sukhothai

Loi Krathong

Many say the best time to visit Sukhothai is mid-November, when Thailand's most beautiful festival, Loi Krathong, is celebrated. It is believed to have started here some 700 years ago, after one of the king's concubines fashioned a lantern from carved fruit and sent it floating down the river, bearing a lighted candle. Now, thousands of people gather by bodies of water all over the country to launch their own candles. But Sukhothai is the festival's spiritual home.

Surrounded by a moat, Wat Mahathat is located within the walls of the Old City

kings was Ramkhamhaeng, who established the Thai script, promoted Theravada Buddhism and established links with China.

The ruins of old Sukhothai lie 13km (8 miles) west of the new town, inside **Sukhothai Historical Park** (daily 6am–6pm; charge). It can be reached easily by songthaew from the new town, although there is a good choice of accommodation near the park. Within the walls of the Old City are the magnificent remains of 21 temples and monuments. The ruins are divided into five zones – north, south, east, west and central – with the most importatant sites found within the Old City walls of the central zone.

The **Ramkhamhaeng National Museum** (www.thailandmuseum. com; daily 9am–4pm; charge), near the gate of the park, is a good start for a tour. It has a fine collection of sculpture, ceramics and other artefacts, plus exhibits from other periods.

The entrance hall is dominated by an impressive bronze walking Buddha, a style that was developed in ancient Sukhothai. The mezzanine has a copy of a famous stone inscription attributed to King Ramkhamhaeng, of which the original is the single most prized exhibit of the National Museum in Bangkok (see p.72).

The historical park itself is divided into five zones covering 100 restored sites; some of the highlights are listed below. Entrance to each zone is B100, or B350 for all five. For an extra charge you can drive a car around, hire bicycles or take an official bus tour.

Central Zone

The central zone is the most impressive, and most people head here first, then gauge their stamina in regard to the rest. The largest and most important temple is **Wat Mahathat**, which is surrounded by a moat, and was the spiritual centre of the kingdom. The original design was typical Khmer, but Ramkhamhaeng's son King Lo Thai had it remodelled around 1345. There are several monumental Buddha images around the site.

Familiar architectural themes are repeated among the 20 other shrines within the walls of the central zone. **Wat Si Sawai**, southwest of Wat Mahathat, was originally a Hindu shrine. Triple towers built in

The huge seated Buddha at Wat Si Chum

a modified Khmer style remain. Just north of Wat Mahathat, **Wat Chana Songkhram** and **Wat Trakuan** both have attractive Sri Lankan-style *chedi*, and further north, beyond the highway, **Wat Sa Si** has a Sri Lankan-style *chedi* and a *bot* (ordination hall) on an island.

Other Zones

About 1km (²/₃ mile) beyond the Royal Shrine gate is **Wat Phra Phai Luang**, in the North Zone. It was probably built in the late 12th century when Sukhothai was still part of the Khmer empire, and might have been the original city centre, as Wat Mahathat came later. A fragmented seated stone Buddha image, dating to 1191, was found here, and is now at the Ramkhamhaeng Museum. Beyond Wat Phra Phai Luang to the west, **Wat Si Chum** has one of the largest seated Buddha images in Thailand.

Wat Chetupon is one of the most interesting sites in the South Zone, for its several walls, bridges and gates made of slate mined nearby. The walking Buddha here is said to be one of the finest of its kind.

In the West Zone, **Wat Saphan Hin** was mentioned in the Ramkhamhaeng inscription, for its '18-cubit image of the standing Buddha'. The image stands on the crest of a low hill, and can be seen from a distance.

Si Satchanalai

About 50km (31 miles) north of Sukhothai, **Si Satchanalai** ⓑ lies on the banks of the Yom River. Founded in the 13th century, it was the seat of Sukhothai viceroys, and was known as

213

Northern Thailand

the twin city of the old capital. It has a wooded setting and an aura attained in few other ancient sites.

Si Satchanalai and the old city of Chaliang, 1km (²/₃ mile) to its east, form the 720-hectare (1,780-acre) **Si Satchanalai–Chaliang Historical Park** (daily 8.30am–5pm; charge). Its most important monument is **Wat Chang Lom**, which has the only surviving *chedi* that can be attributed with certainty to King Ramkhamhaeng. To the south, seven rows of *chedi* at the ruins of **Wat Chedi Jet Thaew** are believed to contain the ashes of the viceroys of Si Satchanalai. Close to the

massive city walls are the remains of **Wat Nang Phya**, the 'Temple of the Queen'. Its fine stucco decoration probably dates from the 16th century.

Phitsanulok

A 1950s fire razed most of old **Phitsanulok** ⑯, some 50km (31 miles) east of Sukhothai, and the new city is dull, save for its location along the Nan River, where there are houseboats and floating restaurants. Fortunately, Phitsanulok's main monastery, **Wat Phra Si Rattana Mahathat** (or Wat Yai), escaped the fire. Its main *viharn* holds the Phra Phuttha Chinnarat, Thailand's second most important Buddha image, after Bangkok's Emerald Buddha. It is a Sukhothai-style bronze image with a flame-like bronze halo around its head and torso, which ends in *naga* (serpent) heads near the base.

Two superb late Ayutthaya wooden pulpits flank the image: the one on the left for monks who chant ancient Buddhist texts in Pali; the other for a monk who translates them into Thai for the congregation.

At a **bronze foundry** on nearby Thanon Wisut Kasat, visitors can watch copies of the Chinnarat Buddha being cast and polished (Wed–Sun 8.30am–4.30pm; free).

Khampaeng Phet

Kamphaeng Phet ⑰, on the Ping River 77km (48 miles) southwest of Sukhothai, was built by King Lu Thai (1347–68), Ramkhamhaeng's grandson, as a garrison town for the Sukhothai kingdom. The ruins of the old city are contained within the walls

Wat Chang Lom in Chaliang Historical Park, Si Satchanalai

Ruins of the old city at Khamphaeng Phet Historical Park

of the **Kamphaeng Phet Historical Park** (daily 8am–5pm; charge), where Wat Phra Kaew, the largest and most important temple, is remarkable for its fragile laterite Buddha images. Nearby, a circular Sri Lankan-style *chedi* marks Wat Phra That, and to the southeast is the **Kamphaeng Phet National Museum** (Wed–Sun 9am–4pm; charge), where the bronze statue of the Hindu god Shiva is one of the finest in Thailand.

Kamphaeng Phet's other ruined monuments are to the northwest of the walled city, where **Wat Phra Si Iriyabot** derives its name from the four postures of its Buddha images (*si*, four, and *iriyabot*, postures) – walking, standing, sitting and reclining. The largely intact standing image is an impressive and unaltered example of Sukhothai sculpture. At another temple, **Wat Chang Rawp**, elephant buttresses surround the base of a laterite *chedi*, a Sri Lankan theme that claims the universe rests on the backs of the beasts.

Textiles and Ceramics

Ban Hat Siaw village southeast of Si Satchanalai is famous for handwoven textiles, characterised by horizontal stripes bordered with rich brocade. They are made by the Thai Phuan, who live in this area, having migrated from Laos around a century ago when Vietnamese invaders occupied their Xieng Khuang homeland. Si Satchanalai is also associated with the famous glazed brown or green Sangkaloke ceramics, with distinctive double-fish designs. Many visitors carry bowls, plates and vases away as souvenirs.

ACCOMMODATION

Given the spectacular setting around the valleys, rivers and mountains of the remote north, it is no disaster that luxury hotels and resorts are thin on the ground. Many of these more modest places have good facilities at bargain prices, with great settings, lots of character and ethnic variation thrown in.

Chiang Rai and East

Anantara Resort and Spa Golden Triangle
229 Moo 1, Wiang, Chiang Saen
Tel: 0-5378-4084
www.goldentriangle.anantara.com
Luxury low-rise resort with spacious and comfortable rooms, sunken baths and large terraces overlooking the Mekong River, Myanmar and Laos. An elephant camp offers elephant treks and elephant training lessons. **$$$$–$$$$$**

Dhevaraj Hotel
466 Thanon Sumonthavaraj, Nan
Tel: 0-5475-1577
www.dhevarajhotel.com
Probably Nan's best hotel, this long-standing favourite is in good condition. All rooms have cable TV, air conditioning and minibar. Other facilities include a pool and sauna. Has a range of good-value accommodation. **$–$$$**

Dusit Island Resort
1129 Thanon Kraisorasit, Chiang Rai
Tel: 0-5360-7999
www.chiangrai.dusit.com
Located near the city centre on an island in the Kok River. Rooms have picture-window views of the city and mountains. Facilities include a large outdoor pool, tennis courts, fitness centre, a steak house, a Thai café and an English pub. **$$$**

Golden Triangle Inn
590/2 Tj/ Phahonyothin
Tel: 0-5371-3981
Sprawling over tropically landscaped grounds, the rooms are nicely trimmed with wood and bamboo. Unlike most hotels, the rooms don't come with TVs, a blessing for those seeking peace and quiet. There is a coffee shop and restaurant. **$–$$$**

Mae Salong Flower Hill Resort
779 Moo 1, Thanon Doi Mae Salong, Mae Salong
Tel: 0-5376-5496
www.maesalongflowerhills.com
Located about 2km (1½ miles) east of the main town, this resort overlooks a stunning valley filled with tea fields. Beautifully manicured gardens with a riot of flowers cover the slopes around the property. Facilities include a pool and restaurant. **$$**

Mae Sai Guest House
Thanon Wiengpangkam, Mae Sai

Anantara Resort and Spa Golden Triangle

Tel: 0-5373-2021
There are a number of good guesthouses by the Sai River, but Mae Sai is a winner. The attractive bungalows are right on the riverbank, so close to Myanmar you can see women washing clothes on the other side each morning. **$**

Naga Hill Resort
83 Moo 8, Ban Pha-U, Chiang Rai
Tel: 08-1818-9684
www.nagahill.com
A French journalist and his Thai-German partner have designed and built a handful of tasteful rustic bungalows amid tropical gardens. Each has an outdoor bathroom, ceiling fan and mosquito net. There's a swimming pool and Wi-fi access. **$–$$**

The Northwest
Belle Villa Resort
113 Moo 6, Thanon Huay Poo-Wiang Nua, Pai
Tel: 0-5369-8226
www.bellevillaresort.com
On a quiet stretch of the Pai River, this is one of the nicest hotels in Pai. Bungalows have cable TV, minibar and well-designed bathrooms – all without forgoing rural Thai charms. **$$$**

Centara Mae Sot Hill Hotel
100 Thanon Asia, Mae Sot
Tel: 0-5553-2601
www.centarahotels.com
Mae Sot's most comfortable accommodation is just outside town, with a lakeside Thai restaurant, Chinese and Western coffee-shop food, a swimming pool, fitness centre and tennis courts. Free shuttle bus. **$$–$$$**

The Dai
158 Toongkongmoo Village, Mae Hong Son
Tel: 0-5361-3964
www.the-dai.com
Owned by a Shan family, The Dai is a lovely property with several Shan-style houses spread across landscaped grounds. The spacious rooms are warmly decorated with bamboo-thatched walls and wood trim. **$–$$**

Fern Resort
64 Moo 10, Tambon Pha Bong, Mae Hong Son
Tel: 0-5368-6110
www.fernresort.info
Shan-inspired wooden bungalows, with walking trails to national parklands. Facilities include a swimming pool and an open-air restaurant serving Thai and local specialities. About 7km (4 miles) south of town, but has a free shuttle service. **$$$**

Pairadise
98 Moo 1, Ban Mae Yen, Pairadise
Tel: 08-9431-3511
www.pairadise.com
Well-maintained, fan-only wooden bungalows with verandas and bathrooms around a spring-fed pond. Perched on a ridge, it offers perhaps the best valley and mountain views of any resort in Pai. **$–$$**

Lower North
Ban Thai
38 Thanon Prawet Nakhon, Sukhothai
Tel: 0-5561-0163
Popular Belgian-owned guesthouse close to new Sukhothai town centre. There is a choice of rooms in a motel-like building or rustic bungalows around a garden. Friendly service and a good open-air restaurant. **$–$$**

Scenic Riverside Resort
325/16 Thanon Tesa 2, Kamphaeng Phet
Tel: 0-5572-2009
www.scenicriversideresort.com
A delightful resort with white-walled adobe cottages in a garden that runs down to the river. All have air conditioning, Wi-fi, LCD TV, and en-suite bathrooms. There is a small café on-site. **$$**

Tharaburi Resort
113 Thanon Srisomboon, Sukhothai
Tel: 0-5569-7132
www.tharaburiresort.com
Stylish resort decorated with Thai crafts and silks, the Tharaburi has spacious villas set amid gardens, a swimming pool and a tour desk. Conveniently located close to the Sukhothai Historical Park. **$$–$$$$**

Listings

RESTAURANTS

Restaurants in the North lean towards the humble shophouse or wooden shack by the river – friendly, with good food made from local produce. There's an occasional surprise, though, like Tex-Mex in Chiang Rai, home-cooked (literally) Italian in Nan, or a bakery that makes its own croissants in Mae Hong Son.

Chiang Rai

Bamboo Riverside
71 Moo 1 Hua Wiang, Chiang Khong
Tel: 0-5379-1234
In a rustic wood-and-bamboo pavilion with stupendous views over the Mekong and Laos, the Thai owners serve excellent Thai salads and curries, plus a smattering of Mexican dishes. **$**

Da Dario
37/4 Thanon Rat Amnuay, Nan
Tel: 0-5475-0258
The Italian owner throws open the dining room inside his own house for some cosily presented family meals. There is a strong local following for his home-made pizza and pasta dishes. **$$**

Jojo Coffeeshop
233/1 Thanon Pahonyothin, Mai Sai
Tel: 0-5373-1662
A relaxed ambience in a small place with shelves lined with wooden Buddha images.

The enduringly popular *pad thai*

The food choice runs to good Thai curries and vegetarian dishes, along with Western breakfasts. **$**

Kae's Casa Burrito
1025/37 Thanon Jet Yot, Chiang Rai
Tel: 08-9755-5225
Tex-Mex restaurant run by Kae, a Thai woman who spent over 40 years in the US. She offers standards like burritos, fajitas, tacos and quesadillas as well as Thai dishes. **$$**

Mae Salong Villa
5 Moo 1, Thanon Doi Mae Salong, Mae Salong
Tel: 0-5376-5114
With a terrific location overlooking the tea terraces, this hotel restaurant serves a nice selection of Yunnanese dishes. Worth trying are local mushrooms, like *het hawm thawt* (deep-fried shiitake mushrooms). **$$**

Salung Kham
384/3 Thanon Paholyothin, Salung Kham
Tel: 0-5371-7192
Northern Thai menu includes Chiang Rai sausage, curries, and steamed herbal chicken with bamboo shoots. The indoor section is nicely decorated with Thai handicrafts and there is also a pleasant garden. **$$**

Wiang Tan
17/9 Thanon Chai Kwan, Phayao
No phone
Wiang Tan is one of the larger and more popular of the lakeside restaurants in town. The menu has a wide range of Chinese, central Thai and northeastern dishes. **$**

The Northwest

Ban Pai Restaurant
7 Thanon Rangsiyanond, Pai
Tel: 05-369-9912
This candlelit wooden café serves good Thai food, steaks and pizzas. Try *tom kha gai*, (chicken with coconut and galangal) or *ho mok plaa* (minced fish with coconut mousse in banana leaves). **$$**

Fern Restaurant
Thanon Khunlum Praphat, Mae Hong Son
No Phone
Serves an impressive variety of northern and central Thai dishes. The house speciality is tasty and crunchy fern shoots, served either stir-fried or as a spicy warm salad. **$$**

Khao Mao Khao Fang
382 Moo 5, Mae Pa, Mae Sot
Tel: 0-5553-3607
A small place located just outside Mae Sot, on the highway north to Mae Sariang. Its spicy Thai food is based on local produce, including wild mushrooms and northern Thai sausage. **$$**

Salween River Restaurant
Thanon Singhanat Bumrung, Mae Hong Son
Tel: 0-5361-2050
Very friendly and popular joint owned by a Shan immigrant from Myanmar. The

Salween offers wonderful Shan cuisine as well as Western and vegetarian dishes, plus coffee, breads and pastries. **$**

Lower North

The Coffee Cup
Moo 3, Old Sukhothai, Sukhothai
No Phone
This is a convenient drop-in for a bracing cup of freshly brewed coffee before an early-morning tour of the old city ruins. They also do Western breakfasts and their sandwiches are an option for picnics beside the temple ruins. **$$**

Dream Café
Thanon Singhawat, Sukhothai
Tel: 0-5561-2081
Full of atmosphere, this eatery is housed in a large wooden building, packed with Rama V-period antiques. Offers an extensive menu of Thai and Western dishes, along with home-made ice cream. **$$**

Fah-Kerah
786 Thanon Phra Ong Dam, Phitsanulok
No phone
Famous throughout the region for delicious Thai-Muslim fare, including rich curries (usually ordered with fried, unleavened flatbread, called *roti*) and strong fragrant tea, laced with fresh goat's milk. **$**

Fresh and wholesome Thai fast food

NIGHTLIFE AND ENTERTAINMENT

The north is devoid of large cities and the entertainment in most towns relies on communal drinks with the neighbours in friendly bars. There will often be live music, a pool table and a TV showing sport. The small town of Pai has more options and a generally livelier scene.

Chiang Rai and East

Cat Bar
Thanon Yet Yod, Chiang Rai
No phone
Small bar with a pool table and an owner who plays guitar every night. Musicians are welcome to jam.

The Northwest

Bebop Bar
188 Moo 8, Tambon Viengtai, Pai
Tel: 0-5369-8046
www.myspace.com/bebopbarpaithailand
Wooden bar with roots blues-style paintings on the walls and nightly sets of live jazz, blues and reggae.

Black & White Bar
Thanon Wiang Mai, Mae Sariang
No phone
An outdoor bar with live music and a basic drinks list.

Crossroads
Thanon Singhanat Bamrung,
Mae Hong Son
No phone
Two-storey bar with a pool table and a Western-Thai menu to wash down with local beers and cocktails.

Ting Tong Bar
55 Moo 4, Tambon Viengtai, Pai
Tel: 08-4807-3781
The laid-back vibe at 'Crazy Bar' involves lying on cushions amid the trees watching the fire jugglers.

Lower North

Chopper Bar
Thanon Prawet Nakorn,
Sukhothai
Tel: 0-5561-1190
Occasional live music and garden seating in Sukhothai new town.

SPORTS, TOURS AND ACTIVITIES

Activities in the north of the country focus on the natural environment in outlying regions of Chiang Rai, Nan and the Myanmar border, and heritage sites around Sukhothai in the lower north. Business in these areas depends largely on tourism, and nearly all hotels and guesthouses offer some kind of tour programme.

Adventure

Eco-Trekking
No 4 Guest House, 736 Thanon Intharakhiri, Mae Sot
Tel: 0-5554-4976
These guided trips to Umphang District include hot springs and bat caves.

Nam Rim Tours
Thanon Khunlum Praphat, Mae Hong Son
Tel: 0-5361-4454

Tours of the local hill-tribe villages, including the famous longneck Padaung.

Thai Adventure Rafting
16 Moo 4, Thanon Rangsiyanon, Pai
Tel: 0-5369-9111
www.thairafting.com
Rubber dinghy trips through the Pai River rapids to Mae Hong Son, with an overnight stay in the jungle. They also have trekking, 4-wheel drive and mountain bikes.

Jungle trekking near Chiang Rai

waterfalls, jungle treks, elephant rides and hill-tribe visits.

Bike Tours

Cycling Sukhothai
Tel: 08-5083-1864
www.cyclingsukhothai.com
Tours of Sukhothai Historical Park and trips to the surrounding countryside. From a few hours to a full day.

Golf

Santiburi Golf Course
12 Moo 3, Tambol Wiang-Chai, Chiang Rai
Tel: 0-5366-2821
www.santiburi.com
A challenging 18-hole course designed by Robert Trent Jones Jr. It has a beautiful mountain backdrop, good greens and plenty of water hazards.

Thom's Pai Elephant Camp Tours
5/3 Moo 4, Thanon Rungsiyanon, Pai
Tel: 0-5369-9286
www.thomelephant.com
Fun with elephants, including bareback riding and jungle treks. You can even get married on one. The agency can combine elephant rides with trekking and rafting trips.

Water Land Golf Course
43/2 Moo 3, Thanon Sripirom,
Phromphiram, Phitsanulok
Tel: 0-5523-3420
www.waterlandgolfresort.com
Located in a resort about 40km (25 miles) from Sukhothai, this cute 18-holer slopes down to the banks of the Nan River.

Trekking Tour Chiang Rai
97/7 Doi Hang, Chiang Rai
Tel: 08-9997-5505
www.trekkingtourchiangrai.com
Tours of the Chiang Rai countryside, with

Listings

FESTIVALS AND EVENTS

Loy Krathong, widely regarded as Thailand's most beautiful festival, is now celebrated countrywide, but has its roots in Sukhothai. Many people head there to watch the candles float at Wat Traphang Thong. Elsewhere, there is a Buddhist initiation ceremony in Mae Hong Son and elephant polo in the Golden Triangle.

March

King's Cup Elephant Polo Tournament
Anantara Golden Triangle Resort, Chiang Rai
www.goldentriangle.anantara.com
Polo on elephant back draws tourists and competitors alike from around the world.

March–April

Poy Sang Long
Mae Hong Son
Boys aged 7–14 parade to a Buddhist

monastery to be temporarily ordained as novice monks.

November

Loy Krathong
The main gathering place for this festival is Wat Traphang Thong, in old Sukhothai, a temple surrounded by water, where people launch small candle-laden boats to seek blessings, forming a beautiful illuminated mini armada.

Northeast Thailand

Northeast Thailand, or Isaan, is the poorest and least-visited region of the country, yet it is full of interesting attractions, from the wildlife of unspoiled Khao Yai National Park, through stunning temple ruins dating from the Khmer empire, to prehistoric cave paintings and village crafts along the banks of the Mekong River. Further north, Loei is known for its rugged mountain scenery.

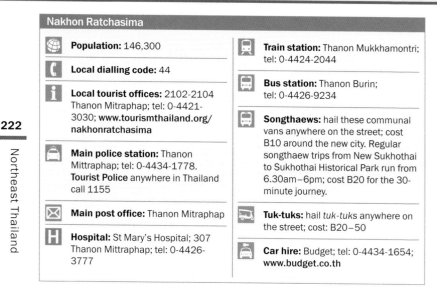

Nakhon Ratchasima

Population: 146,300

Local dialling code: 44

Local tourist offices: 2102-2104 Thanon Mitraphap; tel: 0-4421-3030; www.tourismthailand.org/nakhonratchasima

Main police station: Thanon Mittraphap; tel: 0-4434-1778. **Tourist Police** anywhere in Thailand call 1155

Main post office: Thanon Mitraphap

Hospital: St Mary's Hospital; 307 Thanon Mittraphap; tel: 0-4426-3777

Train station: Thanon Mukkhamontri; tel: 0-4424-2044

Bus station: Thanon Burin; tel: 0-4426-9234

Songthaews: hail these communal vans anywhere on the street; cost B10 around the new city. Regular songthaew trips from New Sukhothai to Sukhothai Historical Park run from 6.30am–6pm; cost B20 for the 30-minute journey.

Tuk-tuks: hail *tuk-tuks* anywhere on the street; cost: B20–50

Car hire: Budget; tel: 0-4434-1654; www.budget.co.th

Northeast Thailand (also known as Isaan) captures only 2 percent of the country's tourism market. Yet the region is a treasure trove of ancient Angkor-era temple ruins, a relatively untouched Lao-Cambodian-Thai culture and pristine national parks.

It occupies a high plateau (the Khorat), home to around one-third of the country's population, and contains three of Thailand's five biggest cities: Khon Kaen, Nakhon Ratchasima (Khorat) and Udon Thani.

The Khmers ruled large parts of the northeast from the 10th to the 13th centuries and subsequently it was part of various Lao kingdoms. Along the Mekong River there are even traces of the French colonialism that engulfed Laos in the 19th century.

Today, northeasterners speak local dialects – mainly related to Lao – but in southern areas, also based on Khmer. The main crop is rice, but yields suffer according to either too much or too little rain. In recent years, droughts have been severe, and large stretches of the Mekong River have run dry, something locals attribute to dams built upriver in China.

Nakhon Ratchasima to Ubon Ratchathani

After spending time in the wilds of Khao Yai National Park, visitors can head east through the Khmer heartlands and magnificent old settlements in Buriram and Si Saket. Also en route are the elephant roundups of Surin and the ruins of Prasat Khao Phra Viharn, across the border in Cambodia, but only accessible from Thailand.

Khao Yai National Park

Three hours' drive northeast of Bangkok, **Khao Yai National Park** ❶ (www.dnp.go.th; daily 8am–6pm;

Rice cultivation in Chiang Khan

Haew Suwat waterfall

charge 🍴) covers 2,100 sq km (837 sq miles) and contains over 100 species of animals and birds, including gibbons, porcupines, wild pigs, black bears and leopards.

Other attractions are the 20m (66ft) Haew Suwat waterfall – which featured in the film *The Beach* – east of the park headquarters, and further south, the larger three-level Haew Narok falls, dropping 150m (500ft). The guides at the park headquarters will probably not speak English, but private ones are bookable in the nearest town, Pak Chong. Hiring one makes sense, as they know the wildlife and can supply equipment such as binoculars.

There is plenty of accommodation in the country lanes outside the park, together with distractions such as golf courses, vineyards and restaurants. The proximity to Bangkok means the park is very crowded at weekends, so is best visited during the week.

Nakhon Ratchasima Town

Highway 2 continues northeast up the Khorat Plateau to **Nakhon Ratchasima** ❷, locally known by its older name, Khorat. It is the capital

223

Northeast Thailand

of Nakhon Ratchasima Province, the richest and largest city in the northeast, and was a base for American bombers during the Vietnam War.

A statue of national heroine **Thao Suranari** (or Khunying Mo) presides over the town square and the old city wall, which dates from the 10th century. Khunying Mo was the wife of an assistant provincial governor in the early 19th century, when a Lao army from Vientiane took the city. Khunying Mo rallied the women, who enticed the Lao soldiers into drunken revelry and then killed them while they slept. Local residents still place offerings at the statue.

There's more local history in the grounds of Wat Suchinda on Thanon Ratchadamnoen, where the **Maha Wirawong National Museum** (www.thailandmuseum.com; Wed–Sun 9am–4pm; charge) has a fine collection of Khmer and central Thai art and artefacts, as well as exhibits on archaeology and folklore.

Around Town

Northeast of Nakhon Ratchasima, just beyond the city limits, is the peaceful monastery of **Prasat Hin Phanomwan** ❸ (daily 8am–6pm; free). Its heavy stone galleries reveal zigzag patterns, a Khmer method adopted to imitate lathed wood. Unlike the majority of Khmer-era ruins, this one contains an active temple. Behind the well-preserved vaulted entrance, the original dark sanctuary is filled with many more recent Buddha images, most of them covered with patches of gold leaf.

Some 50km (30 miles) north of

Thao Suranari memorial in Nakhon Ratchasima

Nakhon Ratchasima, situated on the Mun River (a tributary of the Mekong), are the magnificent 11th-century Khmer ruins of **Prasat Hin Phimai** ❹ (daily 8am–6pm; charge). Some experts suggest Phimai was a prototype for Angkor Wat, in Cambodia, which was built in the following century. As with the Angkor temples, the monuments at Phimai were never inhabited.

The old city gate, likely the main entrance to the sanctuary, still stands at the end of Phimai's present main street. An original 12th-century water tank, called **Sa Kwan**, has also survived. Facing Sa Kwan, the partially open-air **Phimai National Museum** (www.thailandmuseum.com; daily 9am–4pm; charge) displays many of the more beautifully carved lintels and statues found in the area,

Silk and Ceramics

Silk is one of the northeast's most important industries, and there is a production centre about 30km (20 miles) south of Nakhon Ratchasima, at Pak Thong Chai. Around 70 factories here, including the famous Jim Thompson, weave and sell ready-made clothing and accessories like cushion covers and tablecloths.

Also interesting are red ceramics from the very traditional village of Dan Khwian, about 15km (9 miles) southwest of Nakhon Ratchasima, on Route 224.

including an exquisite Buddha-like stone sculpture of King Javarman VII, the last of Angkor's great kings.

Southeast to Buriram

Backtracking south through Nakhon Ratchasima, then east via Highway 24, the road reaches two significant but rarely visited Khmer temple sites in Buriram Province. Three ponds – essential elements of Khmer monumental architecture – surround **Prasat Hin Khao Phanom Rung Historical Park** ❺ (daily 6am–6pm; charge), the largest and best-restored Khmer monument in Thailand. It is a temple complex that historians believe was an important rest stop between Angkor and Phimai during the 11th and 12th centuries. Many generations must have elapsed during its construction, as several stone lintels resemble the mid-11th-century Baphuon style, while the *naga* (serpents) date from the later Angkor Wat period. A stone inscription in Sanskrit mentions King Suryavarman II, the ruler behind the construction of Angkor Wat.

Prasat Hin Khao Phanom Rung includes a Vishnu lintel that was spirited out of Thailand by art thieves in the early 1960s, and later surfaced in

Prasat Hin Phimai, the ancient Angkor-era temple complex near Nakhon Ratchasima

beside the ponds mark the outer boundary of the temple.

Southeast of Phanom Rung, in Ban Ta Miang district on the Cambodian border, is **Prasat Ta Muan Tot** ❼ (daily 6am–6pm; free), one of the most remote and atmospheric Khmer temple sites in Thailand. It was originally part of a healing station on the route to Angkor Wat. The main sanctuary stands in line with an ornate gate and prayer hall built of sandstone and surrounded by a laterite wall.

Surin and Si Saket

Moving north for about 50km (30 miles) on Route 214 leads to Surin, which was primarily known for silk production until 1960, when the first Elephant Roundup was organised (*see box, p.229*). East from here, along Route 226 is the province of Si Saket, and another border with Cambodia.

Si Saket Province's main attraction isn't officially even in Thailand. Ownership of the splendid temple complex of **Prasat Khao Phra Viharn** ❽ (daily 7.30am–4.30pm; charge) has long been disputed between Thailand and Cambodia, and in 1962 the International Court of Justice awarded the temple to Cambodia, where it is known as Prasat Preah Vihear. However, the only practical access for visitors is from Thailand. Ownership is still disputed, and the latest flare-up, in 2009, saw troops of both countries stationed there. As of mid-2010 the site was still closed. To check on the current status, call the TAT office in Ubon at (0-4524-3770).

the US, in a private museum collection. After protracted negotiations, the lintel was returned in the early 1990s and placed in its original position over one of the entrances.

A couple of kilometres east is **Prasat Hin Muang Tam** ❻ (daily 6am–6pm; charge), or Lower Temple, which had cornerstones laid in the 10th century, but wasn't finished until a hundred years later. Muang Tam, which has been beautifully restored, is considered the third most significant Angkor-period site in the northeast (after Phanom Rung and Phimai). It has five *prang*, surrounded by galleries. The huge rectangular stone blocks of the outer walls contain holes, probably used for stone lotus bud motifs. *Naga* serpents

227

Northeast Thailand

Prasat Khao Phra Viharn overlooks the Cambodian countryside

The complex is a 100km (63-mile) drive south on Route 221 from Si Saket, on a 500m (1,650ft) perch of the Dongrak Mountains overlooking the Cambodian plains. When the site was last open, visitors paid fees of B10 for a border pass on the Thai side and B200 on the Cambodian side, plus B400 entrance fee for the temple.

The stairs of the near 1km (²/₃-mile) -long complex alternate between hewn bedrock and stones laid in the 11th century. Each layer has an increasingly large *gopura*, or gate, which ends at the topmost sanctuary, honouring the god Siva.

To the east of the first *gopura*, a precarious trail descends through the jungle to the Cambodian plains. The second *gopura*, shaped like a Greek cross, is superbly carved in 11th-century Khmer style. Its lintels show Vishnu in the Hindu creation myth. The stairs continue in a symbolic ascent to heaven, past another purifiying basin, to the first courtyard with its two palaces, and finally to the second and third courtyards and the main sanctuary. At the end of the long ridge is a breathtaking precipice above the Cambodian countryside, turning a natural site into a stunning work of art.

Ubon Ratchathani

About 60km (40 miles) east of Si Saket, **Ubon Ratchathani** ❾ is usually referred to simply as 'Ubon'. It is the sleepy capital of the province of the same name, and was founded in the late 1700s. Much of the town's 20th-century growth coincided with the American build-up during the Vietnam War – and the military link is still in evidence today. Many of Ubon's inhabitants work for the

Thai military. Strong trade links with nearby Laos and Cambodia have earned Ubon the moniker 'Capital of the Emerald Triangle'. The town hosts Thailand's most famous Candle Festival, every July *(see Listings, p.247)*.

Otherwise, the main attraction is **Wat Thung Si Muang** (daily 8am–5pm; free) on Thanon Luang, which was established by King Rama III, and is notable for its scripture library built of teak and raised on stilts in the middle of a lotus pond, an old method for protecting manuscripts from termites. Slightly southwest on Thanon Kheuan Thani, housed in King Vajiravudh's (Rama VI, r. 1910–25) former country residence,

The city pillar, Ubon Ratchathani

Masters of the Elephant

The village of Ban Ta Klang, 60km (40 miles) north of Surin, is the home of elephant culture in Thailand. Its people, known as the Suay, are known as Thailand's best elephant handlers *(mahouts)*, and train the animals for the famous Surin Elephant Roundup every November. The event features about 400 elephants in re-enactments of famous battles, along with sideshows such as elephant soccer, logging displays and the inevitable Miss Elephant Festival beauty pageant *(see p.247)*.

is **Ubon Ratchathani National Museum** (www.thailandmuseum.com; Wed–Sun 9am–4pm; charge). Its collection of Thai, Lao, Khmer, Vietnamese and Indian artefacts marks it as Isaan's finest museum.

North of town, 1km (²/₃ miles) along Thanon Chayangkun, **Wat Phra That Nong Bua** (daily 8am–5pm; free) has a tall *chedi* modelled on the Mahabodhi Stupa in Bodh Gaya, India.

The Mun River, which flows through Ubon, has an island called **Ko Hat Wat Tai** that is a favourite picnic spot during March and April when the river recedes and exposes a temporary beach.

South of Ubon, Warin Chamrap district has two temples known for their association with famous meditation master, the late Ajahn Cha, who taught and ordained many Western monks. His original monastery, **Wat Nong Pa Phong** (daily 6am–6pm; free), has a *chedi* enshrining his ashes and a small museum. The nearby **Wat**

★ KHMER CONNECTION

Although Thailand is overwhelmingly a Buddhist country, many of its official and religious ceremonies have strong Hindu influences, and temples frequently have Hindu deities such as Vishnu alongside Buddha statues. These cultural quirks are remnants of the Khmer empire that ruled a large part of what is now Thailand 1,000 years ago, from its capital in Angkor, in present-day Cambodia. Over 200 Khmer religious sites remain in northeast Thailand, creating one of the most impressive heritage trails in the country.

The Khmers ruled much of mainland Southeast Asia between the 10th and 14th centuries, occupying lands from the Mekong Delta in the east to as far as Petchaburi and parts of Burma in the west. The capital, at Angkor, connected to the regions via highways that linked major outposts such as Phanom Rung and Phimai, both in Thailand, and Prasat Khao Phra Viharn, which is in Cambodia, but only accessible from Thailand.

Over half of the religious buildings that made up the old Khmer empire are located in northeast Thailand, and, over the last few decades, the Department of Fine Arts has been restoring many of the most important ones.

Khorat and Buriram provinces host the major Khmer complexes of Prasat Hin Phimai and Prasat Hin Khao Phanom Rung. Both have been carefully restored, but Phanom Rung

Prasat Hin Phimai was designed by Khmer architects and predates Angkor Wat in Cambodia

Carving at the Khmer complex Prasat Hin Khao Phanom Rung in Buriram Province

perhaps most impressively, in its spectacular setting atop an extinct volcano. It was built between the 10th and 13th centuries, with the greater part of the work completed in the reign of King Suriyavarman II (1112–52), when Angkor architecture reached its zenith.

Like Angkor Wat itself, these temples were originally constructed as Hindu temples, dedicated to Vishnu and Shiva. It was under Jayavarman VII, in the 12th century, that the shift from Hinduism towards Buddhism began, and temple architecture started to change.

These unique historic treasures remain significant to Thai Buddhists, who traditionally consider them temporary homes for Hindu deities. As such, they are consecrated regularly in elaborate ceremonies performed by Brahman priests, and Phanom Rung is a regular and important place of Buddhist pilgrimage.

The structure that most immediately identifies a site as Khmer is the tall tapering tower, called the *prang*, with longitudinal ridges. These towers were symbolic of Mount Meru, the mythical mountain at the centre of the Hindu universe. Also in the countryside around Phanom Rung are various Khmer *kuti*, or meditation retreats, as well as several unrestored temple complexes, languishing in the forests and undergrowth.

These beautiful and, in many cases, isolated sites are among the greatest treasures of Thailand, and as the tourist footprint in the northeast is so light, they are wonderfully evocative of a long-lost culture that did much to define these lands.

Khmer Connection

The dramatic approach to Prasat Hin Khao Phanom Rung

Population: 141,800

Local dialling code: 42

Local tourist office: 16/5 Thanon Mukmontri; tel: 0-4232-5406; www.tourismthailand.org/udonthani

Main police station: Thanon Naresuan; tel: 0-4221-1077

Main post office: 2 Thanon Wattananuvong

Hospital: Aek Udon International Hospital, 555/5 Thanon Posri; tel: 0-4234-2555; www.aekudon.com

Airport: Thanon Makkang, tel: 0-4222-2845. Taxis from the

airport take around 30 minutes for the 7km (4¼-mile) journey

Train station: Thanon Prajak, tel: 0-4222-2061

Bus station: Thanon Sai Uthit, tel: 0-4222-2916

Songthaews: These communal vans operate on several routes around the city; cost: B8

Car hire: Budget; tel: 0-4224-6805; www.budget.co.th

Samlors: Available anywhere on the street; cost B20–50
Tuk-tuks: Hail *tuk-tuks* anywhere on the street; cost: B20–50

Pa Nanachat Bung Wai (tel: 08-1470-9299; daily 6am–6pm; free), founded by an American student of Ajahn Cha, welcomes day visitors for meditation and religious talks, by appointment.

Some 90km (56 miles) east of Ubon, **Kaeng Tanna National Park**  (www.dnp.go.th; daily 8am–6pm; charge) has a submerged cave system with prehistoric paintings and rapids where the Mun River squeezes through a gorge before joining the Mekong.

North to Loei

The route from Roi Et begins with Thai heritage sites dating back to the 6th century, before reaching Ban Chiang, which was one of the earliest Bronze Age settlements in the world. More contemporary are the dancing plants of Khon Kaen and the

vineyards of Loei, close to a bizarre fertility festival at Dan Sai.

Roi Et and Khon Kaen

Around 150km (95 miles) northwest of Ubon, Route 23 passes through

Weaver in Khon Kaen province

the main livelihoods. Travellers in the region often stop here for a break, taking advantage of the better choice of hotels and restaurants or to get visas from the Lao and Vietnamese consulates.

The well-curated **Khon Kaen National Museum** (www.thailand-museum.com; Wed–Sun 9am–4pm; charge) on Thanon Lang Sunratcha-kan has a collection of Dvaravati-period (6th–10th-century) Buddhist art and artefacts from the ancient settlement at Ban Chiang.

At the southern end of town, following Thanon Klang Meuang, **Wat Nong Wang Muang** (daily 8am–6pm; free) has a beautiful nine-tiered pagoda said to be designed after the Shwedagon Pagoda of Yangon in Myanmar. About 57km (34 miles) southwest is **Chonabot**, a centre for the high-quality, traditional northeastern silk fabric known as *mudmee*.

Udon Thani

From Khon Kaen, it is 110km (70 miles) north on Highway 2 to **Udon Thani ⑬** (Udon for short), which was a base for American airmen in the Vietnam War. Just outside the city limits to the northwest, off Route 2024, the **Udorn Sunshine Nursery** (www.udorn-sunshine.com; daily 7am–6.30pm; free 🏠) is famous for creating the Thai dancing gyrant, a plant whose leaves sway gently when it is spoken or sung to. The nursery developed the plant through selective breeding of a wild herb called Cha

233

Northeast Thailand

Roi Et ⑪, on an artificial lake called Beung Phlan Chai. On Thanon Padung Phanit, **Wat Burapha** (daily 7am–7pm; free) has a 68m (223ft) standing Buddha, with a staircase reaching the figure's knees, from where there are views of the surrounding townscape.

Wat Neua (daily 7am–7pm; free), west along Thanon Padung Phanit, has a *chedi* that may date to the Dvaravati period (6th to 10th centuries) and a stone pillar inscribed in Khmer, suggesting the site was also occupied by the Khmers around the 11th or 12th century.

Lying another 100km (60 miles) northwest along Route 23, **Khon Kaen ⑫** is the only large town in an overwhelmingly rural part of Thailand, where farming and textiles are

Chalor Charu, which was already known to respond to sound. Udorn also blends orchid extracts into natural perfumes.

Around Udon Thani

About 50km (31 miles) east of Udon Thani is **Ban Chiang ⑭**, the most famous archaeological site in Thailand, where bronze artefacts date to around 2,000BC, making this one of the earliest Bronze Age settlements in the world. Ban Chiang is also known for pottery with beautiful whorl designs. It was declared a Unesco World Heritage Site in 1992. Many of the artefacts are at **Ban Chiang National Museum** (www.thailand-museum.com; daily 8.30am 4.30pm; charge), and one of the original excavation pits, at nearby **Wat Pho Si Nai** (daily 8.30am–4.30pm; charge), contains 52 human skeletons that were interred with ceremonial pottery.

North of Udon Thani, 16km (10 miles) and 18km (11 miles), respectively, off Highway 2, are the weaving villages of **Ban Na Kha** and **Ban Thon**. They are well known for hand-loomed textiles called *khit*. Diamond-shaped motifs woven into weft brocade are *khit* hallmarks. Several shops in the two villages offer the textiles for sale.

West of Udon Thani, Route 210 joins Route 201 for a 150km (100-mile) run towards Loei. About 50km (30 miles) before Loei, **Tham Erawan ⑮** (daily 8am–5pm; donation), the 'Triple-Headed Elephant Cave', is a sacred part of Wat Tham Erawan, a small complex of shrine rooms and monastic cells in front of the cave. A life-size statue of Erawan, the triple-headed elephant of Hindu-Buddhist

Excavation of the archaeological prehistoric site of Ban Chiang

Farming by the Mekong River near Nong Khai in Loei Province

mythology, marks the steep 700-step stairway and rocky path to the cave's entrance, and its large sitting Buddha, visible from the plains below.

Loei

The city of **Loei**, with the Loei River flowing through it, is a flourishing centre for the province's cotton trade and low-level commerce with neighbouring Laos. It was once known for Communist insurgents, who hid in the surrounding forests near here, until the 1980s, following the 1976 uprisings in Bangkok.

Around Loei

From Loei, Route 203 plunges 50km (30 miles) into the western wilderness to **Phu Rua National Park** ⑯ (www.dnp.go.th; daily 8.30am–5pm;

charge), dominated by the 1,370m (4,495ft) -high Phu Rua Mountain. A smooth, winding road leads to the summit, from where there are spectacular views of the national forest. Be warned that Loei records the lowest (and the highest) temperatures in the country, and in winter, the mercury at the top of Phu Rua can drop to freezing point. Just beyond the village of Phu Rua, on Route 203, **Chateau de Loei Vineyards** (www.chateaudeloei.com; daily 8am–5pm; free) allows self-tours, offers wine tasting and has a shop.

West of the national park, around 80km (50 miles) from Loei, is **Dan Sai**. This small town is famous for its annual *Phee Ta Khon* Festival, one of Thailand's most curious celebrations (*see box, p237*).

Northeast Plateau landscape

Just outside Dan Sai is the 30m (98ft) **Phra That Si Songrak**, a highly venerated *chedi* constructed in 1560 to commemorate the friendship between Thailand and Vientiane, and to mark the then border between them. Today, there is a de facto border crossing 20km (12miles) away at the tiny town of Na Haew, where Lao and Thai nationals cross the Huang River by raft.

South of Loei

Some 100km (60 miles) south of Loei, along Route 201, **Phu Kradung National Park ⑰** (www.dnp.go.th; daily 8am–6pm, Oct–May; charge) is a 60-sq-km (24-sq-mile) plateau, between 1,200 and 1,500m (4,000–5,000 ft) high. It has over 50km (30 miles) of marked trails, of which the principal one ascends 6km (4 miles) and takes three hours to climb. It is by no means an easy ascent, but ladders enable you to negotiate the steepest boulders, and it's well worth the effort.

North of Loei

After 50km (30 miles), Route 201 north of Loei leads to the Mekong River and the charming riverside town of **Chiang Khan ⑱**, at the border with Laos. Many of the wooden homes lining the river bank are built in French-Lao style, and the town's Buddhist temples show a dominant Lao influence. A cycle or taxi ride 5km (3 miles) east of town are the **Kaeng Khut Khu** rapids.

From Chiang Khan, Route 211 follows the Mekong east through **Sangkhom**, which has excellent river views and two local picnic spots, Than Thip Waterfall and Than Thong Waterfall. Further along Route 211 is the meditation monastery **Wat Hin Mak Peng,** perched on cliffs overlooking the Mekong. Visitors are welcome to visit if they dress modestly.

Around 55km (33 miles) past Sangkhom, the town of **Si Chiang Mai** is directly opposite Vientiane (Yiangchan), the capital of Laos, on the other side of the Mekong. Many of Si Chiang Mai's population, who are mainly of Lao or Vietnamese descent, earn a living by making translucent rice-flour skins for Vietnamese-style spring rolls for export around the world. The wrappers lie drying on bamboo-lattice racks all over town. A small church serves the many Vietnamese Catholic residents.

The Mekong River

The winding road from Nong Khai follows the Mekong River all the way to Khong Jiam in the southeast, passing some of Thailand's most remote destinations. It is a fascinating journey that few travellers undertake, and calls at remote meditation retreats and bordertown markets selling goods from Laos and Vietnam.

Nong Khai

A run of 20km (12 miles) east from Si Chiang Mai, **Nong Khai** ⓭ connects to Laos via the Friendship Bridge across the Mekong River. There is

also a rail link all the way to the Lao capital, Vientiane. The independent Lao kingdoms of Lan Xang and later Vientiane ruled these lands from 1353 to 1694. Nong Khai only became a Siamese protectorate in the late 18th century, and it kept close ties with French-colonised Laos throughout the 19th century. Influences from that period are visible in remnants of Lao-French architecture.

Longtail boats on the Mekong River

Boats can be hired to cruise the Mekong at Tha Sadet Market, on Thanon Rimkong, and further west, **Mut Mee Guest House** on Thanon Kaew Worawut (tel: 0-4246-0717; www.mutmee.net) has dinner cruises on a restored riverboat. One of Thailand's strangest sights happens around Nong Khai each October, when fireballs rise from the Mekong (*see Listings, p.247*).

The town's most popular attraction is **Sala Kaew Ku Sculpture Park** (daily 7.30am–5.30pm; charge), about 4km (2½ miles) southeast of town on Route 212. The park is filled with surreal cement sculptures of Shiva, Vishnu, Buddha and other figures from Hindu and Buddhist religions.

Sala Kaew Ku Sculpture Park

About 70km (42 miles) south-west of Nong Khai, **Phu Phrabat Historical Park** (tel: 0-4225-1352; daily 8.30am–4.30pm; charge) has prehistoric cave paintings, strange natural rock formations and Buddhist temples on a marked trail that takes about two hours to complete.

South Along the Mekong

The road along the Mekong first runs northeast from Nong Khai. A convenient stop 185km (111 miles) en route is Beung Kan, and a side trip to **Wat Phu Thok ⓴** (also called Wat Chedi Khiri Viharn; daily 10am–4pm; free). This meditation monastery sits on a huge sandstone outcrop, with wooden stairs, best avoided by vertigo sufferers, that climb 200m (650ft) above the surrounding plain, past meditation caves and monastic cells.

After another 175km (109 miles), now moving southeast along Route 212, one arrives at **Nakhon Phanom**, northeast Thailand's most remote province. The capital, of the same name, meaning 'City of Hills', is a border crossing to Laos (you need a Lao visa), and is most lively in October for its Fireboat Festival.

Some 44km (26 miles) south, the small town of **Renu Nakhon ㉑** is home to the minority Phu Thai, who are much admired for their *mudmee* patterns, loom-woven in cotton or silk. There is a handicraft market every Saturday near **Wat Phra That Renu Nakhon** (daily 7am–6pm; free), which has a highly revered, centuries-old Lao-style *chedi*. The Phu Thai perform folk dances here on weekends from December to Feburary.

Thai dancers at Wat Phra That Renu Nakhon

About 10km (6 miles) further south, a turn-off onto Route 2031 leads east for 7km (4 miles) to That Phanom, home to the most famous *chedi* in Isaan, at **Wat Phra That Phanom** ㉒, estimated at 1,500 years old, it was built when the province was still part of the Lao kingdom. The *chedi* stands 57m (187ft) tall, and is visible from several kilometres away. The four-sided curvilinear style reflects Lao Buddhist architecture. The short road from the temple to town passes through Pratu Chai (Victory Gate), inspired, on a modest scale, by Paris's Arc de Triomphe, and decorated with Lao motifs.

Towards the Mekong riverfront, many of the town's quaint shophouses date to the French Indochina colonial period, and there's a **Lao market** on the river bank at the north of town. The nearby ferry crossing is open only to Lao and Thai nationals.

Mukdahan

Continuing south on Route 212 along the Mekong leads to the district town of **Mukdahan** ㉓, on the banks of the river and opposite the Lao town of Savannakhet. The Second Thai-Lao Friendship Bridge links the two, and a road runs east from Savannakhet to Danang, in Vietnam. Hence, Mukdahan is a trading centre for Lao timber, agricultural products and gems. Its **Indochina Market** and **Danang Market**, named after the port city in Vietnam, deal in goods from Laos and Vietnam. South of town, on Thanon Samut Sakdarak, the shopping mall **Mukdahan Jewel Hall** has more goods for sale.

Near the river, on Thanon Samran Chaikhong, is **Wat Si Nongkran**, which was built by Vietnamese refugees in 1956. The gates present a curious mixture of Thai contours, Vietnamese writing and Chinese-inspired dragons. A new bridge opened here in 2006.

About 16km (10 miles) south of town, off Route 2034, **Mukdahan National Park** (www.dnp.go.th; daily 8am–6pm; charge) – also known locally as Phu Mu National Park – is famous for its peculiar rock formations, many in the shape of jagged mushrooms.

At Mukdahan, where Route 212 turns inland towards Ubon Ratchathani (*see p.228*), Route 217 continues southeast to the village of **Ban Khon Sai**, where men forge heavy bronze gongs for temples and traditional Thai music ensembles. The most accessible and unusual of several nearby waterfalls cascades in front of **Wat Tham Hew Sin Chai**, a cave monastery off Route 2222, southwest of Khong Jiam.

At Khong Jiam, the Mekong and Mun rivers meet, each flowing a different colour, coining the local name Two-Colour River. Longtail boats can be chartered by the hour for stops at various small islands.

North of Khong Jiam, **Pha Taem National Park** ㉔ (www.dnp.go.th; daily 8am–6pm; charge) is famous for a 200m (650ft) cliff that bears murals of fish, elephants and human figures thought to be at least 3,000 years old. A 500m (1,640ft) trail leads to two platforms for viewing the paintings.

To the south, Route 217 ends at **Chong Mek**, the only official land crossing between Thailand and Laos. Another 5km (3 miles) west of Chong Mek is the Sirinthorn Reservoir. A secluded but famous meditation retreat, **Wat Pa Wana Phothiyan**, sits on an island in the reservoir.

Prehistoric rock paintings at the rock cliff in Pha Taem National Park

ACCOMMODATION

The choice of accommodation may be sparse around the non-touristy northeast, but there are some very good deals to be had considering the facilities. Some of the resorts hugging the Mekong River are delightful, and, as with everything else in Thailand, if you ask for a cheaper price, you may just get it.

Nakhon Ratchasima to Ubon Ratchathani

Khao Yai Garden Lodge
Thanon Thanarat, Km 7, Khao Yai N P
Tel: 0-4436-5178
www.khaoyai-gardenlodge.com
Rooms range from fan-cooled to air-conditioned, all with traditional Thai decor and bathrooms. Spacious grounds include a bird garden and a 40 year-old tortoise, along with a swimming pool with a waterfall. $$

Kirimaya
1/3 Moo 6, Thanon Thanarat, Khao Yai N P
Tel: 0-4442-6099
www.kirimaya.com
Plush resort drawing inspiration from African safaris with four luxury tented villas nestled among buildings with rooms and suites. Right on the edge of the national park, there's also an infinity pool, spa and a golf course. $$$$–$$$$$

Sima Thani Hotel
2112/2 Thanon Mittaphap, Nakhon Ratchasima
Tel: 0-4421-3100
www.simathani.com
Rooms are decorated with Thai and Khmer motifs. There are Chinese and Thai restaurants, plus a café serving Thai, Japanese and Western dishes. A fitness centre, a sauna and a swimming pool fill out the amenities. $$$

Surin Majestic Hotel
99 Thanon Jit Bamrung, Surin
Tel: 0-4471-3980
www.surinmajestichotel.com
This is Surin's best hotel with clean, spacious rooms and a good array of facilities, including free internet, restaurants and swimming pool. Conveniently located for the bus and train station. Good value. $–$$

Tohsang City Hotel
251 Thanon Phalo Chai, Ubon Ratchathani
Tel: 0-4524-5531
www.tohsang.com
A valiant attempt to create a modern, semi-hip hotel, the Tohsang combines contemporary architecture with Isaan silk upholstery in the comfortable rooms. Sprawling landscaped grounds, a restaurant serving Thai and international cuisines, but no swimming pool or fitness centre. $$$

Ubonburi Hotel & Resort
1 Thanon Si Mongkhon, Ubon Ratchathani
Tel: 0-4526-6777
www.ubonburihotel.com
South of the city limits, not far from the railway station, this hotel is set in tropical gardens. On hand are a business centre, a swimming pool, a jogging track, a coffee shop and a Chinese restaurant. $$

North to Loei

Centara Hotel & Convention Centre
Charoensri Complex, Thanon Prajak Silpakorn, Udon Thani
Tel: 0-4234-3555
www.centarahotels.com
Attached to the city's largest shopping mall, this decent provincial city hotel offers large

Entrance to the luxurious Loei Palace Hotel

comfortable rooms, restaurants specialising in northeastern Thai and Cantonese dishes, and a spa. **$$$**

Khon Kaen Hotel
43/2 Thanon Phimphaseut, Khon Kaen
Tel: 0-4333-3222
This clean, no-frills hotel with friendly, attentive service is a bargain. The restaurant serves Thai, Chinese and Western fare. Its Pong Lang Music House has authentic Isaan pop and folk music. **$**

Loei Palace Hotel
167/4 Thanon Charoenrat, Loei
Tel: 0-4281-5668
www.amari.com/loeipalace
The most expensive hotel in Loei is located in a quiet area outside town and has a nice garden. Rooms have cable TV and there is an outdoor swimming pool, jacuzzi and fitness centre. **$$**

Mut Mee Guest House
1111/4 Thanon Kaew Worawut,
Nong Khai
Tel: 0-4246-0717
www.mutmee.net
Well-known guesthouse on the Mekong river bank with a view of Laos from a pleasant garden restaurant that serves some of the best Western food in town. The rustic bungalows offer dorm beds and both fan and air-con rooms. **$**

Phunacome Resort
461 Moo 3, Baan Doen, Dan Sai
Tel: 0-4289-2005
www.phunacomeresort.com
Located just 2km (1½ miles) from the centre of town, this is a change from Dan Sai's otherwise basic accommodation scene. The views are superb, the atmosphere tranquil, and the cuisine organic. Nice pool, too. **$$$$**

Pullman Khon Kaen Raja Orchid
9-9 Thanon Prachasumran, Khon Kaen
Tel: 0-4332-2155
www.pullmankhonkaenrajaorchid.com
Possibly one of the northeast's finest hotels, with large, well-appointed rooms in a building with a temple-inspired facade. Facilities include an authentic Chinese restaurant, a German brewpub and excellent spa. **$$$**

The Mekong River
Nakhon Phanom River View Hotel
9 Thanon Sunthorn Wichit, Nakhon Phanom
Tel: 0-4252-2333
www.nakhonphanomriverviewhotel.com
Good value at Nakhon Phanom's most luxurious accommodation, which overlooks the Mekong River around 2km (1½ miles) south of town. All rooms are air-conditioned and decorated in local Isaan style. **$–$$**

Ploy Palace Hotel
40 Thanon Pitak Phanom Khet, Mukdahan
Tel: 0-4263-1111
www.ploypalace.com
Good rooms at very reasonable rates with park, mountain or river views. Facilities include a nice large pool, karaoke lounge, traditional massage outlet and a rooftop restaurant. **$$**

Tohsang Khong Jiam Resort
68 Moo 7, Baan Huay-Mak-Tay, Khong Jiam
Tel: 0-4535-1174
www.tohsang.com
Some of the best accommodation this side of Bangkok. The beautifully designed rooms, in a mix of Thai, Khmer and Balinese styles, have cable TV and balconies overlooking the Mekong River. **$$$**

Listings

RESTAURANTS

Northeastern food is some of the tastiest in the country, and, as the region is not overly developed for the tourist market, it offers a chance to try some authentic Thai flavours. Whether from roadside stalls or cafés on the Mekong, these are tastes that linger.

Nakhon Ratchasima to Ubon Ratchathani

Chez Andy
5–7 Thanon Manat, Nakhon Ratchasima
Tel: 0-4428-9556
www.chezandy.com
Operating out of the Swiss owner's house, Chez Andy offers a varied menu including salads, schnitzel, beef stroganoff, pasta and Thai dishes. There are BBQ buffets, imported steaks and a small wine selection. **$$**

Indochine
168–170 Thanon Saphasit, Ubon Ratchathani
Tel: 0-4524-5584
True to its name, Indochine serves Lao and Vietnamese food, with a few Thai and Isaan dishes. Most popular is Vietnamese *naem nuang*, a large platter of pork meatballs, thin rice noodles, fresh lettuce, sliced star fruit and condiments. **$$**

Laap Lak Muang
Thanon Lak Muang, Surin
No phone
Open-air place renowned for authentic Isaan fare like its namesake *laab*, spicy minced duck, beef or pork seasoned with lime juice, fish sauce, scallions and dried red chilli. Absolutely delicious. **$**

Samchai Gai Yang
282/1 Thanon Palochai, Ubon Ratchathani
Tel: 0-4520-9118
The most famous restaurant in town for local food, starting with *gai yang* (marinated grilled chicken served with spicy *somtam* (green papaya salad) and sticky rice. Try also fish *laab*, and Isaan sausage. **$**

Thai Pochana
142 Thanon Jomsurangyat, Nakhon Ratchasima
Tel: 0-4424-2840
One of the oldest restaurants in town, this eatery ranks high on the must-do list for many Bangkokians visiting the city. The lengthy menu covers all the usual mainstream Thai options, along with such local specialities as *mee khorat* ('Khorat noodles'), a spicier version of pad Thai. **$$**

North to Loei

Bualuang Restaurant
Thanon Rop Beung Kaen Nakhon, Khon Kaen
Tel: 0-4322-2504
The pleasant lakeside setting and open-air dining areas make this eatery a popular choice for locals and visitors. The menu has an extensive list of northeastern and central Thai dishes. **$$**

Sweet water lobsters

Selecting a snack from a Khon Kaen satay stall

Restaurant Je-Boy
Route 2114 just north of Dan Sai
No Phone
Probably the best place to eat in Dan Sai is this open-air road-side eatery owned by a Thai-Chinese woman who has a good choice of dishes from very spicy Isaan to milder Bangkok fare. **$**

Steve's Bar and Restaurant
254/26 Thanon Prajak Silpakorn, Udon Thani
Tel: 0-4224-4523
This friendly air-conditioned bar and restaurant is popular with the expat community for its Sunday roasts, pie and chips and other Western dishes. Also has satellite TV and organises games like golf, darts and bridge. **$$**

Udom Rot
Thanon Rimkhong, Nong Khai
Tel: 0-4242-1084
One of Nong Khai's oldest restaurants, Udom Rot overlooks the Mekong River. The menu includes *pla sam rot* ('three-flavour fish'), fried and then topped with chillies, garlic and coriander leaves. Very good value. **$$**

The Mekong River
Hat Mae Mun
Khong Jiam
No phone
Attractively perched on the banks of the Mun River, this is the best restaurant in the Khong Jiam area. Be sure to try the delicious *yam met mamuang saam suan*, a roasted cashew-nut salad made with tomatoes, chillies and fresh green peppercorns. **$**

View Khong Restaurant
527 Thanon Sunthornvijit, Nakhon Phanom
Tel: 0-4252-2314
Located on the bank of the Mekong River with a beautiful view of the mountains in Laos, this breezy restaurant offers a variety of Thai foods but specialises in fresh river fish. Try their *laab pla* (spicy-sour minced fish) or the sour fish soup. **$$**

Wine Wild Why
Thanon Samron Chaikhong, Mukdahan
Tel: 0-4263-3122
Lanterns add ambience to this cosy eatery overlooking the Mekong. The mostly Thai menu has spicy Isaan fare, along with 'steak Lao' – grilled beef served with spicy Thai/Lao condiments, called *jaew*. **$$**

NIGHTLIFE AND ENTERTAINMENT

Nightlife is on the quiet side all over Isaan, with most drinking done in quiet bars, while nightclubs are pretty much confined to hotels. Udon Thani has a reasonable choice, including an Irish-themed bar, and in places like Nong Khai, the Mekong River makes an atmospheric and romantic backdrop.

Nakhon Ratchasima to Ubon Ratchathani

Bar Nana
Rachaphruk Grand Hotel, 311 Thanon Mittrapab, Nakhon Ratchasima
Tel: 0-4434-1222
www.rachaphruk.com
A popular hotel nightclub with a live band and DJ. Bar Nana is probably the liveliest place in town, once it gets busy from around 11pm.

Swing Party House
140/1-2 Thanon Chayangkul, Ubon Ratchathani
Tel: 0-4526-5145
Popular bar with live music and a dance floor. There is also sport on TV and a food menu.

Wrong Way Café
49/4-5 Thanon Phadang,
Ubon Ratchathani
Tel: 08-6868-6661
A small, unassuming bar where local expats meet up for drinks and food over games of pool.

North to Loei

Gaia
Mut Mee Guest House
1111/4 Thanon Kaew Worawut, Nong Khai
Tel: 0-4246-0717
www.mutmee.net
Romantic floating bar on the Mekong River with a very laid-back atmosphere. They have Isaan musicians, and an open mike policy, so it's a good place to dust off your plectrum.

The Irish Clock
19/5-6 Thanon Sampantamitr, Udon Thani
Tel: 0-4224-7450
www.irishclock.com
An Irish-theme pub with the usual Guinness and other imported beers, a good Western and Thai menu and a pool table.

Kronen Brauhaus
Pullman Khon Kaen Raja Orchid, Khon Kaen
9-9 Thanon Prachasumran
Tel: 0-4332-2155
www.pullmankhonkaenrajaorchid.com
Microbrewery with a wood-panelled interior, a German menu and good ales brewed on the premises.

SPORTS, TOURS AND ACTIVITIES

The national parks of the northeast lend possibilities for hiking, wildlife watching, and mountain biking to waterfalls with vistas over the countryside. Sports-lovers are well served with golf courses, particularly around Khao Yai. They can also learn a martial art in the modern heartland of *Muay Thai* and have a day at the races in Khorat.

Adventure

Jungle Planet
66 Thanon Mittaparb, Pak Chong, Nakhon Ratchasima
Tel: 08-9282-2280

www.khaoyai-jungle-planet.com
This outfit runs half- and full-day trekking, birdwatching and wildlife tours and night safaris into Khao Yai National Park. They seek out wildlife such as elephants, great

Watching a Muay Thai match

Listings

hornbills and macaques and supply equipment, including binoculars, leech socks and background reading.

Golf
Kirimaya
Kirimaya Resort
1/3 Moo 6, Thanon Thanarat, Pak Chong, Nakhon Ratchasima
Tel: 0-4442-6000
www.kirimaya.com
An exclusive resort with an 18-hole championship golf course designed by Jack Nicklaus. The course is open to visitors and situated right on the edge of Khao Yai National Park. Excellent greens, facilities and views – with prices to match.

Victory Park Golf Country Club
191 Moo 1, Tambol Khai Bok Wan, Nong Khai
Tel: 0-4240-7296
www.victorypark.in.th
Victory Park has a reputation as the best in this part of Isaan. The greens are not top-class, but the scenery is pleasant and the fairways and bunkers decent enough for habitual golfers needing a fix.

Horse Racing
Korat Race Course
Military Stadium, Nakhon Ratchasima
Tel: 0-4424-3716
www.koratracecourse.org
Holds racing on Saturday and Sunday afternoons, with betting allowed, in one of only two sports exempt from anti-gambling laws. The other is *Muay Thai*. There is food and drink available on-site.

Muay Thai
Nongkee Pahuyuth Thai Boxing
24 Thanon Seepetch, Nongkee Pahuyuth, Buriram
Tel: 0-9844-2601
A *Muay Thai* school with accommodation and English spoken by the manager Pramote Hoimook, who has a good reputation as a trainer. Also teaches history and tradition as well as the moves. They don't allow women to train.

Sightseeing
Isan Discovery Travel
Room 305, 311/15 Thanon Klang Muang, Khon Kaen
Tel: 0-4332-1268
www.thaitraveldreams.com
As well as adventure tours of Isaan national parks, they organise homestays in the villages around Khon Kaen and two- or three-day tours of Angkor heritage sites like Phimai, Phanom Rung and Khao Phra Viharn.

Touring
Eco Valley Lodge
199/16 Moo 8, Nongnamdaeng, Pak Chong, Nakhon Ratchasima
Tel: 0-4424-9661
www.ecovalleylodge.com
Tours, some by mountain bike, include the interior of Khao Yai and the surrounding areas, to wineries, caves, waterfalls and the ruins of Phimai.

FESTIVALS AND EVENTS

The northeast has one of Thailand's busiest festival schedules, celebrating a wide range of things, from the area's ancient Khmer heritage to a strange meld of animist and Buddhist beliefs in the ghost festival of Phee Ta Khon. In addition, there are mythological scenes sculpted from candle wax and unexplained fireballs that rise from the Mekong River.

March–April
Thao Suranari Festival
Nakhon Ratchasima

This 12-day celebration of parades, live music, food and bawdy folk drama called *likay*, pays tribute to Khunying Mo and her women followers, who saved the town from 19th-century Lao invaders.

April
Phanom Rung Festival
Buriram

A spectacular night-time sound-and-light show at Phanom Rung, Thailand's best-preserved Khmer ruins.

July
Phee Ta Khon Festival
Dan Sai

Part Buddhist celebration, part animist fertility rite, in which men dressed as ghosts carry large phalluses around the town.

Ubon Ratchathani Candle Festival
Ubon Ratchathani

Held to celebrate the start of Buddhist Lent, on Asanha Bucha Day, this festival sees huge candles, including some elaborately carved into scenes from Buddhist mythology, parade on floats through the streets.

October
Naga Fireball Festival
Nong Khai

Each year, on the October full moon, fireballs rise from the waters of the Mekong River. There is no scientific explanation for this phenomenon, which is traditionally ascribed to mythical serpents called *Naga*.

November
Phimai Festival
Phimai

A lively festival with longtail boat races, sound-and-light shows and cultural performances celebrating one of the country's most important Khmer sites, at Prasat Hin Phimai.

Surin Elephant Roundup
Surin

Over 400 pachyderms take part in historical pageants, games and displays of logging.

Listings

Longtail boats gathering for a race at the Phimai Festival

PRACTICAL ADVICE

Accommodation – *p.250* **Transport** – *p.253*
Health and Safety – *p.258* **Money and Budgeting** – *p.260*
Responsible Travel – *p.262* **Family Holidays** – *p.264*

Accommodation

Thailand has a good range of accommodation and rates vary widely, even at the luxury end, so shop around for bargains. During peak periods, generally November to March, hotels are full, and prices high. Booking well in advance is advisable. Many include a compulsory gala dinner in the room rate at Christmas and New Year.

In low season, ask for a discount – prices are often 50 percent or more off the published rate – though in less visited tourist places such as Khao Lak, hotels close for part of the season.

Hotel Listings	Page
Bangkok and Surroundings	84
Central Thailand	102
Eastern Seaboard	117
Gulf Coast	136
Northern Andaman Coast	160
The Deep South	178
Chiang Mai and Around	193
Northern Thailand	216
Northeast Thailand	241

HOTELS

The top-end hotels and resorts in Thailand's major tourist centres equal the very best, with swimming pools, spas, fitness centres, Wi-fi access and often several restaurants as standard. And even mid-range and budget lodgings will often have a swimming pool and more than one food outlet. There is a star-rating system that is used occasionally, but the approach is fairly cavalier and there is no reliable watchdog to ensure quality.

A slew of new design-conscious hotels, both luxury chains and independent boutique properties, has widened the choice, not only in Bangkok and popular destinations like Hua Hin, Phuket, Ko Samui, Krabi, Ko Lanta and Chiang Mai, but also in more low-key spots such as Petchaburi, Khampaeng Phet and Nakhon Ratchasima. Many of these are very competitively priced.

High-end and mid-range hotels normally charge a standard 10 percent service and 7 percent VAT (Value-Added Tax), so be sure to check whether rates are inclusive. In the budget range, most places are now air conditioned, en-suite, with cable

Mayalay Resort and Spa on Ko Hai

TV, and prices have crept up accordingly, although you can still pick up rooms for a few hundred baht. The term 'resort' in Thailand may merely mean the accommodation is located in the countryside or by the beach, so be wary of low prices in this category, as they may not give all the facilities you expect.

Online sites, like the Thailand Hotels Association (www.thaihotels.org) and Hotels.com (www.hotels.com), are options for finding the best rates.

Stay with a family in a rural village

BUDGET ACCOMMODATION

Travellers on a tight budget will find numerous guesthouses offering clean and decent accommodation, even in high-profile destinations like Bangkok and Chiang Mai, where guesthouses are strewn along the Ping River and in the old city. In most small towns, guesthouses are generally family-run, and mainly found in the vicinity of bus and railway stations, and on main streets.

Once you get to the still untouristy northeast, prices are even lower, and the southern islands around Satun have some beautifully situated beach huts, where you may only get a fan and a cold shower, but the natural scenery makes up for the scant facilities. Generally, prices start around B500 – Thailand is no longer the ultra-cheap destination of yore – but hunt around and you may drop as low as B200, particularly in the low season. Rangers' huts in national parks can be very cheap, although there is a growing upward trend here, too.

Another budget option is youth hostels, which are growing, though not widespread, in Thailand. Bangkok

and Chiang Mai are well served, with accommodation also available in smaller places such as Ayutthaya, Kanchanaburi and Phuket. Prices start around B100. The International Youth Hostel Federation has a Thailand page (www.tyha.org) with more details and a downloadable guide.

OTHER ACCOMMODATION

A good alternative to hotels that can save money and appeals to many for the extra freedom it allows is to rent a serviced apartment. They're often a great choice for families and perfect if you like self-catering. They also have many of the facilities you'd find in a good hotel, such as a gym, swimming pool and often a restaurant. In fact many hotels now offer the service themselves, as do some large shopping malls. You can search for properties by area, from around B800 per night, at www.sabaai.com. You get better deals booking by the week or month.

The beaches and islands are well served with accommodation variants, including villas with most mod cons for around B1,000, up to designer

Pitch a tent in a national park

Accommodation

luxury with butler service for over B20,000. Sea huts on stilts over the waves are available from B400.

As the modern traveller increasingly looks for alternatives to the standard format, Thailand has expanded its options in areas such as home stays and ecotourism, or agrotourism, where visitors get to enjoy closer interaction with the local community. This choice also means that the welcome extra income goes directly to ordinary people, rather than big business.

As you will stay in family homes, mostly in rural communities, facilities vary, with accommodation possibly in a wooden home with a bucket shower. Rather than national umbrella organisations for this type of tourism, in Thailand the arrangements are largely through individual village initiatives, such as Ban Mae Kampong (0-5322-9525) in Chiang Mai, Ban Prasat (0-4436-7075) in Nakhon Ratchasima,

and Ban Rang Jorakae (0-3530-5441) in Ayutthaya. Prices start at around B500 per night, including meals.

With sometimes 10 or more homes participating, large parties of guests can be accommodated, and most homes allow participation in village life, perhaps helping with the harvest, shopping in local markets or learning to cook new recipes. Thai people have an almost legendary warmth and open friendliness that can enhance this type of holiday.

CAMPING

Camping in Thailand is always in tents – the roads are devoid of camper vans and caravans – and pretty much restricted to national parks, many of which offer campsites, and in some cases tents as well. Popular marine national parks with facilities include Ko Tarutao, while the jungles of Khao Yai, Erawan and Doi Inthanon are good choices on the mainland. Prices begin at around B60 for two people, plus an extra B90 for a tent. Facilities will vary, but generally will be meagre. At some sites there may be a shop or a café, but in most cases you will need to take all food and equipment with you.

There are also campsites on some islands, including Bamboo Island, near Ko Phi Phi and Ko Laoliang, close to Krabi, which has luxury tents for hire. Camping is not recommended in the wilds, as robberies are not uncommon.

For a full list of national parks visit www.dnp.go.th, where you can also book accommodation. Alternatively, contact the local TAT office to get detailed information on campsite locations and their rates.

Transport

GETTING TO THAILAND
By Air

There are regular flights to Thailand from several cities in the UK, US and Australia *(see below)*, and nearly 40 international airlines fly into and out of the city's Suvarnabhumi Airport. Bangkok is also a major transportation hub for the rest of Southeast Asia, so even if you do not plan to spend any time in Thailand, the city is the most convenient (and sometimes the only) way to connect to neighbouring countries like Laos, Cambodia and Myanmar. Thailand has four other international airports, at Chiang Mai, Hat Yai, Phuket and Ko Samui *(see p.254)*, although these currently handle flights only within Asia.

From the UK, the main airlines flying direct are British Airways (www.britishairways.com), Qantas (www.qantas.com.au) and Thai Airways

Transport Fact Files	Page
Bangkok	68
Pattaya	109
Phuket Island	144
Deep South Hub Cities	172
Chiang Mai	184

International (THAI) (www.thaiairways.com), all from London Heathrow, with a fligh time of around 11hrs.

From Australia, British Airways and Qantas fly from Sydney (9hrs) and Thai Airways flies from Brisbane (9hrs), Melbourne (9hrs), Perth (7hrs) and Sydney (9hrs).

From the US, Thai Airways flies direct from Los Angeles (17hrs).

In addition, several airlines fly non-direct, often via the Middle East, when prices are usually cheaper. The best deals for all flights are online at sites such as FareCompare (www.farecompare.com) or Travel Supermarket. Com (www.travelsupermarket.com).

Most international flights land at Bangkok's Suvarnabhumi Airport 30km (19 miles) east of the city centre (BKK; tel: 0-2132-1888; www.bangkokairportonline.com), which also handles some domestic routes.

Phuket International Airport (HKT; tel: 0-7635-1122; www.airportthai.co.th), located 28km (18 miles) north of Phuket Town, has flights from Singapore, Hong Kong, Kuala Lumpur and other Asian cities, plus domestic and charter flights.

Samui Airport (USM; www.samuiairportonline.com), in the northeast

Suvarnabhumi Airport sculpture

corner of the island, 5km (3 miles) from Chaweng Beach, operates domestic and some Asian routes, such as Hong Kong and Singapore.

Chiang Mai International Airport (CNX; tel: 0-5327-0222; www.chiangmaiairportonline.com) is 6km (4 miles) west of the city. It handles international flights from Asian cities, including Luang Prabang, Rangoon and Kuala Lumpur, plus domestic routes and charters.

GETTING AROUND THAILAND

Thailand is very easy to get around, by air, train or coach, with regular connections around the country at very cheap prices. Most run fairly close to scheduled times. Integration of transport modes, though, is not a strong point, and for now at least all tickets have to be purchased separately, unless arranged through a travel agency.

Welcome to Ko Samui

Domestic Flights

Domestic flights are fairly inexpensive and THAI is the principal carrier, with daily routes from Phuket, Chiang Mai, Chiang Rai, Mae Hong Son and 11 other major towns. Bangkok Airways (tel: 0-2270-6699; www.bangkokair.com) also covers many local routes.

The arrival of low-cost airlines has brought down domestic prices in recent years. Nok Air (tel: 1318 or 0-2900-9955; www.nokair.com) is partly owned by THAI and services Chiang Rai, Hat Yai, Krabi, and many others. Other budget operators are Air Asia (tel: 0-2515-9999; www.airasia.com) and Orient Thai (tel: 0-2229-4260; www.orient-thai.com). With them you can get to many smaller towns, such as Nakhon Phanom, Phitsanulok and Buri Ram, as well as major centres. Nok Mini (tel: 0-2664-6099; www.nokmini.com) flies between towns in the north and northeast, such as Pai, Nan and Khon Kaen, with Chiang Mai as its hub.

Flight times on the longer routes, from Chiang Mai to Phuket, for instance, are around 1hr 30 minutes. The number of flights increases during the peak season (Nov–Feb).

Don Muang Airport (DMK; tel: 0-2535-1111; www.donmuangairportonline.com), about 30km (19 miles) north of the city centre, handles domestic flights and charters in Bangkok. The airlines often have online saver deals detailed on their websites.

Ferries

The main ferries in Thailand travel from the mainland to the Gulf islands of Ko Samui, Ko Phangan and Ko

Chang. Seatran Ferry (tel: 0-2240-2582), from Surat Thani to Ko Samui and Ko Phangan, runs 12 boats a day, from 5am to 7pm, with tickets at B100 for passengers, B250 for a car. Koh Chang Ferry (tel: 0-3952-8288) runs from Laem Ngop to Ko Chang every 30 minutes from 6.30am to 7pm. Passenger tickets are B120, cars B200.

The ferries can be conveniently booked at travel agents, along with train, bus or plane tickets. This is advisable in the high season. Otherwise you can buy at the ticket booth.

Trains

Thailand's state railway system (tel: 0-2222-0175; hotline: 1690; www.railway.co.th) provides an efficient means of seeing the country, with trains generally running on time. However, for many routes, buses are quicker. Travel agents, hotel desks and the information office at the main (Hualamphong) railway station can advise you on timetables and fares. Bangkok's main stations are: Hualamphong on Thanon Rama IV, for the north, east and northeast and for express trains to the south, and Thonburi on Bangkok Noi (tel: 0-2411-3100) on Thanon Rod Fai, for the west and slower trains to the south.

The northern line passes through Ayutthaya, Phitsanulok and Lampang and terminates at Chiang Mai. The upper northeastern line passes through Ayutthaya, Saraburi, Nakhon Ratchasima, Khon Kaen, Udon Thani and terminates at Nong Khai. The lower northeastern line branches east at Nakhon Ratchasima and passes through Buriram, Surin, Sisaket and terminates at Ubon Ratchathani. The eastern line runs from Bangkok to Aranyaprathet on the Thai–Cambodian border.

The southern line stops at Nakhon Pathom, Phetchaburi, Hua Hin and Chumphon. It splits at Hat Yai; one branch runs southwest through Betong and continues to the western coast of Malaysia to Singapore. The southeastern branch goes via Pattani and Yala to the Thai border. The western route heads for Kanchanaburi and other destinations in western Thailand.

Express and rapid services on the main lines offer first-class air-conditioned (or second-class fan-cooled) carriages with sleeping cabins or berths and dining carriages. There are also special air-conditioned express day trains that travel to key towns along the main lines.

Popular routes include Bangkok to Chiang Mai (first class fare B593), which has six trains from 8.30am to 10pm, journey time from 12 hours, with three of those running between 6pm and 7.35pm; Bangkok to Ayutthaya (B66), 14 trains from 5.45am to 11.40pm, around 90 minutes; and Bangkok to Surat Thani (B519), 11 trains between 8.05am and 10.50pm, from 8 hours 30 minutes.

Train tickets and rail passes can be bought at Hualamphong Railway Station, local stations or at a travel agency. Present them at the ticket gate at the station or to the inspector on board.

Intercity Coaches

The government buses operated by the Transport Company Ltd (tel: 1490; www.transport.co.th) are

The State Railway of Thailand operates five principal routes from Hualamphong Station

generally safer and more reliable than private operators. It is a vast network, known locally as Bor Kor Sor (BKS), and has terminals at every town. Air-conditioned express 42-seaters service many destinations, but VIP coaches with 32 seats spread over two levels have extra legroom and are best for long overnight journeys. Buy tickets (VIP, first class and second class) at any BKS station or online from www.thaiticketmajor.com. Present your ticket to the coach driver. There are no multi-journey passes available.

In Bangkok, BKS terminals are found at: Eastern (Ekamai) Bus Terminal: Thanon Sukhumvit opposite Soi 63 (Soi Ekamai), tel: 0-2391-8097; Northern and Northeastern Bus Terminal: Thanon Kampaengphet 2, Northern: tel: 0-2936-2841; Northeastern: tel: 0-2936-2852; Southern Bus Terminal: Thanon Boromrat Chonnani, Thonburi, tel: 0-2243-1200. Private buses, which are usually more expensive, depart from BKS terminals or their own stations. Several lines depart from Thanon Khao San, in Bangkok.

Popular routes include Bangkok to Surat Thani (8am, 8.20am and 8.30pm; around 11 hours); Bangkok to Phuket (6.30pm and 6.50pm; 14 hours); Bangkok to Chiang Mai (9am and 11pm; 11 hours).

Cycling

Although cycling is difficult in Bangkok's traffic, bikes can be rented at several hotels and guesthouses. In Pattaya, Ko Samui, Phuket and Chiang Mai, bikes and mopeds are more readily available at road-side outlets.

Spice Roads (tel: 0-2712-5305; www.spiceroads.com) has bicycles for hire and organises wide-ranging trips around the country and beyond of up to 14 days, including Bangkok to Chiang Mai.

Driving

Driving in Thailand varies a great deal depending on the time of day and the route taken, but the roads are generally in good condition, and it can be a very rewarding experience. On the negative side, there is only a very rudimentary driving test, so drivers are largely unschooled and rules of the road are often formed by intuition.

Road Conditions

Thailand has a good road system with over 50,000km (31,000 miles) of highways and more being built every year. Road signs are in both Thai and English and you should have no difficulty following a map. Petrol stations are regularly available.

Unfortunately, main routes are very busy and road courtesy is low, with right of way determined by size.

Tailgating and dangerous overtaking are also common. That said, once you are acclimatised, driving in Thailand is not too uncomfortable and some countryside routes are very pleasant.

Regulations

An international driver's licence is required in Thailand. Driving is on the left-hand side of the road; overtake and give way to the right. Seat belts are compulsory. Highway tolls apply to some expressway sections, especially in Bangkok.

Drink driving is against the law, with an alcohol limit of 50mg per 100 millilitres. The speed limit is 50km/h (30mph) in towns, 80km/h (50mph) on main roads, 120km/h (70mph) on motorways. The law requires that if you have an accident, you don't move the vehicle to the side of the road, so police can make an assessment.

Motoring Associations

If you break down, telephone the agency from which you rented the car.

Take a Trang Town *tuk-tuk*

Approximate Driving Times	
Bangkok to Chiang Mai	9hrs
Bangkok to Hua Hin	3hrs
Bangkok to Korat	3hrs
Bangkok to Pattaya	2hrs
Bangkok to Phuket	10hrs

In an emergency dial the Highway Police Patrol Centre, tel: 1193, or the Tourist Police, tel: 1155.

Vehicle Hire

Several international hire companies operate in Thailand, including Avis (www.avisthailand.com) and Budget (www.budget.co.th), with rates starting around B1,500. Local firms will be cheaper, from B800 per day, but it is important to check that insurance is included. You should opt for the full package, including Collision Damage Waiver.

There is plenty of car hire choice, so booking before you leave should not be necessary. It is also possible to hire a car or a van with driver, starting from an extra B300–500 per day, plus a surcharge for overnight stays.

Accessibility

Thailand is a major challenge for disabled travellers, and a travelling with a companion is highly advisable. The pavements are often uneven, crowded with obstructions and there are very few wheelchair ramps in buildings. There are no facilities to speak of in any of the transport networks. Wheelchair Tours to Thailand (tel: 0-2720-5395; www.wheelchairtours. com) specialises in package tours for the disabled.

Health and Safety

Visitors entering Thailand are not required to show evidence of vaccination for smallpox or cholera. Nevertheless, immunisation against cholera, hepatitis A and B and an up-to-date tetanus booster are recommended.

With its thriving nightlife and transient population, Bangkok is a magnet for sexually transmitted diseases. Aids and other diseases are not confined to high-risk sections of the population in Thailand, so practise safe sex.

If you do encounter health problems, it is good to know that private hospitals are of the highest standards in Bangkok, and many other tourist-oriented destinations will have at least one such facility. Doctors are best contacted directly through the local hospital. In cities, some pharmacies are open 24 hours, and are extremely well stocked. Prices for medical services are significantly below equivalent charges in Europe and the US. There are no reciprocal agreements with foreign countries, so arrange insurance before you leave. Most major hospitals accept credit cards.

Hospitals

Bangkok: Bumrungrad Int'l; tel: 0-2667-1000; www.bumrungrad.com. Chiang Mai Ram Hospital; tel: 0-5322-4851, emergency tel: 0-5389-5001; www.chiangmairam.com. Bangkok Pattaya Hospital; tel: 0-3842-7777; www.bph.co.th. Bangkok Phuket Hospital; 0-7624-9400; www.phukethospital.com.

Natural Hazards

Many first-time visitors take a while to adjust to Thailand's tropical heat and intense humidity. Drink plenty of water, especially if you've drunk alcohol, avoid too much sun, use sunblock and wear a hat.

Malaria and dengue fever persist in rural areas but generally not in Bangkok. When in the countryside, especially in the monsoon season, apply mosquito repellent on exposed skin at all times – dengue mosquitoes are at their most active in the day.

There are several species of venomous snake in Thailand, but the chance of being bitten by one is extremely rare. Most trekking is done with a

Embassies and Consulates

Australia: 37 Thanon Sathorn Tai; tel: 0-2344-6300; www.thailand.embassy.gov.au.
Canada: 15/F, Abdulrahim Place, Thanon Rama IV; tel: 0-2636-0540; www.canadainternational.gc.ca.
Ireland Honorary Consul: www.irelandinthailand.com.
New Zealand: M Thai Tower, 14th Fl, All Seasons Place, 87 Thanon Withayu; tel: 0-2254 2530; www.nzembassy.com.
South Africa: 12th Fl, M Thai Tower, All Seasons Place, 87 Thanon Withayu; tel: 0-2659-2900; www.saembbangkok.com.
UK: 1031 Thanon Ploenchit; tel: 0-2305-8333; ukinthailand.fco.gov.uk.
US: 120-122 Thanon Withayu; tel: 0-2205-4000; www.bangkok.usembassy.gov.

guide, who should know the best way to get you to help. If you are bitten while alone, apply a compress (not a tourniquet). Try to remember what the snake looked like, so the doctor can locate the correct antivenom. Then get to a hospital.

There is a risk of rabies. Street dogs are common, but it is best not to approach them.

Despite the devastating 2004 tsunami, Thailand is relatively clear of natural disasters. There is now a tsunami early warning system.

Food and Drink

Water has been declared drinkable in Bangkok but bottled is safest throughout the country. Ice in restaurants and hotels will be fine, though best avoided on the street. Health problems from eating streetfood are rare. However, use common sense. Eat where there is a crowd. Not only is this a recommendation of the food, it ensures there is a high turnover and food is fresher. If you avoid places that

look unhygienic, and stick to freshly cooked food, you should be fine.

Crime

Thailand is generally very safe, although a few precautions are wise. Beware of pickpockets in crowded marketplaces, carry bags away from the roadside to thwart motorbike bag-snatchers, and don't be flash with money, particularly around red-light areas. At the time of writing, many governments advise against visiting the southern provinces of Narathiwat, Yala, Pattani and Songkhla, where there is a high risk of Muslim separatist violence.

Thailand is generally safe for women travellers, even those travelling alone. Thais tend to be non-confrontational, so casual harassment and sexual crimes towards women are not common. That said, like anywhere, it isn't a great idea to be walking alone on quiet streets or beaches late at night.

The police are recognisable by their brown uniforms. There are Tourist Police (TP) units at the major destinations which are specially assigned to assist travellers. Generally, normal police officers won't speak English; it is better to contact the Tourist Police. Thailand has tough drug laws; indulge at your peril.

Directing Bangkok's notorious traffic

Money and Budgeting

Currency

The baht is the principal Thai monetary unit, abbreviated to B. It is divided into 100 units called satang, but only 50 and 25 satang pieces are used. At press time, exchange rates were GB£1: B49, US$1: B32.50, €1: B41.

Foreign currency exceeding US$20,000 either entering or leaving the country should be declared. Thai currency leaving the country is restricted to B50,000.

Cash and Cards

ATMs are available 24 hours at banks, malls, major train and bus stations, and airports. Many accept credit cards and MasterCard and Visa Debit Cards. Banking hours are Mon–Fri 9.30am–3.30pm, but most banks maintain money-changing kiosks in tourist areas. Travellers' cheques can be cashed at all exchange kiosks and banks, and generally receive better exchange rates than cash. There is a charge of B25 for each travellers' cheque cashed.

Tipping

Tipping is not generally a custom in Thailand, although restaurants (not small Thai places) and hotels will add a service charge of 10 percent to your bill. People leave loose change left over from their bill, both in cafés and taxis.

Tax

Thailand adds a 7 percent Value-Added Tax (VAT) to most goods and services (but not at street vendors). You can obtain VAT refunds by shopping at stores with the 'VAT Refund for Tourists' sign, for single purchases over B2,000, with a minimum overall expenditure of B5,000. Present your passport and the sales assistant will complete the refund form. At the airport, present the form, sales receipt and goods bought to Customs. After approval, present your claim to the VAT Refund Counter.

Budgeting for Your Trip

Thailand is inexpensive when compared to most Western countries. After you budget for airline tickets and hotels, you can spend as little as B500 per day on meals and still eat very well, as long as you stick to Thai food. Depending on the exchange rate, international restaurants' prices are similar to those in London. You can get across town for B10 in a bus; a 20-minute taxi ride will cost around B100.

Money-Saving Tips

- Department stores usually have discount cards
- Always ask for a discount wherever you shop
- On Bangkok Skytrain and Metro, Day multi-trip passes are cheaper
- Look for art openings in newspaper listings. There are often free drinks and nobody checking the guest list
- At Bangkok's Grand Palace, the ticket also gets free entry to some attractions in Dusit Park
- Many bars have happy hours, even in hotels. Check their websites

Thai baht banknotes

Low season, economy return flights from New York to Bangkok are $1,300–1,500. High season from $1,500–1,900. First class flights from $12,200–15,500, high and low season.

Low season return flights from Los Angeles are $900–1,200. High season from $1,500–1,700. First-class from $10,500–11,000 high and low season.

Low season from London are £450–500. High season from £770–870. First-class flights from £3,600–4,500, high and low season.

For a budget, backpacker-style holiday you will need to set aside B7,000 (£140/US$220) per person per week. A standard family holiday for four will cost around B70,000 (£1,500/US$2,200) per week. A luxury, no-expense-spared break can cost over B1,500,000 (£30,000/US$46,000) per person per week. Prices include accommodation, but not flights.

Budgeting for Your Trip

- **Top-class/boutique hotel**: B6,000–20,000 for a double
- **Standard-class hotel**: B2,000–4,000 for a double
- **Bed & breakfast**: from B500–1,000 for a double
- **Youth hostel**: B100–150 per person

- **Domestic flight**: B2,200 Bangkok to Phuket
- **Intercity coach ticket**: B510 Bangkok to Chiang Mai
- **Intercity train ticket**: B519 Bangkok to Surat Thani
- **Car hire**: B800–7,000 per day
- **Petrol**: B40 a litre
- **10-minute taxi ride**: B50
- **Airport shuttle bus**: B150
- **Short bus ride**: B5
- **One-day pass**: B120 Bangkok Skytrain

- **Breakfast**: B30–80 (Thai)
- **Lunch in a café**: from B30–100 (Thai)
- **Coffee/tea in a café**: B60–80
- **Main course, budget restaurant**: B80–200 (Thai)
- **Main course, moderate restaurant**: B300–750 (international)
- **Main course, expensive restaurant**: B900–2,500 (international)
- **Bottle of wine in a restaurant**: B800–125,000
- **Beer in a pub**: B50–200

- **Museum admission**: B40–200
- **Daytrip to Ayutthaya**: B500
- **Chiang Mai Zoo**: B100
- **Thai massage**: B200–2,900/hr
- **Theatre/concert ticket**: B200–3,000
- **Tailor-made suit**: B3,000–10,000
- **Nightclub entry**: B500, with two drinks

Money and Budgeting

Responsible Travel

Take care not to litter or pollute

Getting There

A return flight from London to Bangkok leaves a carbon footprint of 4.12 metric tons of CO_2. To offset this amount would cost £70.

A return flight from Los Angeles to Bangkok leaves a carbon footprint of 2.40 metric tons of CO_2. To offset this amount would cost $62.

Carbon Footprint (www.carbon-footprint.com) has several suggestions for ways to offset, including reforestation and renewable energy initiatives.

Ecotourism

There are an increasing number of eco-friendly facilities in Thailand for the responsible tourist. The Thailand Community Based Tourism Institute (www.cbt-i.org) has information about various projects as well as links to partner tour agencies and local tourism programmes. The Educational Travel Center (www.etc.co.th) also has options for community-based holidays.

Other sources of ecotourism and volunteering information include the Gibbon Rehabilitation Project (www.gibbonproject.org), North by North East Tours (www.north-by-north-east.com) and East West Siam (www.ewsiam.com), whose Himmapaan Project promotes reforestation and carbon offsetting at Lisu Lodge, near Chiang Mai.

Ethical Tourism

One of the best ways to ensure your money goes to local people is to use small independent tours, homestays, local shops and restaurants. If you book your holiday through an agent, find out what they actually do to help local communities and the environment.

In order that tourism harms communities as little as possible, local customs need to be respected. Thais do not like (or respect) confrontational behaviour. Appropriate dress in temples is a good idea, even in those that don't specifically demand it. Raised voices and anger are seen as a loss of face for everyone concerned, but especially the perpetrator.

Volunteering/Charities

Volunteering is a good way of leaving something positive behind in the community you have visited. It can range from helping in wildlife sanctuaries to working on hill-tribe projects and teaching deprived children. Visit the Educational Travel Centre (www.etc. co.th) for ideas and contacts.

Thailand's wildlife suffers from illegal poaching, much of which is carried out to satisfy demand for 'magic' potions, charms, and for traditional medicines. The exotic pet trade is also highly lucrative. Charities such as Freeland (www.freeland.org) and Friends of the Asian Elephant (www.elephant-soraida.com) help protect wildlife and educate local communities about conservation. *(See Backpacking, p.27.)*

Things to Avoid

Don't leave litter in national parks, on beaches or in the sea. Not only is it ugly but it is hazardous to wildlife. Feeding wildlife should also be off limits, as eating inappropriate food is harmful. Thailand's coral suffered badly in the 2004 tsunami, but thoughtless tourism is an even greater worry. Don't stand on coral or take any as a souvenir.

VSO volunteer agriculturalist working with children in a school garden, Kanchanaburi

Family Holidays

Practicalities

Thais love children, and will go out of their way to help in most situations should you need it. This might even stretch to waiters playing with your kids while you enjoy a restaurant meal.

Buying nappies, baby food and other supplies is straightforward, with department stores and chemists well stocked. But nappy changing spaces are scarce. In Bangkok, some central department stores have facilities, and they may also have breastfeeding rooms.

Lugging a baby carrier around will feel like twice the weight in the tropical heat, so a stroller is probably a better option, although the pavements are very difficult to negotiate, being often cracked, full of holes and cluttered with street stalls.

If you are hiring a car, international firms such as Budget (www.budget.co.th) have baby seats suitable for ages six months to three years in all locations, but you need to pre-book. There is a small extra charge. There are no car seats for younger children. Cars are fitted with mounting points if you take your own baby seats.

Accommodation

There is a growing range of facilities for children in medium-range hotels and upwards in Thailand, as long as you are in touristed areas. Many hotels in Bangkok, Pattaya, Phuket and Chiang Mai will have at least a kids' pool and babysitting facilities, and resorts, in particular, may have child-dedicated clubs to take

Family Holidays

Travelling with children is a breeze in Thailand

the strain while you go out and have some fun.

You should have no trouble finding something suitable in most popular beach areas of the country. Naturally a lot of families are attracted to these hotels, so there are usually plenty of other kids to mix with.

Beachside resorts are the best choices with children in tow. Not only are the resort facilities better, the air is generally cooler, and there are lots of things to keep children occupied, even just playing in the water and on the sands. Most of the up-market resorts will have private beaches, so there is an added element of safety.

Some resorts will be specifically geared towards family holidays. These will have dedicated clubs for younger children, aged 4–12, which organise activities such as games, parties, and even sleepovers, with tents and camp-fires. They will often have dress-up areas, cinemas, teen internet zones, a kids' pool and adventure programmes.

They should also have qualified supervision. Babysitting services will be available for the youngest, but usually with an added fee.

The other advantage of resorts is that they appeal to teens, too. Many have a water park and windsurfing, sailing and tennis lessons that might keep older kids amused.

Self-catering is a useful option for families, as they are self-contained, and often have facilities such as swimming pool, restaurants and fitness centres also on-site. There is a choice around the country at www.sabaai.com.

Food and Drink

Dining with children in Thailand should be hassle free. Thais themselves don't feed their kids spicy food, and there are lots of dishes that are very mild. There is also a wide choice of international food available in the main tourist centres, including Western fast-food outlets. Most Thai places welcome children. For international restaurants it is worth calling ahead to check.

Attractions and Activities

There are many activities around the country for kids to get involved in. Animal fun includes Siam Ocean World (www.siamoceanworld.com), Safari World (www.safariworld.com) and Dusit Zoo (www.zoothailand. org), all in Bangkok. And in Chiang Mai there are Mae Sa Elephant Camp (www.maesaelephantcamp.com) and

Chiang Mai Zoo and Arboretum (www.chiangmaizoo.com).

Bangkok also has roller coasters at Dream World (www.dreamworld-th. com), including sled rides at Snow Town; Pattaya has elephant battles, lasers and pyrotechnics at Alangkarn Theatre (www.alangkarnthailand. com), and Phuket Fantasea (www. phuket-fantasea.com) has a circus.

There are lots of more adventurous activities available for older kids, such as zip lines through the jungle at Flight of the Gibbon (www.tree-topasia.com) outside Pattaya, and watersports with Kite Boarding Asia (www.kiteboardingasia.com) in several locations, including Hua Hin, Samui and Phuket. Thailand isn't known for safety laws or enforcement of them, so age restriction will be largely down to your own common sense. But check the insurance policy of organisers.

Properly equipped and ready for a go-karting adventure in Patong, Phuket

Family Holidays

SETTING THE SCENE

History – *p.268* **Culture** – *p.276* **Food and Drink** – *p.283*

History

Thailand's long history includes one of the world's earliest Iron Age settlements, followed by violent power shifts between ethnic groups from the west and east, as both the Mon and Khmers ruled large swathes of land in what was to become first Siam, and later Thailand. Small migrating tribes that formed city-states eventually gained ascendance, and two in particular – Sukhothai and Ayutthaya – became the founders of the nation. When Ayutthaya fell to the Burmese, the country – seemingly shattered by the complete destruction of its cultural heart – was resurrected by King Taksin, who relocated the capital to Thonburi and rebuilt. A new ruling dynasty, formed in 1782, made Bangkok the capital. The current King Bhumibol Adulyadej, its ninth king, has overseen some of the most severe crises in the nation's history, as it careers at breakneck speed into the 21st century.

Archaeological finds in Ban Chiang, northeast Thailand, date back over 5,000 years, proving the country was home to one of the world's first Bronze Age civilisations. What happened to those prehistoric people is not known.

As for the Thais: they are descended from many ethnic groups. Around 300BC, Indian traders brought both Hinduism and Buddhism, which became widespread in southern Thailand by the 1st century AD. Another group, the Mon, established the Dvaravati kingdom, which flourished from the 6th to the 11th centuries, with Nakhon Pathom and Lopburi as major settlements.

In the east, the Khmer empire of Angkor, strongly influenced by Indian culture, and forerunner of present-day Cambodia, ruled east of the Chao Phraya valley and north to Laos. By the early 12th century, it had conquered the Dvaravati lands and dominated to Nakhon Si Thammarat, on the Malay Peninsula.

But the group who gave their name to present-day Thailand were the Tai, who migrated in several tribes from China's Yunnan region, probably starting around the 10th century.

They formed principalities, usually vassal states to the Khmer empire, until Sukhothai, in 1238, effectively declared

Ban Chiang pottery fragments unearthed at an archaeological site in Udon Thani

Buddha statues in Kamphaeng Phet
Historical Park near Sukhotai

AYUTTHAYA

Ayutthaya, established in 1350, thrived for over 400 years as one of the East's great civilisations. After driving out the Khmers and overcoming Sukhothai, Ayutthaya became a centre for trade between China, India and Europe. In the 17th century, ambassadors from the court of Louis XIV, in France, were there, along with explorers, zealous Jesuit missionaries and traders. Directors of Britain's East India Company compared it favourably with London, estimating the population to be anything from 300,000 to 1 million. With its palaces, canals and temples, the city acquired a reputation for being the most beautiful in Southeast Asia.

One Greek adventurer, named Constantine Phaulkon, was even appointed King Narai's first minister, and acted as the principal go-between for diplomatic exchanges. Such apparent favouritism sparked jealousy and suspicion, and during a bloody revolt, shortly before the king died in 1688, Phaulkon was arrested and then executed. Thailand, subsequently, reined in contact with the West for 150 years.

Between the 15th and 18th centuries, Siam fought numerous battles against neighbouring Burma, and in April 1767, the Burmese captured Ayutthaya, after a 14-month siege. They pillaged the city and vandalised every aspect of Thai culture and art.

One survivor, a young general called Taksin, rallied the remnants of the Thai army and expelled the Burmese garrison. Ayutthaya had been almost totally destroyed, so Taksin founded a new capital at Thonburi,

independence from Angkor. This event is now widely regarded as the birth of the Siamese, later called Thai, nation.

DAWN OF SIAM

The first great chapter of Thai history began with King Ramkamhaeng the Great, ruler of Sukhothai from c. 1280–1317. His kingdom stretched from Lampang, in the north, to Vientiane, now capital of Laos, and south to Nakhon Si Thammarat. Ramkamhaeng adopted Buddhism as the official religion and introduced the first Thai script, while Sukhothai was a thriving centre for the arts. But Sukhothai was soon usurped by another city power: Ayutthaya.

directly across the Chao Phraya River from a small village called Bang Makok, now known as Bangkok.

Taksin was crowned King of Siam, despite being of Chinese descent. He ruled until 1782, when he was overthrown by a group of elite families. Taksin was beaten to death with a sandalwood club while tied inside a sack, as it was forbidden for royal blood to touch the ground.

FROM THONBURI TO BANGKOK

Taksin was replaced by King Rama I, the first ruler of the Chakri dynasty, which still occupies the throne today. The new king moved his capital from Thonburi to Bangkok, believing it would be easier to defend. He modelled it on Ayutthaya, forming an island with a series of canals and beginning the architectural splendour of the Grand Palace and Wat Phra Kaew.

His son, Rama II, devoted himself to preserving Thai literature, and produced a classic version of the Thai *Ramakien*, based on the epic Sanskrit poem, the *Ramayana*. He also re-established relations with the West. He and his successor Rama III (1824–51) restored or extended some of Bangkok's finest temples, including Wat Arun, Wat Pho and Wat Suthat.

THE KING AND I

King Rama IV (1851–68), also known as King Mongkut, is loosely represented in *The King and I*, a Hollywood film that is deemed disrespectful and banned in Thailand. He was a modern-minded and learned scholar who studied English, Latin, Pali and Sanskrit, as well as history, geography and the sciences. He was also a monk for 27 years before his accession to the throne, which gave him the opportunity to roam as a commoner among the people.

Rama IV made the decision to modernise many of the country's institutions, believing it would bring Siam in line with the West and reduce hostilities. Britain was the first European country to benefit, when an 1855 treaty granted preferential trade conditions. Other Western nations, including France and the United States, followed.

Rama I, founder of the Chakri Dynasty

Together with his son and successor Chulalongkorn, he is considered chiefly responsible for Thailand's continued independence throughout the colonial period. To this day Thais reserve a special affection for both these monarchs.

KING CHULALONGKORN

King Mongkut's son, King Rama V (1868–1910), also called King Chulalongkorn, ascended the throne in 1868 when he was only 15 years old. A great reformer, Chulalongkorn abolished serfdom and ended the ancient custom of ritual prostration in the presence of the ruler. He brought in foreign advisers from abroad, sent his sons to study in Europe, and modernised the medical and education systems.

Chulalongkorn's contributions to the cultural heritage of Bangkok included the construction of Dusit Palace, Ratchadamnoen Avenue and the palace and gardens of Bang Pa-In. When he died in 1910, a grieving nation awarded him the title Phya Maharaj, or Beloved Great King.

With Thailand sandwiched between the colonial powers of France, in Vietnam, and Britain, in Burma, the king compromised and gave up parts of the country to avoid full colonisation. France claimed Laos and western Cambodia, while Britain took the northern Malay territories.

BETWEEN THE WORLD WARS

In 1918, King Vajiravudh (Rama VI) – Cambridge-educated and having served for a time in the British army

Rama V (King Chulalongkorn)

– dispatched troops to France to support the Allied cause. Once the war was over, Siam joined the world community, when it became a member of the League of Nations. Other legacies of Rama VI were compulsory primary education and the use of family names, until then unknown in Siam.

King Prajadhipok (Rama VII) succeeded the throne in 1925. Unlike Rama VI, who was criticised for extravagance, the new king tried to cut public expenditure, which, combined with increased revenue from foreign trade, paid ample dividends. But the worldwide economic crisis of the 1930s again forced the cutting of purse strings, causing unrest in the ranks of civil servants.

In 1932, a coup staged by the People's Party – a military and civilian group masterminded by foreign-educated Thais – ended absolute power in Siam. The chief ideologist

The Bridge on the River Kwai in Kanchanaburi has become a haunting memorial to the POWs who died in World War II

was Pridi Banomyong, a young lawyer trained in France, with the military side led by Plaek Pibun Songkhram (Pibun).

The king moved to England and abdicated in 1935. Ananda Mahidol (Rama VIII), a 10-year-old half-nephew, agreed to take the throne, but remained in Switzerland to complete his schooling. In 1938, Pibun became prime minister, and, increasingly authoritarian, attempted to instil a sense of nationalism. He renamed the country Thailand.

WORLD WAR II

Japan invaded Thailand in World War II, and Pibun declared war on the Allies. Thailand's ambassador in the US, MR Seni Pramoj, collaborated with the Americans and formed a Free Thai movement. In Bangkok, Pridi Banomyong, who had been marginalised by Pibul, established a local resistance movement, the Seri Thai.

Pridi's struggle for power with Pibun and later Seni Pramoj lasted several years. After the now adult King Ananda, on holiday in Thailand, was found shot dead in his palace bedroom in 1946, one of the many rumours and conspiracy theories surrounding this incident claimed Pridi was involved. He fled to Singapore, and after a failed armed rebellion against the Pibun government in 1949, left for China, and never returned.

The circumstances of the king's death have still not been satisfactorily explained; the incident is still discussed; and most people have a theory to this day.

King Ananda was succeeded by his younger brother, Bhumibol Adulyadej (Rama IX), the present monarch, who returned to Switzerland to complete law studies, and did not take up active duties until the 1950s. By then, Thailand had been without a resident king for 20 years.

THE POST-WAR ERA

Since 1932, Thailand has endured 19 coups, and has had nearly 60 prime ministers, although some of these have served several terms. All governments were led by the military between 1946 and 1973, when a clique of generals, Sarit Thanarat, Thanom Kittikachorn and Prapas

Charusathien, employed martial law. Dubbed 'The Three Tyrants', they had grown rich on the large infusions of money flowing into Thailand from the US, which used the country as a base during the Vietnam War.

Following the arrest of student leaders for distributing anti-government leaflets, protests broke out around the country, including 400,000 people at Bangkok's Democracy Monument. Clashes on 14 October 1973 between troops and students left many students dead (the official figure was 77, press estimates 400). The Three Tyrants fled to the US.

After a brief period of civilian governments, in 1976 General Thanom returned to the country, sparking more protests, this time at Thammasat University. On 6 October, police, troops and paramilitary organisations stormed the grounds, raping and killing many people. Within hours the army had seized power.

For the next decade relatively moderate military rule laid the

The Royal Household of King Bhumibol

foundations for new elections, which ushered in a civilian government, until another coup, this one bloodless, in 1991. The following year, in protests against the non-elected leader General Suchinda Kraprayoon, more than 100 pro-democracy demonstrators were wounded or killed.

King Bhumibol brokered reconciliation, and a series of elected governments followed. In 1997, Thailand's economic crash triggered the Asian financial crisis.

THAKSIN SHINAWATRA

In 2001, the newly formed Thai Rak Thai party, led by Thaksin Shinawatra, won a landslide victory. The new leader proved immediately controversial. He faced, and successfully defended, charges of corruption; he was widely condemned after hundreds were killed in his War on Drugs; and he was slammed for suppressing the media. But his populist approach saw loans and cheap health care for the poor. As he became wildly popular in poorer rural areas, his 'CEO style' of government was increasingly annoying traditional powers centred in Bangkok.

In 2005, anti-Thaksin street demonstrators adopted the colour yellow to show allegiance to the monarchy, and became known as the Yellow Shirts. The movement intensified after Thaksin – already the richest man in Thailand – sold his telecommunications company to an arm of the Singapore government for US$1.9 billion and paid no tax. In September 2006, Thaksin was ousted in a military coup.

The following year, the new

Red Shirt anti-government protestors

authorities banned Thaksin from politics and froze his bank accounts. As Thaksin lived in exile, his followers, calling themselves the United Front for Democracy Against Dictatorship (UDD), and wearing red shirts, launched their own protests against the military government.

A Thaksin proxy, the People Power Party (PPP) won the next general election in December 2007, and Thaksin returned the following year, only to later skip bail on corruption charges and flee once again to London.

RED SHIRT, YELLOW SHIRT

Meanwhile, the Yellow Shirt demonstrations resumed. During late 2008, they seized the airport (dubbed without apparent irony 'Operation Hiroshima'), bringing the country to a standstill. In December that year, the courts disbanded the ruling party, and, in a deal largely seen as being brokered by the army, some key Thaksin allies jumped ship. The Democrat Party took office with Abhisit Vejjajiva

as prime minister, bringing the Red Shirts back to the streets.

In April 2009, the Red Shirts disrupted the ASEAN Summit in Pattaya, causing several heads of state to be airlifted to safety, and Songkran riots erupted in Bangkok. In the same month, People's Alliance for Democracy (PAD) leader Sondhi Limthongkul was shot, but survived the assassination attempt.

In February 2010, outstanding corruption charges against Thaksin were finally heard. The courts found him guilty of abuse of power and confiscated assets of B46 billion. In April and May, thousands of Red Shirt demonstrators occupied various parts of the city, closing Pathumwan shopping malls for several weeks. Eighty-five people were killed and nearly 1,500 injured in clashes with the army, mainly on 10 April and 19 May. Banks, department stores and other major buildings were torched in the battles. Thaksin, still abroad, was charged with terrorism.

6–11th century AD
The Dvaravati culture flourishes.

7–11th century
The Khmers rule large parts of what is now Thailand.

1238
Sukhothai kingdom established.

1351
The kingdom of Ayutthaya is founded by Phaya U Thong (Ramathibodi I).

1431
Ayutthaya conquers the Khmer empire centred on Angkor.

1767
Ayutthaya is invaded by the old enemy Burma. General Taksin escapes and is crowned king the following year in Thornburi.

1782
King Rama I, first ruler of the Chakri dynasty, installs the new capital in Bangkok.

1851–68
Rule of King Mongkut (Rama IV).

1868–1910
Chulalongkorn (Rama V) continues his father's initiatives.

1910–25
Rama VI (Vajiravudh) concentrates on political reforms. Britain persuades Siam to fight with the Allies in World War I.

1932
After a military coup, Siam becomes a constitutional monarchy.

1939
Under Prime Minister Pibun Songkhram, Siam adopts a more nationalist stance. The country's name is officially changed to Thailand.

1939–45
During World War II, Thailand is invaded by Japan and declares war on the Allies.

1946
King Ananda dies in mysterious circumstances. His younger brother King Bhumibol ascends the throne as Rama IX.

1945–73
During the Vietnam War, the USA uses Thailand as a base.

1973–76
Political demonstrations lead to several deaths.

1992
Demonstrations against General Suchinda are violently suppressed. The king intervenes.

1997–2001
Thailand's economic collapse sparks the Asian financial crisis. Gradual recovery follows. Democratic government led by Chuan Leekpai.

2004
The Asian tsunami strikes southern Thailand on 26 December.

2006
Opposition parties boycott April elections. A coup unseats Thaksin and installs a temporary military government.

2008
Yellow Shirts seize Bangkok's airport, causing widespread disruption. Abhisit Vejjajiva becomes prime minister.

2009
Red Shirt protestors disrupt ASEAN summit in Pattaya, forcing its cancellation.

2010
Many killed as the Red Shirts occupy parts of Bangkok.

Culture

A warm-hearted demeanour and a sense of calm are among the main Thai qualities that have visitors returning time and again to the Land of Smiles, along with a fascinating cultural landscape.

Like most of Southeast Asia, Thailand's traditional cultural symbols and aesthetics are often most keenly appreciated by people outside the country. Abroad, for instance, Thai dance drama is recognised as among the world's most dazzling and stylistically challenging, yet, in Thailand, performances are relatively rare outside tourist centres, while traditional puppet theatre is struggling to survive. The country's contemporary art scene, on the other hand, is thriving, and also gaining recognition in international circles. Bangkok, in particular, has some good modern art galleries. Meanwhile, Thailand's independent film fraternity gained a shot in the arm in 2010, when the already acclaimed director Apichatpong Weerasethakul won the coveted Palme d'Or at the Cannes Film Festival.

Traditional *wai* greeting

THE PEOPLE

Travellers to Thailand are generally struck by the friendliness of the people, and three concepts, in particular, are significant in forming the Thais' relaxed attitude. The first two, *jai yen* (cool heart) and *mai pen rai* (never mind), are central to the tolerance that allows many fringe lifestyles to exist largely unhassled. To lose your temper or raise your voice in public is seen as a severe loss of face, and Thais will go to great lengths to prevent confrontation. The third, *sanuk* (fun), requires that everything – work, play, tragedy – should have elements of enjoyment, and always with lots of friends.

Thais greet each other with a *wai* (hands pressed together below the chin). Surnames are infrequently used, and even relative strangers will refer to each other by their nickname, often based on animals, like Moo (pig) or Poo (crab), or desirable objects, such as Benz.

Thailand's 64 million population is more than 90 percent Theravada Buddhist. Muslims, who make up around 6 percent, are mainly concentrated in the Deep South. Other immigrant groups include Indians, Khmer, Vietnamese and various hill tribes living in the north. Around 14 percent of

Thais are descended from Chinese immigrants who mostly arrived during the 19th century and first half of the 20th century.

The country has four regions, each with its own dialect, cultural traits and cuisine. Bangkok, in the Central Plains, is the geographical and commercial heart, and home to around one in five people. The central Thai dialect is spoken by educated Thais all over the country.

In the north, people speak a variant called *kham meuang*; in the northeast, they speak Isaan, a language closely related to Lao; and in the south, a southern Thai dialect, plus Malay, spoken by some Muslims. Travellers should check travel advisories before going to the south, as violence associated with Muslim separatist movements continues to escalate.

Thai society is hierarchical, and people use personal pronouns according relative status. The top echelons are known as Hi-So, a Thai slang abbreviated from 'high society'. And at the very top are the king and the royal family, who are greatly revered.

The national anthem is played at 8am and 6pm in public spaces each day, when people will stop what they are doing and stand still as a mark of respect. The king's portrait is prominently displayed in offices, shops and houses, and this respect is enshrined in Lese-majesty, which carry a maximum penalty of seven years' imprisonment for anyone convicted of insulting the royal family.

In recent years the king has endured pockets of unprecedented criticism from some supporters of the fugitive ex-prime minister Thaksin Shinawatra, who believe the traditional elite were involved in his overthrow.

Outside the cities, most people still work in agriculture, although many villagers leave to find work in the big cities as taxi drivers, construction workers and the country's notorious sex industry.

Thailand made prostitution illegal in 1960, although the law is rarely enforced, and sex is openly for sale in go-go bars, brothels and massage parlours. In part this is because it is an accepted and common practice for Thai men to patronise prostitutes or have a *mia noi*, literally 'little wife' ,or mistress on the side.

Sex tourism escalated with American troops taking R&R during the Vietnam War, and, by the 1980s, planeloads of men were flying in for the purpose. Many sex workers, both male and female, come from

At work in a Patong dance bar

northeast Thailand, where incomes are the lowest in the country. Many cross-cultural marriages have started in a Bangkok brothel, and government figures often cite foreign husbands in Northeastern villages as being significant contributors to GDP.

NGOs estimate there are between 200,000 and 300,000 sex workers in Thailand, and, having found that few are motivated to leave the business, no longer focus their primary efforts on extricating them. Organisations such as Empower instead educate bar girls and boys about the dangers of HIV, and teach them English so they are less likely to be exploited by clients.

The non-voluntary side of the sex trade is infinitely more grim. There are an estimated 60,000 child prostitutes in Thailand, many willingly sold by their parents, against whom convictions are rare.

The highly visible nature of sex work is at odds with the otherwise high moral code of behaviour in the country. Women especially are expected to deport themselves modestly, and the Ministry of Culture (much to the outrage of many) is constantly making edicts about appropriate behaviour and dress. Websites that criticise the ministry have been closed down, although in mid-2010 a Facebook page, 'We're sick of Ministry of Culture in Thailand' (sic), was still running.

Thai people are generally sympathetic in their attitude towards sexuality. Consensual adult homosexuality is tolerated, and this extends to transvestites, or *kathoey* (see p.114).

THAI DANCE-DRAMA

The origins of traditional Thai theatrical arts are entwined with court ceremony and religious ritual, some of which can still be seen today in Bangkok's Erawan Shrine or the Lak Muang, where performers are hired to dance as a means of thanksgiving to the spirit gods. Dancers are accompanied by a singer providing a storyline and a *phipat* orchestra (see p.280).

The most identifiable form of dance-drama is *khon*, historically performed by a large troupe of male dancers wearing beautifully crafted masks, and originally staged for the

Traditional dancers at the Erawan Shrine

royal court. These days a condensed version of several episodes from the *Ramakien* – based on the Hindu epic the *Ramayana* – is adapted into a short medley of palatable scenes for tourist dinner shows.

The most graceful dance is *lakhon*, which has two forms. The first, *lakhon nai* (inside *lakhon*), was once performed only inside the palace walls by women. The second, *lakhon nawk* (outside *lakhon*), was performed outside by both sexes.

Village arts are often parodies of the palace arts – more burlesque, with pratfalls and bawdy humour. *Likay* is the village form of *lakhon*, played out against a gaudy backdrop to an audience that walks in and out of the performance, eating and talking at will.

PUPPET THEATRE

It is thought that the movements of dance-drama originated in *nang yai* (shadow puppet) performances of the 16th and 17th centuries, in which huge buffalo hides were cut into the shapes of characters from the *Ramakien*. Against a torch-lit translucent screen, handlers manipulated these puppets so that their silhouettes told the stories. As they moved the figures across the screen, the puppeteers danced the emotions they wanted the figures to convey. A similar form of puppet theatre, *nang thalung*, still survives in the southern provinces (see p.174).

Struggling to survive in Bangkok is the Joe Louis Theatre, which won the Best Performance Award at the World Festival of Puppet Arts in 2008. It was due to leave its home in the Suan

A *nang yai* shadow-puppet performance

Lum Night Bazaar in August 2010, with a new venue as yet unfound.

MODERN THEATRE AND DANCE

The only modern dance company with significant staying power is Patravadi Theatre, run by Patravadi Mechudhon. They often meld classic Thai tales with traditional local dance and theatre and modern Western or other Asian influences, like Japanese *butoh* and Indonesian *wayang kulit*. Some productions tour overseas – notably the landmark *Sahatsadecha*, a mix of *khon* and *nang yai*, which played at the Biennale de la Danse, in Lyon, France. Patravadi Theatre also hosts the annual Fringe Festival of Dance, Drama and Music at venues in Bangkok and Hua Hin.

THAI CLASSICAL MUSIC

Thai classical music works to a scale of seven full steps, each instrument playing the same melody, but in a pattern all its own, and seldom rising in

A classical *phipat* orchestra performing at the Mandarin Oriental Hotel in Bangkok

solo. Rather, in a method sometimes likened to jazz, they challenge and cajole each other and respond according to how others are playing.

A classical *phipat* orchestra has a single-reed instrument, the oboe-like *phinai*, two types of *ranad* (a xylophone of bamboo bars), and two sets of *gong wong* (tuned gongs arranged in a semicircle around the player). The rhythm is set by the *ching*, a tiny cymbal, aided by percussionists who play drums beaten with the fingers. A four-piece *phipat* band also spurs combatants at Thai boxing matches.

THAI ROCK & COUNTRY MUSIC

Thai-style rock and country music comes in three genres. The rock-format *plaeng puer cheewit* (Songs For Life) is rooted in the record collections of Vietnam War American GIs stationed in Thailand. The lyrics developed as protest songs during Thailand's student uprisings of the early 1970s. *Luk thung* (Child of the

Rice Fields) is Thai country music. Its 'real life' lyrics deal with unrequited love, poverty and despair. *Morlam* (Doctor of Rap) is a bawdy, often political, upcountry form sung in the Lao dialect.

OPERA AND WESTERN CLASSICAL MUSIC

Director Somtow Sucharitkul set up the Bangkok Opera in 2002. Among its three or four yearly productions are classics like *The Magic Flute* and Somtow's own works, written in English, such as *Mae Naak*, based on a Thai ghost story.

The Bangkok Symphony Orchestra (BSO) plays concerts throughout the year, including on Sundays in Lumphini Park during the cool season.

CLASSICAL LITERATURE

Unfortunately, most of the country's classical written literature was destroyed when the Burmese sacked Ayutthaya in 1767. At the heart of Thai literature is the *Ramakien*, the

Thai version of the Indian *Ramayana*, and the *Jataka* tales, also of Indian origin, which tell of the Buddha's reincarnations prior to enlightenment. The first tales were translated from Pali script to Thai in the late 15th century. They have generated many other popular and classic stories, such as *Phra Aphaimani*, written by Sunthorn Phu, the 18th-century equivalent of poet laureate.

MODERN LITERATURE

Thai novels were first published in the 1920s, with mainly social or political themes. Military rule in the 1950s, however, brought heavy censorship, and quality fiction practically

Detail from an instructive mural at Bangkok's Wat Traimit

disappeared for 20 years. Many landmark Thai books were translated into English in the early 1990s. The late prime minister and cultural advocate Kukrit Pramoj's *Many Lives*, for instance, gives a good introduction to the Buddhist way of thinking. His *Four Reigns* is a fictional yet accurate account of court life in the 19th and 20th centuries. Also of note are Kampoon Boontawee's *Children of Isaan* and Botan's *Letters from Thailand*.

TRADITIONAL ART

The inner walls of the *bot* (ordination halls) and *viharn* (sermon halls) in Thai temples are traditionally covered with murals. In the days before public education, the temple was the principal repository of knowledge for the common person. Monks were the teachers, and these walls were illustrated lectures, the principal theme being the life of the Buddha.

The murals at Buddhaisawan Chapel in Bangkok's National Museum are among the finest examples of Thai painting. Others include the murals at Wat Suthat and the 19th-century paintings at Wat Bowonniwet.

CONTEMPORARY ART

At the turn of the 20th century, King Chulalongkorn commissioned several European artists for Bangkok projects, a trend the government continued in 1923 when they hired Italian sculptor Corrado Feroci. The Florentine artist proved catalytic in the development of modern Thai art right through the 1960s. Locals gave him the adopted name of Silpa Bhirasri. He is considered to be the forefather of modern art in Thailand, and established the country's first School of Fine Arts, which later became Silpakorn University.

Spirituality and Buddhism have been, and still are, major precepts in contemporary art, whether created by neo-traditionalist painters like Thawan Duchanee and Chalermchai Kositpipat, whose late 20th-century paintings reinvigorate traditional perceptions of Thai identity, or the meditative installations by the late Montien Boonma. Rising artist Sakarin Krue-on uses spiritual metaphors as his basis, appropriating traditional imagery to question the blind adoption of Western trends.

Aside from the spiritual, since the 1997 economic collapse many local artists have begun to question the effects of globalisation on the Thai populace. Rebellious artist Vasan Sitthiket blurs his art with faux political campaigning to highlight his contempt for national policies.

The 11-storey Bangkok Arts and Culture Centre, despite political infighting and being a less than perfect space, is already the most significant exhibition centre in the city, and has run several major shows with both local and international artists since it opened in 2008.

CINEMA

Like most places in the world, Hollywood blockbusters dominate the cinemas, and most independent Thai films don't get the screen time they deserve. This is a shame, as there are some talented Thai directors receiving acclaim on the international circuit. Leading the way is Apichatpong

Scene from the 2006 Apichatpong Weerasethakul film *Invisible Waves*

Weerasethakul, who followed up Cannes prizes for *Blissfully Yours* (2002) and *Tropical Malady* (Sud Pralad) (2004) with the ultimate Palme d'Or in 2010 for *Uncle Boonmee Who Can Recall His Past Lives*. Another significant name is Pen-Ek Ratanaruang, best known for *Last Life in the Universe* (2004) and *Invisible Waves* (2006). Bangkok has several annual film festivals, including the Bangkok International Film Festival, the World Film Festival and the EU Film Festival (which also has a Chiang Mai run).

Customs and Etiquette Tips

- Don't criticise the royal family. Thais find it offensive, and it is also illegal
- Wear appropriate clothes when visiting religious sights (no shorts; no bare shoulders for women)
- Don't point your feet at Buddha images (or people)
- Don't touch people on the head
- Don't blow your nose in public

Food and Drink

Good food in Thailand is ubiquitous. And if you don't like chillies, a statement of '*mai phet*' (not spicy) at the time you order will bring a delicious selection of cooler, more subtle flavours that may include tastes from the sweetness of coconut milk to the pungency of fresh lemon grass or garlic and the saltiness of fermented fish. Added to that are crispy fresh vegetables, lime, a pinch of coriander – and, of course, lashings of culinary inspiration.

Thailand has a very fertile landscape. It is the world's biggest rice producer, has an abundance of seafood and all manner of tasty fruit, with mango, bananas and pineapple being especially favoured, along with the smelly durian. The best meats are chicken and pork.

In cities and tourist-friendly destinations, there will also be a good choice of international restaurants, from Italian and French to Mexican, while cafés, pubs and bars have a long list of local and imported drinks.

REGIONAL CUISINES

Each region of Thailand has its own food style based on local ingredients and the influence of the people who have lived and passed through over centuries (*see Culinary Experiences, p.56*). Popular among northern diners, for instance, is a delicious local curry known as *khao soy*, made with a coconut-based sauce and usually chicken on a bed of noodles with crispy noodles piled on top. The northeast is famed for its *khao niaw* (sticky or glutinous rice), normally served in a bamboo basket as an accompaniment to barbecued meat or spicy salads like *laab*, made of minced meat or fish, lime, fish sauce, roasted ground rice and lots of chilli.

The south produces numerous dishes influenced by the Muslim cooking of the Malays, such as the mild massaman curry, which are often served with fried unleavened flat bread called *roti*. Plus, being surrounded by sea, the south is famous for seafood, including crab, squid, lobster and mussels.

The Central region, dominated by Bangkok, has some of the dishes most familiar to visitors, as the cuisine has travelled most widely. Green curry and *tom yum goong* are both Central specialities.

Isaan food featuring *gai yang* (fried chicken) and *som tam papaya* salad

Tom yum goong soup

CUSTOMS AND COURSES

While Thais usually eat a one-plate individual meal for lunch – most often based on rice or noodles – at dinner, food is served in the middle of the table for everyone to share. It makes for a wonderful chatty to-and-fro between friends and family, with people frequently presenting choice tasty morsels to their companions. Plus, it means you get to try a lot more recipes.

All dishes are served together, and ordered with an emphasis on balance – spicy, mild, sour, salty, sweet – although the menu will often notionally have appetisers listed separately.

Among the favourites for starters are *paw pia tawt*, a Thai spring roll enclosing sweet-and-sour bean sprouts, pork and crabmeat; and *gai hor bai toey*, made of chicken fried with sesame oil, soy sauce, oyster sauce, herbs and a drop of whisky, and presented in a leaf wrapper.

Soups (*tom*) are often very similar in Thailand to curries (*kaeng*), which generally have a less thick sauce than the Indian style. *Tom yam* is a hot-sour soup, made with pork, shrimp, chicken or fish, which should be accompanied by plenty of steamed rice to soak up the chilli heat. *Kaeng jeud* is a less pungent soup made of chicken, pork and shrimp combined with Chinese-style vegetables, glass noodles and Thai herbs and spices. *Tom kha gai* is a spicy chicken soup with a coconut milk and lemon grass base.

Lunch-time noodles are almost a ritual on Thailand's streets. *Bah mee nam* is a tasty broth with thin noodles, pork or chicken, mixed with herbs, bean sprouts and subtle spices. You can also order dishes like this dry (*bah mee haeng*), with just a light sauce. *Pad thai* is served many ways, but is basically flat rice-flour noodles sautéed with garlic, onion, tamarind juice and a variety of spices, and served with vegetables. *Mee grob* is crispy fried rice noodles with pork, egg, bean sprouts, shrimp, and a sweet-and-sour flavour.

Thailand has 3,000km/2,000 miles of coastline and abundant rivers, so fish and seafood are never far away from the table in recipes like *hor mok pla*, a fish curry with vegetables and coconut milk, served wrapped in banana leaves. *Pla preow wan* is fried fish covered in a thick sweet-and-sour sauce; *pla samlee daet deow* is whole deep-fried cotton-fish traditionally served with a tangy mango salad. Or try *goong tod* – crispy fried prawns, usually with a choice of sauces.

Among meats, Chicken and pork are the best, although the lower quality of beef is often mitigated by the fact that meats are usually served chopped or minced, so there is no chewy steak to negotiate. Delicious meat dishes include *kaeng ped gai naw mai* (red chicken curry with bamboo shoots, lime and basil leaves), *kaeng ped* (roast duck curry, sometimes served with slices of fried aubergine) and *khao nah gai*, which is sliced chicken with spring onion, bamboo shoots and steamed rice.

When eating dishes hot with chillies, take a local tip and have plenty of steamed rice, which helps to soothe the stomach and will smother the fire. Nothing else is as effective, and cold drinks are the worst antidote possible – they just fan the fire.

Thai dessert of mango and coconut cream

THAI SWEETS

Don't worry if you have a sweet tooth, you're not likely to go hungry. Many Thai sweets are based on rice flour, coconut milk, palm sugar and sticky rice, and just about all of them are tasty, including *salim*, a refreshing blend of sugared noodles with coconut milk and crushed ice, and *khao tom mad*, sticky rice with coconut cream and bananas. Ice cream sometimes comes in original and natural flavours. A local variation of a sundae, for instance, is coconut ice cream sprinkled with peanuts and kernels of corn.

Tropical fruits form a large proportion of dessert ingredients, as well as being a refreshing street snack. Among the most popular are *som o* (pomelo), which is a tropical cousin of the grapefruit, and is served divided into sections. *Sapparot* (pineapple) may be familiar in the West, but it is twice as tasty on its home ground.

More exotic local fruits are found at markets and street stalls. Just point if you don't know the name. *Ngor* (rambutan) looks like a hairy and overdeveloped strawberry; *lamut*, a light-brown fruit, is syrupy sweet inside, with a taste reminiscent of fresh figs. Durian, that green monster with spiky thorns, contains bits of custard-like flesh around egg-shaped piths. It is an acquired taste, with a smell often compared to a rubbish tip, or worse, although its creamy interior is sweet, and gives off a heating sensation. Try local oranges, bananas, mangoes, papayas – almost every fruit imaginable, except apples and pears, which don't grow here and are expensive.

Food and Drink

Restaurant in a Bangkok food market

WHERE TO EAT

Food vendors line the streets everywhere in Thailand, and sometimes it may seem as if everybody is eating or drinking round the clock. Local markets teem with them, selling items such as nuts, dried meats and sweets. If you are feeling adventurous, skip the hotel breakfast and stroll through an open-air market sampling the various treats.

Food stalls buy their ingredients fresh and inexpensively at the market in the early morning and prepare their best dishes. There are usually no menus, as each offers a few specialities. Buying from food stalls poses no language difficulties, as you simply point at what you want.

The stalls may look dubious, but in terms of health hazards, Westerners who have spent some time in Thailand have complete faith in them. The rule of thumb is to trust your eyes (fresh is best; if it looks old, don't eat it) and dine where there is a crowd.

Some vendors operate from glass-fronted carts on wheels; others with just large pans, maybe filled with curry, on a blanket on the ground. Plastic tables and chairs will be available nearby, which are communal, so sit at any space available.

Don't expect to find knives on Thai tables. A spoon is used instead. But do expect sauces, there to season your dish in the manner of salt and pepper. One of them is *nam pla*, a salty caramel-coloured fish sauce with tiny chilli segments in it. *Nam phrik*, 'pepper water', is a much-prized concoction of pounded red chillies, shrimp paste, black pepper, garlic and onions mixed with tamarind, lemon juice, ginger and fish in an early state of fermentation. There will also be sugar, and possibly small bowls of roasted chillies for diners with a more robust constitution.

A variation on the street stall is the *raan aharn* (food shop), which might have a similar short repertoire of specialities or a longer menu with a bit of everything. They are sometimes more expensive – definitely so if they are glassed in and have airconditioning – but dishes are rarely over B100, unless they contain whole fish.

For a change of both taste and scenery, try one of the Asian outlets that serve a spectrum of different cuisines, particularly near borders, where you'll find Cambodian, Malaysian, Burmese, Lao and in some cases Vietnamese. Chinese food is everywhere.

In cities, especially Bangkok, and tourist-friendly areas such as Phuket,

Pattaya and Samui, there will be a good choice of international food. Italian is the most popular non-Asian food by far, but there should also be options for French, German, even Mexican and Californian, plus pub grub, Indian and lots more.

The quality of international food is steadily improving, although prices are moving accordingly, and some restaurants are very high end, including several spectacular rooftop outfits in Bangkok.

DRINKS

Fruit juices, available from street stalls, are a great pick-me-up on a hot day's walk. Another option is to drop into a café, which these days will usually have airconditioning. The cities have undergone a shot of coffee culture in recent years, and there are a lot of

Most foods are available year-round, but some are best at certain times.

Lychee	Apr–June
Mango	Apr–May
Mangosteen	Apr–Sept
Durian	May–Aug
Rambutan	May–Sept

Starbucks-style joints to choose from.

With meals, iced water is frequently served and is almost bound to be safe to drink in any decent restaurant. If in doubt, ask for a bottle of water and skip the ice. Thais usually drink water or cold tea *(cha jin yen)* throughout their meal, along with beer or whisky with dinner, usually served as a 'set' with ice and soda. Thai whisky – Mekhong is the best-known brand – is weaker and cheaper than you'd think, though too much can result in a frighteningly bad hangover.

Thai beer brand names to try are Singha, Kloster and Chang – all palatable with food, and quite strong, particularly Chang. Because of high import duty, wines are very expensive. Many restaurants have a good range, up to *premier cru classé*, but even a poor bottle of plonk might cost more than your whole dinner.

Tourist areas will have plenty of British- and American-style pubs, clubs and bars, usually with some imported beers on tap, cocktails and sometimes a very impressive spirits list. Thai bars are cheap and very cheerful, and often tiny. There are even some in Bangkok that operate from the back of a camper van by the road side.

287

Food and Drink

Fruit juices often get a splash of syrup unless you request otherwise

PHRASE BOOK

Pronunciation – *p.290* **Phrases** – *p.292* **Menu Reader** – *p.297*

Phrase Book

For centuries, the Thai language, rather than tripping from foreigners' tongues, has been tripping them up. Its roots go back to the place from which Thais originated in the hills of southern China, but these are overlaid with Indian influences. From the original settlers come the five tones that seem designed to frustrate visitors. While an increasing number of people in Bangkok speak English, negotiating the rest of Thailand will need a little phrase-book help. The official language, Thai, is spoken all over the country, although people in many areas also speak regional dialects.

PRONUNCIATION

This section is designed to familiarise you with the sounds of Thai using our simplified phonetic transcription. You'll find the pronunciation of the Thai letters and sounds explained below, together with their 'imitated' equivalents. This system is used throughout the phrase book; simply read the pronunciation as if it were English, noting any special rules below.

Standard Thai, sometimes called Central Thai or Siamese, part of the Tai family of languages, is a tonal language with a highly complex orthographic system. Written Thai does not use space to mark word boundary: 'thaileavesnospacebetweenwords'. And, though punctuation marks exist, they are generally not used in writing. Standard Thai is the official language of Thailand, though it has several different forms, which are used in special social situations, especially in informal, formal, religious and royal contexts.

Consonants

The way Thai consonants are written in English often confuses foreigners. An h following a letter like p and t gives the letter a soft sound; without the h, the sound is more explosive. Thus, ph is not pronounced f but as a soft p; without the h, the p has the sound of a very hard b. The word thanon (street) is pronounced tanon in the same way as Thailand is not meant to sound like Thighland.

Similarly, final letters are often not pronounced as they look. The letter j at the end of a word is pronounced as t, while l is pronounced as an n. To complicate matters further, many words end with se or r, which are not pronounced; for instance, Surawongse, one of Bangkok's main thoroughfares, is simply pronounced Surawarong.

Vowels

Following are the approximate pronunciation of short and long vowels: i as in sip, ii as in seep, e as in bet, a as in pun, aa as in pal, u as in pool, o as in so, ai as in pie, ow as in cow, aw as in paw, iw as in you, oy as in toy.

Two Thai letters, ๐ and ๅ, function as both consonants and vowels. When they are used as consonants they will always be initial consonants in a syllable and take an initial sound as listed in the consonant table. But when they are used as vowels their sounds will be as follows:

– ฮ has an or sound as in torn and can be in the middle or at the end of a syllable.

– ฺ has an oar sound as in boar and will always be in the middle of a syllable.

Pronouns
In Thai, the pronouns I and me are the same word, but it is indicated differently for males and females. Men use the word *pom* when referring to themselves, while women say *di chan*. Men use *khrap* at the end of a sentence when addressing either a male or a female to add politeness, or in a similar manner as 'please' (the word for 'please', *karuna*, is seldom used directly), ie *Pai nai, khrap* (Where are you going sir?). Women add the word *kha* to their statements, as in *pai nai, kha*.

Tones
Thai is a tonal language. Therefore when you mispronounce a word, you don't simply say a word incorrectly: it is another word entirely. The phonetic transcriptions in this phrase book include the following tone marks:

Tone	Pitch	Symbol
mid tone	normal speaking with the voice at a steady pitch	no mark
high tone	pitched slightly higher than normal	´
low tone	pitched slightly lower than normal	`
falling tone	pitched high and falling sharply	^
rising tone	pitched low and rising sharply	ˇ

To ask a question, add a high tone *mai* to the end of the phrase ie *rao pai* (we go) or *rao pai mai* (shall we go?).

To negate a statement, insert a falling tone *mai* between the subject and the verb ie *rao pai* (we go), *rao mai pai* (we don't go).

'Very' or 'much' are indicated by adding *maak* to the end of a phrase ie *ron* (hot), *ron maak* (very hot), or *phaeng* (expensive), *phaeng maak* (very expensive), and the opposite *mai phaeng* (not expensive).

Here are examples of how tone changes the meaning of a word:

Thai Script	Pronunciation	Tone	Meaning
คา	kar	mid tone	to dangle
ข่า	kàr	low tone	galanga (spice)
ฆ่า	kâr	falling tone	to kill
ค้า	kár	high tone	to trade
ขา	kăr	rising tone	a leg

English	Thai	Pronunciation
How much?	เท่าไหร่?	tôu • rì

A simplified pronunciation guide follows each Thai word or phrase. Read it as if it were English. Where an expression varies according to the gender of the speaker, the alternative versions are followed by an M (masculine) and an F (feminine) in square brackets. Among the English phrases, American-English equivalents of British-English expressions are given in square brackets.

General

0	๐ sŏ on	100	๑๐๐ nùehng róry	
1	๑ nùeng	500	๕๐๐ hâr róry	
2	๒ sŏ rng	1,000	๑๐๐๐ nùeng pahn	
3	๓ să rm	1,000,000	๑๐๐,๐๐๐ nùeng să en	
4	๔ sèe	Monday	วันจันทร์ wahn jahn	
5	๕ hâr	Tuesday	วันอังคาร wahn ahng • karn	
6	๖ hòk	Wednesday	วันพุธ wahn púht	
7	๗ jèht	Thursday	วันพฤหัสบดี wahn páh • rúe • hàht • sàh • bor • dee	
8	๘ bpàet	Friday	วันศุกร์ wahn sùhk	
9	๙ gôw	Saturday	วันเสาร์ wahn sŏ u	
10	๑๐ sìhp	Sunday	วันอาทิตย์ wahn ar • tíht	

Hello!	สวัสดี!	sah • wàht • dee
How are you?	เป็นยังไง	bpehn yahng • ngi
Fine, thanks.	สบายดี ขอบคุณ	sah • bie dee kòrp • kuhn
Excuse me!	ขอโทษ!	kŏ r • tôet
Do you speak English?	คุณพูดภาษาอังกฤษได้ไหม?	kuhn pôot par • să r ahng • grìht dîe mí
What's your name?	คุณชื่ออะไร?	kuhn chûee ah • ri
My name is...	ผม [M]/ฉัน [F] ชื่อ...	pŏ m [M]/chán [F] chûee...
Nice to meet you.	ยินดีที่ได้รู้จัก	yihn dee têe dîe róo • jàhk
Where are you from?	คุณมาจากไหน?	kuhn mar jàrk ní
I'm from the US/UK.	ผม [M]/ฉัน [F] มาจาก อเมริกา/อังกฤษ	pŏ m [M]/chán [F] mar jàrk ah • me • rih • gar/ahng • grìht
What do you do?	คุณทำงานอะไร?	kuhn tahm • ngarn ah • ri
I work for...	ผม [M]/ฉัน [F] ทำงานที่...	pŏ m [M]/chán [F] tahm • ngarn têe...
I'm a student.	ผม [M]/ฉัน [F] เป็นนักศึกษา	pŏ m [M]/chán [F] bpehn náhk • sùek • să r
I'm retired.	ผม [M]/ฉัน [F] เกษียณแล้ว	pŏ m [M]/chán [F] gah • sě an láew
Do you like...?	คุณชอบ...ไหม?	kuhn chôrp...mí
See you later.	แล้วเจอกัน	láew jer gahn

Arrival and Departure

I'm on holiday [vacation]/business.	ผม [M]/ฉัน [F] มา เที่ยว/ธุระ *pŏ m [M]/cháhn [F] mar têaw/túh • ráh*
I'm going to...	ผม [M]/ฉัน [F] จะไปที่... *pŏ m [M]/cháhn [F] jah bpi têe...*
I'm staying at the... Hotel.	ผม [M]/ฉัน [F] พักอยู่ที่โรงแรม... *pŏ m [M]/cháhn [F] páhk yòo têe roeng • raem...*

Money and Banking

Where's...?	...อยู่ที่ไหน? *...yòo têe • nĭ*
– the ATM	– ตู้เอทีเอ็ม *dtôo e • tee • ehm*
– the bank	– ธนาคาร *tah • nar • karn*
– the currency exchange office	– ที่รับแลกเงิน *têe ráhp lâek ngern*
When does the bank open/close?	ธนาคาร เปิด/ปิด เมื่อไหร่? *tah • nar • karn bpèrt/bpìht mûea • rì*
I'd like to change dollars/pounds into baht.	ผม [M]/ฉัน [F] อยากแลกเงิน ดอลลาร์/ปอนด์ เป็น เงินบาท *pŏ m [M]/cháhn [F] yàrk lâek ngern dohn • lǎr/bporn bpehn ngern bàrt*

Transportation

How do I get to town?	ผม [M]/ฉัน [F] จะเข้าเมืองยังไง? *pŏ m [M]/cháhn [F] jah kôu mueang yahng • ngi*
Where's...?	...อยู่ที่ไหน? *...yòo têe • nĭ*
– the airport	– สนามบิน *sah • nǎ rm • bihn*
– the railway [train] station	– สถานีรถไฟ *sah • tǎ r • nee rót • fi*
– the bus station	– สถานีขนส่ง *sah • tǎ r • nee kǒ n • sòng*
– the underground [subway] station	– สถานีรถไฟใต้ดิน *sah • tǎ r • nee rót • fi tĭe dihn*
– the skytrain station	– สถานีรถไฟฟ้า *sah • tǎ r • nee rót • fi • fár*
Where do I buy a ticket?	ผม [M]/ฉัน [F] จะซื้อตั๋วได้ที่ไหน? *pŏ m [M]/cháhn [F] jah súee dtǒ ar dîe têe • nĭ*
A one-way/return [round-trip] ticket to...	ตั๋ว เที่ยวเดียว/ไปกลับ ไป... *dtǒ ar têaw deaw/bpi glàhp bpi...*
How much?	เท่าไหร่? *tôu • rì*
Which...?	...ไหน? *...nĭ*
– gate	– ประตู *bprah • dtoo*
– line	– แถว *tǎ ew*
– platform	– ชานชาลา *charn • char • lar*
Can I have a map?	ผม [M]/ฉัน [F] ขอแผนที่หน่อยได้ไหม? *pŏ m [M]/cháhn [F] kǒ r pǎ en • têe nòhy dî mí*

Accommodation

I have a reservation.	ผม [M]/ฉัน [F] จองห้องไว้ *pŏ m [M]/cháhn [F] jorng hôhng wí*
My name is...	ผม [M]/ฉัน [F] ชื่อ... *pŏ m [M]/cháhn [F] chûee...*
Do you have a room...?	คุณมีห้อง...ไหม? *kuhn mee hôhng...mí*
– for one/two	– สำหรับ คนเดียว/สองคน *sǎ hm • ràhp kon deaw/sǒ rng kon*

– with a bathroom	ที่มีห้องน้ำ *têe mee hôhng nárm*
– with airconditioning	ที่มีแอร์ *têe mee ae*
For...	สำหรับ... *sǎ hm • ràhp...*
– tonight	คืนนี้ *kueen née*
– two nights	สองคืน *sǒ rng kueen*
– one week	หนึ่งสัปดาห์ *nùeng sàhp • dar*
Is there anything cheaper?	มีอะไรที่ถูกกว่านี้ไหม? *mee ah • ri têe tòok gwàr née mí*
Can I have my bill/a receipt?	ขอ บิล/ใบเสร็จ ด้วยได้ไหม? *kǒ r bihn/bi • sèht dôary dî mí*

Can I access the internet/check email here?	ผม [M]/ฉัน [F] ใช้อินเตอร์เน็ต/เช็คอีเมล ที่นี่ได้ไหม? *pǒ m [M]/cháhn [F] chí ihn • dter • nèht/chéhk ee • mew têe • nêe dî mí*
How much per hour/half hour?	ชั่วโมงละ/ครึ่งชั่วโมง เท่าไหร่? *chôar • moeng lah/ krûeng chôar • moeng tôu • rì*
Hello. This is...	ฮัลโหล นี่... *hahn • lǒ e nêe...*
Can I speak to...?	ขอพูดกับคุณ... *kǒ r pôot gàhp kuhn...*
Can you repeat that?	พูดอีกทีได้ไหม? *pôot èek tee dî mí*
I'll call back later.	ผม [M]/ฉัน [F] จะโทรกลับมาใหม่ *pǒ m [M]/cháhn [F] jah toe glàhp mar mì*
Where's the post office?	ที่ทำการไปรษณีย์อยู่ที่ไหน? *têe • tahm • garn bpri • sah • nee yòo têe • nǐ*
I'd like to send this to...	ผม [M]/ฉัน [F] อยากจะส่งของนี้ไปที่... *pǒ m [M]/cháhn [F] yàrk jah sòng kǒ rng née bpi têe...*

Where's the tourist information office?	สำนักงานท่องเที่ยวอยู่ที่ไหน? *sǎ hm • náhk • ngarn tôhng • têaw yòo têe • nǐ*
What are the main attractions?	มีอะไรที่น่าสนใจบ้าง? *mee ah • ri têe nâr • sǒ n • ji bârng*
Do you have tours in English?	คุณมีทัวร์ที่เป็นภาษาอังกฤษไหม? *kuhn mee toar têe bpehn par • sǎ r ahng • grìht mí*

Where's the market/shopping centre [mall]?	ตลาด/ศูนย์การค้า อยู่ที่ไหน? *dtah • làrt/sǒ on • garn • kár yòo têe • nǐ*
I'm just looking.	ผม [M]/ฉัน [F] แค่ดูเฉยๆ *pǒ m [M]/cháhn [F] kâe doo chǒ ey • chǒ ey*
Can you help me?	ช่วยผม [M]/ฉัน [F] หน่อยได้ไหม? *chôary pǒ m [M]/cháhn [F] nòhy dî mí*
I'm being helped.	ผม [M]/ฉัน [F] มีคนช่วยแล้ว *pǒ m [M]/cháhn [F] mee kon chôary láew*
How much?	เท่าไหร่? *tôu • rì*
A receipt, please.	ขอใบเสร็จด้วย *kǒ r bi • sèht dôary*

Culture and Nightlife

What's there to do at night?	ที่นี่มีอะไรให้ทำตอนกลางคืนบ้าง? *têe nêe mee ah • ri hî tahm dtorn glarng • kueen bârng*
Do you have a programme of events?	คุณมีโปรแกรมกิจกรรมไหม? *kuhn mee bproe • graem gìht • jah • gahm mí*
Where's ...?	...อยู่ที่ไหน? *...yòo têe • nǐ*
– the town centre [downtown area]	– ย่านใจกลางเมือง *yârn ji • glarng mueang*
– the bar	– บาร์ *bar*
– the dance club	– คลับเต้นรำ *klàhp dtên • rahm*
Is there a cover charge?	มีค่าเข้าไหม? *mee kâr • kôu mí*

Business Travel

I'm here on business.	ผม [M]/ฉัน [F] มาธุระ *pǒ m [M]/cháhn [F] mar túh • ráh*
I have a meeting with...	ผม [M]/ฉัน [F] มีประชุมกับ... *pǒ m [M]/cháhn [F] mee bprah • chuhm gàhp...*
Where's...?	...อยู่ที่ไหน? *...yòo têe • nǐ*
– the business centre	– ศูนย์บริการทางธุรกิจ *sǒ on bor • rih • garn tarng túh • ráh • giht*
– the convention hall	– ห้องคอนเวนชั่น *hôhng kohn • wen • chârn*
– the meeting room	– ห้องประชุม *hôhng bprah • chuhm*

Travel with Children

Is there a discount for children?	มีส่วนลดสำหรับเด็กไหม? *mee sòarn • lót sǎ hm • ràhp dèhk mí*
Can you recommend a babysitter?	คุณช่วยแนะนำพี่เลี้ยงเด็กให้หน่อยได้ไหม? *kuhn chôary ná • nahm pêe • léang dèhk hî nòhy dî mí*
Do you have a child's seat/highchair?	คุณมีที่นั่งเด็ก/เก้าอี้เด็กไหม? *kuhn mee têe • nâhng dèhk /gôu • êe dèhk mí*
Where can I change the baby?	ผม [M]/ฉัน [F] จะเปลี่ยนผ้าอ้อมให้เด็กได้ที่ไหน? *pǒ m [M]/cháhn [F] jah bplèan pâr • ôrm hî dèhk dîe têe • nǐ*
Are children allowed?	เด็กเข้าได้ไหม? *dèhk kôu dîe mí*
My child is missing.	ลูกของผม [M]/ฉัน [F] หาย *lôok kǒ hng pǒ m [M] cháhn [F] hǐ e*

Disabled Travellers

Is there...?	มี...ไหม? *mee...mí*
– access for the disabled	– ทางเข้าออกสำหรับคนพิการ *tarng kôu òrk sǎ hm • ràhp kon píh • garn*
– a wheelchair ramp	– ทางขึ้นสำหรับรถเข็นคนพิการ *tarng kûen sǎ hm • ràhp rót • kě hn kon píh • garn*
– a disabled- [handicapped-] accessible toilet	– ห้องน้ำสำหรับคนพิการ *hôhng • nárm sǎ hm • ràhp kon píh • garn*
– the meeting room	– ห้องประชุม *hôhng bprah • chuhm*

Emergencies

Help!	ช่วยด้วย! *chôary dôary*

Go away!	ไปให้พ้น! *bpi hî pón*
Stop, thief!	หยุดนะ ขโมย! *yùht náh kah • moey*
Get a doctor!	เรียกหมอให้หน่อย! *rêak mŏ r hî nòhy*
Fire!	ไฟไหม้! *fi mî*
I'm lost.	ผม [M]/ฉัน [F] หลงทาง *pŏ m [M]/cháhn [F] lŏ ng tarng*
Can you help me?	คุณช่วยผม [M]/ฉัน [F] หน่อยได้ไหม? *kuhn chôary pŏ m [M]/cháhn [F] nòhy dî mí*
Call the police!	ช่วยเรียกตำรวจให้หน่อย! *chôary rêak dtahm • ròart hî nòhy*
There was an accident/attack.	มี อุบัติเหตุ/คนถูกทำร้าย *mee uh • bàht • dtih • hèt/kon tòok tahm • ríe*
I'm innocent.	ผม [M]/ฉัน [F] บริสุทธิ์ *pŏ m [M]/cháhn [F] bor • rih • sùht*
I need...	ผม [M]/ฉัน [F] ต้องการ... *pŏ m [M]/cháhn [F] dtôhng • garn...*
– an interpreter	– ล่าม *lârm*
– to make a phone call	– โทรศัพท์ *toe • rah • sàhp*
– to contact the consulate	– ติดต่อสถานกงสุล *dtìht • dtòr sah • tã r gong • sŭ hn*

Health

I'm ill [sick]	ผม [M]/ฉัน [F] ไม่สบาย *pŏ m [M]/cháhn [F] mî sah • bie*
I need an English-speaking doctor.	ผม [M]/ฉัน [F] ต้องการหมอที่พูดภาษาอังกฤษได้ *pŏ m [M]/cháhn [F] dtôhng • garn mŏ r têe pôot par • sã r ahng • grìht dîe*
Where's the chemist [pharmacy]?	ร้านขายยาอยู่ที่ไหน? *rárn • kĩ e • yar yòo têe • nĩ*
What time does it open/close?	ร้านขายยา เปิด/ปิด กี่โมง? *rárn • kĩ e • yar bpèrt/bpiht gèe moeng*
Can you make up [fill] this prescription?	ช่วยจัดยาตามใบสั่งยาให้หน่อยได้ไหม? *chôary jàht yar dtarm bi • sàhng • yar hî nòhy dî mí*
What would you recommend for...?	คุณมียาที่แนะนำสำหรับอาการ...ไหม? *kuhn mee yar têe ná • nahm sã hm • ràhp ar • garn...mí*
– diarrhea	– ท้องร่วง *tórng rôarng*
– insect bites	– แมลงกัดต่อย *mah • laeng gàht • dtòry*
– sunburn	– แดดเผา *dàet pŏ u*

Eating Out

A table for ..., please.	ขอโต๊ะสำหรับ...คน *kŏ r dtó sã hm • ràhp...kon*
Where's the toilet [restroom]?	ห้องน้ำไปทางไหน? *hôhng • nárm bpi tarng nĩ*
A menu, please.	ขอเมนูหน่อย *kŏ r me • noo nòhy*
I'd like ...	ผม [M]/ฉัน [F] อยากได้... *pŏ m [M]/cháhn [F] yàrk dîe...*
The bill [check], please.	เช็คบิลด้วย *chéhk bihn dôary*
Is service included?	รวมค่าบริการแล้วหรือยัง? *roarm kâr bor • rih • garn láew rúe yahng*
The wine list/drink menu, please.	ขอเมนู ไวน์/เครื่องดื่ม หน่อย *kŏ r me • noo wie/krûeang dùeem nòhy*
Thank you!	ขอบคุณ! *kòrp • kuhn*

apple	แอ๊ปเปิ้ล *áp • bpêrn*	lemongrass	ตะไคร้ *dtah • krí*
banana	กล้วย *glôary*	lobster	กุ้งมังกร *gûhng • mahng • gorn*
bean	ถั่ว *tòar*	mackerel	ปลาทู *bplar too*
bean sprout	ถั่วงอก *tòar • ngôrk*	mango	มะม่วง *mah • môarng*
beef	เนื้อวัว *núea woar*	milk	นม *nom*
beer	เบียร์ *bea*	mineral water	น้ำแร่ *nárm râe*
boiled sticky rice in coconut milk	ข้าวเหนียวเปียก *kôw • ne᷆aw bpèak*	mushroom	เห็ด *hèht*
bread	ขนมปัง *kah • no᷆m • bpahng*	mussels	หอยแมลงภู่ *ho᷆ ry mah • laeng • pôo*
broccoli	บร็อคโคลี่ *bróhk • koe lêe*	noodle soup	ก๋วยเตี๋ยวน้ำ *go᷆ary • te᷆aw nárm*
cabbage	กะหล่ำปลี *grah • làhm • bplee*	omelet	ไข่เจียว *kì jeaw*
chicken	ไก่ *gì*	orange juice	น้ำส้ม *nárm sôm*
chicken satay	สะเต๊ะไก่ *sah • dtéh gì*	papaya	มะละกอ *mah • lah • gor*
chilli	พริก *príhk*	peanut	ถั่วลิสง *tòar líh • so᷆ng*
clear soup with fish balls	แกงจืดลูกชิ้นปลา *gaeng • jùeet lôok • chíhn bplar*	pork	เนื้อหมู *núea • mo᷆o*
coconut	มะพร้าว *mah • prów*	potato	มันฝรั่ง *mahn • fah • ràhng*
(hot/iced) coffee	กาแฟ (ร้อน/เย็น) *gar • fae (rórn/yehn)*	red wine	ไวน์แดง *wie daeng*
crab	ปู *bpoo*	rice	ข้าว *kôw*
deep-fried, battered vegetables	ผักชุบแป้งทอด *pàhk chúhp bpâeng tôrt*	sea bass	ปลากะพงขาว *bplar grah • pong ko᷆ w*
duck	เป็ด *bpèht*	seafood	อาหารทะเล *ar • ha᷆ rn tah • le*
egg noodle	บะหมี่ *bah • mèe*	prawn [shrimp]	กุ้ง *gûhng*
featherback (fish)	ปลากราย *bplar grie*	snakehead (fish)	ปลาช่อน *bplar • chôrn*
fish stew with soy sauce	ปลาต้มเค็ม *bplar dtôm • kehm*	spinach	ผักโขม *pàhk • ko᷆em*
fresh spring roll	เปาะเปี๊ยะสด *bpor • bpéa sòt*	squid	ปลาหมึก *bplar • mùek*
fried rice with pork/ prawn [shrimp]	ข้าวผัด หมู/กุ้ง *kôw pàht mo᷆o/ gühng*	stir-fried chicken/ pork with ginger	ไก่/หมู ผัดขิง *gì/mo᷆ opàht • ki᷆ hng*
fruit	ผลไม้ *po᷆ n • lah • mí*	stir-fried rice noodles with prawn, tofu and peanuts (pad thai)	ผัดไทย *pàht • ti*
ginger	ขิง *ki᷆ hng*	tofu	เต้าหู้ *dtôu • hòo*
gourami (freshwater fish)	ปลาสลิด *bplar sah • lìht*	tuna	ปลาทูน่า *bplar too • nâr*
green curry	แกงเขียวหวาน *gaeng ke᷆ aw • wa᷆ rn*	vegetable	ผัก *pàhk*
lemon	มะนาว *mah • now*	white wine	ไวน์ขาว *wie ko᷆ w*

297

Phrase Book

Index

A

Abhisit Vejjajiva 274
accessibility 257
accommodation **250–2**,
    264–5
    Bangkok 84–5
    beaches and islands 29–31
    Central Thailand 102–3
    Chiang Mai and Around 193
    Deep South 178–9
    Eastern Seaboard 117
    Gulf Coast 136–7
    Northeast Thailand 241–2
    Northern Andaman Coast
        160–2
    Northern Thailand 216–17
adventure activities 17,
    36–43, 105, 166, 220–1,
    245–6
age restrictions 11
air travel 253–4
Amphawa 101
Ananda Mahidol (Rama VIII)
    272
Ancient City 100
Ang Thong Marine National
    Park 35, **131**
Angkor 230, 231, 268, 269
antiques 46
Ao Bang Thao (Phuket) **148**,
    163–4
Ao Chalok Ban Kao (Ko Tao)
    135
Ao Hin Khok (Ko Samet)
    111–12, 118
Ao Kantiang (Ko Lanta) 158
Ao Khlong Chak (Ko Lanta) 158
Ao Lo Dalam (Ko Phi Phi) 155
Ao Maya (Ko Phi Phi) 156
Ao Phai (Ko Samet) **112**, 117,
    119
Ao Phang Nga Marine National
    Park **153**, 160
Ao Phra Ae (Ko Lanta) **158**,
    162, 165, 166
Ao Phrao (Ko Samet) **111**, 118
Ao Ton Sai (Ko Phi Phi) **155**,
    166
Ao Tub Tim (Ko Samet) 112
Ao Wong Deuan (Ko Samet)
    112
apartments 252
art 281–2
ATMs 260
Ayutthaya 17, **94–7**, 268, **269**
    accommodation 102–3

festivals and events 15, 105
restaurants 103–4

B

backpacking 22–7
Ban Bang Bao (Ko Chang) 113
Ban Chiang **234**, 268
Ban Hat Siaw 215
Ban Khon Sai 240
Ban Na Kha 234
Ban Sala Dan (Ko Lanta) 157
Ban Ta Klang 229
Ban Tai (Ko Phangan) **132**,
    136
Ban Thawai 191
Ban Thon 234
Ban Wan 191
Bang Pa-In 95
Bang Saen 106–7
Bangkok 16, 17, **66–81**, 270
    accommodation 84–5
    day trips 82–3
    festivals and events 14–15,
        76, 91
    nightlife and entertainment
        23, 79, **88–9**
    restaurants 86–7
    shopping 16, 44, 77–8
    sport and activities 89–90
    tours 90
    transport 68
    Chatuchak Weekend Market
        16, **44**, 82, **83**
    Chinatown 16, 45, 74–5,
        80–1
    Dream World 82–3
    Erawan Museum 83
    Golden Mount 72
    Grand Palace and Wat Phra
        Kaew **67–9**, 70
    Jim Thompson House
        Museum 76
    Khao San Road 22, **23–4**,
        73
    Lak Muang **69**, 70
    Lumphini Park 76
    Maha Uma Devi Temple 78
    Mandarin Oriental Hotel 78
    MR Kukrit Pramoj Heritage
        Home 79
    National Museum 71, **72**
    National Museum of Royal
        Barges 73
    Prasart Museum 83
    Rattanakosin 70–1
    Safari World 83

Siam Discovery Museum 72
Snake Farm 77
Thanon Sukhumvit 79
Vimanmek Mansion 75
Wat Arun 73
Wat Benjamabophit 75
Wat Mangkon Kamalawat
    74, 80
Wat Pho 53, 72
Wat Suthat 72
Wat Thammamongkhon 83
Wat Traimit **74**, 80
bargaining 46
beaches 28–35
Bhumibol Adulyadej (Rama IX)
    268, 272, 273
bird watching 43
Bo Sang 16, 47, **190**, 197
boat trips 121, 141, 197
Bridge on the River Kwai 15,
    26, **93**
Bronze Age 268
Buddhism **204–5**, 231, 268
budgeting 260–1
bullfighting 172, 173
bungy jumping 41, 120
Buriram 226–7
Burma Banks 143, **145**

C

Cambodia 223, 227–8, 229,
    268
camping 253
car hire 257
Central Thailand 92–105
ceramics 16, 48, 191, 215,
    226
Cha-am **124–5**, 136, 137
charities 263
Chiang Dao Elephant Training
    Centre 189
Chiang Khan 236
Chiang Khong 202
Chiang Mai 17, 25, **182–8**,
    199
    accommodation 193
    festivals and events 197
    nightlife and entertainment
        195–6
    restaurants 194
    shopping 44, 47, 185
    sports and activities 196
    tours 197
    transport 184
    ethnic diversity 184
    National Museum 188

Night Bazaar 16, 45, **185**
Wat Bupparam 185
Wat Chiang Man 183–4
Wat Phra Singh 184
Wat Srisuphan 185
Wat Suan Dok 188
Wat U Mong 188
Zoo and Arboretum 188
Chiang Rai 17, **198–201**, 216,
217, 218, 220, 221
Chiang Saen **201–2**, 216
children 32, 264–5
China 202
Chinese community 74,
276–7
Chonabot 233
Chong Mek 240
Chulalongkorn (Rama V) 271
Chumphon 126
cinema 282
climate 12–13
clothes and fashion 48–9
coach travel 255–6
colonialism 271
cookery schools **58–9**, 105,
196
crafts 47–8, 124, 184, 191,
215
credit cards 260
crime 259
cuisine 283–5
cultural shows 89, 196
culture 276–82
currency 10, 260
cycling 196, 197, 221, 246,
256

D

Damnoen Saduak 103
Dan Khwian 16, 226
Dan Sai 14, **235**, 237, 242,
244, 247
dance 174–5, 278–9
Death Railway 26, 94
Deep South 170–81
deep-sea fishing **35**, 166
disabled travellers 257
diving 29, 32–3, 43, 120,
133, 140, 166–7
Doi Chang Dao Wildlife
Sanctuary 190
Doi Inthanon National Park 39,
190–1
Doi Phu Kha National Park
206
Doi Suthep 189

drinks 59, 287
driving 256–7
drugs 259, 273
dugongs 176

E

Eastern Seaboard 106–21
eco-tourism 27, 37, 220, 253,
262
electricity 11
Elephant Palace and Kraal
(Ayutthaya) 95, **97**
Elephant Village (Pattaya) 109
elephants 36, **186–7**, 189,
192, 221, 229
embassies and consulates
18–19, 258
emergency contacts 11, 259
entertainment see nightlife
and entertainment
entry requirements 18
Erawan National Park 39, **94**
etiquette 282
events see festivals and
events

F

ferries 254–5
festivals and events **14–15**,
26, 30, 57
Bangkok 91
Central Thailand 105
Chiang Mai and Around 197
Deep South 181
Eastern Seaboard 121
Gulf Coast 141
Northeast Thailand 237,
247
Northern Thailand 221
film and TV locations 29
Fish Foot Massage 53
floating markets 101
food and drink **56–9**, 259,
265, **283–7**, 297
Full-Moon Parties **26**, 27, 132,
155

G

gems and jewellery 46–7
go-karting 89, 120, 140
Golden Triangle 17, 201–3
golf 90, 120, 140, 167–8,
221, 246
guesthouses 251
Gulf Coast 122–41
gyms 90

H

Hat Bangrak (Ko Samui) 127
Hat Bophut (Ko Samui) **127**,
136, 139, 140
Hat Chang Lang (Trang) 177
Hat Chaweng (Ko Samui) **127**,
136, 138, 139, 140, 141
Hat Karon (Phuket) **149**, 163,
165
Hat Kata (Phuket) **149**, 163
Hat Khlong Dao (Ko Lanta)
157–8, 162
Hat Khlong Khong (Ko Lanta)
158
Hat Khlong Nin (Ko Lanta)
158, 162
Hat Khlong Phrao (Ko Chang)
113
Hat Kuat (Ko Phangan) 133
Hat Lamai (Ko Samui) 127
Hat Maenam (Ko Samui) **126**,
138
Hat Pak Nam (Ko Phi Phi) 156
Hat Patong (Phuket) **149**, 161,
163, 164, 165
Hat Railay (Krabi) **154**, 161–2,
164, 166
Hat Rin (Ko Phangan) **132**,
139
Hat Sai Kaew (Ko Samet) 111
Hat Sai Khao (Ko Chang) **113**,
117, 119
Hat Sai Ree (Ko Tao) **134**, 137,
139, 140
Hat Tha Nam (Ko Chang) 113
Hat Yai **173**, 178, 180
Hat Yao (Ko Phangan) **133**, 140
health 23, 258–9
high/low season 13
hilltribes 37–8, 184, 188,
201, 220, 276
Hinduism 230–1, 268
history 268–75
Hnag Dong 191
home stays 253
horse racing 246
hospitals 258
hot air balloons 41
Hot Springs Waterfall (Krabi)
154
hotels see accommodation
Hua Hin 17, 34, **122**, **125**,
136, 138, 139, 140, 141

I

itineraries 16–17

299

Index

K

Kaeng Krachan National Park 39, **124**, 141
Kaeng Tanna National Park 232
Kamphaeng Phet **214–15**, 217
Kanchanaburi 15, 25, **92–4**, 102, 103, 104, 105
kayaking *see* sea canoeing
Khao Lak **145**, 160, 163, 167, 168
Khao Phra Taew National Park 151
Khao Sam Roi Yot National Park 39, 43, **125–6**, 141
Khao Sok National Park 39, **145**
Khao Yai National Park 39, **223**, 241, 245
Khmers 222, 223, 225, 226, **230–1**, 268, 269
Khon Kaen **233**, 242, 243, 245, 246
Khong Jiam **237**, 242, 244
Khun Yuam 208–9
Khunying Mo 225
kite-boarding **33–4**, 120, 140
Ko Adang 176
Ko Bon 151
Ko Bubu 159
Ko Chang 28, 33, 35, **112–16**
  accommodation 117
  nightlife 119
  restaurants 118
  sports and activities 120
  tours 121
Ko Chang (Northern Andaman) **143**, 160
Ko Hae 151
Ko Hai **177**, 179
Ko Jum 159
Ko Kradan 177
Ko Kret 82
Ko Kut 116
Ko Lanta **157–9**, 162, 165, 166
Ko Libong 177
Ko Lipe **176**, 179
Ko Mak 116
Ko Muk **177**, 179
Ko Nang Yuan (Ko Tao) 134
Ko Phangan 28, **131–3**
  accommodation 136–7
  nightlife 26, 27, 32, 133, **139**
  restaurants 138
  sports and activities 33, 34, 133, **140**
Ko Phi Phi **155–7**
  accommodation 162
  nightlife 166
  restaurants 164–5
  sports and activities 33, 167
Ko Samet 28, **110–12**, 117, 118, 119
Ko Samui 17, 28, **126–31**
  accommodation 136
  nightlife 32, **139**
  restaurants 138
  sports and activities 33, 34, **140**
  tours 141
Ko Si Chang 107–8
Ko Tao 28, **134–5**
  accommodation 137
  nightlife 32, **139**
  restaurants 138
  sports and activities 33, 140
Ko Tarutao Marine National Park 17, 31, **176**, 178, 181
Ko Wai 116
Krabi **153–5**
  accommodation 161–2
  nightlife 166
  restaurants 164
  sports and activities 42, **168–9**
Kukrit Pramoj, MR 79, 281

L

lady-boys (*kathoeys*) 114–15
Lampang **192**, 195
Lamphun **191–2**, 195
language 277, 290–7
Laos 201, 202, 229, 235, 236–7, 239
literature 280–1
Loei 232, **235**, 242
Loi Krathong 15, 211, 221
Lopburi **100**, 103, 104, 105, 268

M

Mae Hong Son 17, 207, **208**, 217, 219, 220
Mae Sa Elephant Camp 189
Mae Sai **203**, 216–17, 218
Mae Salong **199–201**, 216, 218
Mae Sariang **209**, 220
Mae Sot **209**, 217, 219, 220
maps and books 19

markets and bazaars 44–5, 56, 101
Mekong River 17, 202, 236, **237–40**
menu reader 297
merbok (zebra doves) 177
military rule 272–3
Mini Siam (Pattaya) 109
Mon 268
money 260–1
Mongkut (Rama IV) 270–1
Mu Ko Lanta Marine National Park 158–9
Mukdahan **239–40**, 242, 244
music 234, 279–80
Muslims 276, 277
Myanmar 201, 203, 207, 209
Myawadi (Myanmar) 209

N

Nakhon Pathom **93**, 103, 268
Nakhon Phanom **238**, 242, 244
Nakhon Ratchasima **222–5**, 241, 243, 245, 246, 247
Nakhon Si Thammarat **170–2**, 268, 269
  accommodation 178
  festivals and events 181
  restaurants 179
  transport 172
Nan **203–6**, 216, 218
Narai, King 269
national parks 39
nightlife and entertainment 32, 174–5
  Bangkok 88–9
  Central Thailand 104
  Chiang Mai and Around 195–6
  Gulf Coast 139
  Northeast Thailand 245
  Northern Andaman Coast 165–6
  Northern Thailand 220
Nong Khai **237–8**, 242, 244, 245, 246, 247
Nonthaburi 82
Northeast Thailand 222–47
Northern Andaman Coast 142–69
Northern Thailand 198–221

O

off-road tours 39–40
opening hours 11
opium 189, 201, 202

P

packing list 19
Padaung (longneck) villages 207
Pai **207**, 217, 219, 220, 221
Pak Thong Chai 16, 226
Pattaya 28–9, **106**, **108–10**
  accommodation 117
  festivals and events 121
  nightlife 110, 119
  restaurants 118
  shopping 108
  sports and activities 34, 109–10, 120
  tours 121
  transport 109
people 276–8
performance art 174–5, 278–80
Pha Taem National Park 240
Phaulkon, Constantine 269
Phayao **201**, 218
Phee Ta Khon Festival (Dan Sai) 14, 235, **237**, 247
Phetchaburi **123–4**, **128–9**, 136, 137
Phimai 17, **225–6**, 247
Phitsanulok **214**, 219, 221
Phra Nakhon Khiri Historical Park (Phetchaburi) 124, **129**
Phra Pathom Chedi (Nakhon Pathom) 93
Phra That Si Songrak 236
Phrae 206
phrase book 290–7
Phu Kradung National Park 39, 236
Phu Phrabat Historical Park 238
Phu Rua National Park 235
Phuket 28, **142**, **147–53**
  accommodation 161
  festivals and events 15, 30, 59, 169
  nightlife and entertainment 165–6
  restaurants 163–4
  shopping 147
  sports and activities 34, 35, 166–9
  tours 166
  transport 144
  Aquarium and Marine Biological Research Centre 150

  Chinatown 147
  Phuket Fantasea 149
  Sanjao Sam San 147
  Seashell Museum 150
  Wat Chalong 150
  Wat Phra Thong 151
  Wat Put Jaw 147
Pibun Songkhram 272
politics 273–4
postal services 11
Prajadhipok (Rama VII) 271–2
Pranburi 31, 141
Prasat see temples
Pridi Banomyong 272
public holidays 12
puppet theatre 172, 174, 175, 279

R

rail travel 255
Raksawarin Park Hot Springs 143
Rama I, King 270
Rama II, King 270
Rama III, King 270
Ramakien 174, 280–1
Ramkamhaeng, King 269
Ranong **143**, 145, 160–1, 163
Red Shirts 274
religion 204–5, 276
Renu Nakhon 238–9
responsible travel 262–3
restaurants 57–8
  Bangkok 86–7
  Central Thailand 103–4
  Chiang Mai and Around 194–5
  Deep South 179–80
  Eastern Seaboard 118
  Gulf Coast 137–8
  Northeast Thailand 243–4
  Northern Andaman Coast 163–5
  Northern Thailand 218–19
road travel 255–7
rock climbing **41–2**, 168, 196
Roi Et 233

S

safety 23, 258–9
sailing **34–5**, 120, 140
Salak Phet (Ko Chang) **116**, 118
Samut Prakan Crocodile Farm & Zoo 100

Samut Sakhon 100
Samut Songkhram **101**, 104
Sanctuary of Truth (Pattaya) 108
Sangkhlaburi **94–5**, 102, 210
Sao Din 206
Satun **173–6**, 178–9, 180, 181
sea canoeing **35**, 168–9, 181
Sea Gypsies (*Chao Lay*) **33**, 156
Seni Pramoj 272
sex trade 277–8
shipping 49
shooting 169
shopping 16, **44–9**
Si Chiang Mai 236–7
Si Kaew 234
Si Saket 227–8
Si Satchanalai 213–14
Siam 269–72
silk 16, 49, 124, 226
Silpa Bhirasri 281–2
Similan Islands Marine National Park 17, 29, 33, 35, **145–7**
Sirinat National Park 148
sky diving 40–1
Sondhi Limthongkul 284
Songkhla **172–3**, 178, 180, 181
Songkran 14
Sop Ruak 202–3
spas and treatments 50–5
sports and activities **36–43**, 117
  Bangkok 89–90
  Central Thailand 105
  Chiang Mai and Around 196
  Eastern Seaboard 120
  Gulf Coast 140
  Northeast Thailand 245–6
  Northern Andaman Coast 166–9
  Northern Thailand 220–1
Sriracha Tiger Zoo 107
street food 56 7, 286
Sukhothai 17, **210–13**, 268–9
  accommodation 217
  nightlife 220
  restaurants 219
  tours 221
Surin **227**, 241, 243

Surin Elephant Roundup 15, 227, **229**, 247
Surin Islands Marine National Park 17, 29, 33, **143–4**

T

Taksin, King 268, 269–70
Tattoo Festival 22, **26**
tax 260
telephone numbers 11, 259
temples
  Maha Uma Devi (Bangkok) 78
  Prasat Hin Khao Phanom Rung Historic Park 17, **226–7**, 230–1, 247
  Prasat Hin Muang Tam 227
  Prasat Hin Phanomwan 225
  Prasat Hin Phimai 17, **225**, 230, 247
  Prasat Khao Phra Viharn **227–8**, 230
  Prasat Ta Muan Tot 227
  Sanjao Sam San (Phuket) 147
  Wat Arun (Bangkok) 73
  Wat Benjamabophit (Bangkok) 75
  Wat Bupparam (Chiang Mai) 185
  Wat Chalong (Phuket) 150
  Wat Chetupon (Sukhothai) 213
  Wat Chiang Man (Chiang Mai) 183–4
  Wat Kamphaeng Laeng (Phetchaburi) 123, **128**
  Wat Ko Keo Sutharam (Phetchaburi) 123, **128**
  Wat Mahathat (Phetchaburi) 123–4, 128
  Wat Mahathat (Sukhothai) 213
  Wat Mangkon Kamalawat (Bangkok) **74**, 80
  Wat Pho (Bangkok) 53, 72
  Wat Phra Kaew (Bangkok) **67–9**, 70
  Wat Phra Kaew (Chiang Rai) 201
  Wat Phra Mahathat (Ayutthaya) 95, **97**
  Wat Phra Phai Luang (Sukhothai) 213
  Wat Phra Si Iriyabot (Kamphaeng Phet) 215
  Wat Phra Si Rattana

  Mahathat (Phitsanulok) 214
  Wat Phra Singh (Chiang Mai) 184
  Wat Phra Sri Sanphet (Ayutthaya) 95, **96**
  Wat Phra That Doi Suthep 189
  Wat Phra That Phanom 239
  Wat Phra Thong (Phuket) 151
  Wat Phu Thok 238
  Wat Put Jaw (Phuket) 147
  Wat Ratchaburana (Ayutthaya) 95, **97**
  Wat Saphan Hin (Sukhothai) 213
  Wat Si Sawai (Sukhothai) 213
  Wat Srisuphan (Chiang Mai) 185
  Wat Suan Dok (Chiang Mai) 188
  Wat Suthat (Bangkok) 72
  Wat Tham Seua (Krabi) 154
  Wat Thammamongkhon (Bangkok) 83
  Wat Traimit (Bangkok) **74**, 80
  Wat U Mong (Chiang Mai) 188
  Wat Yai Suwannaram (Phetchaburi) 123, **128**
textiles 215, 234
Thai Boxing (Muay Thai) 37, **42**, 91, **98–9**, 169, 196, 246
Thai massage **50–4**, 188
Thai people 268
Thaksin Shinawatra 74, 273–4, 277
Tham Erawan 234–5
Tham Lot 208
Tham Mai Kaeo (Ko Lanta) 159
Thanom Kittikachorn 272
theatre 89, 278–9
Thompson, Jim 76, 226
Thonburi 73, 269–70
Three Tyrants 273
Tiger Temple 22, **25**, 26
time zone 10
tipping 260
tourist information 19
tours
  Bangkok 90
  Central Thailand 105
  Chiang Mai and Around 197

  Deep South 181
  Eastern Seaboard 121
  Gulf Coast 141
  Northeast Thailand 245–6
  Northern Andaman Coast 166
  Northern Thailand 220–1
Trang **176–7**, 179, 180, 181
transport **253–7**
  Bangkok 68
  Chiang Mai 184
  Nakhon Si Thammarat 172
  Pattaya 109
  Phuket 144
trekking **37–9**, 120, 197, 220, 221, 245–6

U

Ubon Ratchathani **228–9**, 241, 243, 245, 247
Udon Thani **232–4**, 241, 244, 245
Um Phang 210–11

V

Vajiravudh (Rama VI) 271
Vegetarian Festival (Phuket) 15, 30, 59, 169
Vietnam 237, 239
Viharn Phra Mongkhon Bophit (Ayutthaya) 95, **96**
Viking Cave (Ko Phi Phi) 156
villas 252
visas 18
volunteering 27, 263

W

Wat *see* temples
water sports 32–5, 42–3
weather 12–13
websites 19
whitewater rafting 40, 220
wind-surfing **33–4**, 120
wine 59
women travellers 259
World War I 271
World War II 93–4, 209, 272

Y

Yellow Shirts 274
yoga **54**, 90
youth hostels 251

Z

zip lines 41, 140

Accommodation Index

Alila Cha-am 136
Amanpuri (Phuket) 161
Anantara Resort & Spa Golden
   Triangle (Chiang Saen) 216
Anantara Si Kao (Sikao) 179
Apple Guest House 102
Arun Residence (Bangkok) 84

Baan Saladaeng (Bangkok) 84
Baan Sukchoke Country Resort
   (Damnoen Saduak) 103
Bamboo Bungalows (Ko
   Phayam) 160
Banyan Tree (Phuket) 161
Barali Beach Resort (Ao Khlong
   Phrao) 117
Belle Villa Resort (Pai) 217
BP Samila Beach Hotel &
   Resort (Songkhla) 178

Cashew Resort (Ko Chang) 160
Centara Hotel & Convention
   Centre (Udon Thani) 241–2
Centara Mae Sot Hill Hotel 217
Chiang Mai Plaza Hotel 193
CoCo Cottage (Ko Hai) 179
Cocohut Village (Ban Tai) 136–7

Dai, The (Mae Hong Son) 217
Dhevaraj Hotel (Nan) 216
Dusit Island (Chiang Rai) 216

Eugenia, The (Bangkok) 84

Felix River Kwai Resort 102
Fern Resort (Mae Hong Son)
   217
Four Seasons Chiang Mai 193

Galare Guest House (Chiang
   Mai) 193
Golden Triangle Inn (Chiang
   Rai) 216
Grand Park Hotel (Nakhon Si
   Thammarat) 178

Haad Son Resort (Hat Son) 137

Jai Restaurant and Bungalows
   (Khao Lak) 160
JW Marriott (Bangkok) 84

Karinthip Village (Chiang Mai)
   193
Kaya House (Phuket) 161
Khao San Palace (Bangkok) 84

Khao Yai Garden Lodge 241
Khon Kaen Hotel 242
Kirimaya (Khao Yai N P) 241
Ko Tao Grand Coral Resort (Hat
   Sai Ree) 137
Ko Tarutao National Park 178
Koh Chang Kacha Resort & Spa
   (Hat Sai Khao) 117
Koh Mook Charlie Beach Resort
   (Ko Muk) 179
Krabi Mountain View Resort (Ao
   Ton Sai) 161
Krungsri River Hotel (Ayutthaya)
   102–3

Lanta Sand Resort & Spa (Ao
   Phra Ae) 162
Le Bua at State Tower (Bangkok)
   84–5
Lee Pae Resort (Ko Lipe) 179
The Lodge (Hat Bophut) 136
Loei Palace Hotel 242
Lopburi Inn Resort 103

Mae Sai Guest House 216–17
Mae Salong Flower Hill 216
Mandarin Oriental (Bangkok) 85
Mandarin Oriental Dhara Dhevi
   (Chiang Mai) 193
Mercure Pattaya 117
Mut Mee Guest House (Nong
   Khai) 242

Naga Hill (Chiang Rai) 217
Nakhon Phanom River View
   Hotel 242
New Season Hotel (Hat Yai) 178
Novotel Bangkok 85
Novotel Hat Yai Centara 178

Old Bangkok Inn 85

P Guest House (Sangkhlaburi)
   102
Pairadise (Pai) 217
Pavilion Songkhla Hotel 178
Phang Nga Guest House 160
Phi Phi Andaman Resort (Hat
   Hin Khom) 162
Phi Phi Banyan (Ao Ton Sai) 162
Phi Phi Island Village Resort &
   Spa (Ao Lo Bakao) 162
Phunacome (Dan Sai) 242
Pinnacle Tarutao (Satun) 179
Ploy Palace Hotel (Mukdahan)
   242

Poppies Samui (Chaweng
   Beach) 136
Pullman Khon Kaen Raja Orchid
   242

Rabieng Rim Nam Guesthouse
   (Petchaburi) 136
The Rachamankha (Chiang
   Mai) 193
Railay Village Resort (Hat Railay
   West) 161
Rawi Warin Resort & Spa (Hat
   Khlong Nin) 162
Rayavadee (Hat Tham Phra
   Nang) 161
River Kwai Jungle Rafts
   (Kanchanaburi) 102
River Kwai Restotel
   (Kanchanaburi) 102
River View Place Hotel
   (Ayutthaya) 102

Samed Villa (Ao Phai) 117
Sand Sea Resort (Hat Railay
   West) 162
The Sarojin (Khuk Khak) 160
Scenic Riverside Resort
   (Kamphaeng Phet) 217
Sheraton Pattaya 117
Siam Guest House (Pattaya)
   117
Sima Thani Hotel (Nakhon
   Ratchasima) 241
Six Senses Hideaway (Ao Phang
   Nga) 160
Sofitel Central Hua Hin 136
Southern Lanta Resort (Hat
   Khlong Dao) 162
Sukhumvit 11 Hostel (Bangkok)
   85
Surin Majestic Hotel 241

Take a Nap (Bangkok) 85
Tharaburi (Sukhothai) 217
Thavorn Beach Village and Spa
   (Patong) 161
Thumrin Thana (Trang) 179
Tinidee Hotel @ Ranong 160–1
Tohsang City Hotel (Ubon
   Ratchathani) 241
Tohsang Khong Jiam 242
Twin Lotus Hotel (Nakhon Si
   Thammarat) 178

Ubonburi Hotel & Resort (Ubon
   Ratchathani) 241

Index

Credits for Berlitz Handbook Thailand

Written by: Howard Richardson
Series Editor: Alexander Knights
Commissioning Editor: Alyse Dar
Cartography Editor: Zoë Goodwin
Map Production: Stephen Ramsay and Apa Cartography Department
Production: Tynan Dean, Linton Donaldson and Rebeka Ellam
Picture Manager: Steven Lawrence
Art Editors: Richard Cooke and Ian Spick
Photography: Alamy 5TL, 6MR/TL/TR, 7B/MR, 9BL, 12, 27T, 35, 36, 47, 70, 75, 84, 87, 99T, 104, 113, 115/T, 117, 119, 125, 127, 133, 138, 145, 153, 155, 156, 157, 159, 160, 169, 173, 179, 180, 181, 186, 188, 190, 193, 194, 195B, 197, 202, 210, 214, 216, 221, 223T, 225, 227, 228, 231/T, 232, 233, 234, 238, 239, 240, 242, 246, 247, 248/249, 263, 264, 268, 279, 286; Corbis 1, 273, 274; Rene Ehrhardt 27B; Laughlin Elkind 71B; Mary Evans 271; Getty Images 121; Robert Harding 187T; APA John Ishii 6BL, 9BR, 13, 18, 24, 28, 29, 30, 31, 32, 33, 34, 38, 39, 41, 43, 48T, 53, 54, 56, 99, 106, 109, 111, 118, 125, 131, 134, 135, 136, 137, 140, 141, 161, 162, 164, 167, 181T, 262, 265; iStockphoto 4B, 4TR, 5BR, 7TL, 8BL, 10/11, 14, 15, 23, 90, 91, 100, 139, 170, 183, 189B, 206, 212, 213, 218, 219, 237, 243, 251, 252, 256, 281, 287; Leonardo 102; Courtesy Mandarin Oriental 85; Photolibrary 112, 114, 116, 144, 174, 175/T, 177, 191, 192, 195T, 205T, 211, 215, 250, 257; Davis Sim 26; APA Peter Stuckings 2TR, 3TL, 4TL, 5BL, 5ML, 5TR, 6BR, 7TR, 8BR, 8T, 16, 20/21, 22, 25, 37, 42, 44, 45, 46, 48, 50, 52, 55, 57, 58, 59, 67/T, 71T, 72, 73, 74, 76, 77, 78, 79, 80, 81, 82, 83, 88, 93, 95, 96, 97, 98, 101, 129, 185, 187, 199/T, 201, 203, 204, 205, 207, 208, 209, 223, 226, 229, 230, 235, 236, 244, 253, 254, 259, 261, 266/267, 272, 276, 278, 280, 283, 284, 285; Thai Flying Club 40; TIPS Images 128; Topfoto 269, 270; APA Nikt Wong 17, 51, 60/61, 147, 149, 165, 166, 168, 277
Front cover: photolibrary.com
Printed by: CTPS-China

© 2011 APA Publications GmbH & Co. Verlag KG (Singapore branch)
7030 Ang Mo Kio Ave 5
08-65 Northstar @ AMK
Singapore 569880

apasin@singnet.com.sg

First Edition 2011

Contacting Us
At Berlitz we strive to keep our guides as accurate and up to date as possible, but if you find anything that has changed, or if you have any suggestions on ways to improve this guide, then we would be delighted to hear from you. Write to Berlitz Publishing, PO Box 7910, London SE1 1WE, UK or email: berlitz@apaguide.co.uk

Worldwide: APA Publications GmbH & Co. Verlag KG (Singapore branch), 7030 Ang Mo Kio Ave 5, 08-65 Northstar @ AMK, Singapore 569880; tel: (65) 570 1051; email: apasin@singnet.com.sg
UK and Ireland: GeoCenter International Ltd, Meridian House, Churchill Way West, Basing-stoke, Hampshire, RG21 6YR; tel: (44) 01256-817 987; email: sales@geocenter.co.uk
United States: Ingram Publisher Services, 1 Ingram Boulevard, PO Box 3006, La Vergne, TN 37086-1986; email: customer.service@ingrampublisherservices.com
Australia: Universal Publishers, 1 Waterloo Road, Macquarie Park, NSW 2113; tel: (61) 2-9857 3700; email: sales@universalpublishers.com.au
New Zealand: Hema Maps New Zealand Ltd (HNZ), Unit 2, 10 Cryers Road, East Tamaki, Auckland 2013; tel: (64) 9-273 6459; email: sales.hema@clear.net.nz

www.berlitzpublishing.com